1850 Census
of
Rowan County, North Carolina:

A Genealogical Compilation of All Six Schedules

by

Jo White Linn, C.G., C.G.L.

Library of Congress Catalog Card Number 91-077702
International Standard Book Number 0-918470-21-8
Printed in the United States of America

TABLE OF CONTENTS

Introduction

Maps

Population Schedule with additions from other schedules
    and compiler's files   1

Leftovers 128

Mortality Schedule with additions from newspaper notices,
    cemetery listings, and compiler's files 129

Social Statistics Schedule 135

Slave Schedule 137

Agriculture Schedule 137

Manufacturing Schedule 138

Compilation of Schedules 138

Index 139

Other books by the compiler 148

INTRODUCTION

<u>Description</u>: The seventh decennial census of the United States was
the first to list all free persons by name. The population
schedule also gives the birthplace (by state or country), occupation (of males over fifteen), age, sex, and color, the value of the
real estate owned, whether the persons were married within the year
or attended school within the year, whether those over twenty were
literate. Numbering every abode and family, the census also
spelled out those who were deaf and dumb, blind, insane, idiotic,
paupers, and convicts. Of the six schedules that make up the 1850
census, the population and mortality schedules are those most often
employed by genealogists.

<u>Source</u>: This transcription was made from the microfilm of the
original schedule with the following abbreviations employed:

        B - free black
        MB: marriage bond
        Mu - mulatto
        m - married within the year
        S - attended school
        (X) - over 21 and illiterate
        WB - Rowan County will book
        WC - <u>Western Carolinian</u> newspaper pub. Salisbury
        CW - <u>Carolina Watchman</u> newspaper pub. Salisbury
        unimpr - unimproved land

<u>Arrangement</u>: Selected statistics of genealogical value from the
slave, agriculture, and manufacturing schedules are included with
the household as shown in the population schedule. Editor's notes
also include marriage bonds, parentage, citations of wills, and
other details for many households. Persons wishing the additional
details from the agriculture and manufacturing schedules will
simply have to turn to the microfilm of the original census.

The mortality schedule is presented separately since there was no
way to determine from which household each of the deceased came.
Details of death dates from the <u>Carolina Watchman</u> and cemetery
records (some indicating relationships) are included in some cases,
as well as some information from the compiler's files. Where hh
identification has been made, the index and the mortality schedule
provide that information.

A description of each of the special schedules follows the
population and mortality schedules.

The format was selected because the editor would prefer to have all
the information with the household when she is using the census
rather than looking through six schedules separately.

<u>Problems</u>: Elkanah D. Austin, the Asst. Marshall, did not follow the same order in the five special schedules as he did in the population schedule. The writing in the special schedules is cramped and, in part, illegible. Great effort was made to place the statistics with the correct household. Names of some persons appear in the special schedules and do not appear in the population schedule. Conversely, there are households where the manufacturing schedule is not included, although industry is indicated by the occupation and valuation of the household. Further, there are households where the numbers simply do not match. "Leftovers" appear at the end of the population schedule and are indexed.

Further, Mr. Austin became mixed up on the numbering of households, repeating the household numbers 1582-1591. A notation on the pages affected seeks to remedy the confusion.

The census is hearsay at best and enormously valuable if its evidence is not overweighted in the evaluation that determines proof of lineage acceptable to a reasonable person.

<u>Index</u>: A surname index was employed because a full-name index would have created so many additional pages as to put price of the book too high for most libraries, genealogists, and social historians. The numbers in the index are for the household unless preceded by <u>p.</u>, which indicates a page number.

<u>Conclusions</u>: Persons who doubt that people married their neighbors and relatives are encouraged to examine the households closely.
   This compilation puts to rest the theory that part of the original population schedule of the Rowan County 1850 census is not extant. The household numbers come out to 1842. The Assistant Marshall said he turned in 238 pp. and 10 lines, precisely what exists, with the addition of a family on p. 238 which he added with a note to that effect.
   Household #1292 appears to show a quadruple birth. The incidence of twins in Rowan is much less than in the Lincoln County, NC, 1850 Census published by M/M Judson Crow.

<u>Appreciation</u>: To Jean Kirk Ramsey for making the print-out of the population schedule at the office of the Register of Deeds available to your editor; to William D. Bennett who cheerfully read the undecipherable names from the original special schedules at the North Carolina Archives when all else failed; to those of you who have been patient while the exercise was being completed.

Jo White Linn
Jo White Linn, C.G., C.G.L., R.G.
P. O. Box 1948
Salisbury, NC 28144
January, 1992

Maps of Rowan County

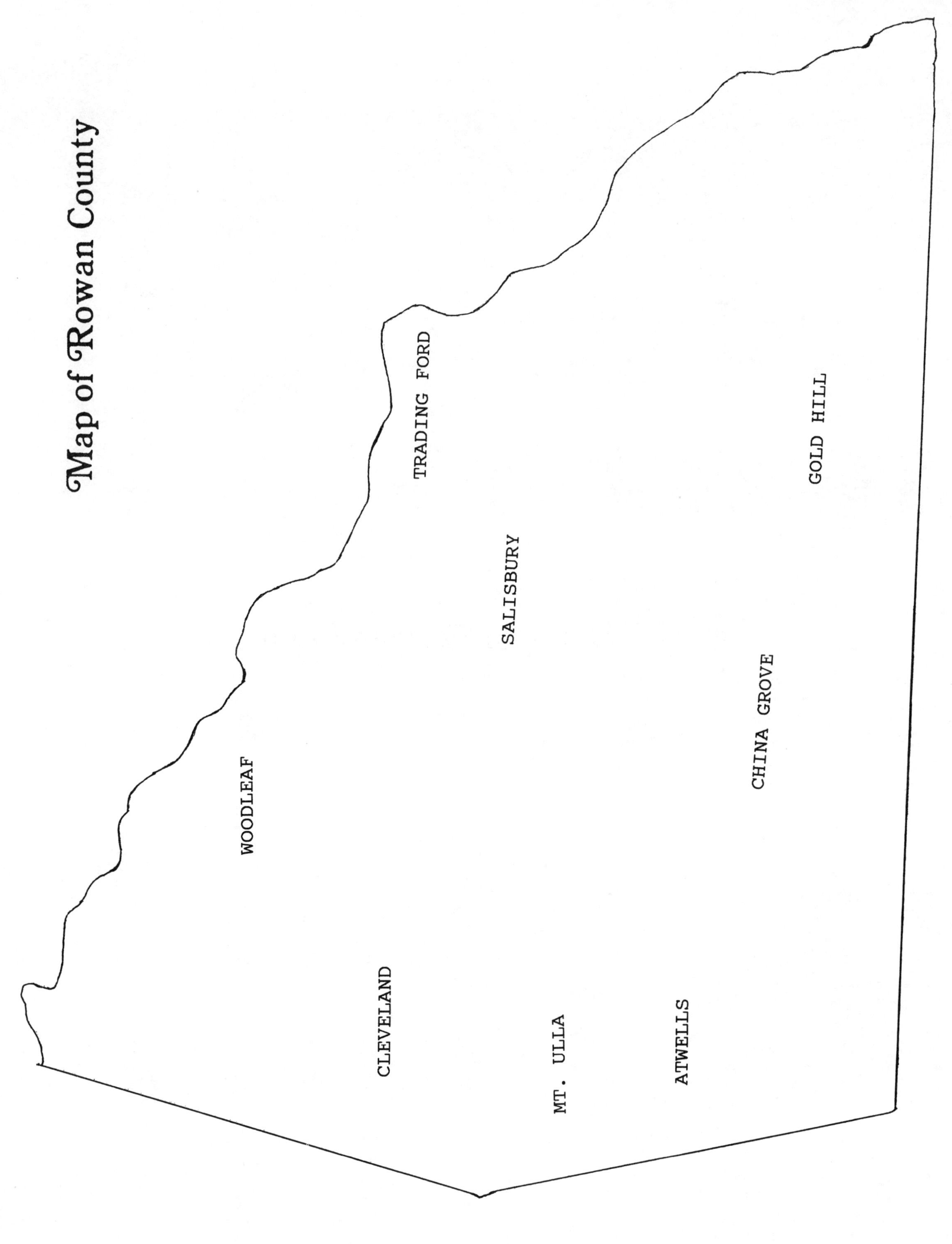

Map of Rowan County
TRADING FORD
GOLD HILL
SALISBURY
WOODLEAF
CHINA GROVE
CLEVELAND
MT. ULLA
ATWELLS

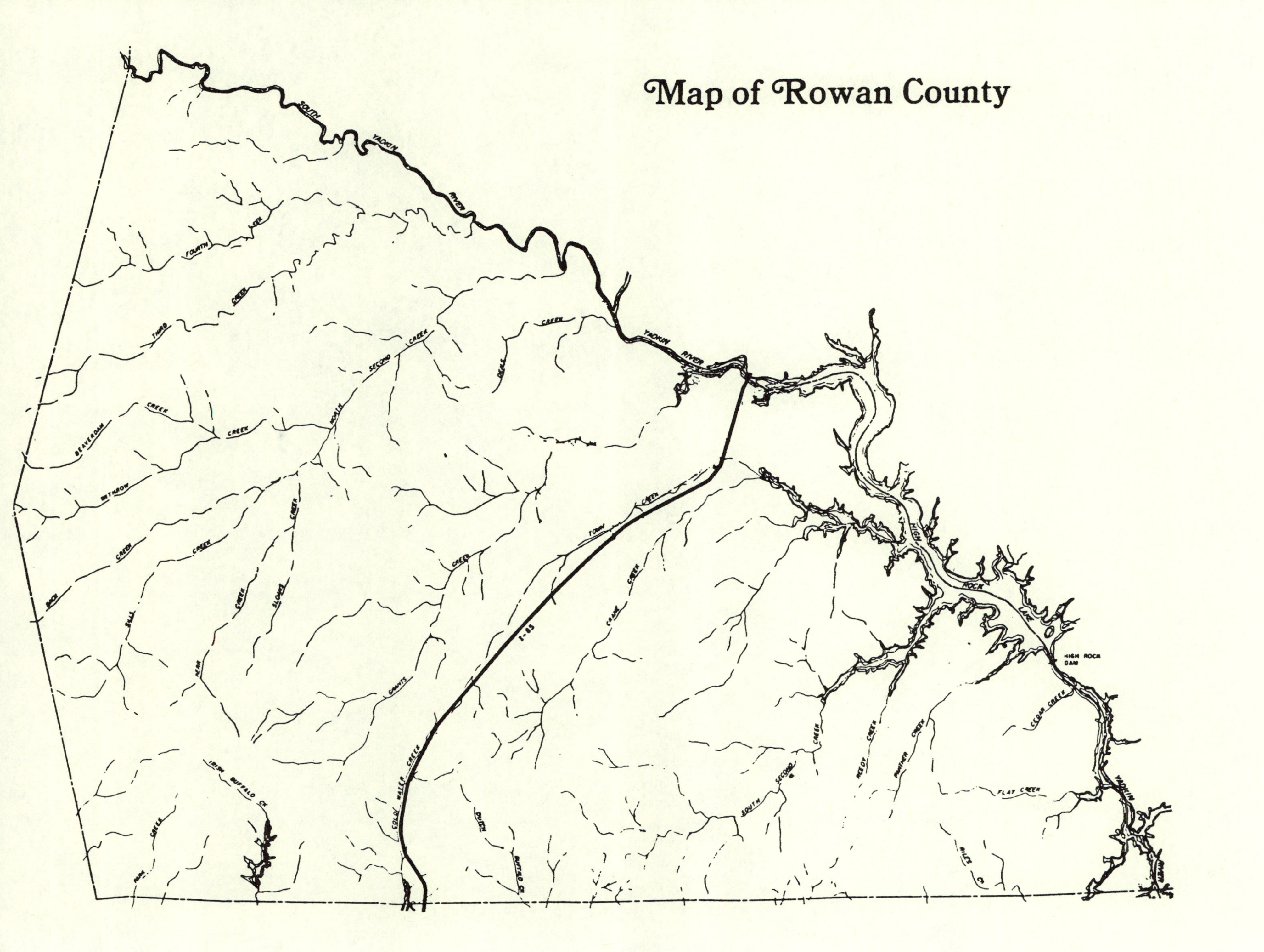

Map of Rowan County
SOUTH YADKIN RIVER
YADKIN RIVER
HIGH ROCK DAM
HIGH ROCK LAKE
CLEAR CREEK
FLAT CREEK
RILES CR.
PANTHER CREEK
REEDY CREEK
SECOND CREEK
SOUTH
FOURTH CREEK
THIRD CREEK
SECOND CREEK
BEAVERDAM CREEK
WETHROW CREEK
NORTH CREEK
DEAL CREEK
CREEK
TOWN CREEK
CRANE CREEK
I-85
GRANTS CREEK
COLD WATER CREEK
DUTCH
BUFFALO CR.
IRISH BUFFALO CR.
PARK CREEK
BELL CREEK
BEAR CREEK
SLOWS CREEK
CREEK
HIGH ROCK
DAM

<u>p. 111, School District 42, 20 July 1850</u>
E. D. Austin, ass't Marshall

1.1 Dawalt LENTZ   46 M NC farmer 525
    Sarah LENTZ   50 F NC (X)
    Edmund D.   20 M NC S farmer
    Rufus W.   18 M NC S labourer
    Aaron G.   16 M NC S labourer
    Mary S.   14 F NC S
    Joseph C.   13 M NC S
    Margaret M.   11 F NC S
    Hannah C.   9 F NC S
    Abram   8 M NC
    Sarah Jane   6 F NC

    [MB: Dawalt Lentz to Sally Lipe 28 Jan. 1828]
    100 A improved land, 422 unimpr, valued at $525

2.2 Peter E. FOUTZ 20 M NC farmer m
    Rebecca FOUT<u>S</u>   21 F NC S m

    [<u>CW</u>: Peter E. Fouts to Rebecca Kirk, dau. of
    Stephen, 29 Dec. 1849]

3.3 James E BASENGER 43 M NC (X) farmer 170
    Anna BASSINGER   44 F NC
    Richard T.   20 M NC S (X) labourer
    John C.   18 M NC S labourer
    Drury W.   16 M NC S labourer
    William A.   14 M NC S labourer
    James I.   12 M NC S labourer
    Emanuel P.   10 M NC S labourer
    Barum P.   8 M NC S labourer
    Howel M.   6 M NC
    Elisabeth C.   4 F NC

    45 A improved land, 115 unimproved, valued at $170

4.4 Conrod MILLER   50 M NC (X) blacksmith 825
    Susanna MILLER   42 F NC
    Alexander M.   22 M NC labourer
    Aaron W.   21 M NC labourer
    Jacob A.   17 M NC S (X) labourer
    Henry D.   14 M NC S labourer
    Rufus S.   11 M NC S labourer
    Crawford A.   8 M NC S
    Doctor F.   7 M NC
    Catharine L.   1 F NC

    [MB: Conrod Miller to Susanna Lentz 9 Jan. 1826]
    75 A improved land, 340 unimproved, valued at $825

5.5 Caleb MILLER   45 M NC farmer 600
    Mary MILLER   43 F NC
    Emely L.   17 F NC S
    Pleasant   15 M NC S labourer

    [MB: Caleb Miller to Mary Lopp 23 Aug. 1828]
    1 slave

6.6 Jacob MILLER   48 M NC farmer
    Anna MILLER   42 F NC (X)
    Levi   22 M NC S labourer (cont.)

Mary   20 F NC
Triphener   14 F NC S
Enock   13 M NC S
John W.   4 M NC

    1 slave

7.7 Polly COX   47 F NC
    Charity B.   27 F NC (X)
    Feribee   17 F NC S
    Susannah   14 F NC S
    Patsy Jane   11 F NC

    [MB: Mark Cox to Polly Curkhead 5 Dec. 1820]

8.8 Nancy MILLER   34 F NC (X) 125
    William P.   12 M NC S
    Catherine L.   11 F NC S
    Mary J.   9 F NC S
    Abram D.   7 M NC S

9.9 Catherine PARKER 55 F NC (X)
    David C.   25 M NC (X) farmer
    Wm L.   16 M NC S labourer
    Drury B.   14 M NC S

    120 A improved land, 130 unimpr, valued at $300
    3 slaves

10.10 Howell PARKER 31 M NC farmer 300
    Joice PARKER   20 F NC
    James C.   1 M NC

    10 A improved land, 140 A unimpr, valued at $300

11.11 Jessee BOGGS   51 M NC farmer
    Terissa BOGGS   30 F NC (X)
    Priscilla   18 F NC S
    Martha   14 F NC S
    Malinda   12 F NC S
    Mary J.   10 F NC S
    Peter   8 M NC
    Harris   4 M NC
    Sarah   3/12 F NC

12.12 Richard PARKER 47 M NC (X) farmer 400
    Ruth PARKER   28 F NC
    Elisabeth D.   8 F NC S
    William   6 M NC
    Jeremiah   4 M NC
    Richard   2 M NC

    200 A improved land, 200 A unimpr, valued at $400

13.13 Willis McLENDON 44 M NC shoemaker
    Barthena McLENDON 26 F NC (X)
    Ellen   14 F NC S
    Martha   10 F NC
    Clementine   8 F NC
    Mary   7 F NC
    Young   4 M NC
<u>p.112, School District #42, 22 July 1850</u>
    Martha Anne   2 F NC

14.14 Abram SHAVER   60 M NC farmer
      Christiana SHAVER 48 F NC
      Noah   18 M NC S labourer
      Isaac M.   17 M NC S labourer
      Christiana A   13 F NC S
      David   12 M NC S
      Alexander SHAVER 10 M NC
      Olla J.   8 F NC S
      Eliza BRADDY   23 F NC (X)

      [MB: Abraham Shaver to Christena Fouts 24 Jan.
        1824]
      no land, 1 slave

15.15 James PARKER   46 M NC farmer
      Caroline PARKER   44 F NC (X)
      Eliza A.   21 F NC S
      John C.   14 M NC S
      James A.   6 M NC
      Martha J.   2 F NC

      no land, 1 slave

16.16 Charles CANUP   39 M NC (X) labourer
      Mira E. CANUP   25 F NC (X)
      Sarah J.   3 F NC
      Emanuel A.   1 M NC
      Calvin   1/12 M NC

17.17 Drura PARKER   40 M NC (X) farmer 300
      Rhoda PARKER   45 F NC
      Emanuel P.   13 M NC S

      [MB: Drury Parker to Rhoda Eller 11 Feb. 1836]
      50 A improved land, 50 A unimpr, valued at $300

18.18 Jacob REDWINE   36 M NC farmer 800
      Eliza A. REDWINE 32 F NC (X)
      William R.   12 M NC S
      Polly A.   8 F NC S

      [MB: Jacob Redwine to Eliza Reed 29 Oct. 1835]
      100 A improved land, 300 A unimpr, valued at $800
      10 slaves

19.19 David CANUP   49 M NC (X)
      Catherine CANUP   30 F NC
      Elizabeth   17 F NC S
      Alexander   16 M NC S
      Polly   12 F NC S
      Daniel   10 M NC
      John   3 M NC

20.20 Littleberry STOKES 42 M NC farmer 700
      Priscilla STOKES   35 F NC
      Pleasant G.   17 M NC
      Calvin H.   16 M NC
      Louisa   12 F NC
      Obadiah   10 M NC
      Williams STOKES   5 M NC
      Littleberry W STOKES 2 M NC

      [MB: Littleberry Stokes to Priscilla Henley 4 May
        1832] (cont.)

200 A improved land, 200 A unimpr, valued at $700
4 slaves

21.21 Washington HENDLY 42 M NC farmer
      Sophia HENDLY   40 F NC
      John W.   20 M NC (X) labourer
      Burrell   18 M NC S labourer
      Rachal L.   16 F NC S
      Eve C.   12 F NC S

      [MB: Washington Hendley to Sophia Fraley 21 Dec.
        1826], no land

22.22 John HENDLY   55 M NC (X) farmer
      Middy HENDLEY   35 F NC (X)
      Charlotte   16 F NC S
      Miles   15 M NC labourer
      Margaret HENDLEY 13 F NC
      Penelope   11 F NC
      Robby   6 M NC
      Greenberry   5 M NC
      Pinkney   1 M NC

23.23 William STOKES   66 M NC farmer 2,000
      Elisabeth STOKES 65 F NC
      Thomas   25 M farmer
      Rebecca   22 F NC
      Elisabeth M.   20 F NC

      60 A improved land, 639 A unimpr, valued at $1,200
      12 slaves

24.24 Jacob FRALEY   25 M NC farmer
      Polly FRALEY   30 F
      Rachel   63 F NC (X)

25.25 Peter MILLER   52 M NC farmer
      Sophia MILLER   46 F NC
      Olla C.   22 F NC
      Henry W.   20 M NC labourer
      Jacob C.   18 M NC S labourer
      Albert   16 M NC S labourer
      Philip   14 M NC S
      Abram M.   12 M NC S

26.26 Otho HARTMAN   35 M NC farmer
      Rose Ann HARTMAN 27 F NC (X)
      Thomas   14 M NC S
      Alfred   10 M NC S
      John   9 M NC S
      Franklin   4 M NC
      Mary J.   2 F NC
      Julius A.   4/12 M NC
      George BROWN   19 M NC labourer

      [CW: Otha Hartman to Mrs. Roseana Brown 17 July
        1845]
      18 A improved land, 80 A unimpr, valued at $100
      Otho Hartman's manager: 550 A improved land, 440
        A unimproved, valued at $4,000

27.27 John HARTMAN   70 M NC farmer 290 m
p. 113, School District #42, 23 July 1850
   Sarah HARTMAN   59 F NC (X) m
   West H.   38 M NC farmer

   [CW: John Hartman to Sarah Rogers 10 Mar. 1850]
   100 A improved land, 130 unimpr, valued at $230
   1 slave

28.28 Sophia HILL   31 F NC (X)
   Hannah   21 F NC (X)
   Henry   18 M NC
   Sally   16 F NC
   Polly   11 F NC
   Jane   8 F NC

29.29 William HOOKS   45 M NC (X) labourer
   Chana HOOKS   27 F NC
   Daniel   10 M NC
   James   8 M NC
   Elizabeth   5 F NC
   Barbara   3 F NC
   Margaret)   5/12 F NC
   Hariet   ) twins   "

29.30 John EARNHART   35 M NC (X) farmer
   Sally EARNHART   33 F NC (X)
   Moses   15 M NC labourer
   Catharine   14 F NC
   Miles   12 M NC
   Jacob   10 M NC
   Thomas   6 M NC
   Eliza J.   3 F NC

   [MB: John Earnhart to Sally Pool 31 Aug. 1833]
   75 A improved land, 227 A unimpr, no valuation

30.31 Jacob POOL   32 M NC farmer (X)
   Martha POOL   29 F NC
   Henery   9 M NC
   Elisabeth   4 F NC
   Alexander   2 M NC

   [MB: Jacob Pool to Martha Cambell 30 Nov. 1839]
   12 A improved land, 155 unimproved, valued at $13

31.32 Elisabeth Malt   30 F NC (X)
   James P.   9 M NC
   Isac C.   6 M NC
   Ruth BRADDY   73 F NC

   [MB: William Malt to Elizabeth Brady 12 May 1840]

32.33 John BLACK   25 M NC (X) farmer
   Susanna BLACK   23 F NC (X)
   Henery H.   6 M NC
   Thomas M.   4 M NC

33.34 James TROUTMAN   39 M NC (X) farmer 75
   Catherine TROUTMAN   32 F NC (X)
   Travis   13 M NC
   Emeline   6 F NC
   Catherine L.   2 F NC   (cont.)

[MB:James Troutman & Catharine Earnheart 27 Oct
   1835]
   40 A improved land, 100 A unimpr, valued at $125

p.113, School District #43, 23 July 1850

34.35 Henry MORGAN   55 M NC (X) labourer
   Polly MORGAN   45 F NC (X)
   Margaret   26 F NC (X)
   Amy   21 F NC (X)
   Jerusha   18 F NC (X)
   Lucretia   16 F NC
   Mary   14 F NC
   McCamy W.   10 M NC
   Julia A. C.   1 F NC
   John C. F.   3 M NC

   [MB: Henry Morgan to Mary Hofner 10 Jan. 1821]

35.36 James McCOMBS   38 M NC farmer 100
   Polly McCOMBS   36 F NC
   Catharine A.   15 F NC S
   Elisabeth N.   13 F NC S
   William M.   10 M NC S
   Martha C.   7 F NC
   James M.   4 M NC
   Catherine Cole   66 F NC (X)

36.37 Polly BEAN   53 F NC (X)
   Nancy BEAN   22 F NC (X)
   Polly   20 F NC
   Rebecca   17 F NC
   Susan   15 F NC (X)
   William H.   11 M NC S
   Harriet   9 F NC
   Margaret   7 F NC

37.38 William SHIPTON   38 M NC (X) labourer
   Uphrania SHIPTON   23 F NC (X)
   John   7 M NC
   Maria   4 F NC
   Elisabeth   2 F NC

38.39 Wilson MORGAN   27 M NC m farmer 50
   Mary MORGAN   20 F NC m (X)

   [MB: Wilson Morgan to Mary Trexler 25 Feb. 1850]
   10 A improved land, 40 A unimpr, valued at $50

39.40 George CROTZER   45 M NC (X) blacksmith
   Sally CROTZER   40 F NC (X)
   Margaret   20 F NC (X)
   Rose M.   19 F NC
   Catherine   16 F NC
   David   12 M NC
   Caleb   9 M NC
   Eve S.   5 F NC
   Joseph   2 M NC

   [MB: George Crotzer to Sally Pame 16 Sept. 1828]
   110 A improved land, 50 A unimpr, valued at $700

4   Linn, 1850 Census, Rowan County, NC

<u>p. 114, School District #43, 23 July 1850</u>

40.41 John GOODMAN   26 M NC (X) farmer
   Susanna Goodman 30 F NC (X)
   Nancy   2 F NC
   Lydia   5/12 F NC

[MB: John Goodman to Susannah Camp 3 Feb. 1846]

41.42 Tobias GOODMAN 28 M NC (X) farmer
   Anna GOODMAN   27 F NC
   Rosanna C.   6 F NC
   Rachel E.   3 F NC
   George A.   1 M NC

[MB: Tobias Goodman to Anna Keply 14 Mar. 1842]
no land but livestock

42.43 William CANUP 47 M NC (X) shoemaker
   Nancy CANUP   42 F NC (X)
   Minta   18 F NC S
   Daniel   16 M NC S
   Nancy   14 F NC
   Joice   10 F NC
   Caleb   5 M NC
   William   11/12 M NC

no land but livestock

43.44 John CANUP   61 M NC farmer 535
   Polly CANUP   62 F NC (X)
   Polly L.   13 F NC
   Rolin   10 M NC
   Solomon   8 M NC
   Susanna CANUP 23 F NC (X)

[MB: John Knup to Polly Stoner 8 July 1818]
150 A improved land, 113 A unimpr, valued at $326

44.45 David CAMPBELL 35 M NC labourer
   Anna Campbell   42 F NC (X)
   William   10 M NC
   Milly   8 F NC
   Susanna   6 F NC
   John   4 M NC
   Samuel   2 M NC

45.46 James KIRK 49 M NC farmer 1,200
200 A improved land, 360 unimpr, valued at $1,200
16 slaves

46.47 John KIRK   46 M NC farmer 1,500
   Sally KIRK   41 F NC
   William P.   17 M NC
   Penewell   16 M NC labourer
   Mary A.   13 F NC
   Eliza   11 F NC
   Calvin J.   9 M NC
   Elisabeth   6 F NC
   Lucy HITMAN   26 F B NC

100 A improved land, 500 A unimpr, valued at $1200
5 slaves

47.48 Paul HARKEY   46 M NC (X) farmer
   Leana HARKEY   33 F NC (X)
   Sally   16 F NC
   George W.   12 M NC
   Robert W.   10 M NC
   Casander   8 F NC
   Richard   7 M NC
   Jackson   5 M NC
   Henery   1 M NC

48.49 Jeremiah MILLS   36 M NC (X) shoemaker
   Jane MILLS   37 F NC (X)
   Eliza E.   14 F NC S

49.50 Polly GALIMORE   19 F NC (X)
   Leah HOFNER   19 F NC (X)
   Tabitha F. L. GALIMORE 1 F NC
   Margaret E. GALIMORE 5/12 F NC

50.51 Joel JACKSON   48 M NC (X) shoemaker
   Rachel JACKSON   40 F NC (X)
   Henry H.   7 M NC
   Mary N.   5 F NC
   Rachel C.   3 F NC

51.52 Christian BRINGLE   66 M farmer NC
16 A improved land, 100 A unimpr, valued at $200
1 slave

52.53 Isac RIBELIN   49 M NC gunsmith 2,000
   Polly RIBELIN   45 F NC (X)
   Paul RIBELIN   24 M NC cabinetmaker
   Crease C.   20 F NC
   Nancy S.   17 F NC
   Elisabeth   13 F NC
   William H. H.   9 M NC
   Caroline   6 F NC
   George W.   4 M NC
   Sarah J.   1 F NC

[MB: Isaac Ribelin to Polly Agle 10 Aug. 1822]
60 A improved land, 518 unimpr, valued at $1,200
7 slaves, manufactured 30 rifles valued at $400

53.54 Catherine JONES 20 F NC (X)
   George A.   1 M NC
   Jessy   1/2 M NC

54.55 Moses EARNHART 38 M NC farmer 1,200
   Adelaid ELLA   25 F NC (X)

45 A improved land, 65 A unimpr, valued at $300
2 slaves

55.56 Alexander FINK 20 M NC farmer 200
   Emeline FINK   18 F NC (X)
   Mary J.   7/12 F NC
   57 Wiley FINK   22 M farmer 200 NC
   Susanna FINK   20 F NC
   James A.   1 M NC

40 A improved land, 250 A unimpr, valued at $400

```
56.58 Wiley CANUP      26 M NC farmer
[115]Elisabeth CANUP 23 F NC (X)
   Luther A.          3 M NC
   Elin A.J.          1 F NC (helpless, cause un
                        known)
   Charlotte A.    5/12 F NC
```

[MB: Wila Knup to Elizabeth Arey 20 Mar. 1846]
30 A improved land, 230 unimpr, valued at $400

p. 115, School District #43, 23 July 1850

```
57.59 John MILLER       30 M NC farmer 75
   Elisabeth A MILLER  22 F NC (X)
```

1 A improved land, 39 A unimproved, valued at $75

```
58.60 William B RABON 32 M NC carpenter
   Matilda L. RABON   33 F NC (X)
   Matilda L.         14 F NC S
   Mary A.E.S.        11 F NC S
   Moses B.F.          6 M NC S
   Lucy C.             4 F NC
   Bartholomew T.      2 M NC
```

Sawmill, lumber worth $1,000

```
59.61 Henery TROUTMAN 48 M NC farmer
   Margaret TROUTMAN 56 F NC (X)
   Nancy             14 F NC
   Henry PARNELL     23 M NC labourer
```

10 A improved land, 34 A unimpr, valued at $100

```
60.62 Martin HOFNER   33 M NC farmer
   Leah HOFNER        30 F NC
   Lavinia            13 F NC
   Atlas              10 M NC
   Rebecca M.          8 F NC
   William             6 M NC
   Rachel           2/12 F NC
```

[MB: Martin Hofner to Lea Hofner 13 Mar. 1838]
no land but livestock

```
61.63 Durant A. PARKER 21 M NC labourer

62.64 Bilson J WHITLOCK 19 M NC labourer
   Paul S. HEILIG      22 M NC farmer 1,000
   David W. HONEYCUT   27 M NC clerk 200
   Alfred E. HANNAH    22 M NC labourer
   Albert F. NASH      22 M NC labourer 61
   Jacob SHANKLE       22 M NC labourer
   John STOKER         22 M NC clerk 250
   Stokes ADDERTON     20 M NC clerk
```

Paul Heilig, ore grinding, gold worth $500

```
63.65 William W. REED    26 M NC 800
   James M. REED        25 M NC
   John W. REED         20 M NC S
   Ruffin ELIOTT        17 M M NC
   Jacob CAUSEY         13 M M NC
   Alfred CAUSEY        12 M M NC
```

```
   Oliver MITCHEL       12 M B NC
   Amanda DUNIN         16 F M NC

   3 slaves
```

```
64.66 Joseph A  WORTH 30 M NC farmer 2,000
   Fatinia WORTH      26 F NC
   Albert H.           9 M NC
   Miriam C.           7 F NC
   John M.             2 M NC
   Eliza NOAH         18 F NC
```

3 slaves
ore grinding, sandwashing, $12,000

```
65.67 Horatio G CARTER  31 M NC farmer 50
   Elizabeth J CARTER   18 F NC
   James M.           1/12 M NC
   Joel CROWELL         22 M NC
```

[MB: H.G.Carter to Elizh. J. Morphis 20 Dec. 1847]
2 slaves

```
66.68 George A.E. PAPE 26 M GER 400
   Martha A. PAPE      18 F NC
   Asa FISHER          35 M NC carpenter
```

```
67.69 Hugh KELLEY      35 M NC physician 2,000
   Amelia KELLY        34 F NC
   Cornelia E.          9 F NC
   Rebecca B KELLY     19 F NC tuteress
```

3 slaves

```
68.70 Edward G. GATLIN    32 M NC shoemaker
   Harriet E. R. GATLIN 23 F NC
   Susan E. R. GATLIN    3 F NC
```

```
69.71 Henry GATLIN        29 M NC miner
   Susanna GATLIN        50 F NC (X)
   Susan GATLIN          13 F NC S
   George W. GATLIN       8 M NC S
```

```
70.72 Abram McCARN      31 M NC miner 100
   Phebe McCARN         28 F NC (X)
   Loveless D.           6 M NC S
   Margaret J.           4 F NC
   Hanible H.            1 M NC
```

```
71.73 John D. GATLIN    27 M NC miner 50
   Rebecca GATLIN       30 F NC (X)
```

```
72.74 James MONTGOMERY      35 M NC manager
   Archibald MONTGOMERY 22 M NC labourer
.75 John MONTGOMERY         33 M NC labourer
   Eliza J. MONTGOMERY  28 F NC
   Sarah Ann            12 F NC S
   Columbus A.           3 M NC
```

James Montgomery: 5 slaves

73.76 Elias LINK   26 M NC blacksmith
    Phillipene LINK   25 F NC
    Margaret A.   5 F NC S
    Mary A.   3 F NC
    John H.   1 M NC
    David LINK   55 M NC (X) blacksmith

<u>p.116, Gold Hill District #44, 23 July 1850</u>

74.77 Hartwell S. LOVE 29 M NC
    Sarah B. LOVE   29 F NC
    Hamilton J. LOVE   7 M NC
    Franklin   4 M NC S
    Jane M.   3 F NC
    Stanhope P.   3/12 M NC

75.78 George MOOSE   24 M NC miner 50 m
    Elisabeth H. MOOSE 20 F NC (X) m

76.79 John V BARINGER 23 M NC labourer 50
    Mary A. BARINGER 21 F NC
    George W.   6/12 M NC

77.80 Archibald HONEYCUT 31 M NC miner 275
    James PASCOE   27 M NC miner 25

    Pascoe: 1 slave
    Ore grainding: gold worth $2,200

78.81 Acril GRIFFIN 52 M NC (X) labourer
    Eliza GRIFFIN   40 F NC (X)
    Lany A.   14 F NC
    Wesley   15 M NC miner
    Frances   12 F NC
    Sidney   9 M NC
    Emeliza GRIFFIN   7 F NC
    Temperance H.   4 F NC

79.82 William C BLALOCK 25 M NC labourer
    Mary BLALOCK   21 F NC
    John E.   2 M NC
    P. William P   1/12 M NC

80.83 Benjamin WILLIS 42 M NC (X) labourer
    Sarah WILLIS   32 F NC
    William   9 M NC S
    James H.   3 M NC
    Clarissa BOWERS 26 F NC
    John J. BOWERS 3/12 M NC

81.84. Henery JONES 49 M NC (X) wagonmaker
    Sarah E. JONES   39 F NC (X)
    Martha   13 F NC
    Leanna   11 F NC S
    Happy   9 F NC S
    Willy B.   11 M NC
    James W.   9 M NC
    Elisabeth C.   5 F NC
    Doctor   4 M NC
    John P.   5 M NC

82.85 Samuel JONES 21 M NC
    Martha JONES   30 F NC (X)

83.86 Samuel GRIFFIN 41 M NC labourer
    Mary GRIFFIN   38 F NC (X)
    Mary   17 F NC
    Nancy   15 F NC S
    John   13 M NC
    James   10 M NC
    Abner   6 M NC
    John W.   3 M NC

84.87 Alexander M WEBB 29 M NC labourer 100
    Linna A. WEBB   27 F NC
    Margaret E.   2 F NC
    Zachariah TUCKER 69 M NC labourer

85.88 Green L WREN   49 M NC innkeeper
    Mary A. WREN   33 F NC
    John A.   11 M NC S
    Elisabeth   9 F NC
    Mary P.   5 F NC
    James   3/12 M NC (Practicing
    Archibald M. NESBITT 24 M M.D.(Physician NC
    William A. McCORKLE 19 M NC merchant 550
    William IDLER   35 M NC miner
    Roseana IDLER   28 F NC
    Jacob   13 M NC
    Mary   5 F NC
    Rosa   3 F NC
    William   1 M NC
    Clement IDLER   27 M NC miner
    Celestine RINGLE 28 M NC miner
    David ELIAS   35 M NC merchant
    Eleanor ELIAS   24 F NC
    Jennette   4 F NC
    Rachel   2 F NC
    James DIAL   57 M NC (X) labourer

    Wren: 7 slaves

86.89 Edward B RICE 30 M NC physician 1,500
    Gardner STEARNS   49 M NC labourer
    Nancy STEARNS   38 F NC
    Sarah   18 F NC
    Jane   17 F NC
    George C.   15 M NC
    Alfred   13 M NC
    Thomas   11 M NC
<u>p.117, Gold Hill District $44, 24 July 1850</u>
    Caroline   9 F NC
    Henery   6 M NC
    William   4 M NC
    James   2 M NC

    Gardiner Starnes: 9 slaves

87.90 James MOSELEY 27 M NC (X) labourer
    Nancy MOSELY   35 F NC
    Elisabeth   8 F NC S
    William   6 M NC S
    Sarah Ann   2 F NC
    Moritz LEERS   25 M NC
    Richard S. ADDERTON 18 M NC

88.91 Aaron WOOLWORTH 46 M NC silversmith

89.92 James ELWOOD   37 M NC labourer
  Sophia ELWOOD   31 F NC (X)
  Sarah A.   13 F NC S
  Mary C.   9 F NC S
  Thomas   6 M NC S
  John M.   1 M NC

90.93 Calvin JONES   24 M NC labourer
  Mary JONES   22 F NC
  James   5 M NC

91.94 James JOHNSON 35 M NC labourer
  Jane JOHNSON   32 F NC
  Richard M.   12 M NC
  David A.   10 M NC
  James M.   8 M NC
  William L.P.   6 M NC
  Rufus, M.D.   4 M NC
  Mary A.   1/12 F NC

92.95 Bezal GALLAMORE 26 M NC (X) labourer
  Rachel GALAMORE 25 F NC (X)

[MB:Bozwell Gallimore & Rachel Mesimer 7 Nov 1846]

93.96 Susan MASK   40 F NC (X)
  Marian   14 M NC
  Henry   12 M NC
  Nancy   10 F NC
  Dudly   8 M NC

94.97 John JONES   19 M NC labourer
  Amanda MASK   18 F NC

95.98 Benjamin BEAVER 41 M NC (X) labourer
  Ransom SIDES   19 M NC labourer m
  Catherine SIDES   21 F NC m
  Mary C. CULP   2 F NC
  Leah GROANER   54 F NC (X)

[MB: Ransom Sides to Catharine E Culp 2 Mar 1850]

96.99 Martha ARNELL   22 F NC (X)
  Julian A. DAVIS 28 M NC (X)

97.100 Ann FELTS   34 F NC 50
  Susanna STIKELEATHER 72 F NC
  John SELLS   52 M NC (X) labourer
  Caleb PENDERGRASS 35 M NC (X) miner

98.101 Elisabeth PARNELL 55 F NC (X)
  Alexander PARNELL   24 M NC
  Margaret PARNELL   26 F NC
  David F.   13 M NC
  Margaret   6 F NC

99.102 Charles REEVES   22 M NC (X) miner
  Mary A. REEVES   22 F NC (X)
  Margaret   1 F NC

100.103 Mary A CAMPBELL   26 F NC (X)
  Margaret C.   7 F NC
  Nicoles LUDEWICK 45 M NC

101.104 John SULIVAN   21 M NC (X) labourer
  Elisabeth SULLIVAN 21 F NC (X)
  Julia A. RIGINS   5 F NC

102.105 Ann BIRD   28 F NC (X)
  Haris MILTON   26 M NC (X) labourer

103.106 Tilman AUSTIN   27 M NC
  Amelia AUSTIN   24 F NC
  Josaphine   6 F NC S
  Elisabeth   4 F NC S
  Henry   2 M NC
  Cornelius   1/12 M NC

104.107 John VANDERBURG   32 M NC labourer
  Catherine VANDERBURG 30 F NC (X)
  Israel   12 M NC
  Christina   10 F NC
  Francis   8 M NC
  Elisabeth   6 F NC
  James M.) twins   4 M NC
  Eliza   )   4 F NC
  108. Eli NOAH   29 M NC (X) labourer
  Rebecca NOAH   28 F NC (X)
  Eliza   19 F NC
  Lundy   18 F NC S
  Alexander   11 M NC

p. 118, Gold Hill District #4, 24 July 1850
  Susanna   10 F NC
  Adaline   8 F NC
  Mary C.   ) twins 6 F NC
  Margaret C.)   6 F NC
  Rebecca E.   4 F NC
  John W.   1 M NC
  James C.   2/12 M NC
  Margaret NOAH   40 F NC (X)

105.109 Tabitha JOHNSON 24 F NC (X)
  William   6 M NC
  George W.   3 M NC

106.110 William A LAMB   22 M NC (X)
  Sarah J. LAMB   28 F NC (X)
  Calvin   9 M NC
  Nancy   8 F NC
  Mary Ann   2 F NC
  Adaline RIGGINS 24 F NC (X)

107.111 Mary SIMPSON   44 F NC
  Elisabeth   21 F NC (X)
  Jacob   13 M NC S
  Miles   15 M NC
  Catharine   9 F NC S
  Green M.   7 M NC

108.112 Daniel LUDWICK   26 M NC miner
  Martha M. Ludwick 32 F NC

109.113 William J LISK   33 M NC (X) labourer
  Temperance LISK 35 F NC
  Henry   14 M NC
  Thomas   12 M NC
  Cornelius   11 M NC   (cont.)

```
            Starlin L.         9 M NC
            Margaret E.        6 F NC S
            Susan F.           2 F NC

110.114 John H WEANT     48 M NC labourer
        Delilah WEANT    58 F NC (X)
        George W.        14 M NC S
        Sarah E.         13 F NC S
        Hugh A.           2 M NC
        Christianna PENCE 34 F NC (X)


[MB: John H. Weant to Delilah Crider 20 Dec. 1832]


111.115 Burten R DRIVER  24 M NC labourer


112.116 Whitson NASH     22 M NC labourer 450
        Jane NASH        20 F NC
        Reuben C.         1 M NC


113.117 Ephraim WHITLOCK 22 M NC (X) labourer
        Apsy WHITLOCK    20 F NC (X)
        Eliza D.          4 F NC
        Daniel            1 M NC
        Wilson SMART     21 M NC labourer


114.118 Doctor BENNETT   24 M NC Mu carpenter
        Amanda BENNETT   38 F M NC
        John H. SHEPPARD 15 M M NC labourer


115.119 Daniel KERNS     37 M NC blacksmith
        Litha            39 F NC
        Obadiah          18 M NC blacksmith
        Edward F.        16 M NC blacksmith
        Mary             12 F NC S
        George W.        11 M NC S
        Daniel            9 M NC S
        Jacob             7 M NC
        Susan             4 F NC
        Jane S.           2 F NC
        Mary A. WISE     31 F NC

    Coal worth $35.00


116.120 Lewis P ROTHROCK 36 M NC miner
        Rebecca ROTHROCK 35 F NC
        Anne A.           8 F NC S
        Wallace H.        7 M NC S
        Susan A.          6 F NC
        Margaret D.       4 F NC
        James L.          1 M NC
        Catharine Bunn   21 F NC

    1 slave


117.121 Joseph McCANLESS 38 M NC
        Catharine McCanless 33 F NC
        Wm L.            10 M NC
        James C.          9 M NC
        David A.          6 M NC
        Laura A.          1 F NC

    3 slaves
```

```
118.122 John MESEMER    52 M NC (X) labourer
        Hannah MESEMER  50 F NC (X)
        Polly           37 F NC (X)
        Nancy           23 F NC (X)
        Belford         18 M NC labourer
        Henery          15 M NC labourer
        George          10 M NC


119.123 George OWEN     25 M NC (X) labourer
[119]   Eleoner OWEN    17 F NC
        Casper           1 M NC
        Miles A. OWEN   19 M NC labourer
```

p. 119, Gold Hill District #44

```
120.124 Andrew TROUTMAN 34 M NC labourer
        Catharine TROUTMAN 29 F NC (X)
        Rufus            8 M NC
        Delia T.         3 F NC
        Elisabeth     3/12 F NC


[MB: Andrew Troutman to Catharine Aronheart
22 Jan. 1839]

121.125 James MORPHIS    43 M NC miner 500
        Permilia MORPHIS 58 F NC
        Cornilus A.      20 M NC S labourer
        Sarah Ann        15 M NC S

    3 slaves, gold worth $750


122.126 John BARTLET    24 M NC labourer
        Rachel BARTLET   23 F NC (X)


123.127 Henry B KINGSBERY 28 M NC tailer 150
        Lucy A. KINGSBERY  28 F NC
        Maria WALL        20 F NC


[MB:Henry Kingsbury to Lucy Ann Walls 2 Apr. 1842]

124.128 Samuel G BOYDEN 35 M NC MA physician 200
        Letitia C. BOYDEN   20 F NC


[CW: Dr. Samuel C. Boyden to Letitia C. Bruner 23
    July 1850]

125.129 Ruben J HOLMES  27 M NC merchant 1,200
        Moses L. HOLMES  33 M NC merchant 260
        Daniel CULP      19 M NC
        Delila WORTH     45 F NC Mu

    3 slaves
    Holmes & Earnhart: 6 slaves


126.130 Richard H. UMSTEAD 47 M MD saddler
        Lavinia UMSTEAD   35 F NC
        Mary              16 F NC
        Lucinda            4 F NC
        Maria              2 F NC

127.131 Michael SWICEGOOD  28 M NC shoemaker
        Elisabeth SWICEGOOD 22 F NC
        Daniel L           2 M NC
```

128.132 Francis W. SCOTT   26 M ENG tailer
   Elisabeth J. SCOTT   21 F TN
   John F.   1 M NC

129.133 Eliza RICHARDS   __ F NC

130.134 John VOLENTINE   35 M NC Mu
   Mary VOLENTINE   20 F NC Mu

131.135 John CROOK   23 M NC labourer
   Elisabeth CROOK   25 F NC
   Henry   3 M NC
   Wila   1 M NC
   Richard   1/12 M NC

[MB: John Crook to Elizabeth Park 8 Feb. 1847]

132.136 Gerry ANDERSON 34 M NC (X) labourer
   Eve ANDERSON   33 F NC (X)
   William   12 M NC
   George   10 M NC
   Lewis   5 M NC
   Monroe   1/12 M NC

133.137 William JINKINS   31 M ENG miner
   Elisabeth JINKINS   29 F ENG
   Mary A.   4 F ENG
   John   9/12 M NC

134.138 James PHILLIPS   27 M ENG miner
   Caroline PHILLIPS   29 F NC
   James   2 M NC
   William J.   1 M NC

135.139 George WALTON   28 M NC tailor
   Catharine WALTON   29 F NC
   Junius F.   1 M NC

Cloth valued at $200, made various articles

136.140 Eli CARROLL   24 M NC
   Thomas TIPPETT   45 M NC labourer
   Stimson MILLS   21 M NC labourer
   James MILLS   19 M NC labourer
   James A. CAMPBELL   20 M NC shoemaker

137.141 Daniel MANN   55 M NC labourer
   Charlotte MANN   55 F NC (X)
   William   17 M NC labourer
   Cornelia V.   3 F NC
   John C. McCARN   1/12 M NC

138.142 Jacob PENCE   36 M NC labourer
   Mary PENCE   30 F NC
   Thomas H.   6 M NC

139.143 John SOLOMON   21 M NC
   Eliza SOLOMON   21 F NC

140.144 Abigail BOLITHO 34 F NC (X)
   Martha J.   4 F NC
   Fatima A.   6/12 F NC
   John PARKER   22 M NC   (cont.)

   Adelade GRAHAM   25 F NC Mu

141.145 William H THRIFT 29 M NC (X) miner
   Jane THRIFT   27 F NC
   Laura A.   9 F NC
   Mary L.   7 F NC
   Sarah A.   6 F NC
[120] Emely Jane   4 F NC

p. 120, Gold Hill District #44, 24 July 1850

142.146 Polly CASTLE   24 F NC
   Mary Jane   6 F NC
   William H   1 M NC
   Love FREEMAN   20 F M NC

143.147 John SCOTT   27 M NC (X) Mu chairmaker
   Sarah An SCOTT   26 F NC Mu
   Ann Emeline   9 F NC Mu
   William A.   6 M NC Mu
   Jane M.   3 F NC Mu
   John M.   1 M NC Mu
   Lucinda S.   4 F NC Mu

144.148 John LENTZ   29 M NC labourer
   Sophia LENTZ   25 F NC
   Luther A.   3 M NC
   Solomon HEILIG   29 M NC clergyman

[MB: John Lentz to Sophia Hielick 24 May 1841]
3 slaves

145.149 Martha McCARNES   34 F NC (X)
   James F.   15 M NC
   Margaret J.   12 F NC
   George Washington   8 M NC
   Moses H.   4 M NC

146.150 John W. GORDEY   25 M NC labourer
   Hester M. GORDEY   22 F NC
   Lindsay M.   0/12 M NC

147.151 James MOSELY   27 M NC (X) labourer
   Nancy MOSELY   35 F NC
   Elisabeth C.   7 F NC S
   William F.   5 M NC S
   Sarah A.   3 F NC
   Rebeca MOSELY   78 F VA (X)

148.152 Nicholas SMITH   24 M NC (X) miner
   Sophia SMITH   22 F NC
   Charles   3 M NC
   Benjamin F.   1 M NC

149.153 Oren L. BASS   23 M NC labourer
   Catherine BASS   24 F NC
   Robert MOREAU   23 M NC labourer
   Burges KILPATRICK 22 M NC (X) labourer

150.154 Alexander EARNHEART 40 M NC (X) labourer
   Polly EARNHEART   30 F (X)
   Clark   11 M NC S (cont.)

Rosana   7 F NC S
Jane   5 F NC

151.155 Julia A. BURKET   20 F NC Mu
        Housten   6 M NC Mu

152.156 John CASPER   21 M NC (X) labourer
        Mary C. CASPER   22 F NC
        Elisabeth J.   2 F NC
        Lucinda   0/12 F NC
        Rachel L. FREESE   9 F NC S

153.157 Rachel CASPER   30 F NC (X)
        Soleman D.   10 M NC idiot

154.158 David CASPER   28 M NC (X) labourer
        Lavinia CASPER   23 F NC
        Margaret S.   4 F NC
        Barbara C.   2 F NC

[MB: David Casper to Lavinia Casper 19 Feb. 1844]

155.159 Conrod CASPER   62 M NC carpenter
        Rachel CASPER   55 F NC (X)
        Elisabeth GRIFFIN   24 F NC
        Rachel   8 F NC
        Mary C.   6 F NC
        Thomas   4 M NC
        Elisabeth   3 F NC
        Anna CASPER   21 F NC
        Adeline   4 F NC
        Polly PHILLIPS   18 F NC
        Luther A.   1 M NC
        Levi A. CASPER   5 M NC

[MB: Conrod Casper to Rachel Morgan 12 Sept. 1821]

156.160 Levi CASPER   35 M NC carpenter
        Catharine CASPER   33 F NC (X)
        Elisabeth   9 F NC
        Polly   6 F NC
        Nancy   1 F NC
        Jacob   0/12 M NC

157.161 David MARTIN   30 M ENG miner
        Hannah MARTIN   27 F NC
        William H.   6 M NC
        Susan M.   5 F NC
        Mary MARTIN   18 F NC
        Henry MARTIN   32 M NC miner

158.162 John PETERS   36 M ENG miner 200
        Sidney PETERS   26 F MD
        Hugh   4 M NC

159.163 Martin STEVENS   43 M ENG miner
[121]Jane STEVENS   30 F ENG
        Martin S.   8 M NC
        Elisabeth A.   6 F NC
        Mary Jane   4 F NC
        Mathew W.   3 M NC
        Joseph TYACK   25 M ENG miner
        Francis TYACK   27 M ENG miner

p.121, Gold Hill District #44, 25 July 1850

160.164 Jacob C BARNHART 23 M NC merchant 700
        Hervy H. COLTHARP   26 M SC
        John M. BARNHART   27 M NC miner
        John W. YONTZ   19 M NC labourer
        Eli YONTZ   22 M NC labourer

1 slave, Gold mining, gold worth $19,000
Heilig, Barnhart & Co.
Barnhart, Moos & Co., sandwashing Gold worth
$1,473

161.164 Mathew MOYLA   20 M miner ENG
        Eliza MOYLA   25 F ENG
        John   6 M NC
        Henry   4 M NC
        Julia   2 F NC
        Mathew   0/12 M NC
        Joshua DAVIS   21 M NC miner
        John DAVIS   23 M NC miner
        Thomas TRALOAR   18 M NC labourer

162.166 John M. COFFIN 35 M mining NC
        Clarkson COFFIN   25 M mining NC
        Martin RICHWINE   25 M NC

11 slaves, Coffin, Worth & Co., ore grinding,
sandwashing, gold worth $12,000

163.167 Daniel M. MOYER   32 M NC labourer
        Elisabeth MOYER   24 F NC
        Sarah A.C.   7 F NC
        Elsa C.   4 F NC
        Milton H.G.   1 M NC

164.168 John MOODY   52 M CN
        Mary A. MOODY   45 F SC
        John A.   22 M NC
        George L.   17 M NC S labourer
        Janes F.   15 M NC labourer
        Cornelia F.   13 F NC S
        William A.   12 M NC S
        Daniel W.   8 M NC S
        Charles A.B   5 M NC

165.169 Samuel FRALEY   50 M NC ginmaker
        Loretta FRALEY   38 F NC
        Margaretta   17 F NC
        William   16 M NC

[MB: Samuel Fraley to Loretta Gheen 24 Apr. 1828]

166.170 William FLETCHER   25 M miner NC
        Elisabeth FLETCHER   26 F NC (X)
        John F. MARTIN   27 M miner ENG
        William A. MARTIN   23 M miner ENG
        Benjamine T. MARTIN 16 M miner ENG
        James MARTIN   28 M miner ENG
        John ANDREUS   30 M miner ENG
        William MARTIN   35 M miner ENG
                    (cont.)

Peters & Martin & Co., see also 167.171,.172
Martins: gold worth $5,110 and $900

167.171 Elisabeth LUCKEY   46 F ENG
    John B. STIDAFOR   24 M ENG miner
    Samuel M. STIDAFOR   21 M ENG miner
    William R. LUCKEY   5 M MA
    Lucy H. LUCKEY   2 F NC
    James PETERS   32 M ENG miner
    Nannie PETERS   3 F NC

168.172 Hugh PETERS   38 M ENG miner
    Eliza PETERS   39 F ENG
    Emma   18 F ENG
    Elisabeth   11 F ENG
    Eliza J.   3/12 F NC

    See 166.170 also

169.173 Nathan BROWN 49 M NC carriagemaker
    Sarah BROWN   40 F NC
    Robert M. BROWN   18 M NC carriagemaker

[MB: Nathan Brown to Sally Jones 26 June 1827]
Made various articles worth $600

170.174 Thomas SAWYER   27 M NC blacksmith
    Margaret SAWYER   30 F NC
    Elisabeth   10 F NC S
    Mary   8 F NC S
    William   5 M NC S
    Sarah   2 F NC
    Henery OLIVER   19 M ENG blacksmith

171.175 Robert A MOREAU   23 M NC labourer
    Andrew KILPATRICK   21 M NC wagonmaker
    William BOYD   35 M NC labourer

172.176 David STOKER   39 M NC labourer
    Sarah C. STOKER   39 F NC
    James A.   18 M NC S
    Philo White   15 M NC S
    Wade   12 M NC S
    Davidson   8 M NC S
    Robert D.   6 M NC S
    Eliza AUSTIN   21 F NC S
    George W. HIPP   27 M NC silversmith

<u>p.122, District #44 Gold Hill, 25 July</u>

173.177 John CAUBLE   29 M NC labourer
    Charlotte CAUBLE 32 F NC
    Jane   4 F NC
    Martha I.   2 F NC

[MB:John Cauble to Charlotte Walton 24 July 1844]

174.178 Andrew BUCHART   21 M NC

175.179 Charles L EARNHART 40 M NC farmer 500
    Lavinia EARNHART   40 F NC (X)
    Julia Ann   16 F NC
    Jane   13 F NC
    Alfred   11 M NC
    Amanda   7 F NC
    Martha   4 F NC
    George HOPMAN   20 M labourer NC

[MB:Charles Earnhart to Levina Thomas 26 June 1833]
50 A improved land, 75 A unimpr, valued at $500

176.180 Jacob EARNHART 65 M NC (X) farmer 1,000
    Catherine EARNHART 58 F NC (X)
    Chlotilda   15 F NC

    23 A improved land, 100 A unimpr, valued at $200

177.181 Jacob EARNHART 30 M NC (X) farmer
    Anna M. EARNHART   24 F NC
    Crawford A.   5 M NC
    Nacy C.   4 F NC
    Jiles L.   2 M NC

[MB: Jacob Earnheart to Ann Troutman 10 July 1843]

178.182 James UDY   36 M NC carpenter
    Sophia UDY   37 F NC (X)
    Albert A.   15 M NC S
    Pierdy M.   12 F NC
    John J.   9 M NC
    William C.   7 M NC
    Mary Jane   3 F NC

179.183 William TOMPKINS 43 M ENG (X) miner
    John   9 M ENG S
    Mary Ann   7 F NC S
    Ann TOMPKINS   62 F ENG (X)
    John DENNIS   55 M ENG miner
    James DENNIS   29 M ENG (X) miner

180.184 Bryant CELLARS   24 M NC labourer
    Sarah CELLARS   22 F NC (X)
    Catharine   7/12 F NC

181.185 Will<u>a</u> THOMPSON 37 M labourer NC (X)
    Mary THOMPSON   36 F NC (X)
    Julia Ann   14 F NC S
    Calvin   12 M NC S
    Henry   10 M NC S
    Sylvester   4 M NC
    Caroline   2 F NC

182.186 Lucinda BUNN   41 F NC (X)
    James C.   17 M NC
    Joseph Wesley   16 M NC
    Unice   13 F NC
    Nancy Helen   11 F NC
    Eliza J.   8 F NC
    William F.   3 M NC
    Grandberry WILLIAMS 38 M NC labourer

183.187 Peter HARTMAN   45 M NC (X) farmer 1,100
     Sally HARTMAN   42 F NC
     Charles   22 M NC labourer
     Catherine   19 F NC S
     Jesse   17 M NC S
     Mary Ann   14 F NC S
     Tobias   12 M NC S
     Melinda   10 F NC S
     Nancy   7 F NC S
     John   4 M NC
     William   1 M NC

     [MB: Peter Hartman to Sally Hoffman 17 Apr. 1827]
     90 A improved land, 198 unimpr, valued at $1,100

184.188 Henry HARKEY   55 M NC farmer 450
     Barbara HARKEY   45 F NC
     John HARKEY   23 M NC farmer 175
     Margaret HARKEY   21 F NC 175
     Daniel   19 M NC labourer
     [MB: Henry Harkey to Barbara Miller 19 Dec. 1829]
     Henry: 40 A improved land, 50 A unimpr, valued at
          $50, 2 slaves
     John: 25 A improved land, 35 A unimpr, value
          $175

185.189 George HARKEY   31 M NC farmer 175
     Elisabeth HARKEY   31 F NC
     Julia Ann   7 F NC
     Daniel   5 M NC
     Elisabeth   1 F NC

     [MB:George Harkey & Elizabeth Goodman 29 Nov 1837]
     30 A unimproved land, 30 A unimpr, valued at $175

186.190 George GOODMAN   61 M NC farmer 620
     Elisabeth GOODMAN   57 F NC
     Lucinda   31 F NC
     Catharine   21 F NC S
     Celia Ann   17 F NC S
     Christopher   24 M NC S
     Abram   14 M NC S
     Caleb   10 M NC S

     [MB: George Goodman & Elizabeth Hill 25 June 1812]
     100 A improved land, 200 A unimpr, valued at $620

187.191 Jacob HARKEY   30 M NC farmer 175
     Lavinia HARKEY   32 F NC
     Paul R.   7 M NC
p.123, School District #40, 31 July 1850
     Margaret E.   4 F NC

     30 A improved land, 20 A unimpr, valued at

188.192 Daniel HOFFMAN   35 M NC farmer 1,500
     Anna HOFFMAN   32 F NC
     Lettitia M.   13 F NC S
     William A.   9 M NC S
     Michael C.   4 M NC
     Mary J.   1 F NC
     Malinda C.   1/12 F NC

     [CW: D. Hoffman to Anne Williams 24 Sept. 1835]
     60 A improved land, 100 A unimpr, valued at $1,000
     2 slaves

189.193 Wilson KESTLER   25 M NC farmer 350
     Nancy KESTLER   35 F NC (X)
     John HOFFMAN   18 M NC S labourer
     Adam HOFFMAN   16 M NC S labourer
     David HOFFMAN   14 M NC S
     Henry HOFFMAN   8 M NC
     Joseph KESTLER   1 M NC
     Nelly ELLER   45 F NC (X)

     60 A improved land, 57 A unimpr, valued at $350

190.194 Christiana BULLEN 33 F NC (X) 250
     Eve Ann   15 F NC S
     Sally C.   13 F NC S
     Elisabeth   1 F NC
     Mary A.   19 F NC

     85 A improved land, 95 A unimpr, valued at $250

191.195 Henry WILHELM   34 M NC farmer 300
     Sophia WILHELM   24 F NC
     Louisa   9 F NC S
     Margaret E.   6 F NC S
     Sophia C.   1/12 F NC

     80 A improved land, 116 unimpr, valued at $300

192.196 Jonathon STONER   52 M NC (X) wagonmaker 66
     Easter STONER   37 F NC (X)
     William   16 M NC S labourer
     Daniel   14 M NC S
     Aveline   12 F NC S
     Nancy   10 F NC S
     Mildred   9 F NC S
     Julia A.   8 F NC S
     Alfred   6 M NC
     Monroe   4 M NC
     Leah   1 F NC

     [MB:Jonathan Stoner/Easter Lutewick 26 Apr 1830]
     60 A improved land, 800 A unimpr, valued at --

193.197 William ALMON   25 M NC (X) labourer
     Polly ALMON   20 F NC (X)
     Archibald ALMON   17 M NC labourer

194.198 David LUDEWICK 30 M NC (X) labourer

195.199 John W TREXLER 25 M NC farmer 75
     200 A improved land, 146 unimproved, valued at

196.200 George BAIM   38 M NC (X) wagonmaker 500
     Lavinia BAIM   33 F NC (X)
     Levi   11 M NC S
     David   9 M NC S
     Polly   6 F NC
     Catharine   4 F NC
     Jerusha   1 F NC   (cont.)

Charlotte   5/12 F NC
David Trexler   21 M NC labourer

[MB: George Baim to Lovinia Earnhart 16 Dec. 1837]
50 A improved land, 150 A unimpr, valued at $500

197.201 Jesse RIBELIN 27 M NC gunsmith
    Elisabeth RIBELIN 32 F NC (X)
    Penna L.   2 F NC
    Samuel A.   9/12 M NC

no land but livestock

198.202 Solemon EAGLE 37 M NC cooper 200
    Agness EAGLE   33 F NC (X)
    Mary   13 F NC S
    John   12 M NC S
    Joseph   10 M NC S
    George   8 M NC S
    Nancy   6 F NC S
    Daniel   1 M NC

[MB: Solomon Eagle & Agness N. Hodge 18 Dec 1834]
60 A improved land, 140 A unimpr, valued at

199.203 Daniel LUDEWICK 31 M NC (X) farmer
    Crissy LUDEWICK   30 F NC (X)
    Easter   7 F NC

[MB: Daniel Ludwick to Crissey Paine 16 Oct. 1840
13 A improved land, 22 A unimpr, valued at $100

200.204 Charles STONER 39 M NC (X) farmer 125
    Leah STONER   34 F NC (X)

[MB: Charles Stoner to Leah Lotwick 25 Mar 1833]
30 A improved land, 52 A unimpr, valued at $125

201.205 Willa MORGAN jr 32 M NC farmer 200
    Susanna MORGAN   32 F NC
    Daniel R.   9 M NC S
    Mary   6 F NC S
    Abram A.   3 M NC
    Nathan R.   0/12 M NC
    Philopena ICEHOUR 30 F NC

[CW: Willie Morgan & Susannah Icehour of Cabarrus
   Co. 17 Oct. 1839 in Cabarrus]
50 A improved land, 100 A unimpr, valued at $200

202.206 Levi TREXLER   36 M NC farmer 520
    Elisabeth TREXLER 34 F NC (X)
    Allen   12 M NC S
    John   11 M NC S
    Daniel M.   4 M NC
    Mary Jane   3 F NC
    Henry C.   6/12 M NC

[WC: Levi Trexeler to Elizabeth Frick 5 Apr. 1835]
15 A improved land, 175 A unimpr, valued at $220

p. 124, School District #41, 31 July 1850

203.207 Willa MORGAN Sr 37 M NC farmer 700
    Catherine MORGAN   32 F NC (X)
    Sophrona J.   12 F NC S
    Elisabeth C.   10 F NC S
    Polly S.   7 F NC S
    Sally A.   5 F NC
    Jesse Austin   2 M NC

50 A improved land, 100 A unimpr, valued at

204.208 James BUCHANAN   60 M SC farmer 2,000
    John BUCHANAN   22 M NC farmer
    Malinda BUCHANAN   21 F NC
    Peter WALLER   48 M NC labourer
    Henry C. WALLER   13 M NC S
    Margaret   11 F NC
    Mary BUCHANAN   21 F NC
    Cornelius A.   1 M NC

125 A improved land, 475 unimpr, valued at $1,200

205.209 David PARKS   46 M NC carpenter
    Polly PARKS   35 F NC (X)
    Eliza BOST   21 F NC
    William A. BOST   25 M NC blind
    David TREXLER   22 M NC (X)labourer
    George PARKS   18 M NC S farmer
    Osborn   16 M NC S labourer
    Daniel   10 M NC S
    Elisabeth)twins   13 F NC
    Mary   )   13 F NC
    Rose D.   2 F NC
    Loretta BOST   3 F NC
    David A.   1 M NC

30 A improved land, 56 unimproved, valued at

206.210 Edward SHEPARD   22 M NC labourer 150
    Rachel H. SHEPARD 20 F NC S
    Siles   14 M NC S
    Rachel SHEPARD   50 F NC

25 A improved land, 15 A unimpr, valued at $150

207.211 Henry MORGAN   31 M NC farmer 300
    Polly MORGAN   25 F NC
    Sally   5 F NC
    John   3 M NC
    Penna E.   1 F NC

25 A improved land, 140 A unimpr, valued at $300

208.242 Moses G MORGAN   37 M NC farmer 1,200
    Barbara MORGAN   35 F NC
    Nathan   17 M NC S
    John   15 M NC S
    McCamy   13 M NC S
    Mary   11 F NC S
    Rhoda   9 F NC S
    Moses G.   7 M NC S
    Noah   5 M NC
    Jacob   3 M NC   (cont.)

```
      Loveless              1 M NC
      Rachel SHAVER        37 F NC idiot

75 A improved land, 175 A unimpr, valued at $600
3 slaves


209.213 John MORGAN       56 M NC shoemaker 1,000
      Sarah MORGAN        50 F NC
      Elisabeth           23 F NC S
      Nathaniel           21 M NC S
      John G.             19 M NC S
      Abram               15 M NC S
      Eveline             14 F NC S
      Sarah                8 F NC S

[MB: John Morgan to Sally Hill 31 Aug. 1816]
70 A improved land, 240 unimpr, valued at $1,000


210.214 Nathan THOMSON    30 M NC farmer 60
      Rachel THOMSON      28 F NC
      Elisabeth C.         3 F NC
      James D.             1 M NC
      Martha J.         9/12 F NC


   75 A improved land, 47 A unimpr, valued at $150


211.215 Lawrence BRINGLE  42 M NC farmer 1,500
      Elisabeth BRINGLE   26 F NC
      Clementine          13 F NC
      John                 8 M NC
      Mary A.              4 F NC
      Catharine            2 F NC


[MB:Lawrence Bringle & Elizabeth Shepherd 25 Feb
1846]   50 A improved land, 123 A unimpr, valued at
$1,200   Lawrence A Bringle: 1 slave


212.216 John SHAVER   48 M NC farmer 1,000
      Rebecca SHAVER  44 F NC
      Barbara         22 F NC
      Mary C.         18 F NC S
      Susanna J.      14 F NC S
      Rachel D.       12 F NC S
      John I.          6 M NC S


[MB: John Shaver to Rebecca Reed 3 Jan 1826]
100 A improved property, 100 A unimpr, value $200


213.217 David C REED 29 M NC farmer 1,000
      Caroline REED  25 F NC
      Moses L.        1 M NC


125 A improved land, 115 unimpr, valued at $1,000
9 slaves


214.218 Hugh MORGAN      53 M NC farmer
      Polly MORGAN      48 F NC
      Joice             27 F NC
      Patsy             22 F NC S
      Omy               20 F NC S
      Miles             18 M NC S labourer
      Solomon           17 M NC S          (cont.)
```



```
      Pena D.           14 F NC S
      Ivy               10 M NC S
      Elisabeth          8 M NC
      Omy MORGAN        90 M NC

[MB: Hughey Morgan to Polly Poole 28 Sept 1816]

215.219 Samuel BADGET  40 M NC (X) carpenter
      Nancy BADGET     25 F NC (X)


216.220 Caleb SHAVER   45 M NC farmer
      Leah SHAVER      37 F NC
      Jane             16 F NC S
      Paul             14 M NC S
      Mary             12 F NC S
      Abram            10 M NC S
      Pena      )twins  8 F NC S )
      Catharine )       8 F NC S )
      Salome            5 F NC
      John E.           3 M NC
      Joice             1 F NC


217.221 Aaron MILLER   37 M NC 1,500
      Nancy MILLER     37 F NC
      Emanuel          14 M NC S
      Jeremiah M.      12 M NC S
      David            10 M NC S
      Jane              8 F NC
      Abram             5 M NC
      Needum L.         4 M NC


[NCMB: Aron Miller to Nancy Reed 19 Nov. 1833]
170 A improved land, 188 unimpr, valued at $200
9 slaves


218.222. Sophia MILLER  60 F NC 800
      Daniel Miller    25 M NC farmer
      Abram            17 M NC S labourer
      Sophia           12 F NC S


100 A improved land, 450 A unimpr, valued at $800
9 slaves


219.223 George A PARK  43 M NC farmer 100
      Hannah PARK      40 F NC (X)
      William A.       19 M NC S labourer
      Ruhama J.        15 F NC S
      Delila A.        13 F NC S
      Jesse A.         11 M NC S
      Mary              8 F NC S
      John F.           6 F NC


[Note: George A Park to Hannah Hodge 21 Dec 1829]
110 A improved land, 60 A unimpr, valued at $100


220.224 Michael MILLER  29 M NC farmer 700 m
      Sarah C MILLER   18 F NC m


2 slaves
```

221.225 Charles MORGAN 28 M NC farmer 400
   Joannah MORGAN   27 M NC
   Calvin R.   3 M NC
   Mary J.   2 F NC
   Elizabeth C.   3/12 F NC

   [MB: Charles Morgan to Joanna File 16 Oct. 1844]
   65 A improved land, 85 A unimpr, valued at $400

222.226 John C BENSON 28 M NC farmer 1,000
   Mary L. BENSON   24 F NC
   Mary J.   4 F NC
   James H.   1 M NC
   Martha Ann   5/12 F NC

   [CW: Jphn C. Benson to Mary Lundy Adderton 13 July
     1847]
   80 A improved land, 150 A unimpr, valued at $800

223.227 Daniel M SHAVER 22 M NC farmer 500
   Joice E. SHAVER   22 F NC (X)
   Nancy J.   1 F NC

   [MB: Daniel Shaver to Joyce Crowell 12 Nov. 1847]
   50 A improved land, 357 unimproved, valued at $500

224.228 William HILL   33 M NC (X) farmer
   Avelina HILL   25 F NC (X)
   Henry G.   7 M NC
   Mary A.   5 F NC
   William S.   1 F NC

   [MB: William Hill to Avaline Black 30 Aug. 1847]
   no land, but livestock

225.229 David MORGAN   59 M NC farmer
   Elisabeth MORGAN   57 F NC (X)
   Polly   33 F NC
   Jacob   31 M NC labourer
   Elisabeth   26 F NC
   Ally   24 F NC
   David   21 M NC S labourer
   Nancy   17 F NC S
   Levi   16 M NC S labourer
   Francis D.   10 M NC S

   [MB: David Morgan to Elizabeth Hofman 9 Feb. 1813]
   150 A improved land, 450 A unimpr, valued at $1000

226.230 Jane SHAVER 57 F NC 200
   1 slave

227.231 Jesse HODGES 57 M NC 700
   Sally M.   20 F NC S
   Abram A.   17 M labourer NC S
   John F.   15 M labourer NC S

   75 A improved land, 565 unimproved, valued at $700

228.232 Wilson AIRY 30 M NC (X) labourer 110
   Eliza AIRY   22 F NC
   Mary E.   4 F NC
   John A.   2 M NC   (cont.)
   Prisy J.   5/12 F NC

   40 A improved land, 10 A unimpr, valued at $110

229.233 Joseph HODGES   63 M NC 250
   Mary HODGES   67 F NC (X)
   William   42 M NC nearly helpless
   Elisabeth   39 F NC nearly helpless

   124 A improved land, 30 A unimpr, valued at $200

230.234 Richard HODGES 24 M NC
   Sarah HODGES   20 F NC
   Nancy Jane   7/12 F NC

<u>p. 126, School District #39, 1 Aug 1850</u>

231.235 Henry F. MILLER 29 M NC 1,500
   Nancy MILLER   25 F NC
   Adam   2 M NC
   Stephen L.   5/12 M NC
   Sevens MILLER   20 F NC S
   John Fite   6 M NC S

   80 A improved land, 137 A unimpr, valued at $1,000
   15 slaves

232.236 Ivy MILLER   29 M NC farmer
   E. E. Miller   24 F NC (X)
   John F.   1 M NC
   Susan WALLACE   8 F NC

   40 A improved land, 120 A unimproved, valued at $5
   1 slave

233.237 John SHEPARD   24 M NC (X) labourer
   Sally SHEPARD   24 F NC (X)
   Jerome   4 F NC [sic]
   Rachel   1 F NC
   Jessee WILHELM   25 M NC

234.238 Willa BEAN   32 M NC farmer 1,000
   Elisabeth BEAN   31 F NC
   Clarinda A.   12 F NC S
   Mary Ann   10 F NC S
   Moses L.   8 M NC S
   Nancy E.   6 F NC S
   Richard KINNEY   24 M NC labourer

   50 A improved land, 137 A unimproved, valued at ?
   3 slaves

235.239 Polly JACKSON 72 F NC (X)
   Polly   35 F NC (X)

236.240 Demsy PARKS   46 M NC 400
   Nancy PARKS   45 F NC (X)
   Catharine   25 F NC (X)
   Ebenezer   23 M NC chairmaker
   Augustus W.   20 M NC (X) chairmaker
   Ally   16 F NC S
   Nancy M.   12 F NC S
   Caroline A.   11 F NC S
   Willa W   6 M NC   (cont.)

[MB: Dempsey Park to Nancy Bean 20 Jan 1824]
50 A improved land, 65 A unimpr, valued at $400

237.241 Huldah BURRAGE   70 F 75 NC (X)
   George BURRAGE   40 M NC wheelwright
   Polly BURRAGE   25 F NC (X)

238.242 James BURRAGE   32 M NC cabinetmaker 200
   Susanna BURRAGE   24 F NC (X)
   John H.   3 M NC
   Edward   1 M NC

   20 A improved land, 36 A unimpr, valued at $200

239.243 John SHEPARD   45 M NC farmer 30
   Luraney SHEPARD   38 F -- (X)
   Rebecca   18 F NC
   Malinda   16 F NC S
   George   14 M NC S
   Polly   12 F NC S
   Daniel   10 M NC S
   Elisabeth   6 F NC
   Hannah   4 F NC
   John   2 M NC

[MB: John Shepherd to Lurana Wall 17 Dec. 1827]
no land, but livestock

240.244 James SHEPPARD   30 M NC (X) farmer 275
   Lavinia SHEPPARD   24 F NC (X)
   Lavinia   10/12 F NC
   Eveline FRICK   10 F NC S

   20 A improved land, 30 A unimpr, valued at $275

241.245 Thomas WYATT   26 M NC m (X)
   Louisa WYATT   25 F NC m (X)

242.246 Amos PARKS   60 M NC (X)
   Mildred PARKS   70 F NC (X)

[MB: Amos Parks to Milly Brigs 27 Aug. 1800]

243.247 Ebenezer PARKS   85 M NC farmer
   Sarah PARKS   60 F NC
   Elisabeth PARKS   24 F NC

244.248 Alexander PARKS   22 M NC 500
   Sarah PARKS   23 F NC
   Joseph McC.   10/12 M NC
   William JACKSON   13 M NC S

[MB: Alexander Park to Sarah Bean 3 May 1849]
35 A improved land, 358 unimproved, valued at ?

245.249 Noah WYATT   45 M NC farmer 600
   Polly WYATT   44 F NC
   Thomas   21 M NC S labourer
   William W.   19 M NC S labourer
   James M.   18 M NC S labourer
   Delilah   16 F NC S
                                    (cont.)

   Rachel E.   14 F NC S
   Siles   12 M NC S
   Mary A.   11 F NC S
   Eli   9 M NC S
   Noe C.   7 M NC S
   Rhoda E.   5 F NC
   John P.   3 M NC
   Amanda J.   1 F NC

   100 A improved land, 192 unimpr, valued at $600

246.250 Brantly WYATT   35 M NC farmer
   Julia A. WYATT   32 F NC (X)
   Pleasant L.   12 M NC S
   James I.   10 M NC S
   Calvin   7 M NC

[MB: Brantly Wiatt to Juley Daniell 5 Apr. 1836]
50 A improved land, 93 A unimpr, valued at $600

p. 127, School District #39, 3 Aug 1850

247.251. Brantly SKEEN   26 M NC farmer 600
   Rebecca SKEEN   28 F NC (X)
   Mary A.   2 F NC
   Mary A. LEFLER   17 F NC

[MB: Brantly Skeen to Rebecca Henly 4 May 1847]
50 A improved land, 93 A unimpr, valued at $420

248.252 Miles PARKS   22 M NC (X) farmer
   Anna PARKS   19 F NC (X)

[MB: Milas Park to Anny Wiatt 17 Apr. 1849]

249.253 Israel MISENHIMER   37 M NC farmer
   Sarah MISENHIMER   36 F NC (X)
   Eve E.   11 F NC S
   Jacob W.   9 M NC S
   Christina M. A.   7 F NC S
   Isaac A.   3 M NC
   Leah M.   4/12 F NC

250.254 Noah PARKS   25 M NC 200
   Mary Ann PARKS   19 F NC
   Nancy PARKS   20 F NC

251.255 George MILLER   60 M NC farmer
   Christina MILLER   45 F NC (X)
   Jacob O.   18 M NC S
   Margaret M.   14 F NC S
   George   4 M NC S
   Daniel KESLER   15 M NC S labourer

   36 A improved land, 30 A unimpr, valued at $325

252.256 John BAIM   25 M NC (X) m millwright 200
   Polly BAIM   25 F NC (X) m

[MB: John Bame to Mary Ketchey 11 Apr. 1850]

253.257 Miles MILLER   25 M NC farmer 800
   Elisabeth MILLER   24 F NC (S)
   Stephen J.   2 M NC
   Christina R.   11/12 F NC

[MB: Miles Miller & Elizabeth Beaver 11 Mar 1846]
36 A improved land, 216 unimproved, valued at $650

254.258 Lewis FRICK   36 M NC farmer 600
   Polly FRICK   34 F NC (X)
   Mary J.   7 F NC S
   Daniel   4 M NC
   Caroline   10/12 F NC

74 A improved land, 30 A unimpr, valued at $250

255.259 Lenard HOFNER   36 M NC farmer 600
   Jerusha HOFNER   37 F NC
   William W.   12 M NC S
   Nathan I.   9 M NC S
   Elisabeth J.   7 F NC S
   John O.   5 M NC
   Joseph G.   1 M NC

100 A improved land, 236 unimpr, valued at $600

256.260 Green MOWRY   25 M NC farmer 500
   Barbara F. MOWRY   21 F NC (X)
   Jane C.   3 F NC

[MB: Green Mowry to Barbara Miller 8 July 1844]
40 A improved land, 60 A unimpr, valued at $500

257.261 Eli C. FILE   27 M NC blacksmith 400
   Rhoda FILE   26 F NC
   Elisabeth C.   5 F NC
   Green W.   3 M NC
   Nathan C.   3/12 M NC
   George MISAMER   28 M NC farmer 250
   Barbara MISAMER   30 F NC (X)
   *Archibald MISENHIMER   33 M NC farmer
   Mann R.   18 M NC farmer
   Elisabeth   15 F NC S
   Elisabeth MISAMER   55 F NC
   *Mary A.   1 F NC
   Elisabeth MISENHIMER   56 F NC

[MB: Eli File to Rhoda Morgan 7 Aug. 1843
George Misamor to Barbara Wiatt 1 Jan. 1848]
File: 35 A improved land, 65 A unimpr, valued at
   $400; Misamer: 15 A improved land, 55 A unimpr-
   oved, valued at $400

258.262 Daniel J. MISENHIMER   22 M NC farmer
   Eliza M. MISENHIMER   20 F NC (X)

[MB:Daniel J Misenhimer & Eliza Lentz 30 Oct 1849]

259.263 Morgan MISENHIMER   20 M NC farmer
   Lucinda MISENHIMER   15 F NC
   Mary Jane   1 F NC

[MB:Morgan Misenhamer & Lucinda Casper 14 Aug 1847]

260.264 Jessee WYATT   50 M NC farmer
   Sarah WYATT   42 F NC (X)
   Noah   17 M NC

261. 265 Adam HARTMAN   31 M NC farmer 700
   Catharine HARTMAN   30 F NC (X)
   Daniel   9 M NC S
   John   8 M NC S
   Jessee   5 M NC
   Samuel   3 M NC
   Mary Ellen   1 F NC
   Lydia C. PIERCE   14 F NC S
   Moses A. HULEN   13 M NC S

[MB: Adam Hartman & Catharine Harkey 16 Oct. 1839]
35 A improved land, 115 A unimpr, valued at $700

262.266 Henry HARTMAN   56 M NC (X) farmer
   Lydia HARTMAN   53 F NC (X)
   Elisabeth   18 F NC S
   John   16 M NC S
   Susan C.   13 F NC S
   Camiline PIERCE   8 F NC S 400

[MB: Henry Hartman to Liddy Misomer 7 Apr. 1816]
25 A improved land, 102 A unimpr, valued at $400

263.267 Alexander HULEN   32 M NC (X) labourer
   Eve Ann HULIN   27 F NC (X)
   Lydia C.   3 F NC

264.268 Henry GOODMAN   21 M NC farmer
   Sophia GOODMAN   21 F NC (S)
p. 128, School District #39, 5 Aug 1850
   John GOODMAN   0/12 M NC

[MB: Henry Goodman & Sophia Hartman 13 Apr. 1849]

265.269 Samuel BADGET   40 M NC (X) carpenter m
   Nancy BADGET   25 F NC (X) m

266.270 Martin DAVIS 35 M NC (X) shoemaker
   Polly DAVIS   31 M NC (X)

267.271 Buckner CROWELL 41 M NC farmer 1,000
   Augustus D. HICKS   21 M NC S farmer 2,000

Crowell: 109 A improved land valued at $1,000
10 slaves

268.272 Celia BRUNER   55 F NC (X)
   Elisabeth   17 F NC S
   Rachel   10 F NC S

269.273 Riley STONER   32 M NC farmer 250
   Edith STONER   24 F NC (X)
   Clark   4 M NC

[MB: Riley Stoner to Edy Eller 27 Nov. 1841]
20 A improved land, 107 unimpr, valued at $250

270.274 James W DOBY   35 M NC (X) labourer
   Mary DOBY   35 F NC (X)
   Pleasant   11 M NC
   Lavinia DOBY   6 F NC

271.275 Michael FILE   21 M NC farmer m
   Elisabeth FILE   19 F NC m
   Jessee PARKS   20 M NC S farmer
   Noah FILE   20 M NC S farmer
   Sarah PARKS   18 F NC S
   Christena HARTMAN 14 F NC S
   Mary HARTMAN   12 F NC S
   Pinkney A. HARTMAN 6 M NC S
   Patience FILE   16 F NC S
   Ivy FILE   14 M NC S
   William H. File   5 M NC
   Michael R. FILE   3 M NC

[MB: Michael File & Elizabeth Hartman 17 Sept 1849]

272.276 Moses LEMLY   44 M NC farmer 725
   Sarah LEMLY   44 F NC
   Philip   19 M NC S labourer
   Jacob   16 M NC S labourer
   David A.   14 M NC S
   Benjamin F.   11 M NC S
   Margaret S.   5 F NC S
   Mary A. WHITE   15 F NC
   Samuel J. WHITE   9 M NC

[MB: Moses Lemly to Sally Bruner 19 Oct. 1827]
105 A improved land, 107 unimpr, valued at $725
1 slave

273.277 Sally ROUGH   22 F NC
   Henderson   2 M NC
   Sarah S.   4/12 F NC
   Cornelius M. CASPER 17 M NC S farmer
   no land but livestock

274.278 Jacob FILE   54 M NC farmer 8,000
   Elisabeth FILE   53 F NC (X)
   Alexander CASPER   15 M NC
   Margaret FILE   16 F NC S

[MB: Jacob File to Betsey Eddleman 15 Mar. 1817]
150 A improved land, 160 A unimpr, valued at
12 slaves . $2,000

275.279 Catharine WILHELM 26 F NC 500
   Moses PEELER   8 M NC
   George L. WILHELM   3 M NC
   John H.   8/12 M NC

[MB:John Wilhelm to Catherine Peeler 18 Feb. 1846]
50 A improved land, 100 A unimpr, valued at $500

276.280 Caleb GOODMAN 31 M NC (X) blacksmith
   Rose Ann   3 F NC
   John Wesley   1 M NC
   Elvira GOODMAN   26 F NC

277.281 Charles ALMON 28 M NC (X) farmer
   Barbara ALMON   30 F NC (X)
   Margaret   3 F NC
   Mary Axiem   8 F NC

278.282 George A WILHELM   21 M NC farmer 250 m
   Sarah WILHELM   18 F NC (X) m

279.283 Samuel STONER 46 M NC farmer 600
   Margaret STONER   50 F NC (X)
   Charles W.   19 M NC S
   Catharine   15 F NC S
   Christiana   14 F NC S
   Margaret   9 F NC
   John HISS   8 M NC

[MB: Samuel Stoner to Peggy Wilhelm 3 Apr. 1830]
92 A improved land, 1 A unimproved, valued at $150

280.284 Alexander POOL 30 M NC farmer 200
   Lavinia POOL   29 F NC
   Henry C.   6 M NC
   Abram H.   4 M NC
   Loretta   1 F NC

40 A improved, 35 A unimproved land, valued $250

281.285 Elvira HARTMAN 32 F NC (X) 275
   Lucrease   14 F NC S
   Elisabeth   12 F NC S
   Rose   9 F NC S
   Jacob   6 M NC S
   Margaret   4 F NC
   William   1 M NC

55 A improved land, 50 A unimpr, valued at $275

282.286 John ELLER 67 M NC 750
   Eve ELLER   42 F NC (X)
   Mary N. ELLER   26 F NC (X)

200 A improved land, 178 unimpr, valued at $750
1 slave

283.287 Abram LENTZ 56 M 1,200 NC
   Edith LENTZ   47 F NC
p. 129, School District #38, 6 Aug 1850
   Equla CASPER   19 F NC
   Lucas B. LENTZ   12 M NC

105 A improved land, 280 A unimpr, valued at $1,200
4 slaves

284.288 Catharine LINEBARRIER 33 F NC (X)
   James MAXWELL   6 M NC

285.289 Edward POOL 34 M NC shoemaker 225
   Susanna POOL   33 F NC (X)
   Joseph   10 M NC S
   Miles M.   8 M NC S
   John C.   4 M NC
   David   1 M NC

[MB: Edward Pool to Susanna Hartman 24 Apr. 1839]
65 A improved land, 50 A unimpr, valued at $250

286.290 Tobias KESLER   35 M NC 2,727
    Nancy KESLER   28 F NC
    Anna L.   7 F NC S
    John W. H.   4 M NC
    Infant   0/12 F NC
    Mary ROSEMAN   20 F NC

[MB: Tobias Kesler to Nancy Roseman 13 Sept. 1841]

305 A improved land, 145 A unimpr, valued at $2,727
8 slaves

287.291 Henry CANUP   50 M NC farmer
    Eve CANUP   47 F NC
    Miles A.   25 M NC farmer
    Benjamin F.   24 M NC labourer
    Henry T.   17 M NC S labourer
    Samuel LUTHER   1 M NC
    Margaret KETCHEY   12 F NC S

[MB: Henry Canup to Eve Earnheart 17 June 1826]
65 A improved land, 50 A unimpr, valued at $400

288.292 Mary E. EARNHEART 80 F NC (X)
    Rosena   50 F NC (X)
    Julia Ann   13 F NC S
    Adam   18 M NC S

289.293 Thomas EARNHEART   35 M NC 300
    Casy M. EARNHEART   23 F NC (X)
    Sarah   7 F NC helpless
    Thomas M.   5 M NC
    Stephen A.   4 M NC
    Lewis   1 M NC
    Mary Jane   0/12 F NC
    Sophia FITE   13 F NC S

290.294 Peter CASPER   56 M farmer NC (X) 450
    Elisabeth   17 F NC
    Adam W.   13 M NC
    Christina   11 F NC S
    Charlott   8 F NC S
    Jane   6 F NC

70 A improved land, 79 A unimpr, valued at $450

291.295 Alexander LYERLA 21 M NC farmer m
    Sophia LYERLA   18 F NC m

[MB:Alexander Lyerly & Sophia Hartman 6 June 1849]

292.296 Charles LYERLA 47 M NC wagonmaker 900
    Barbara LYERLA   42 F NC
    Adaline E.   14 F NC
    Polly   16 F NC
    Michael Holtshouser 16 M NC

[MB: Charles Lyarly to Barbara Kesler 1 Dec. 1826]
199 A improved land, 100 A unimpr, valued at $900

293.297 Solomon J PEELER 37 M NC farmer 5,000
    America L. PEELER   20 F NC
    Theodore L.   2 M NC
    Susan J. SMITH   13 F NC S
    Henry T. FITE   10 M NC S

[MB:Solomon Peeler & America L Smith 14 July 1845]
300 A improved land, 240 A unimpr, valued at $5,000
4 slaves

294.298 Jacob CRESS   26 M NC farmer 1,100
    Susanna L. CRESS   20 F NC
    Martha J.   1 F NC

70 A improved land, 75 A unimpr, valued at $1,000
1 slave

295.299 John AREY   62 M NC hatter 2,000
    Nancy AREY   39 F NC
    Sarah   18 F NC S
    Charles KESLER   20 M NC S
    Maria   14 F NC S
    Joice   10 F NC S
    Tobias OWEN   21 M NC
    John   5 M NC
    Abram   2 M NC

275 A improved land, 100 A unimpr, valued at $1,500
1 slave

296.300 Mary A. REDWINE   32 F NC 500
    Joice C.   11 F NC S
    Pleasant A. SMITH   14 M NC S
    George M.   12 M NC S
    Thomas J.   9 M NC S

50 A improved land, 44 A unimpr, valued at $500
3 slaves   [JWL note: Mariah Annah Barringer,
widow of Pleasant Redwine whom she m 10 Dec 1835.
He d 22 Feb 1845.]

297.301 Elizabeth MAHALA   51 F NC
    Frederick MAHALA   55 M NC labourer
    Charles M.   21 M NC labourer
    Theophilus A.   17 M NC labourer
    David F.   15 M NC
    John P.   12 M NC
    Louisa   10 F NC
    Selina   5 F NC

298.302 Milford G. MILLER 31 M NC farmer 600
    Margaret MILLER   29 F NC
    Margaret S.   1 F NC
    Alison H. Mowry   17 M NC S labourer

40 A improved land, 12 A unimpr, valued at $300

299.303 Levi THOMAS   38 M NC farmer 1,000
    Sophia THOMAS   33 F NC (X)

75 A improved land, 65 A unimpr, valued at $1,000

<u>p. 130, School District #30, 7 Aug. 1850</u>

```
300.304 Samuel PEELER   45 M NC (X) farmer 2,000
    Sarah PEELER        46 F NC (X)
    Eli A.              20 M NC
    Henry M.            18 M NC
    Alfred M.           15 M NC
    John D.              5 M NC

    145 A improved land, 245 unimpr, valued at $1,200

301.305 Henry BARINGER   29 M NC 1,100
    Maria BARRINGER      26 F NC (X)
    Rufus A.              5 M NC S
    George M.            1 M NC

    [MB: Henry Barringer to Maria Brown 12 Feb. 1844]
    75 A improved land, 80 A unimpr, valued at $900
    4 slaves

302.306 Jacob BROWN   40 M NC farmer 1,000
    Louisa BROWN      29 F NC (X)
    Eliza C.           3 F NC
    Pleasant A.        1 M NC

    [MB: Jacob Brown to Lewisy Arey 7 June 1845]
    100 A improved land, 104 A unimpr, valued at $1,000
    3 slaves

303.307 Cornelius LINEBARRIER 45 M NC wagonmaster 150
    Sally LINEBARRIER        42 F NC (X)
    Lucy Ann                 17 F NC S
    Catharine                14 F NC S
    Delia                     9 F NC
    John                      7 M NC
    David                     3 M NC
    William F.             4/12 M NC

MB:Cornelius Linebarrier & Sarah Glover 21 Mar 1832

304.308 Otho POOL       26 M NC wagonmaker 225
    Lucrese POOL       19 F NC
    Edith LINEBARRIER 8 F NC S

    [MB: Otho Pool to Lucressa Lentz 27 Mar. 1848]
    45 A improved land, 35 A unimpr, valued at $225

305.309 Michael ELLER  24 M NC farmer 350
    Anna ELLER         25 F NC (X)

    25 A improved land, 105 A unimpr, valued at $350

306.310 Lucinda ELLER   33 F NC (X)
    Polly              13 F NC S
    Charlotte          11 F NC S
    Jane                8 F NC S
    Peter               4 M NC
    Leah L.          0/12 F NC

307.311 Catherine ELLER  48 F NC (X) 150
    John                20 M NC S
    Cornelius           17 M NC S
    Eli                 15 M NC
    Samuel              12 M NC          (cont.)
```

```
    Matilda               8 F NC

    75 A improved land, 25 A unimpr, valued at $150

308.312 John HESS     40 M NC (X) carpenter
    Elisabeth HESS   42 F NC (X)
    Mary A. L.       19 F NC S
    John             17 M NC S labourer
    Charles          16 M NC S labourer
    Richard          14 M NC S
    Benjamin          5 M NC
    Eve A. C.         2 F NC
    Eve M. ELLER     25 F NC (X)

309.313 Noah PEELER    34 M NC farmer
    Delinda PEELER    27 F NC
    Wiley HEDINGER    14 M NC S
    Eliza HEDINGER    10 FNC

310.314 Charles ELLER   45 M 400 NC (X) farmer
    Sophia ELLER       43 F NC
    Moses              22 M NC S labourer
    Catharine          20 F NC
    Mary               17 F NC
    James              15 M NC S
    David              14 M NC S
    Christiana         12 F NC
    Eveline            10 F NC
    Jacob               8 M NC
    Benjamin            6 M NC
    Michael             4 M NC
    John                2 M NC
    Jane             0/12 F NC

    [MB: Charles Eller to Sophia Brown 29 Oct. 1826]
    60 A improved land, 45 A unimpr, valued at $400

311.315 Mary FRALEY   50 F NC (X) 200
    Polly ELLER      33 F NC (X)
    Caleb ELLER      14 M NC S

    50 A improved land, 25 A unimpr, valued at $200

312.316 John M. ELLER  39 M NC farmer 800
    Chloe ELLER       32 F NC (X)
    Julia A.          14 F NC S

    45 A improved land, 45 A unimpr, valued at $300

313.317 Tobias LENTZ   26 M NC farmer 800
    Lydia LENTZ      23 F NC
    Mary J.           2 F NC
    Ebenezer          1 M NC
    Rosena TREXLER   24 F NC S

    [MB: Tobias Lentz to Lydia Hill 18 Oct. 1845]
    100 A improved land, 90 A unimpr, valued at $800

314.318 Abram HILL       49 M NC farmer 2,000
    Elisabeth A. HILL  49 F NC
    Mary Ann HILL      20 F NC S
    Sarah              19 F NC S
    Dorothy            17 F NC S          (cont.)
```

Guy   15 M NC S
Anna L.   13 F NC S
p. 131, School District #38, 8 Aug. 1850
  Abram A.   11 M NC S
  Eveline   8 F NC S
  George L. WILHELM   21 M NC S

[MB:Abram Hill to Elisabeth A Hill 25 Mar 1818]
130 A improved land, 98 A unimpr, valued at $2,000

315.319 John L. HILL   26 M NC farmer
  Sarah HILL   28 F NC (X)
  William F.   3 M NC
  Elisabeth C.   1 F NC
  Amanda L.   4/12 F NC

20 A improved land, 10 A unimpr, valued at $60

316.320 Henry W. HILL   28 M NC farmer 1,200
  Elisabeth HILL   23 F NC (X)
  Joseph A.   3 M NC
  David L.   1/12 M NC
  Rollin MILLER   13 M NC labourer

[MB: Henry W. Hill to Elizabeth Pool 13 Jan. 1847]
111 A improved land, 178 unimpr, valued at $1,200

317.321 Alexander ELLER 28 M NC labourer
  Nancy ELLER   24 F NC (X)
  Mary J.   3 F NC
  William S.   2/12 M NC

[MB: Alexander Eller to Nancy Cox 16 Mar. 1846]

318.322 Sene BASSINGER 33 F NC (X)
  Reems   11 M NC
  Daniel   9 M NC S
  John   7 M NC
  Thomas   1 M NC

319.323 Mathias LUTEWICK 48 M NC (X) farmer 60
  Dianna LUTEWICK   46 F NC (S)
  Eveline   18 F NC
  Jane   16 F NC
  Leah   13 F NC
  Burrel R.   4 F NC

[MB:Mathias Lutewick & Dianna Glover 20 Feb 1827]
17 A improved land, 3 A unimproved, valued at $60

320.324 Ann STARNS   54 F NC
  Rolin H.   17 M NC S
  Samuel R.   15 M NC S
  Anna MAX   17 F NC

75 A improved land, 85 A unimpr, valued at $350

321.325 Nathan ALMON   50 M NC (X) farmer
  Nancy ALMON   40 F NC (X)
  Archibald   17 M NC
  Robert   12 M NC S
  Caster   7 F NC hands deformed
  Cornelius   21 M NC deformed & nearly
                                   helpless

322.326 George HARTMAN 28 M NC labourer
  Louisa HARTMAN   21 F (X)
  John   2 M NC
  Magdalena D.   10/12 F NC
  Cealy A. LUTEWICK   19 F NC

323.327 Moses KESLER   25 M MC farmer 150 m
  Elisabeth KESLER   19 F NC m
  Benjamin   12 M NC S

[MB: Moses Kesler & Elizabeth Brown 16 Apr 1850]

324.328 Anna KESLER   35 F NC (X)
  Henry R.   8 M NC S
  Eliza M.   3 F NC S [sic]

no land, but livestock

325.329 Miles KESLER   29 M NC farmer
  Catharine KESLER   34 F NC
  Daniel M.   9 M NC S
  George W.   5 M NC
  Michael R.   1 M NC

[MB:Miles Kesler to Catharine Huffman 8 Feb 1841]

326.330 Bostian LENTZ   90 M PA farmer 500
  Catharine LENTZ   40 F NC (X)
  Nancy   22 F NC

160 A improved land, 100 A unimpr, valued at $500
5 slaves

327.331 Henry LENTZ   57 M NC farmer 800
  Catharine LENTZ   37 F NC

70 A improved land, 176 unimpr, valued at $800
3 slaves

328.332 George ELLER   29 M NC (X) farmer 400
  Rose A. ELLER   28 F NC (X)
  John A. ELLER   7 M NC
  Martha A. S.   4 F NC
  George H. M.   2 M NC
  Michael D.   0/12 M NC

[MB: George Eller & Rosena Goodman 29 Dec 1842]
125 A improved land, 125 unimpr, valued at $400

329.333 Rose AGNER   61 F NC 300 (X)
  1 slave

330.334 James GOODMAN   38 M NC farmer 1,000
  Frances GOODMAN   38 F NC
  Rose   12 F NC S
  Daniel A.   10 M NC S
  Mary   6 F NC
  James C.   3 M NC
  Charlotte   1 F NC

65 A improved land, 68 A unimpr, valued at $1,000
4 slaves
tannery: 1,600 sole leather worth $400, 1,100
harnesses worth 300, 250 pieces ? worth $400

331.335 Pleasant MAY   43 M NC cabinetmaker m   40 A improved land, 50 A unimpr, valued at $300
    Eliza MAY   19 F NC m (X)
                                                  338.342 John MAY   33 M NC
    [MB: Pleasant May to Eliza A. Michals 2 May 1850]   Anna MAY   37 F NC (X)
                                                      Fanny   8 F NC S
                                                      Lunda   5 F NC S
332.336 Mary MAY   60 F NC   Leah EARNHART   24 F NC (X)
    Christena   24 F NC   Polly   22 F NC (X)
    Chainey   22 F NC   Elizabeth MILES 14 F NC S
    Nancy   20 F NC S
    Mary   16 F NC S   [MB: John May to Ann Earnhart 25 Oct. 1835]

    [MB: John May to Mary Basinger 14 June 1805] 339.343 Susanna EARNHART 61 F NC (X) $1,200
    250 A improved land, 50 A unimpr, valued at $700   John   26 M NC S
    2 slaves   Catherine H.   18 F NC S
                                                      Rosanna Cauble   8 F NC S
                                                      Catharine HONBARRIER 29 F NC (X)
333.337 Henry EARNHART 58 M NC (X) farmer   Elizabeth   11 F NC S
    Sally EARNHART   53 F NC (X)   John   9 M NC S
    Moses   25 M NC (X) farmer   Henry   3 M NC
                                                      Mary Earnhart   24 F NC (X)
                                                      Elisabeth   22 F NC (X)
334.338 Peter LENTZ   44 M NC tailer 400   Christiana   20 F NC (X)
p. 132, School Dist. #37, 9 Aug. 1850
    Polly LENTZ   39 F NC   200 A improved land, 62 A unimpr, valued at $800
    Lutitia   16 F NC S
    Robert   14 M NC S   340.344 Lenard KLUTTS   49 M NC wagonmaker
    Joice   12 F NC S   Elizabeth KLUTZ   49 F NC
    Julia A.   10 F NC S   Eve C.   17 F NC S
    Rose   7 F NC   Leah E.   15 F NC S
    Alford   4 M NC   Christiana C.   13 F NC S
                                                      Camilla L.   10 F NC S
    [MB: Peter Lentz to Polly Keisler 8 Aug. 1833]   Moses GOODMAN   14 M NC S
    100 A improved land, 95 A unimpr, valued at $400
    1 slave   125 A improved land, 260 unimpr, valued at $1,000
                                                      1 slave
335.339 Charles ROUGH 39 M NC farmer
    Rosanna ROUGH   42 F NC (X)   341.345 George EARNHART 38 M NC farmer
    Joseph   2 M NC   Mary J.   13 F NC S
    Elizabeth   1/12 F NC   Thomas   12 M NC S
    Dorothy KESLER   15 F NC   Linna E.   9 F NC S
    Sylvester ?STENP?   4 M NC   James P.   7 M NC S
                                                      Henry   5 M NC
    [MB: Charles Rough to Rosanna Stouck 7 Feb. 1848]
                                                      50 A improved land, 100 A unimpr, valued at $400
336.340 Jesse MAY   44 M NC farmer
    Anna MAY   35 F NC   342.346 Michael PEELER 52 M NC farmer 2,000
    Mary   15 F NC S   Elisabeth PEELER 50 F NC
    Abram   13 M NC S   Moses   22 M NC S labourer
    Robert   11 M NC S   Eve Ann   18 F NC S
    Maria   8 F NC   Paul   17 M NC S
    Amanda   6 F NC   Elisabeth   14 F NC S
    William F.   4 M NC   Polly   11 F NC S
    Louis H.   8/12 M NC   [MB:Michael Peeler to Elizabeth Brown 6 Jan 1821]
                                                      341 A improved land, 500 A unimpr, valued at $2000
337.341 Jacob POOL   43 M NC farmer 300   1 slave
    Elizabeth POOL   23 F NC (X)
    John   14 M NC S   343.347 Christiana AGNER 40 F NC (X)
    Catherine   16 F NC S   John   17 M NC farmer 150
    Loretta   12 F NC S   Elisabeth   15 F NC S
    Michael   8 M NC S   Lunda   12 F NC S
    William   6 M NC S   Daniel   7 M NC   (cont.)
    Mumford   1 M NC
    Ellen WALKER   7 F NC S   (cont.)

Nancy   5 F NC

41 A improved land, 9 A unimproved, valued at $150

344.348 Felix FRITS   28 M NC (X) farmer
  Mary A. FRITS   18 F NC
  Rose AGNER   10 F NC S

345.349 Cornelius KESLER 25 M NC farmer 500
  Ann KESLER   23 F NC (X)
  Sophia   3 F NC
  Mary Loretta   1 F NC
  Mary A. CAUBLE   23 F NC (X)

[MB:Cornelius Kesler & Anna Hartman 29 July 1845]
no land, but livestock, $500

346.350 Adam EARNHART 19 M NC labourer

<u>p.133, School District #37, 10 Aug. 1850</u>
347.351 Caleb EARNHART 41 M farmer NC
  Polly Earnhart   23 F NC (X)
  Jesse BAIM   13 M NC S

[MB:Caleb Earnheart & Polly Hotchins 29 Feb 1848]

348.352 Edward RUFTY   43 M NC millwright 700
  Elisabeth RUFTY   35 F NC (X)
  Jane   15 F NC S
  Lucetta   13 F NC S
  Miles   11 M NC S
  Rufus   9 M NC S
  Amanda   7 F NC S
  Milton   1 M NC

100 A improved land, 193 A unimpr, valued at $700

349.353 John WALLER   32 M NC farmer
  Eliza WALLER   25 F NC (X)
  Catherine   7 F NC S
  Jane   4 F NC
  Lewis   2 M NC

[WC: John Waller to Eliza Mull 10 Nov. 1840]

350.354 Frederick WALLER 25 M NC m (X) 400
  Christena M. WALLER   27 F NC m (X)
  Michael A.   0/12 M NC
  Elisabeth WALLER   61 F NC

[MB:Frederick Waller/Crisey M Cauble 21 Jul 1849]

351.355 Eve WALLER   57 F NC (X) 120
  Elisabeth WALLER   45 F NC
  Polly WALLER   41 F NC (X)
  Nancy   39 F NC (X)
  Milly   34 F NC (X)
  Henry A.   16 M NC S
  Talmon   11 M NC S
  Sarah A.   1 F NC
  Susanna   12 F NC S
  Henry POOL   21 M NC m (X)
  Catherine POOL   20 F NC m (X)   (cont.)

[MB: Henry Poole & Catharine Cauble 13 Apr 1850]

352.356 John WALLER   54 M NC farmer 50
  Eve WALLER   53 F NC
  John   22 M NC labourer
  George   21 M NC S labourer
  Mary A.   18 F NC
  Christena   14 F NC
  Laura   12 F NC
  Loretta   8 F NC
  Polly WALLER   4 F NC

353.357 Harriet JAMES   25 F NC (X)
  Francis   4 M NC

354.358 Jacob WALLER   21 M NC (X) labourer
  Margaret A.   23 F NC (X)
  Eve An   23 F NC (X)

355.359 Andrew BARGER   26 M NC
  Sarah C. BARGER   21 F NC

72 A improved land, 200 A unimpr, valued at $1,500

356.360 Jacob LYERLA   26 M NC m farmer
  Anna LYERLA   22 F NC m

[MB:Jacob Lyerly to Annie L Fisher 30 July 1849]

357.361 Peter EARNHART   36 M NC (X)
  Susanna EARNHART   38 F NC (X)
  Crawford   7 M NC
  Adam TREXLER   4 M NC

358.362 James EARNHART 37 M NC (X) farmer
  Sophia EARNHART   26 F NC (X)
  Catharine   13 F NC S
  Julia A.   11 F NC S
  Wila   9 M NC S
  Jacob   3 M NC

[MB:James Earnheart to Sophia Klutts 14 Aug 1837]
no land, but livestock

359.363 Tobias HARKEY 45 M NC (X) farmer
  Sophia HARKEY   46 F NC (X)
  Polly   18 F NC
  Moses G.   17 M NC
  Barbara   15 F NC
  Alexander   13 M NC
  Miles   10 M NC

[MB:Tobias Harkey to Sophia Hartline 15 Jan 1824]

360.364 David WORMINGTON   24 M NC (X)
  Celia WORMINGTON   23 F NC (X)

[MB:David Wormington & Celia Earnheart 9 Aug 1848]

361.365. Charles EARNHART 35 M farmer NC
  Elizabeth EARNHART   30 F NC
  Jane   8 F NC   (cont.)

Drucilla   5 F NC
Triphena   2 F NC
Elisabeth HUDGINS   21 F NC

115 A improved land, 100 A unimpr, valued at $800

362.366 Benjamin CHANDLER   30 M NC labourer
Elisabeth CHANDLER   27 M NC
Henry W.   6 M NC
John D.   3 M NC
Margaret A. S.   2 F NC
Julia F.   0/12 F NC

p.134, School District #37, 10 Aug. 1850

363.367 Clark REDWINE   24 M NC farmer 900
James WORMINGTON   14 M NC
Deberry CHANDLER   24 M NC
Polly HICKMAN   12 F B NC
Samuel WORMINGTON   19 M NC

140 A improved land, 75 A unimpr, valued at $800
2 slaves

364.368 Jacob FULENWIDER   60 M NC farmer 1,500
Polly FULLENWIDER   41 F NC
Eliza   32 F NC
John   21 M NC labourer S
Eve   17 F NC S
Jacob   16 M NC labourer S
Camilla   14 F NC S
Adam   11 M NC S
Monroe   7 M NC S
Alfred B.   4 M NC S
Elisabeth WORMINGTON   15 F NC

200 A improved land, 200 A unimpr, valued at $1800

365.369 George A HORNBARIER   35 M NC labourer
Polly HORNBARIER   30 F NC (X)
Jeremiah   4 M NC
John L.   2 M NC
Eliza BOST   35 F NC (X)

[MB: George A Hornbarringer to Mary Fullenwider 18 June 1839]

366.370 John TREXLER   35 M NC farmer 1,000
Leah TREXLER   35 F NC
Mary C.   13 F NC S
Catherine C.   8 F NC S
Sophia C.   4 F NC

60 A improved land, 48 A unimpr, valued at $1,000

367.371 John TREXLER Senr 40 M NC farmer 400
Margaret TREXLER   38 F NC (X)
Lavinia   17 F NC S
Alexander   15 M NC S
Polly   14 F NC S
Rufus   12 M NC S
Miles   10 M NC
Rose A.   7 F NC
Alfred   5 M NC   (cont.)

Lawson A.   3/12 M NC

[MB:John Trexler & Peggy Holshouser 26 Jul 1831]
150 A improved land, 80 A unimpr, valued at $400
2 slaves

368.372 Mary TREXLER   62 F NC (X)
Moses TREXLER   25 M NC farmer 1,000
Lawson   1 M NC

Moses Trexler: 75 A improved land, 125 A unimpr,
valued at $1,000

369.373 Caleb TREXLER   23 M NC farmer 800
120 A improved land, 85 unimpr, valued at $800

370.374 Henry MILLER   25 M NC farmer

p.134.5, Salisbury District, 12 Aug. 1850

371.375 Thomas L COWAN   69 M NC merchant 23,865
                        Salisbury, NC
Elizabeth COWAN   64 F NC
Mary COWAN   26 F NC
Joel H. JENKINS   42 M merchant NC
Charlotte C. JENKINS 38 F NC
Elizabeth C. JENKINS 7 F NC
Ella   4 F NC
Thomas L.C.   2 M NC
Sallie   1 F NC
Thomas C. McNEELY   22 M NC clerk in store
William G. McNEELY   18 M NC clerk

[MB:Thomas L Cowan & Elizabeth Brown 26 Apr 1810]
Thyatira: 400 A improved land, 240 unimpr, valued
     at $1,960, 16 slaves, 14 slaves, 13 slaves
13 slaves, Salisbury
Joel H. Jenkins: 2 slaves

372.376 John B LORD   33 M NC attorney-at-law 5,000
Ann S. LORD   28 F NC
William C.   12 M NC S
Mary S.   10 F NC S
Stephen F.   4 M NC
Margaret   1 F NC

[MB: John B. Lord to Ann S. Ferrand 7 Feb. 1838]
200 A improved land, 224 unimpr, valued at $1,215
64 slaves

373.377 William J PLUMER   32 M NC saddler
Mary PLUMMER   28 F NC
Franklin E.   7 M NC S
William   5 M NC S
Mary   3 F NC
Margaret A.   1 F NC
Samuel KESLER   18 M NC saddler
Sylvester WALL   17 M NC saddler

1 slave
150 pr harness valued at ?
160 saddles valued at ?

374.378 Edmund WADE   48 M NC stage driver
    Susan WADE   43 F NC (X)
    Elisabeth   24 F NC (X)
    Letha A.   21 F NC (X)
    Jessee   18 M NC blacksmith
    George   15 M NC blacksmith
    Edward   13 M NC
    James   6 M NC
    Laura   5 F NC
    Archibald   4/12 M NC
    Martha McCANN   23 F NC B

375.378 John SHUMAN   55 M NC carpenter 600
    Elmina SHUMAN   34 F NC
    Anson P.   23 M NC carpenter
    Mary   21 F NC (X)
    Rebecca   17 F NC
    Stephen A.   4 M NC
    Valeria F.   2 F NC

[MB:John Shuman Sr/Elmira Williamson 12 Oct 1844]

376.380 Phillipina HUIE 45 F 350 NC
    Elias   22 M labourer NC
p. 135, Salisbury, 12 Aug. 1850
    James HUIE   18 M NC S carriage painter m
    Polly HUIE   18 F NC S m
    Catharine WALTON   28 F NC
    Samuel CRESON   21 M NC blacksmith
    John FRALEY   17 M NC carpenter

    Philipina Huie: 1 slave
    James Huie: 2 slaves

377.381 Michael DAVIS 45 M NC carpenter 500
    Sarah DAVIS   41 F NC (X)
    Jacob A.   21 M NC S carpenter
    Mary A.   17 F NC S
    John B.   13 M NC S
    Luther M.   10 M NC S
    Laura E.   8 F NC S
    Michael   4 M NC
    James R.   1 M NC
    Samuel LINN   23 M NC carpenter
    William J. BARINGER 14 M NC

[MB: Michael Davis & Sally Trexler 31 Aug 1826]
    Davis: 1 slave

378.382 Mary BODENHAMMER 42 F NC 75
    Eliza J.   15 F NC
    McKinza G.   13 M NC
    Elmina B.   11 F NC S

379.383 James D. GLOVER 41 M NC shoemaker
    Nancy GLOVER   36 F NC
    Richard   14 M NC S
    May E. MORIS   14 F NC S
    Mary A. GLOVER   12 F NC S
    James L.   10 M NC S
    Margaret J. GHEEN 16 F NC S

[MB:James D Glover & Nancy Morris 16 Sept 1845]

380.384 John A STOCKTON 26 M NC tailor
    Mary E. STOCKTON   26 F NC (X)
    Mary M.   5 F NC S
    John F. A.   3 M NC
    Martha A.   1 F NC
    Lavinia GHEEN   18 F NC

381.385 William REYNOLDS 26 M VA (X) m
    Jane REYNOLDS   20 F NC m

[MB:William Reynolds to Jane Huie 21 Nov 1849]

382.386 Frederick MOWRY 51 M NC blacksmith 2,100
    Elizabeth MOWRY   44 F NC
    George MOWRY   18 M NC labourer
    Andrew   14 M NC
    Susan   11 F NC S
    Marcellus   3 M NC
    Lawson A. BURRIS   16 M NC blacksmith

60 A improved land, 138 unimpr, valued at $1,300

383.387 William HELFER   20 M NC (X) blacksmith
    Christina HELFER   24 F NC
    Martha H.   4 F NC

384.388 Alfred SAPHENFIELD 27 M NC (X) shoemaker
    Sarah SAPHENFIELD   25 F NC
    Sarah A.   2 F NC

385.389 Anna SHOFF   46 F NC (X)
    Susan   14 F NC
    Lucina   8 F NC S
    William BRINKLEY   21 M NC weaver
    Polly LEFLER   21 F NC (X)

386.390 Peter WARREN   27 M NC casder
    Margaret WARREN   19 F NC
    James S.   0/12 M NC
    Robert L. WARREN   3 M NC

[MB:Peter Warrne to Margt. Shoaf 26 Apr 1849]

387.391 Hervy M SAUCERMAN 26 M NC carriagemaker
    Nancy SAUCERMAN   22 F NC (X)
    Sarah SAUCERMAN   24 F NC (X)
    Rachel WADESWORTH 24 F NC (X)
    James H. SAUCERMAN 21 M NC carriagemaker (X)
    Levi POWLASS   19 M blacksmith
    Margaret WADESWORTH 20 F NC (X)
    Nancy J. FOSTER   19 F NC (X)
    Joseph H. SAUCERMAN 13 M NC

388.392 James G CAIRNS 50 M NC manager in factory
                                        b Scotland
    Lucie CAIRNS   30 F MA
    George A.   14 M NC student
    Mary D.A.   13 F NC S
    Juliett R.   10 F NC S
    Theodore E.   8 M NC
    Isabella T.   2 F NC
    John   1/12 M NC   (cont.)

Mary ADAMS   76 F Rhode Island
1 slave

389.393 Caroline CASPER 26 F NC (X) 360
    William F.   12 M NC
    Henry CASPER   22 M NC shoemaker
    Mary FRALEY   17 F NC
    George WIRE   35 M NC shoemaker
    Richard WALTER   55 M NC shoemaker

389.394 James TAYLOR   40 M NC cabinetmaker
    Eveline TAYLOR   34 F NC
    Elisabeth   13 F NC
    Henry C. TAYLOR   4 M NC

[MB:James Taylor to Eveline Hughes 27 Jan 1836]

p.136, Salisbury, 12 Aug. 1850

390.395 Richard B PENDLETON 22 M VA printer
    Mary A. PENDLETON   20 F NC

[MB:Richard B Pendleton & Mary Wade 22 Mar 1848]

391.396 Mace C PENDLETON 46 M VA printer 6500
    Susan PENDLETON   39 F NC
    Hamilton J. PENDLETON 18 M NC S drug store clerk
    Mace C. ", Jr.   11 M NC S
    Christina WEST   55 F Germany

    Mace C. Pendleton: 5 slaves
    Christina West: 1 slave

392.397 Rachel VOLENTINE 25 F NC B
    Franny   27 F NC B

393.398 Dolpin A DAVIS   47 M NC cashier, Bank of
                            Cape Fear 6,000
    Mary E. H. DAVIS   30 F NC
    Ann W.   23 F NC
    Mary B.   20 F NC
    Louisa M.   7 F NC
    William   4 M NC
    Jane E.   2 F NC
    John R.   9/12 M NC

[MB: D.A. Davis to Mary E. Horah 12 Nov. 1844]
15 slaves

394.399 George VOGLER 61 M NC gunsmith 3,000
    Mary VOGLER   66 F NC
    Alpheus SEERS   20 M NC B labourer
    2 slaves

395.400 Cyrus WEST   54 M NC carriagemaker
    Cyrus   18 M NC S
    Lueco   15 M NC S
    Cornelius   12 M NC S

40 A improved land, 100 A unimpr, valued at $1000
5 slaves

396.401 Horatio L ROBARDS 34 M NC attorney at
                            law 12,500
    Bettie Jane ROBARDS   32 F VA
    Annie Keiling   9 F NC 2,500
    William BARGE   23 M NC student
    James AXUM   11 M NC
    William AXUM   8 M NC S
    Alexander BRANDON   58 M NC merchant 6,000
    Abram CRESS   30 M PA hunter/fisher-
                             man 6,000

    Samuel B. HARRISON   22 M NC cabinetmaker
    John C. HARGRAVE   26 M NC clerk in store
    Alfred L. JOHNSON   24 M NC carpenter
    Henry A. WILSON   17 M PA silversmith
    Milo LESSLY   24 M NC carriage maker
    James R. McDONALD   23 M NC clerk in store
    William M. ELIOTT   35 M NC merchant
    Samuel B. WILLIAMS   31 M NC millwright
    John N. OWIN   35 M NC carriagemaker
    James G. MERONEY   22 M NC clerk
    Thomas C. JOHNSON   30 M NC portrait painter

    17 slaves
    Alfred L. Johnson: various articles

397.402 Ann CHAMBERS   46 F NC 13,200
    John H. PARKER   39 M NC clergyman E

    250 A improved land, 950 A unimpr, valued at $3600
    19 slaves

398.403 Burrell B ROBERTS 31 M NC merchant
    Jane E. ROBERTS   26 F NC
    Mary Jane   3 F
    Thomas P. RICHARDS   29 M MD clergyman ME
    Anna M. RICHARDS   22 F NC
    Frances J.   3/12 F NC
    John W. CLEMMONS   20 M NC
    Aquilla J. MOCK   20 M NC clerk
    4 slaves

399.404 Nancy KESLER   52 F NC
    Caroline   20 F NC
    Mary C.   13 F NC
    Laura   11 F NC
    Margaret REEVES   17 F NC
    Moses WISEMAN   19 M NC blacksmith

400.405 John M VOGLER   37 M NC silversmith
    Maria L. VOGLER   38 F NC
    George E.   12 M NC S
    James A.   8 M NC S
    Henrietta L.   6 F NC
    Lewis M.   2 M NC

[WC:John U. Vogler of Lincolnton to Miss Maria
    Louisa Reich of Salem 25 June 1835 in Salem]

401.406 Jeremiah M BROWN 42 M NC carpenter 3,000
    Charlotte BROWN   27 F NC
    William T.   15 M NC carpenter
    Mary A.   13 F NC S   (cont.)

Amanda F.   11 F NC S
Louisa H.   9 F NC S
Charles M.   1 M NC
Margaret COUGHENOUR   14 F NC
Barbary   10 F NC
Hiram SHARPE   35 M NC carpenter
James EAGLE   22 M NC carpenter
Peter SWINK   21 M NC carpenter
.407. Jacob OVERCASH   44 M NC carpenter
Elizabeth OVERCASH   41 F NC
Teressa   22 F NC
Margaret   21 F NC
Elizabeth   16 F NC

p.137, Salisbury, 13 Aug. 1850
Sophrona   14 F NC
Jacob   12 M NC
Solaman   10 M NC
Christina   8 F NC
Abner   5 M NC
Mary   2 F NC
Martha P.   5/12 F NC

4 slaves
5 houses, no amount

402.408 HIRAM LAWSON   59 M NC farmer
Penina LAWSON   48 F NC (X)
Eliza E.   33 F NC (X)
Abram N.   25 M NC blacksmith
David H.   20 M NC (X) carriagemaker
 John A.   17 M NC in the Factory
Ruth A. O.   14 F NC
Nancy E.   12 F NC
William H.   10 M NC
Margaret N.   7 F NC
.409 Catherine BEVINS   53 F NC (X)
Rachel   25 F NC
Susanna) twins   21 F NC (X)
Martha A)   21 F NC (X)
Joseph N.   16 M NC
Polly LENTZ   20 F NC
Matilda TUCKER   18 F NC
Laura E. SWISHER   7 F NC
Julia C. SWISHER   5 F NC

403.409 David BARNETT   43 M NC labourer
Rebecca BARNETT   53 F NC (X)
Mary D.   23 F NC (X)
Jane B.   21 F NC
Margaret M.   19 F NC
Louisa R.   17 F NC
Isabella S.   15 F NC

Robert E.) twins   12 M NC
Martha L.)   12 F NC
Nancy A.   8 F NC
Ester H   6 F NC

404.401 Samuel REEVES   52 M NC farmer 1,650
Mary A. REEVES   52 F NC
Henry PORTER   22 M NC B

[MB:Samuel Reeves/Catherine Coldiron 8 Dec 1817]
85 A improved land, 42 A unimpr, valued at $800
10 slaves

405.412 Ann SHAVER   52 F NC (X)   500
Mary SHAVER   29 F NC
Margaret   22 F NC
Jane   3 F NC
Bettie   2 F NC

406.413 Sophia RIMER 35 F NC (X)
Elizabeth   5 F NC

407.414 Everett G ALLEN 40 M NC town watch
Mary ALLEN   35 F NC (X)
Jacob   21 M NC labourer in factory
Mary   19 F NC
Elizabeth   17 F NC
George W.   12 M NC
Delphine SITTON   24 F NC (X)
Mahala   19 F NC
Moses KESLER   18 M NC
Ellenor SECREASE   20 F NC

408.415 Eleanor BROWN 62 F NC (X)
Rebecca   36 F NC (X)
Nancy M.   15 F NC

409.416 William KESTER   25 M NC weaver
Perlina KESTER   26 F NC (X)
Catherine   16 F NC
Elsa   10 F NC S
Mary A. MIRES   23 F NC (X)
Sarah A. FOSTER   22 F NC

410.417 Martha COX   27 F NC (X)
Siveley   21 F NC (X)

411.418 Minta BROWN   53 F NC (X)
Elisabeth   26 F NC (X)
Maria   20 F NC (X)
Elanora   17 F NC
William   12 M NC S

412.419 Charlotte GRIFFIN 44 F NC (X)
Micah   46 M NC carpenter
Josiah   17 M NC carriage painting
Noah   13 M NC
Samuel   10 M NC
Serena YARBORROUGH   21 F NC (X)
Minerva MIRES   24 F NC (X)
Margaret WEST   18 F NC
Lidia PHILLIPS   16 F NC
Elizabeth PHILLIPS   14 F NC
Adam SWINK   22 M NC labourer
p.138, Salisbury, 13 August 1850
.420 John SULIVAN   39 M NC labourer
Rachel   33 F NC (X)
Mary Ann   17 F NC
Lydia J.   15 F NC
Rhuhama   13 F NC
Louisa   11 F NC   (cont.)

(cont.)

```
      Allison M.K.          8 M NC
      Jerusha P.            6 F NC
      Missouri M.           3 F NC
      John B.           11/12 M NC
      Jane REDWINE         20 F NC (X)
      Selena FRALEY        23 F NC (X)
      Eliza                15 F NC
      Catherine TEMPLES    18 F NC

413.421 Peter KETCHEY     46 M NC millwright
      Lydia KETCHEY        36 F NC (X)
      Mary L.              18 F NC
      Sarah E.             16 F NC
      Margaret C.          14 F NC
      Rebecca L.           12 F NC
      John I.              10 F NC
      Julius M.             5 M NC
      Henery J.             2 M NC
      .422. Jacob WEAVER   31 M NC
      Lavinla WEAVER       25 F NC (X)
      Mary J.               7 F NC S
      James D.              4 M NC
      Anna E.           7/12 F NC
      Rosanna WEAVER       32 F NC
      Mary A.S.            11 F NC S

414.425 Rachel HILL   44 F NC (X)
      Lydia A.             23 F NC (X)
      Catherine            21 F NC (X)
      Elizabeth M.         20 F NC (X)
      George W.            16 M NC
      Celia F.             14 F NC
      Margaret R.           4 F NC
      .424. Nancy C. MONTGOMERY 16 F NC

415.425 Robert COX    42 M NC brickmason
      Sarah COX            42 F NC
      Susan      )twins    21 F NC
      Pheby E.   )         21 F NC
      Margaret             17 F NC
      Burges A.            14 M NC
      Nancy S.             11 F NC
      William POOL         21 M NC brickmason

416.426 Joseph BROWN   26 M NC (X) shoemaker
      Christina BROWN      19 F NC (X)
      John H.               1 M NC

[MB:Joseph Brown & Chrisy Cauble 23 Dec 1847]

417.427 Alexander SMITH 24 M NC (X) shoemaker 300
      Adalade SMITH        22 F NC
      Mary J.           10/12 F NC

418.428 Sophia HILTBRANT 52 F NC (X) 500
      Ann HILTBRANT        29 F NC (X)
      Melvina              25 F NC
      Sarah A. BOWERS       6 F NC

419.429 Ezekiel SEGRAVES  33 M NC (X) brickmason
      Lydia SEGRAVES       44 F NC
      William G. MOWREY    18 M NC brickmason
      George M.         1/12 M NC
```

```
      Robert HENDRICKS     19 M NC brickmason
      William MORGAN       20 M NC brickmason
      James LIKES          18 M NC brickmason
      James BENSON         22 M NC Mu
```

[MB:Ezekial Segraves & Lidia Mowry 3 Oct 1844]

```
420.430 James DOUGHERTY  51 M NC blacksmith 1,200
      Elizabeth CLARY      63 F NC 1,300
      David POOL           37 M NC silversmith

9 slaves
horse shoeing, other articles valued at ?

421.431 William H HORAH 61 M NC silversmith 4,322
      William H. HORAH, Jr 28 M NC clerk
      James HORAH          23 M NC silversmith
      Franklin             21 M NC cabinetmaker
      Ann                  17 F NC S
      Henry                15 M NC student
      Rowan                14 M NC S
      Joseph               11 M NC S
      George                9 M NC S
      John M. HORAH        26 M NC clerk in bank 1,200
      Margaret S. HORAH    23 F NC
      Amelia L.             1 F NC
      Isabella MURPHEY     57 F NC
```

[MB:William H Horah/Louisa Furrer 6 Jan 1814]
200 A improved land, 678 A unimpr, valued
      at $3222, 20 slaves

```
422.432 Mary G. BROWN   69 F NC 2,100
3 slaves

423.433  James MURPHY   27 M NC merchant 2,500
      Elizabeth C. MURPHY 25 F NC
      Mary E. CHUNN         8 F NC S
```

[MB:James Murphy & Elizabeth C Chunn 20 Dec 1848]
4 slaves

```
424.434 Jane GHEEN      58 F NC (X)
      Lavinia              26 F NC (X)
      Susan                20 F NC (X)
      Catharine            15 F NC
      Christiana LEFLER    17 F NC
      .435 Mary MINER      63 F NC (X)
      Phebe                23 F NC (X)
      Susan                19 F NC
      Pascal               18 M NC carriagemaker
      Wesley ROBBARDS      18 M NC labourer
      Nathan SIKES         30 M NC well digger

425.435 John CORRELL    35 M NC cabinetmaker
      Catherine Correll    28 F NC
      Samuel W.             5 M NC S
      Mary S.               3 F NC
      Sophia JAMES         54 F NC (X)
      Margaret S.          12 F NC S
      Sarah SHAVER         18 F NC
```

[MB:John Correll/Mary Catherine James 16 Jul 1844]

426.437 Martha E S BILES   27 F SC 1,500
  Catharine W   8 F SC
  5 slaves

427.438 William ROWZEE 40 M VA cabinetmaker 1,500
  Caroline ROWZEE   39 F NC
  Claudius W.   17 M NC S
  Alison H.   10 M NC S
  Elizabeth U.   5 F NC
  Cornelia F.   2 F NC
  Mary J.   6/12 F NC
  Richard HARRISON   20 M NC cabinet maker
  Maxwell BENSON   18 M NC cabinet maker

  3 slaves. Rowzee & Harrison: 11 fine beauros,
  value $333; other articles valued at $2,667

428.439 Priscilla WILLIAMSON   55 F NC
  Lavina WILLIAMSON   35 F NC
  Daniel B.   4 M NC

429.440 JAMES SMITH   50 M NC shoemaker
  Ann Smith   45 F NC (X)

430.441 John THOMPSON 40 M NC shoemaker
  Jane THOMPSON   32 F NC
  Susan V.   12 F NC S
  William H.   9 M NC S
  John F.   8 M NC S
  Mary Jane   5 F NC
  Cornelia   3 F NC
  Perlina   9/12 F NC
  Amy PORTER   50 F NC B
  2 slaves

431.442 Thomas T MAXWELL 35 M NC merchant 1,200
  Maria E.   6 F NC S
  Lavina   5 F NC
  John L.   3 M NC
  Louisa L. LEECH   19 F NC
  James A. CRUMP   20 M NC clerk

  [CW:Thomas T Maxwell & Rebecca Pool 30 Nov 1842
  6 slaves

432.443 Matthias BOGER   38 M NC merchant 3,300
  William   6 M NC
  Mary J.   4 F NC
  Sarah   1 F NC
  Henry B. REESE   24 M NC clerk
  John K. POTTS   17 M NC clerk
  Jane WOODSIDES   50 F NC
  4 slaves

433.444 George W BROWN 49 M NC Merchant 8,500
  Cornelia BROWN   30 F NC
  Elizabeth C.   16 F NC
  Peter Alexander   12 M NC
  George W. Junr   6 M NC
  Robert L. McCONNAUGHEY 21 M NC clerk
  James J.   18 M NC clerk   (cont.)

[CW:George W Brown & Cornelia K Long, dau Dr.
  Alexander Long 28 May 1843]
125 A improved land, 390 unimpr, valued at $3000
18 slaves

434.445 Calvin S BROWN 23 M NC merchant 6,000
  Ann E. BROWN   20 F NC
  Walter S.   5/12 M NC
  Benjamin F. CROSSLAND 24 M SC clerk
  Jane G. McCONNAUGHEY   16 F NC

  [MB:Calvin S Brown & Anne E McConnaughey 25 May
  1847] 4 slaves

435.446 Pleasant HENDERSON 47 M NC physician 4,000
  Rebecca F. HENDERSON   28 F VA
  Francis Marion   24 M NC physician

  [She was Rebecca Wimbish; bur. Old English Cem.]
  6 slaves

436.447 Moses RIMER   30 M NC shoemaker
  Sarah M. RIMER   27 F NC
  Mary E.   7 F NC S
  John L.   4 M NC
  Milten F.   3 M NC
  Joseph S.   6/12 M NC

  [MB: Moses Rimer to Sarah M Weant 16 June 1842]

437.448 David F CALDWELL 55 M NC judge S.C.M.E.
                        15,000
  Rebecca R. CALDWELL 59 F NC
  Archibald H.   25 M NC attorney at law
                        2,000
  Andrew J.   20 M NC farmer
  Fannie M.   15 F NC S

  [She is Rebecca M. (Nesbit) Troy]
  125 A improved land, 1100 A unimpr, valued at
  $5000, 21 slaves

438.449 Joseph J. SUMMERELL 30 M NC physician 1,000
  Elen H   26 F NC
p.140, Salisbury, 13 August 1850
  Anna M.   4 F NC
  John M.   1 M NC
  Sarah E. PETERSON   12 F NC S
  Mary E.   10 F NC S
  3 slaves

439.450 Jane CALDWELL 55 F NC 20
  James C.   26 M NC merchant
  Maxwell C.   23 M NC merchant
  David   18 M NC clerk
  3 slaves

440.451 John J. BRUNER 33 M NC printer 1,000
  Mary A. BRUNER   25 F NC
  Clarissa   5 F NC S
  William H.   3 M NC
  Mary B.   1 F NC
  James BOWERS   11 M NC S   (cont.)

[MB:John J Bruner & Mary Ann Kincaid 26 Jan 1843]
2 slaves. Bruner & James: 750 newspapers valued
at $1,400, advertising, $600.

441.452 William BROWN 25 M NC tinner 1,200
    Ann B. BROWN   23 F NC

    Brown & Baker, tin & coppersmith: 9 stills, tin
       ware, other articles

442.453 John E BOGER 29 M NC silversmith 1,100
    Mary A. BOGER   21 F NC
    Margaret M.   15 F NC S
    William C.   6/12 M NC
    3 slaves

443.454 John D BROWN 42 M NC merchant
    Jane BROWN   29 F NC
    John A.   7 M NC
    Alice   3 F NC
    Mary E.   6/12 F NC
    James SLATE   18 M NC clerk
    4 slaves

444.455 Archibald BAKER 37 M SC clergyman P 2,500
    Sarah BAKER   26 F NC
    Hinton J.   4 M NC
    Catharine M.   2 F NC
    Laura T.   0/12 F NC
    Ann M. JAMES   50 F NC
    Betsy FREEMAN   30 M̲ NC
    4 slaves

445.456 Gilbert MORGAN 55 M NY clergyman P 5,000
    Maria MORGAN   44 F NY
    Gilbert   21 M NY student
    Charlotte   19 F NY
    Margaret   17 F NY
    Emely   14 F NY
    Andrew G. KER   28 M PA music teacher
    3 slaves

446.457 Claudius B WHEELER 38 M MA physician
    Ann J. WHEELER   31 F NC
    Elizabeth A.   12 F NC S
    William A.   10 M NC S
    Henery C.   8 M NC S
    George W.   6 M NC
    Charles H.   2 M NC
    Stephen B. WESCT   18 M NY druggist

    [MB:Claudius B Wheeler & Ann J Chaffin 7 Dec
1835]
    52 A improved land valued at $3000
    6 slaves

447.458 William OVERMAN 37 M NC carriage trimmer 500
    Mary E. OVERMAN   23 F NC
    Laura J.   7 F NC S
    Charles A.   4 M NC
    William H.   3 M NC   (cont.)

    John F.   6/12 M NC
    Albert OVERMAN   24 M NC carriage maker
    Alphonso HOLDER   25 M NC carriage trimmer
       RUMPELT   22 M NC wheelwright
    Rowan SLATER   15 M NC clerk
    Samuel HOLTSHOUSE   19 M NC Mu labourer

    7 slaves
    Overman Brown: 25 carriages, 25 buggies

448.459 Maxwell CHAMBERS 70 M NC 37,000
    Catherine B. CHAMBERS 65 F NC

    [MB:Maxwell Chambers & Katherine B Troy 14 Jan
1830]
    350 A improved land, 1350 A unimpr, valued at
       $13000, 69 slaves, shirting worth $50,000,
       cotton yarn worth $1000, batting worth $832

449.460 Michael BROWN 56 M NC merchant 2,000
    Susan   26 F NC
    Edward   25 M NC physician
    Leonidas   20 M NC law student
    Virginia W.   17 F NC
    Mary L.   13 F NC
    Alexander H.   8 M NC
    Joseph J. BURKE   19 M NC clerk
    53 slaves

450.461 John S JOHNSON 34 M NC attorney
                                 at law 2,500
    Sarah JOHNSON   28 F NC
    Mary Ann   9 F NC S
    Thomas P.   4 M NC S
    Charles LINEBARRIER 12 M NC S
    Harriet JOHNSON   2 F NC

    3 slaves
    5 wagons, 30 carriages

451.462 John A WISEMAN 24 M PA tailor
    William WISEMAN   22 M PA
    Mary Jane   3 F Philadelphia
    Jenette   8/12 F NC
    James SCROGGS   17 M NC tailor

    John A. Wiseman:various articles valued at $2,200
    1 slave

452.463 Marcellus WHITEHEAD 29 M VA physician 3,000
    Virginia WHITEHEAD   26 F VA
    Anna E.   2 F NC
    Norah A.   1 F NC
    11 slaves

p. 141, Salisbury, 13 August 1850

453.464 Samuel REEVES 21 M NC town clerk 1,800
    Margaret A REEVES 20 F NC
    Mary L. E.   2/12 F NC
    2 slaves

454.465 Hand JAMES 24 M NC physician 3,900
 Harriet I JAMES 21 F NC
 Laura B.   1 F NC
 Hinton M.   1/12 M NC
 John ENNIS   17 M NC clerk in drug store
 6 slaves

455.466 Wilson C. HACKET 26 M NC carpenter
 Jane M. HACKET   25 F NC
 Mary CONRAD   7 F NC
 3 slaves

456.467 Nancy SUTTON   49 F VA (X)
 Thomas M. SUTTON   21 M NC blacksmith
 Nancy E.   11 F NC S

457.468 Augustus ELLER 25 M NC (X) stage driver
 Tranquilla ELLER   23 F NC (X)
 Martha A. TREXLER   16 F NC
 John I.   4 M NC

458.469 William HOWARD 61 M NC collecting officer
 Elen HOWARD   53 F NC
 Mary L   32 F NC
 Christina   27 F NC
 Elen L.   25 F NC
 Rosabella C.   19 F NC
 Jane A.   14 F NC
 Catherine L.   10 F NC S

[MB: William Howard & Elinor Beard 19 Sept 1818]
 1 slave

459.470 Mary BEARD   75 F NC
 Christina BEARD   50 F NC
 Julia   26 F NC

 4 A improved land
 3 slaves

460.471 Charles BEARD 48 M NC farmer
 Adam SWINK   23 M NC farmer

 tannery: 400 Pcs Leather value $800

461.472 Samuel W. JAMES 29 M NC farmer
 Mary M JAMES   20 F NC
 Henery T.   1 M NC
 Alice V.   2/12 F NC
 Elizabeth WALL   50 F NC
 James HENDERSON   18 M NC
 Ann VALENTINE   29 F NC Mu
 Randal TWOPENCE   41 M NC B

[MB: Samuel W James to Mary W Wall 21 Dec 1847]

462.473 Farley ELLIS 35 M NC (X) wagoner
 Eliza ELLIS   38 F NC (X)
 Frank DOLAND   8 M NC Mu
 Mathew EARNHART   10 M NC

[MB: Farley Ellis to Eliza Courtney 7 Jan. 1830]
 1 slave, no land but livestock

463.474 James E KERR   40 M NC attorney at law
 Catherine L. KERR 36 F NC
 Sarah   15 F NC S
 Mildred C.   11 F NC S
 William H.   8 M NC spasmodic fits
 James H.   7 M NC S
 Mary R.   5 F NC S
 Jane A.   3 F NC
 Paulina   1 F NC

[MB:James E Kerr & Catharine L Huie 18 Sept 1833]
 4 slaves

464.475 Lenora HAMPTON 65 F NC 400
 Susanna   46 F NC
 Elen WOOLWORTH   21 F NC
 Julia A.   16 F NC
 .476 Wade W. HAMPTON 43 M NC tailor
 Caroline C HAMPTON 27 F NC
 Mary E.   10 F NC S
 Elen M.   7 F NC S
 John S.   5 M NC
 Arabella L.   3 F NC
 George C.   2 M NC
 Julia L.   10/12 F NC

[MB:John Hampton to Leonora Faust 23 Oct. 1800]

465.477 George M. SMITH 40 M NC wagon maker
 Mary   28 F NC (X)
 Willam A.   14 M NC S
 Julius L.   10 M NC S
 Francis C.   7 F NC S
 Laura E.   4 F NC S
 Jane E.   2 F NC
 Lucinda M.   8 F NC S

466.478 Richard FOX 30 M VA cabinet maker
 Delitha   25 F VA
 Thomas   6 M VA S
 William LITLE   8 M NC S
 Jacob CORRELL   25 M NC cabinet maker
 Levi KELLER   22 M NC cabinet maker
 Peter MILLER   17 M NC cabinet maker
 2 slaves

467.479 Sarah A. WATSON 27 F NC
 Pinkney WATSON   9 M NC S
 Albert   5 M NC S
 John MONROE   21 M NC carriage driver
 .480 Samuel BROWN   25 M NC shop keeper
p. 142, Salisbury, 14 August 1850
 Joseph ELLER   35 M NC (X) stage driver
 Caroline   26 F NC
 .481 Darkes ROUGH   30 F NC
 William ROUGH   30 M NC carpenter
 William   9 M NC
 John   6 M NC
 Franklin   4 M NC
 Franklin HARTLY   19 M NC carpenter
 Samuel MOON   26 M NC carriage painter
 1 slave

468.482 William BARKER   28 M VA carriage
                                trimmer 1,200
  Angelina A. BARKER   20 F NC
  Cicero R.   2 M VA
  Virginia   0/12 F NC
  Martha SMITH   55 F NC
  Margaret MICHAEL   21 F NC
  Theophilus HOLDER   21 M NC carriage trimmer
  4 slaves

469.483 Caleb KLUTTS   39 M NC sheriff 1,000
  Elisabeth KLUTTS   28 F NC
  Alfred W.   11 M NC
  Charlotte L.   8 F NC
  Milly A.   6 F NC
  John H.   3 M NC
  Theodore F.   1 M NC
  Jacob E. MOOSE   24 M NC deputy sheriff
  Jesse STOKER   27 M NC carpenter
  Lucinda MOOSE   20 F NC
  John H. COFFMAN   23 M NC clergyman Lu
  Ansalem KESTER   18 M NC labourer in jail
  Sally DOBY   24 F NC (X) in jail

[MB:Caleb Klutts to Amelia Holshuser 14 July 1837
Caleb Klutts to Elizabeth Moose 20 Apr 1841]
Caleb Klutts - 3 slaves
Jesse A. Stoker - 6 slaves

470.484 Benjamin BROWN   25 M NC
  Louisa BROWN   25 F NC
  Josaphine   2 F NC
  Walter G.   1 M NC
  Mary SUTTON   16 F NC
  Josephas MAHALA   25 M NC carpenter
  Elen PARKS   26 F NC
  Miles BROWN   17 M NC

[MB: Benjamin Brown to Louisa Parks 21 May 1846]
1 slave

471.485 Abner PACE   27 M NC harness maker
  Julia PACE   24 F NC
  John F.   5 M NC

472.486 Benjamine JULIAN   39 M NC postmaster 2,000
  Clarissa C. JULIAN   20 F NC
  Francis D.   2 M NC
  Virginia E.   11/12 F NC

[MB:Benjamin Julian & Clarissa E Gibson 5 Oct 1846]
4 slaves

473.487 William LAMBETH 34 M VA shoemaker
  Amanda LAMBETH   34 F VA

474.488 Elizabeth GILES   52 F NC
  Susan F. GILES   49 F NC
  Ellen M. FULTON   35 F NC
  2 slaves

475.489 Alexander W BUIS 48 M NC confectioner 4,000
  Malinda BUIS   41 F NC (X)   cont.

  Martha C.   18 F NC S
  William A.   15 M NC S
  John H.   13 M NC S
  Lewis H.   10 M NC S
  George M.   3 M NC
  Margaret   1/12 F NC

[MB:Alexr W Buis to Marenda Fraley 12 July 1831]
5 slaves, 3,000 pounds candy, $660; bread, $260,
other articles, $450

476.490 John I SHAVER   41 M NC hotel keeper 19,000
  Mary E. SHAVER   28 F NC
  Edwin   8 M NC
  Elizabeth E.   7 F NC
  Elizabeth HARIS   18 F NC
  Robert MURPHY   24 M NC merchant 4,000
  Mary A. MURPHY   23 F NC
  Alice W.   2 F NC
  John   11/12 M NC
  Myer MYRES   28 M NC trader
  Ezekiel MYERS   17 M NC merchant
  Abram   26 M NC clerk
  William W.   15 M NC clerk
  James H. ENNIS   26 M NC merchant
  William SHEMWELL   27 M NC merchant
  Joseph CHAMBERS   26 M NC merchant
  Robert G. ALLISON   43 M NC teacher
  Alexander HENDERSON   41 M NC physician
  Julius RAMSEY   23 M NC clerk
  John W ELLIS   M NC judge of S.C.S.E.
  William WILSON   29 M NC silversmith
  Joseph HAWKINS   24 M NC tailor
  Archibald COATY   27 M NC stage driver
  John LONG   23 M NC stage driver
  Isaac LAYERLY   38 M NC carpenter
  Joel SULLIVAN   37 M NC saddler
  David TOM   37 M NC carpenter
<u>p.143, Salisbury, 15 August 1850</u>
  William J PALMER   30 M NC stage contractor
  Steven STEEL   25 M NC B waiter
  Luke BLACKMER   35 M NC attorney at law

[MB:John I Shaver & Mary E Lemly 14 Jan. 1840]
400 A improved land, 425 A unimpr, valued at $6500
53 slaves
blacksmith with 5 road wagons valued at $500
5 other wagons valued at $625, 3 carriages valued
at $2,000, a lot of timber valued at $1,000

477.491 Nathaniel BOYDEN   52 M MA attorney at law
  Jane C. BOYDEN   44 F NC
  Nathaniel A   18 M NC S
  Ruth M.   14 F NC S
  Sallie Mitchel   12 F NC S
  Lueco   11 M NC S
  Archibald H. BOYDEN   3 M NC
  Laura HENDERSON   18 F NC

[MB:Nathaniel Boyden & Jane C Mitchell 2 Dec 1845]
20 A improved land, 50 A unimpr, valued at $500
64 slaves

478.492 Henderson BARRETT 35 M NC (X)
  Martha BARRETT   25 F NC
  Isaac G.   7 M NC
  James A.   4 M NC
  Virginia T.   9/12 F NC

479.493 George M WEANT   41 M NC shoemaker 300
  Julia WEANT   36 F NC (X)
  Mary E.   19 F NC
  William A.   10 M NC S
  Matthew J.   12 M NC S
  Laura A.   8 F NC
  Julia A.   2 F NC

480.494 William A LYERLA   29 M NC housepainter
  Mary P. LYERLA   23 F NC (X)
  Jane E.   4 F NC S
  Laura C.   3 F NC
  Alice B.   8/12 F NC
      1 slave
  .495 Hue CULVERHOUSE   42 M NC saddler
  Rebecca CULVERHOUSE   36 F NC
  Margaret C.   13 F NC
  Rue R.   10 M NC S
  William O.   8 M NC S
  Hariet R.   2 F NC
  Margaret A. WOOD   57 F NC

[MB:Hugh Culverhouse & Rebecca Wood 22 Dec 1838]
1 slave

481.496 Lorenza D BENCINI 25 M NC carriage painter
  Hariet BENCINI   21 F NC
  Moses A.   4 M NC
  Ann M.   1 F NC
  Mira SHAVER   21 F NC (X)
  John HESS   19 M NC mail carrier
  William JARETT   13 M NC B
  Alfred C. McLAND   47 M NC house painter
  Elizabeth McLAND   40 F NC
  Caroline C. McCELLAND   18 F NC S
  John G.   17 M NC S house painter
  Sarah C.   13 F NC S
  John SIMPSON   20 M NC house painter
  Rodolph McCELLAND   28 M NC house painter
  Ann   26 F NC
  Eliza   3 F NC

[MB:Lorenzo D Bencini/Harriet C Brown 4 May 1844]
Alfred C. McClelland: 2 slaves

483.498 Horace H BEARD   44 M NC tailor 5,000
  Margaret L BEARD   42 F PA
  Lewis H.   14 M NC S
  Julia M.   12 F NC S
  William   7 M NC S
  Maria   4 F NC
  Susan B.   2 F NC
  Lenora   3/12 F NC
  George MONROE   17 M NC tailor
  Daniel JOHNSON   9 M NC S
  John L. KERR   22 M NC tailor
  Mary Ann SWINK   24 F NC (X)   cont.

55 A improved land, 20 A unimpr, valued at $320
4 slaves
Various articles valued at $1,000

484.499 Mary P. HOLLAND 60 F NC

485.500 Alexander LONG 60 M NC physician
  Mary LONG   56 F NC
  Julia E.   26 F NC
  Robert W.   25 M NC clerk
  Hellen W.   19 F NC
  Hamilton W   13 M NC S
  Hogan H HELFER   29 M NC
  Elizabeth C HELFER   22 F NC
  Hinton F.   9/12 M NC

[She was Mary Williams of Hillsboro]
6 slaves

486.501 Moses L. BROWN   49 M NC tanner
  Letitia BROWN   41 F NC
  Laura A.   18 F NC
  Rebecca   16 F NC
  Hue L.   14 M NC student
  Sarah A.   9 F NC S
  Julia A.   7 F NC S
  Thomas M. HAINS   20 M NC

[MB:Moses L Brown & Letitia Hartman 3 Aug 1826]
18 slaves
2,000 soles at $300, 830 harnesses at $250, other
articles valued at $1,250

487.502 James SMITH   30 M NC Mu carpenter
  Sophia SMITH   29 F NC Mu
  Wesley   26 M NC Mu
P.144, Salisbury, 25 Aug.1850.
  Henry MITCHELL   22 M NC Mu matrass maker
  Lucinda A   18 F NC Mu
  Sarah A Valentine   15 F NC Mu

James Smith: house carpenter, 5 houses valued at
$1,800, other articles valued at $250

488.503 William H. SMITH 49 M KY 2,000
  Nancy SMITH   49 F NC (x)
  Susan C.   15 F NC S
  Franklin COUGHENOUER   18 M NC S black smith
  Sally TROTT   25 F NC

[MB: William H Smith to Nancy Smith 4 Jan 1827]
6 slaves

489.504 Charles H. BAKER 23 M NC coppersmith
  Margaret A. BAKER   25 F NC
  Mary E.   2/12 F NC
  Richard PARKS   18 M NC tinner

[CW: Charles F. Baker to Margaret Ann Owen
6 June 1849] 3 slaves

490.505 Henery SMITH   52 M NC farmer 3,800
  Ann SMITH   55 F NC   cont.

Charles D. SMITH   23 M NC carpenter
Robert H. SMITH   20 M NC carriage maker

80 A improved land, 181 unimpr, valued at $1600
4 slaves

491.506 Henery A. SMITH   27 M NC carpenter 500
  Sarah A. SMITH   23 F NC
  Mary Ann   5 F NC S
  Laura K.   3 F NC
  George A.   11/12 M NC
  James B. EARNHEART   18 M NC carpenter

[MB:Henry A Smith to Sarah Ann Weant 1 Aug 1843]
2 slaves

492.507 Martha PAGE 19 F NC (X)
  Nancy   16 F NX (X)

493.508 David TREXLER   42 M NC wagoner 200
  Rachel TREXLER   38 F NC
  Alexander   18 M NC
  Mary L. MOYER   16 F NC
  Daniel MOYER   13 M NC
  Jane TREXLER   3 F NC

[MB:David Trexler to Rachel Moyer 7 June 1849]
3 slaves

494.509 Mary SWINK   64 F NC 500
  Joice LEWIS   19 M NC
  Laura   1 F NC
  Elen SWINK   11 F NC S
  Mathew JACOBS   20 M NC blacksmith
  Margaret JACOBS   26 F NC 500

495.510 Otho SWINK   23 M NC harness maker
  Catherine SWINK   22 F NC

[MB: Otho Swink to Catharine Cauble 29 Mar 1849]

496.511 Jane TANNER 50 F VA
  Louisa   22 F VA
  Isabella MADISON   21 F VA
  Susan R.   0/12 F VA
  Branch T. L. TANNER 15 M VA S bricklayer
  Whitfield   13 M VA S
  Ann C   11 F VA S

497.512 Mary BROWN 65 F NC
  Mary A. C.   24 F NC

498.513 Tobias WIRE   34 M NC (X) labourer
  Polly WIRE   29 F NC (X)
  Henery A.   10 M NC S

499.514 William A. SWINK 26 M NC harness maker
  Sarah SWINK   28 F NC
  Mary J.   2 F NC
  Sarah P.   7/12 F NC
  Rebecca TREXLER   14 F NC

[MB:William A Swink & Sarah Sawyers 6 May 1847]

500.515 Charity BROWN 26 F NC

501.516 Henry A JACOBS 27 M NC blacksmith
  Elizabeth JACOBS   25 F NC
  John   3 M NC
  Selena   22 F NC
  David TREXLER   19 M NC blacksmith

[MB:Henry A Jacobs & Elisabeth Williamson 24 Dec
  1845]

502.517 Obadiah WOODSON 34 M NC clerk S.C.
  Ann M. WOODSON   28 F NC
  ANN M.   8 F NC S
  Margaret H.   7 F NC S
  Horatio N.   5 M NC S
  Mary Louisa   3 F NC
  Otis C.   1 M NC

[MB:Obadiah Woodson & Ann Maria Fraley 15 Dec 1840]
1 slave

503.578 Daniel W. SMITH   39 M NC carriage maker
  Nancy SMITH   37 F NC (X)
  William L.   12 M NC S
  Gerand R.   7 M NC S
  Calvin B.   4 M NC
  David W.   9/12 M NC
  Michael D.   19 M NC S carpenter
  Margaret WALTON   25 F NC (X)
  Albert T. WALTON   19 M NC (X) carriagement

[MB:Daniel Smith to Nancy Walton 3 Jan 1833]

504.579 Samuel CAUBLE   40 M NC farmer
  Elizabeth CAUBLE   43 F NC (X)
  Rose M.   18 F NC
  Michael   14 M NC labourer
  Horace G.   12 M NC S
  Benjamin D.   9 M NC S
  John B. WATSON   3 M NC

[MB:Samuel Cauble/Elizabeth Godfrey 18 Jan 1825]
renter, 48 A improved land valued at $140

p.145, Salisbury, 15 Aug. 1850

505.520 Margaret EARNHART   45 F NC 1,000
  Newton EARNHART   26 M NC carriage maker
  Lettitia EARNHART   22 F NC
  John H.   1 M NC
  Thomas   0/12 M NC
  Peter EARNHART   14 M NC
  Caroline   12 F NC

506.521 Evander CALVIN   28 M SC Mu house painter
  Mariah J. CALVIN   26 F NC Mu
  Mary E.   2 F NC Mu
  Eliza CANADA   48 F NC Mu
  Henry CANADA   19 M NC Mu painter
  Solomon CANADA   20 M NC Mu house painter
  Henderson EVANS   30 M NC Mu house painter

507.522 Julian Ann MURR 47 F NC 200
    Celia   22 F NC
    Michael A.   21 M NC carpenter
    Moses B.   13 M NC S
    William   7 M NC S
    Joice A.   6 F NC S

[MB:George W Murr & Juliana Trote 14 Feb 1822]

508.523 Jessee H. HOWARD 29 M NC shoe maker
    Susan HOWARD   27 F NC
    Hugh A.   4 M NC
    George M.   2 M NC
    Ann M.   4/12 F NC
    Margaret REDWINE   14 F NC S
    William SWINK   21 M NC shoemaker

[MB:Jesse H Howard to Susan Murr 30 Nov 1844]
Howard & Swink: 150 pr. boots, 85 pr. shoes

509.524 Rufus SWINK   30 M NC blacksmith
    Nancy SWINK   28 F NC
    Mary J.   8 F NC
    Henry   6 M NC
    Michael   4 M NC
    Henry SWINK   19 M NC blacksmith
    525. Wila BROWN   24 M NC shoemaker
    Jerusha BROWN   20 F NC
    John BROWN   18 M NC
    Mary A. DEATON   F NC

510.526 Jacob LEFLER   24 M NC
    Sally C. LEFLER   28 F NC (X)
    Mary A.   15 F NC S
    Sarah C.   12 F NC S
    Martha E.   8 F NC S
    Susan E. LEFLER   5 F NC S
    Jacob R.   3 M NC
    Nancy R.   1 F NC
    Daniel BASSINGER   11 M NC
    Green KESLER   49 M NC shoemaker
    2 slaves

511.527 Howel PARKER 30 M NC (X) stagedriver
    Sarah D. PARKER   26 F NC (X)
    William P.   8 M NC
    Alexander   5 M NC
    Sarah M.   1 F NC

[MB:Howel Parker to Sarah Dixmukes 27 Dec 1842]

512.528 Catharine BROWN 34 F NC
    Clementine   15 F NC
    Henry   13 M NC
    Sarah   8 F NC S
    Mary E.   4 F NC S

513.529 Robert BROWN 33 M NC (X) shoemaker
    Sarah BROWN   26 F NC
    Lettitia KESLER   8 F NC S

514.530 Franklin PINKSTON   30 M NC carriage painter
    Sarah   16 F NC
    Mary   13 F NC S
    Susan CRITTENTON   37 F NC (X)

515.531 Levi BROWN   35 M NC carder in factory
    Emely BROWN   30 F NC
    Richard   17 M NC carder
    Levi   15 M NC carder
    Caroline BENSON   19 F NC
    Franklin BENSON   14 M NC
    Robert BENSON   12 M NC

[MB:Levi Brown to Emily Williamson 31 Dec 1846]

516.532 John WILLIAMSON   60 M NC carpenter 500
    Hester WILLIAMSON   50 F NC
    Mary A.   27 F NC
    Jane   20 F NC
    Martha   18 F NC
    John F.   16 M NC
    William C.)twins   11 M NC
    Isaac M.   )   11 M NC
    Elizabeth A. LITTLE   9 F NC
    Thomas H. PIERCE   29 M NC carpenter
    James H. PIERCE   22 M carpenter

517.533 William MURPHY   38 M NC merchant
    Susan W. MURPHY   24 F NC
    p.146, Salisbury, 15 Aug. 1850
    Jane E.   2 F NC
    Laura C.   11/12 F NC
    William   12 M NC S
    Mary   15 F NC S
    Thomas D. CHUNN   19 M NC medical student
    William C.   13 M NC S
    Ann E. COUGHENOUR   23 F NC
    Amos SHARPE   22 M NC
    William WATTS   22 M NC
    Julius BLACK   25 M GER

[MB:William Murphy & Susan W Chunn 25 July 1845]
240 A improved land, 400 A unimproved, valued at
    $5,000, 17 slaves

518.534 Mary SMITH 56 F NC (X) 300
    Mary A.   18 F NC

519.535 Mary MURPHY 54 F NC
    Andrew   18 M NC student
    Elizabeth MURPHY   49 F NC
    William SUMPTER   22 M NC
    11 slaves

520.536 Susanna B. HOLMES   66 F PA 400
    Rebecca SMITH   29 F NC
    Samuel   10 M NC S
    1 slave

521.537 John J. BELL 45 M NC
    Mary C. BELL   35 F NC
    Lunda W.   21 F NC   cont.

Jane C.   10 F NC S
William COUGHENOUR 14 M NC S
Thomas A.   4 M NC

[MB:John J Bell & Mary C Coughenour 16 May 1850]
7 slaves

522.538 Margaret DICKSON 49 F NC 1,000
    Thomas   26 M NC tailor
    Isabella   23 F NC
    William   20 M NC tailor
    Mary   18 F NC
    Martha   16 F NC
    Barbara W.   12 F NC
    Thomas WAMACK   55 M NC (X) tailor
    Asberry P. LEACH   16 M NC tailor

5 slaves
Thomas: various articles valued at $200

523.539 John UTZMAN 30 M NC saddler 4,000
    George UTZMAN   63 M NC tin & coppersmith

125 A improved land, 225 A unimpr, valued at
$4000, 5 slaves

524.540 Benjamin F FRALEY 41 M NC tailor 800
    Jane P. FRALEY   42 F NC
    Cameron E.   10 M NC
    Jane U.   9 F NC
    Roxanna O.   7 F NC

60 A improved land, 15 A unimpr, valued at $500
20 slaves

525.541 Catharine DILLOW 75 F NC (X)
    1 slave

526.542 Robert E. LOVE 35 M NC attorney at law
    Laura E. LOVE   25 F MD
    Mary V.   8 F NC S
    Betsy McKAY   6 F NC S
    William C.   2 M NC
    Alice McC   3/12 F NC

[WC: Robert E Love to Laura A Cone 31 Jan 1842
    in Tuscaloosa, AL]

527.543 Margaret BRYANT 49 F NC (x)
    Frances   20 F NC
    Linsey   9 M NC S

528.544 Jacob MYERS 53 M NC 100
    Mary A MYERS   50 F NC
    Christina   10 F NC

[MB:Jacob S Myers to Mary Cauble 8 Feb 1838]

529.545 James I. KINDER 19 M NC Mu
    Sarah S. KINDER   20 F NC Mu
    John C.P.   6/12 M NC Mu

530.546 John L. BEARD 54 M NC
    Patience E. BEARD   26 F NC (X)

531.547 Christian MAHALA 63 M NC (X) farmer
    Eve MAHALA   61 F NC (X)
    Lawrence   21 M NC labourer
    Susan D.   15 F NC S

532.548 Polly SAWYER 25 F NC 75

533.548 Elizabeth MORE 44 F NC
    Sarah MORE   23 F NC

534.550 Polly HANNANS 28 F NC (X)
    Rachel KRIDER   35 F NC
    Mary R.   7 F NC
    Barbara ELLER   60 F NC
    John ELLER   52 M NC (X)labourer

535.551 Cyrus WEST Jr. 26 M NC (X) carpenter 300
    Caroline WEST   23 F NC
    William   1 M NC
    Alexander WEST   12 M NC
    Elizabeth)twins   7 F NC
    Albertine)   7 F NC
    Martha PHILLIPS   26 F NC (X)

[MB:Cyrus West & Caroline Griffin 11 Aug 1847]

536.552 Sophia THOMAS 39 F NC 500
    Mary L.   15 F NC
    Delia C.   13 F NC
    Calistia   10 F NC
    Charles   7 M NC
    Daniel H.   4 M NC

p.147, Salisbury 16 Aug. 1850.

537.553 Mary E. EARNHART 41 F NC 500
    Martha H.   16 F NC
    Lewis P.   11 M NC
    H. SHAVER   62 M VA

538.554 Mary SEERS 44 F NC (X)
    Sandy C.   1 M NC

539.555 David PORTER 28 M NC B
    Peggy PORTER   24 F NC B
    William VALENTINE   38 M NC B

540.556 Eliza DUSTAN 25 F NC Mu
    Joseph   4 M NC Mu
    Lenora   2 F NC Mu
    Lolly MITCHELL   70 F NC Mu
    James M.   23 M NC Mu house painter
    Margaret HICKMAN   6 F NC B

541.557 Henrietts W. LOVE 33 F NC
    William H.   5 M NC

542.558 Charles F. FISHER 34 M NC farmer
    Frances C.   4 F NC
    Frederick)twins   9/12 F NC
    Annie   )   9/12 F NC
    Christina   23 F NC   cont.

200 A improved land, 200 A unimpr, valued at $2000
corn mill - 3,300 bu. valued at $132
saw mill - 300,000 ft of lumber valued at $2,250

543.559 Moses HODGES   80 M NC B

544.560 Archibald HENDERSON   39 M NC farmer 9,000
  Mary S. HENDERSON   30 F NC
  Lenard A.   8 M NC S
  John S.   4 M NC
  Archibald   2 M NC
  Jane C.   0/12 F NC
  Joseph HENDERSON   18 M NC student
  Suzanna STEEL   80 FB NC

[MB: A Henderson to Mary S Ferrand 14 Dec 1840]
200 A improved land, 400 A unimproved land,
  valued at $3,000, 35 slaves

545.561 Joseph R. WEST   38 M NC farmer 2,000
  Alice WEST   42 F NC
  Albert   8 M NC
  Antoinett   6 F NC
  Frances   4 F NC

[CW:R J West to Mrs. Alice Slater 22 Dec 1840]
120 A improved land, 120 unimpr, valued at $2000
5 slaves

546.562 Christiana CRAWFORD   39 F NC 2,000
  Thomas M.   18 M NC S farmer
  William H.   15 M NC
  James B.   12 M NC
  Robert R.   9 M NC
  Leonidas   8 M NC

250 A improved land, 463 A unimpr, valued at $2000
10 slaves

p. 148, School District #20, 21 Aug. 1850

547.563 Jacob MENUS   37 M NC farmer 325
  Harriet E.   11 F NC S
  James F.   10 M NC S

40 A improved land, 47 A unimpr, valued at $325

548.564 Thomas T LOCKE   24 M NC farmer 5,000
  Elizabeth A.   21 F NC
  Margaret   19 F NC
  Mathew   15 M NC S

700 A improved land, 700 A unimpr, valued at $5000
45 slaves

549.565 Joseph E. TODD   61 M NC farmer
  Giles   17 M NC labourer

50 A improved land, 115 unimpr, valued at $495
11 slaves

550.566 Thomas WOOD   53 M NC farmer
  Catherine   47 F NC   cont.

Daniel WOOD   24 M NC
Jane M. WOOD   22 F NC
Margaret C.   1 F NC
Richard L.   11/12 M NC
Lydia YOUNG   25 F NC
Thomas A. KRIDER   28 M NC
Thomas M. MATTHEWS   12 M AL

[MB:Thomas Wood & Catherine Young 20 Dec 1824]
400 A improved land, 587 unimpr, valued at $4000
39 slaves

551.567 Margaret BURKHEAD   35 F NC 3,000
  Julia A. BURKHEAD   15 F NS S
  James A.   12 M NC S
  William H. M.   10 M NC S
  Charity E.   6 F NC
4 slaves

552.568 Ferand WATSON 35 M NC farmer
  Nancy Watson   36 F NC
  Elisabeth   8 F NC S
  Mary J.   6 F NC S
  Thomas F.   1 M NC
  Annie WATSON   11 F NC S

[MB:Ferrand Watson & Mary M Thompson 8 Apr 1850,
to Nancy Dent 31 Jan 1848; Mary d 19 Nov 1844 CW]
200 A improved land, 200 A unimpr, valued at
  $2500

553.569 Joseph BLACKWELL 45 M NC farmer 600
  Sarah A. BLACKWELL   35 F NC

[MB:Joseph Blackwell & Sarah A Howard 8 Dec 1831]
75 A improved land, 75 A unimpr, valued at $600
7 slaves

554.568 David WATSON   43 M NC 3,500
  Mary WATSON   41 F NC
  William F.   15 M NC S
  Henry W.   12 M NC S
  Thomas C.   10 M NC S
  James A.   8 M NC S
  Mary A.   5 F NC S
  James T. BELL   18 M NC S
  Ishmael McDANIEL   70 M NC B

100 A improved land, 184 A unimpr, valued at $2500
11 slaves

555.571 David HUNT   28 M NC 325
  Elizabeth HUNT   29 F NC
  William E. HUNT 4/12 M NC

60 A improved land, 80 A unimpr, valued at $600

p. 148, School District #20, 19 Aug. 1850

556.572 Henry COON   69 M NC (X) farmer 300
  Eve COON   64 F NC (X)
  Rosena   42 F NC (X)
  Elizabeth   32 F NC
  Henry   21 M NC S   cont.

James   19 M NC S
Margaret   13 F NC S

60 A improved land, 110 A unimpr, valued at $300

557.573 James H. SMITH   33 M NC 1,000
Margaret G. SMITH   38 F NC
William A.   6 M NC deficient
Eliza C.   4 F NC
Delia L.   2 F NC

[MB: James H Smith & Margt G Locke 24 Sept 1842]
1 slave

558.574 Richard LOWRY   48 M NC farmer 4,000
Elizabeth LOWRY   50 F NC
William B.   12 M NC S
Mary HENLY   65 F NC
Sarah E. ERVIN   16 F NC

400 A improved land, 400 A unimpr, valued at $4000
26 slaves

559.575 Charles ROSANKRANTZ 50 M GER shoemaker
Sophia ROSANKRANTZ   32 F NC (X)
Elizabeth   21 F GER (x)
Henry A.   7 M NC
William   6 M NC
Catharine   3 F NC

14 A improved land valued at $100

560.576 John JULIAN   50 M NC farmer 800
Abigail JULIAN   36 F NC
Mary   12 F NC
Matilda   11 F NC
Clementine   9 F NC
Benjamine   7 M NC
Caroline   5 F NC
James   3 M NC
Isaac   11/12 M NC
William   13 M NC
Samuel HARE   20 M NC
John HARE   26 M NC (X)

75 A improved land, 95 A unimpr, valued at $800
1 slave

561.577 Thomas KINCAID   49 M NC farmer 1,000
Clarissa H. KINCAID   60 F NC
Lucinda   39 F NC
William   15 M NC S

[MB: Thomas Kincaid & Claracy Brandon 15 Jul 1824]
100 A improved land, 150 A unimpr, valued at $1000
6 slaves

562.578 James MORRIS   29 M NC M farmer
Mary L. MORRIS   23 F NC M

[MB:James R Morris & Mary L Holshouser 12 Nov 1849]

563.579 William W JACOBS   31 M NC Mu farmer
Hannah JACOBS   22 F NC Mu (X)

564.580 Jesse KINCAID   51 M NC farmer
Hannah KINCAID   50 F NC
Newton TOMLINSON   16 M NC S labourer

[MB: Jesse Kincaid & Hannah Kincade 4 Nov 1823]
100 A improved land, 108 A unimpr, valued at $600
9 slaves

565.581 Burgess CRANFORD 32 M NC (X) farmer 400
Lavinia CRANFORD   32 F NC (X)
William WINDERS   22 M NC labourer

30 A improved land, 66 A unimpr, valued at $400
2 slaves

566.582 Jacob FESTERMAN   37 M NC farmer
Margaret J. FESTERMAN 21 F NC
Nathan G.   16 M NC
Jane I.   11 F NC
John F.   9 M NC

[MB:Jacob Fesperman to Margaret J Gibbons 15 Jan
    1849]
70 A improved land, 40 A unimpr, valued at $520

567.583 Samuel OWEN   42 M NC well diger
Jane OWEN   43 F NC
Martha A.   13 F NC S
Henry C.   10 M NC S
Mary J.   8 F NC S

[MB:Samuel Owen to Jane Winders 17 Feb 1836]

568.584 Mary COX   48 F NC (X)
George W.   23 M NC farmer
Elvira   19 F NC
Mary E.   13 F NC S
Burges C.   11 M NC S
Margaret .   9 F NC S
Alexander GIBBONS   20 M NC labourer
Martha GIBBONS   22 F NC (X)

[MB:Alex Gibbins & Martha Cox 20 July 1850]

569.585 Sophia SAWYER   29 F NC
William   7 M NC
Robert   5 M NC
Mary E.   1/12 F NC
Maria PIERCE   22 F NC

[MB:James Sawyers to Sophia Agner 9 July 1840
James Sawyers d 17 Apr 1850 CW]

570.586 Jane McCAY   61 F DC
Reason MAKEW   55 M DC labourer 100

150 A improved land, 11 slaves

571.587 William R FRALEY   27 M NC farmer 250
Jane E. FRALEY   23 F NC   cont.

```
William W                    4 M NC
Thomas B.                    1 M NC

40 A improved land, 29 A unimpr, valued at $250
1 slave

572.588 Anthony COZART   39 M NC carpenter 800
  Mary A. COZART         39 F NC
  Sarah L.               18 F NC
  Laura J.               16 F NC S
  Amelda A.              14 F NC S
p. 149, School District #28, 21 Aug. 1850
  William F.             12 M NC S
  Sophia E.              10 F NC S
  Mary M.                 8 F NC S
  Margaret L.             4 F NC S
  Emily E.                2 F NC
  Hariet E.               1 F NC
  Clarisy M.              6 F NC S
  William JULIAN         19 M NC S labourer

  60 A improved land, 50 A unimpr, valued at $800

573.589 John THOMASON    40 M NC farmer 800
  Hariet THOMASON        22 F NC
  Almina                  1 F NC
  Davidson               12 M NC S

  50 A improved land, 58 A unimpr, valued at $800
  2 slaves

574.590 Aaron RAINEY     49 M NC (X) farmer 450
  Mary RAINEY            51 F NC (X)
  Sarah J.              12 F NC S
  Fanny Lelila           7 F NC
  William T.             5 M NC
  Barbara A.) twins      1 F NC
  Mary E.   )            1 F NC

[MB:Aaron Rainey & Mary Ann Julian 28 Dec 1838]
75 A improved land, 75 A unimpr, valued at $450

575.591 Richard THOMASON   31 M NC 400
  Mary THOMASON         25 F NC
  Margaret               7 F NC S
  William                5 M NC S
  George                 2 M NC
  James KNOX            17 M NC labourer

[MB:Richard Thomason to Mary E Krider 22 Jan 1842]
16 A improved land, 14 A unimpr, valued at $400
1 slave

576.592  Thomas FOARD  66 M VA 550
  Elizabeth FOARD     51 F NC

30 A improved land, 90 A unimpr, valued at $360

577.593 William JULIAN  54 M NC farmer
  Mary JULIAN          36 F NC (X)
  Elisabeth            31 F NC (X) idiotic
  James                15 M NC S labourer
```

```
Jane M.                  8 F NC S
Mary C. FRALEY          15 F NC idiotic
John H. FRALEY           9 M NC S
Alphonzo                15 M NC labourer

75 A improved land, 100 A unimpr, valued at 900
1 slave

578.594 Jehu FOSTER     39 M NC 5,000
  Jane H. FOSTER        39 F NC
  Thomas J.             15 M NC
  Laura A.              11 F NC
  Julia                  7 F NC
  Jehu                   4 M NC
  Lucy J.                1 F NC
  Ann HIGDON            60 F NC

[MB: Jehu Foster to Jane Higdon 14 Dec 1833]
320 A improved land, 228 unimpr, valued at $5000
17 slaves

579.595 Radford BAILY   41 M NC 2,000
  Nancy C. BAILY        26 F NC
  John A.                1 M NC
  Clara CRAIG            7 F NC S

[MB:Radford Bailey to Nancy C Howard 12 Jan 1848]
150 A improved land, 200 A unimpr, valued at $2000
5 slaves

580.596 Elizabeth ROBERTSON   60 F NC

581.597 Abram BOST   57 M NC hatter
  Catherine BOST     62 F NC
  Leah QUILMAN       28 F NC 525

[MB:Abraham Bost/Catharine Quillman 19 Oct 1847]
40 A improved land valued at $200

582.598 Lewis JACOBS   35 M NC  farmer
  Camilla JACOBS       23 F NC

[MB:Lewis Jacobs to Camilla Gheen 19 Dec 1948]
67 A improved land, 10 A unimpr, valued at $200

583.599 Elisabeth WEANT   61 F NC
  Edward SWINK            2 M NC
  Peter SWINK             9 M NC
  Louisa SWINK            4 F NC

584.600 Willa W. SWINK   41 M NC (X) farmer
  Mary SWINK             38 F NC (X)
  Angeline               17 F NC S
  Mary A.                16 F NC S
  George A. P            13 M NC S
  Sarah A.               10 F NC S
  Wila E.                 9 F NC S
  James D.                7 M NC
  Lesley D.               5 M NC
  Molsey M.L.S.           2 F NC

585.601 George SWINK   66 M NC (X) farmer 900
  Nancy C. SWINK       15 F NC       cont.
```

Mariah L. HOWLET   30 F NC

586.602 Peter R. SWINK   32 M NC (X) farmer
   Mary C. SWINK   32 F NC
   Jane C.   11 F NC
   Susanah   10 F NC
   Mary M.   8 F NC
   Martha C.   6 F NC
   George R.   4 M NC
   Clarky D.   2 F NC

587.603 Johnson C SWINK 40 M NC (X) farmer
   Mary A. SWINK   30 F NC (X)
   Peter J.   8 M NC
   Louisa   6 F NC
   Edward   3 M NC

[MB:Johnson E Swink/Mary Ann Sanders 21 May 1849

p. 150, Scool District #28, 21 Aug. 1850

588.604 John H CRESS   24 M NC farmer 500
   Eve Ann CRESS   23 F NC
   Plesent R.   1 M NC

589.605 David WEANT   21 M NC   labourer
   Elsa W. WEANT   22 F NC (X)

590.606 Fanny WEST   62 F NC (X)
   Starlin WEST   20 M NC (X) labourer
   B. Franklin WEANT 18 M NC labourer
   Polly WEANT   20 F NC

591.607 Charles A. WEANT 23 M (X) labourer
   Rebecca WEANT   25 F NC
   William A.   3 M NC
   Nancy C.   3 F NC

[MB:Charles A Weant to Rebecca West 22 Feb 1845]

592.608 William B. COUGHENOUR   28 M NC farmer 500
   Elizabeth COUGHENOUR   20 F NC (X)

22 A improved land, 90 A unimpr, valued at $500

593.609 Tobias HUNEYCUT   23 M NC (X) labourer
   Clementine HUNEYCUTT 20 F NC
   Latitia   1 F NC
   Margaret SWINK   7 F NC

594.610 John COPE   38 M NC labourer
   Elisabeth L. COPE 32 F NC
   Henery H.   9 M NC
   Julia A.   7 F NC
   Sarah A.   5 F NC
   Mary E.M.   3 F NC

595.611 George COON   32 M NC (X) M farmer
   Mary M. COON   23 F NC (X) F
   Cornelia SWISHER   2 F NC
   Margaret SWISHER   17 F NC
   William SWISHER   20 M NC S labourer

596.612 Michael H. SWINK 55 M NC farmer
   Mary SWINK   55 F NC
   Eve   Leonora   24 F NC
   Nancy S.   17 F NC
   Margaret E.   15 F NC
   Moses P . . .   13 M NC

[MB:Michl Swink to Mary E Sloan 12 Aug 1829]

597.613 James W CLARK   27 M NC M trader 2,900
   Ann E. CLARK   29 F NC M
   Mary M. PINKSTON   8 F NC S
   Margaret D. PINKSTON 3 F NC
   Susanah SROAT   49 F NC

200 A improved land, 250 A unimpr, valued at $1200
9 slaves

598.614 Jones SWISHER   46 M NC farmer 300
   Polly SWISHER   44 F NC
   Mary C. SWISHER   22 F NC
   Angelina   19 F NC
   James C.   16 M NC farmer
   Milus A.   13 M NC
   Claudius W.   9 M NC
   Barbara J.   5 F NC

[MB:Jonas Swisher to Mary Jacobs 14 Dec 1826]
60 A improved land, 33 A unimpr, valued at $300

599.615 Jacob COON   26 M NC (X) overseer 300
   Sarah COON   34 F NC
   David F.   14 M NC nearly helpless
   George H.)twin   1 M NC
   Jacob M.   )   1 M NC
   Adam CABLE   23 M NC (X) labourer

[MB: Jacob Coon to Sarah Pence 28 Dec 1844]

600.616 James BLUE   30 M NC (X) shoemaker
   Christina BLUE   20 F NC (X)
   Henry J.   2 M NC
   David Rowan   11 M NC
   Susan C.   8 F NC
   Elisabeth   15 F NC

[MB:James Blue & Christina Correll 22 Sept 1846]

601.617 William PARNELL   23 M (X) M overseer
   Rosita M. PARNELL   24 F NC M
   John H.   2/12 M NC

602.618 Leslie FORD   34 M NC farmer
   Susan FORD   35 F NC
   Newton A.   1 M NC

603.619 Peter ROUGH   28 M (X) labourer
   Polly ROUGH   28 F NC (X)
   George A.   15 M NC
   Benjamin C.   13 M NC
   Cornelia E.   11 F NC
   Steven A   9 M NC
   Christina   19 F NC   cont.

[MB: Peter Rough & Polly Wise 7 Feb. 1834]

604.620 Lewis WATKINS   33 M NC (X) miller
  Polly WATKINS   36 F NC (X)
  Lucy A.   7 F NC S
  Sarah J.   2 F NC
  Lucy BARNETT   84 F NC

605.621 Alexander EARNHEART 25 M NC (X) farmer
  Mary S. EARNHEART   40 F NC
  Theodore L. EDWARD   6 M NC S 300

  11 A improved land, 39 A unimpr, valued at $300

606.622 Logan A. EDWARDS   23 M NC farmer
  Elizabeth B. EDWARDS   37 F NC
  Catherine T.   1/12 F NC

[MB:Logan L Edwards & Elizabeth Hulin 29 Mar 1849]

p.151, School District 28, 22 Aug. 1850

607.623 Michael CORL   41 M NC M labourer
  Sarah CORL   35 F NC M (X)
  Mary E.   16 F NC S 400
  Adam David   8 M NC 400

[MB: Michael Corl to Sally Swink 18 June 1834]

608.624 John FISHER   37 M NC farmer
  Sophia FISHER   36 F NC (X)
  George H.   12 M NC S
  Levine   11 F NC S
  Margaret C.   6 F NC S
  Sarah   3 F NC
  Mara   9/12 F NC

  40 A improved land, 85 A unimpr, valued at $600
  1 slave

609.625 Robert HULEN   57 M NC (X) farmer
  Catherine HULEN   63 F NC (X)
  Martha   17 F NC
  Robert T.   15 M NC labourer
  Tabitha   12 F NC

[MB:Robert Hulin to Catharine Cauble 1 Feb 1848]
  36 A improved land, 20 A unimpr, valued at $100

610.626 Lenord KRIDER   30 M NC farmer 500
  Lenora C. KRIDER   25 F NC
  Julia   4 F NC
  David BUTNER   12 M NC S

[MB:Leonard Krider & Leonora Bost 30 Jan 1845]
  70 A improved land, 30 A unimpr, valued at $400

611.627 Silass EARNHEART 43 M NC farmer
  Caroline EARNHEART   23 F NC
  Nathaniel   11 M NC
  Silass L.   7 M NC
  Turner   3 M NC   cont.

  Julius   1 M NC
  Tobias EARNHEART   21 M NC (X) labourer

[MB:Silas Earnheart & Caroline Goodman 5 Apr 1837]
  35 A improved land, 72 A unimpr, valued at $500

612.628 Mary MYERS   36 F NC (X) 50
  Hariet J. A.   15 F NC
  Charlotte C.   12 F NC
  Rebeckah E.   10 F NC
  John H.   8 M NC
  William A.   5 M NC
  Frances N.   3 F NC
  Julius C.A. BUTNER 1 M NC

613.629 Henery J SWINK 31 M NC (X) farmer 900
  Sophia SWINK   26 F NC
  David A.   1 M NC

  45 A improved land, 94 A unimpr, valued at $900

614.630 Daniel HENLY   36 M NC labourer
  Mary HENLY   26 F NC
  Cicero   8 M NC
  Mary   6 F NC
  John   3 M NC

615.631 Sarah CAUBLE   33 F NC (X) 50
  John   16 M NC S
  Nancy   12 F NC S
  Jane M.   10 F NC S
  Daniel M.   7 M NC S
  Henery M.   2 M NC

616.632 James A. SMITH 30 M NC farmer 100
  Sarah SMITH   23 F NC (X)
  Stephen T.   2 M NC

[MB: James A Smith to Sarah Myers 14 Feb 1846]

617.633 George CASPER 55 M NC (X) farmer
  Nancy CASPER   52 F NC (X)
  John   23 M NC labourer
  Jacob A.   17 M NC
  David   21 M NC labourer
  Elizabeth   25 F NC
  Sarah   19 F NC
  Polly L.   16 F NC

[MB: George Casper & Nancy Leonard 5 Mar 1819]

618.634 Margaret CRAIG 56 F NC (X) 1,500
  Peter MONROE   22 M NC farmer
  Mariah C. MONROE   21 F NC

  150 A improved land, 250 A unimpr, valued at $1500
  2 slaves

619.635 Susan SRIVER   58 F NC
  Mary BLUE   21 F NC

620.636 John CAUBLE 56 M NC farmer 1,200
    Elener CAUBLE   57 F NC
    Miles   28 M NC labourer
    Otho   22 M NC S labourer
    Delinda   17 F NC S
    John L.   5 M NC
    Pinckney A.   1 M NC
    William F.   1/12 M NC

    40 A improved land, 100 A unimpr, valued at $200

621.637 David CAUBLE 21 M NC farmer
    Louisa CAUBLE   20 F NC

    [MB:David A Cauble & Louisa E Winders 9 Feb 1848]
    50 A improved land, 80 A unimpr, valued at $600

622.638 Nancy PINKSTON 44 F NC 375
    Mesheck W.   22 M NC S
    William F.   20 M NC (X)
    Sarah S.   17 F NC
    Jesse R.   14 M NC S
    Turner   7 M NC

    50 A improved land, 100 A unimpr, valued at $375
    3 slaves

623.639 Robert N. CRAIG 45 M NC farmer 2,000
    Mary L. CRAIG   34 F NC
    Margaret E.   5 F NC
    p. 152, School District #29, 23 Aug. 1850
    William W.   4/12 M NC
    Sarah CRAIG   11 F NC S
    John CRAIG   43 M NC farmer 1,500
    George   13 MNC S
    Cletus   5 M NC

    175 A improved land, 200 A unimpr, valued at
       $2,000, 6 slaves

624.640 Susan J CRAIG 33 F NC 3,000
    Mary S.   10 F NC S
    Thomas D.   8 M NC S
    David LOOKINBEE   39 M NC overseer

    [MB:Thomas H Craig & Susan Jones 15 Mar. 1838
    He d. 4 Mar. 1847 CW.]
    200 A improved land, 225 A unimpr, valued at $300
    5 slaves

625.641 Hiram W. COZORT 35 M NC farmer
    Rachel COZORT   38 F NC
    Malinda B.   10 F NC S
    Mary R.   8 F NC S
    David F.   5 M NC S
    Jesse A.   3 M NC
    Charles S.   1 M NC
    Charles COZORT   32 M NC labourer

    [MB:Hiram W Cozart & Rachel Philips 8 June 1837]
    30 A improved land valued at $100

626.642 Elizabeth WINDERS 43 F NC (X)
    Thomas C.   18 M NC S farmer
    Lucinda E.   14 F NC S
    Abner C.   11 M NC S
    Mary A.   6 F NC S
    Amanda L.   4 F NC

    [MB:A C Winders & Elizabeth B Kincaid 12 Jul
    1827]
    30 A improved land valued at $100

627.643 Joseph WILLIAMS 59 M NC farmer 450
    Dorothy WILLIAMS   43 F NC (X)
    Milass   24 M NC labourer
    John H.M.   2 M NC
    Mildred S. JOHNSON 11 F NC

    100 A improved land, 100 A unimpr, valued at $425

628.644 Michael SWISHER 50 M NC (X) labourer

629.645 Mary SWINK 53 F NC 600

    90 A improved land, 90 A unimpr, valued at $600
    2 slaves

630.646 William HEATHMAN 51 M NC farmer 1,500
    Darkus HEATHMAN   47 F NC
    Elisabeth   23 F NC
    James F.   21 M NC S labourer
    William G.   19 M NC S
    Thomas   16 M NC S
    John M.   14 M NC S
    Lawson D.   12 M NC S
    Darkus M.   9 F NC S

    [MB: William Heathman & Dorcas Dent 27 Mar 1821]
    112 A improved land, 379 A unimpr, valued at $1500
    8 slaves

631.647 Sabrit S TROTT 43 M NC farmer 1,000
    Elizabeth TROTT   41 F NC
    William H.   19 M NC S labourer
    John H.   6 M NC S
    John M. WATSON   14 M NC S
    Margaret A. DENT   49 F NC

    [MB: Sabert S Trott to Elizabeth Dent 3 Jan 1839]
    80 A improved land, 181 A unimpr, valued at $1000
    3 slaves

632.648 Lucinda DENT 28 F NC 100
    Ann   4 F NC
    Martha J.   1 F NC

633.649 Caleb FREEZE 25 M NC farmer
    Maria FREEZE   29 F NC

634.650 Samuel TURNER 52 M NC farmer 1,500
    Charlotte TURNER   49 F NC
    James M.   25 M NC teacher
    Sarah A.   21 F NC
    Thomas K.   19 M NC S   cont.

Hezekiah   17 M NC S
John P.   15 M MC S
David B.   13 M NC S
Mary E.   7 F NC S

150 A improved land, 350 unimpr, valued at $1500
7 slaves

635.651 Fortune GREEN 35 M NC (X) shoemaker
   Leutitia GREEN   22 F NC (X)
   William D.   1 M NC

636.652 Moses BROWN 39 M NC farmer
   Phebe BROWN   57 F NC
   Elizabeth F.   17 F NC S
   Henry MOWRY   39 M NC (X) blacksmith

[MB: Moses Brown to Phoebe Biles 14 Oct 1830]

637.653 Elias LEE   52 M NC farmer 700
   Catharine LEE   51 F NC
   William F. OWEN   21 M NC farmer
   Charlotte COLE   23 F NC
   Nathaniel ENNISS   22 M NC labourer
   John MAY   12 M NC S

54 A improved land, 72 A unimpr, valued at $400

638.654 William BLACKWELL 34 M NC farmer
   Sarah M. BLACKWELL   32 F NC
   Sarah A.   10 F NC S
   Mary M.   7 F NC S
   William J.   4 M NC

[MB:Wm Blackwell/Sarah M Thomason 29 Aug 1837]
66 A improved land, 60 A unimpr, valued at $500
1 slave

639.655 Miles A. GHEEN 25 M NC farmer
   Rachel GHEEN   23 F NC (X)
   Margaret L.   4/12 F NC

[MB: Milas A Gheen & Rachel McCrary 7 Aug 1848]
180 A improved land, 200 A unimpr, valued at $1000

640.656. James FORD 58 M NC
   Lydia FORD   54 F NC
   Beverly D. BILES   4 M NC
   Mazy M. BILES   1 F NC

<u>p.153, School District #19, 24 Aug. 1850</u>

641.657 Barbara JACOBS 66 F NC (X)
   Kendal JACOBS   71 M NC (X) farmer 300
   Polly BEEFLE   68 F NC (X)

642.658 Lewis JACOBS sr 76 M NC (X) farmer 300
   Elisabeth JACOBS   72 F NC
   George W.   21 M NC labourer
   Susanna   47 F NC (X)
   Elisabeth   20 F NC
                                        cont.

[MB:Lewis Jacobs & Elizabeth Walton 14 Sept 1840]
67 A improved land, 10 A unimpr, valued at $200

643.659 George THOMASON 69 M VA farmer 500
   Sarah THOMASON   73 F NC (X)
   David CRAIG   11 M NC S
   Margaret JACOBS   45 F NC (X)

60 A improved land, 75 A unimpr, valued at $500

644.660 Thomas GHEEN 50 M NC (X) farmer 500
   Margaret GHEEN   40 F NC (X)
   Providence   18 F NC
   Mary   13 F NC S
   David   11 M NC S
   Catharine   9 F NC S
   Hampton   5 M NC S

45 A improved land, 98 A unimpr, valued at $500

645.661 George W THOMASON 36 M NC farmer 400
   Lavinia THOMASON   28 F NC (X)
   Turner P.   3 M NC

[MB:George W Thomason & Lavina Jacobs 6 Oct 1842]
45 A improved land, 66 A unimpr, valued at $400

646.662 Rachel WAGONER 35 F NC 400
   Louisa   21 F NC
   David   20 M NC teacher
   Charles   17 M NC S
   William   14 M NC S
   Christian   12 M NC S

50 A improved land, 76 A unimpr, valued at $500

647.663 Burges THOMASON 38 M NC farmer 400
   Nancy THOMASON   36 F NC (X)
   Sarah E.   6 F NC S
   Ann L.   3 F NC

[WC:Burgess Thomason of Rowan to Miss Nancy Barnes of Davidson Co, 16 Jan 1840 in Davidson Co]
10 A improved land, 70 A unimpr, valued at $450

648.664 Mary HALL 47 F NC (X)
   Sarah L.   21 F NC (X)
   Mary C.   16 F NC
   Elen C.   14 F NC
   Abner L.   13 M NC
   John A.   9 M NC

125 A improved land, 76 A unimpr, valued at $600
2 slaves

649.665 John ELLIOTT senr 76 M NC 300
   Sarah ELLIOTT   69 F NC (X)
   Abner ELLIOTT   29 M NC 500

John: 6 slaves
Abner: 85 A improved land, 87 A unimpr, valued at
   $300

650.666 William TOWNSLEY 41 M NC (X) ditcher 400
    Delitha TOWNSLEY   42 F NC (X)
    Julius   15 M NC S
    Mary A.   13 F NC S
    Giles S.   10 M NC S
    Martha J.   8 F NC S
    Margaret C.   4 F NC
    Maria E.   2 F NC

    35 A improved land, 70 A unimpr, valued at $400

651.667 Sally OWEN 35 F NC
    Elisabeth   13 F NC

652.668 Nancy KINCAID 73 F NC (X)
    Andrew KINCAID   33 M NC
    Martha   9 F NC
    Mary   6 F NC

653.669 Richmond WYATT 46 M NC farmer
    Lucy WYATT   44 F NC
    Thomas W.   26 M NC 100
    Angeline   22 F NC S (X)
    Emeline   19 F NC S
    Amanda C.   16 F NC
    Lucy E.   11 F NC
    Wilson M.   7 M NC S
    Richmond R.   4 M NC

    [MB:Richmond Wyatt & Lucy Foster 23 Feb 1822]
    11 A improved land, 27 A unimpr, valued at $100

654.670 Thomas KINCAID 50 M NC (X) labourer
    Hannah   10 F NC
    Susanah ELLIOTT   50 F NC (X)

655.671 John G ELLIOTT 39 M NC farmer 1,000
    Cicero TODD   22 M NC blacksmith

    Elliott: 70 A improved land, 78 A unimpr, valued
        at $1,000, 2 slaves

656.672 Joseph T BURRIS 51 M NC 1,900
    Elisabeth BURRIS   57 F NC
    Joseph A.   17 M NC S
    Maria F.B. McCRARY   23 F NC
    Joseph F.   3 M NC
    Elizabeth A.   7/12 F NC
    Mary DOBIN   61 F NC (X)
    Nancy E.   10 F NC S
    Margaret A.   7 F NC S

    [MB:Joseph T Burris/Elizabeth Dobbins 22 Dec 1824]
    65 A improved land, 111 A unimpr, valued at $800
    2 slaves

657.673 Elenor DUNN 46 F NC (X) 125
    George   23 M S labourer
    Mary   22 F NC (X)
    William   16 M NC S labourer

p. 154, School District #19, 26 Aug. 1850

658.674 Milass A AGNER 30 M NC farmer 250
    Lucy A. AGNER   35 F NC

    [MB:Milas A Agner & Lucy Ann Winders 2 May 1844]
    60 A improved land, 18 A unimpr, valued at $250

659.675 John RAINY 60 M NC (X) farmer
    Catherine RAINY 50 F NC
    Henery   30 M NC (X) labourer
    Franklin   35 M NC (X)

    20 A improved land, 6 A unimpr, valued at $100

660.676 Hilary ELLIOTT 44 M NC cabinetmaker 75
    Mary R. ELLIOTT   40 F NC
    John H.   14 M NC S
    Jane E.   12 F NC S
    David L.   2 M NC

    [MB:Hilary Elliott & Mary Phillips 11 Dec 1834]

661.677 George RAINY 40 M NC (X) farmer
    Permilla RAINY   40 F NC (X)
    Maria KING   22 F NC

    57 A improved land valued at $285

662.678 Samuel MOOR 37 M NC farmer
    Sarah MOOR   61 F NC (X)
    Maria KING   22 F NC

    35 A improved land valued at $135

663.679 Elizabeth HULEN 28 F NC
    Margaret HULEN   21 F NC
    James A. HULEN   16 M NC farmer

664.680 George H GHEEN 44 N NC farmer 1,400
    Mary H. GHEEN   43 F NC
    Thomas T.   17 M NC S labourer
    David B.   15 M NC S
    Margaret E.   14 F NC S
    Mary E.   12 F NC S
    Rachel C.   11 F NC S
    Jane M.   8 F NC S
    George H.   5 M NC S
    Lucrecia A.   3 F NC
    Rachel PINKSTON   61 F NC
    Tobias THOMISON   64 M NC farmer
    Leonard RIMER   30 M NC (X) labourer
    John NOBLE   16 M NC Mu labourer

    [WC: George H Gheen to Miss Mary Ann Rutherford 17
        July 1830 in Rowan]
    92 A improved land, 300 A unimpr, valued at $1265
    1 slave

665.681 Samuel KINCAID 65 M NC farmer 150
    Gordon WISE   40 M NC (X) farmer
    Elisabeth WISE   30 F NC (X)
    Alexander   4 M NC
    Lydia   0/12 F NC
    Henery J. WISE   12 M NC   cont.

Lydia U. SWINK   15 F NC

666.682 Hezekiah C. GRAHAM 26 M NC
  Caroline C. GRAHAM   21 F NC
  Mary GRAHAM   2 F NC
  Thomas C.   8/12 M NC
  Mary ORR   43 F NC

  [MB: Hezekiah C Graham & Caroline Chambers 19 Mar
      1846]
  Thomas C: 1 slave

667.683 Conrad FESTERMAN   36 M NC (X) farmer
  Lydia FESTERMAN   36 F NC (X)
  Mary A.   15 F NC S
  Rosena   12 F NC S
  Catherine   9 F NC S
  Crawford   8 M NC S
  Christina   6 F NC
  Monroe   4 M NC
  David   2 M NC

  40 A improved land, valued at $225

668.684 David CANUP   51 M NC farmer 1,000
  Pena CANUP   51 F NC S
  Sophia   24 F NC
  Elisabeth   21 F NC
  Salome   19 F NC S
  David   17 M NC S
  Henery   14 M NC S
  Alexander   11 M NC S
  Salena C.   3 F NC
  Julius H.   2 M NC
  Eli C.   1 M NC

  [MB:David Canup & Philpena Miller 13 Feb 1845]

669.685 George HENLY   40 M NC farmer
  Sally HENLY   35 F NC (X)
  Alfred   14 M NC S
  Daniel   12 M NC S
  Margaret E.   9 F NC S
  Charles   8 M NC S
  Sarah   6 F NC S
  Cinthia   3 F NC
  George   1 M NC

670.686 Joseph GHEEN   55 M NC farmer 500
  Elisabeth GHEEN   67 F NC
  William H.   21 M NC S labourer

  120 A improved land, 75 A unimpr, valued at $500
  2 slaves

671.687 Peter JOSEY   -- M NC
  Polly JOSEY   51 F NC
  Caleb   30 M NC
  Salome   28 F NC
  Lavinia   20 F NC
  Clementine   17 F NC
  Malinda   11 F NC   cont.

[MB: Peter Josey & Polly Klutz 21 Dec 1818]
100 A improved land, 100 A unimpr, valued at $500

p.155, School District #19, 26 Aug. 1850

672.688 Alexander MOWRY   34 M NC (X) farmer 450
  Margaret MOWRY   24 F NC (X)
  Christina L.   8 F NC
  Mary J.   5 F NC
  Nancy R.   3 F NC

[MB:Alexander Mowry & Margret Hoffner 4 Sept 1839]
50 A improved land, 44 A unimpr, valued at $400

673.689 John O. TOWNSLY 45 M NC (X) 450
  Polly TOWNSLY   43 F NC (X)
  Elizabeth   18 F NC
  Mary A.   17 F NC
  Angeline   13 F NC
  Martha G.)   6 F NC
  Lucinda   ) twins   6 F NC
  George W.   4 M NC

  61 A improved land, 40 A unimpr, valued at $400

674.690 Michael ANDERSON   61 M NC farmer 800
  Jinsey ANDERSON   59 F NC (X)
  Nancy   29 F N (X)
  Margaret   19 F NC
  John   27 M NC (X) labourer

[MB:Michael Anderson & Jensy Hartley 29 Oct 1814]
100 A improved land, 50 A unimpr, valued at $800
1 slave

675.691 Andrew MOWRY   36 M NC (X) farmer
  Elisabeth MOWRY   37 F NC (X)
  Angeline   12 F NC S
  Chrisa   10 F NC S
  Andrew Jackson   7 M NC
  Mary E.)twins   1 F NC
  Nancy J.)   1 F NC

  20 A improved land, 14 A unimpr, valued at $200

676.692 Hamilton BYERS   22 M NC (X) labourer
  Nancy J. BYERS   21 F NC (X)
  William F.   1 M NC

[MB:Hamilton Byres & Nancy Downsley 2 Mar 1848]

677.693 William LINK   49 M NC farmer 225
  Nancy LINK   49 F NC (X)
  Sally   22 F NC
  Oliver   20 M NC S
  Polly   14 F NC S
  John   12 M NC S
  Davidson COZART   6 M NC

[MB:William Link & Nancy Townsley 4 Nov 1824]

678.694 Margaret LOGAN   55 F NC (X) 50
    Sally TOWNSLY   32 F NC (X)

679.695 Thomas B. COWAN   30 M NC farmer 825
    Mary CHAMBERS   60 F NC

    45 A improved land, 150 A unimpr, valued at $825
    4 slaves

680.696 John D. HENLY   31 M NC farmer
    Sarah HENLY   44 F NC

    4 slaves

681.697 Robert B. TOWEL   37 M NC carpenter
    Elisabeth TOWEL   32 F NC
    Mary J.   11 F NC S
    William A.   8 M NC S
    Louisa L.   4 F NC
    John C.   1 M NC

    [MB:Robert B Towel & Elizabeth Innis 19 Dec 1837]

682.698 Tilman CRANFORD 35 M NC constable 125
    Martha E. CRANFORD 26 F NC
    Harriet A.   12 F NC S
    Patron C.   11 M NC S
    Abner K.   10 M NC S
    Henry Giles   8 M NC S
    Martha J.   3 F NC
    Laura E.   4/12 F NC

    [MB:Tilman Cranford & Martha E Green 4 Mar 1846]
    no land but livestock

683.699 Henery EARNHEART 31 M NC (X) farmer 300
    Anna EARNHEART   27 F NC (X)
    Elisabeth S.   4 F NC
    Laura J.   2 F NC
    William COLE   15 M NC S

    60 A improved land, 31 A unimpr, valued at $300

684.700 Andrew LYERLA 55 M NC M farmer 1,200
    Charity LYERLA   21 F NC (X) M
    Andrew   21 M NC S labourer
    Jacob   19 M NC S labourer
    John   16 M NC S labourer
    Jane   )twins   13 F NC S
    Elisabeth)   13 F NC S
    Martha   10 F NC S
    Alexander   4 M NC
    Susanah GHEEN   27 F NC (X)
    Milford L.   2 M NC
    John W.   1 M NC

    125 A improved land, 190 unimpr, valued at $1200
    1 slave

685.701 Barbara L JOHNSON 42 F NC (X) 400
    William A.   13 M NC S
    Delia Loretta   12 F NC S   cont.

    Clinton H.   9 M NC S
    George W.   5 M NC

686.702 Moses A POWLAS   31 M NC farmer 400
    Anna M. POWLAS   21 F NC
    Laura C.   1 F NC

    [MB:Moses Powlass & Anne Trexler 24 Aug 1849]
    25 A improved land, 31 A unimpr, valued at $450

687.703 Adam TREXLER   49 M NC farmer 400
    Mary A. TREXLER   32 F NC
    Eliza c.   19 F NC
    Elisabeth   17 F NC
    [156] Margaret L.   15 F NC
    Julius A.   5 M NC
    Obidiah STARR   21 M NC
    James KINCAID   9 M NC

    100 A improved land, 7 A unimpr, valued at $400
    5 slaves
    saw mill: 100,000 ft of lumber valued at $700

<u>p.156, School District #17, 27 Aug 1850</u>

688.704 Michael CLIFFORD   25 M NC miller
    Catherine CLIFFORD   21 F NC
    Lydia C.   3 F NC
    Joseph W.   1 M NC

689.705 Henry ROBISON -- M NC farmer 1,800
    James K.   23 M NC labourer

    100 A improved land, 270 unimpr, valued at $1200
    4 slaves
    flouring: 364 bu flour valued at $1,640
    corn mill: 2750 bu valued at $1,100

690.706 Jesse LYERLY 28 M NC farmer
    Elisabeth LYERLY   24 F NC

    [MB: Jesse Lyerly to Elizt Barger 19 Apr 1849]
    31 A improved land valued at $200

691.707 Daniel LYERLY 54 M NC farmer 4,000
    Margaret LYERLY   45 F NC (X)
    Samuel   26 M NC S farmer
    Joseph   20 M NC S labourer
    Henery   18 M NC S labourer
    Margaret   16 F NC S
    Polly   14 F NC S
    Nancy   12 F NC S

    [MB:Daniel Lyerly & Peggy Barrier 27 Mar 1821]
    100 A improved land, 207 unimpr, value:$3671

692.708 John A WHITMAN 27 M NC (X) farmer 700
    Sarah A. WHITMAN   33 F NC
    Amanda C.   6 F NC
    Eliza C. WHITMAN   3 F NC
    Marie J.   5/12 F NC
    William D. WHITMAN   13 M NC
    James F. ROBISON   10 M NC   cont.

Joseph A. ROBISON   8 M NC

[MB:John A Whitman & Sarah Ann Roberson 8 Aug 1844]
31 A improved land, 54 A unimpr, valued at $700

693.709 William CAMPBELL 25 M NC farmer
    Elizabeth CAMPBELL   21 F NC (X)
    Mary Jane   1 F NC

[MB: William Campbell & Elizath Lyerly 5 Feb 1848]

694.710 John FREEZE   51 M NC   farmer 1,100
    Susanna FREEZE   48 F NC (X)
    Penelope   23 F NC
    Benjamin   21 M NC
    Christiana   19 F NC
    Hainla E.   17 F NC
    Cleodora   15 F NC
    Jacob   12 M NC
    Phillip   10 M NC
    Willa   8 M NC
    Polly   6 F NC
    Amanda M.   2 F NC

[MB:John Freeze to Susan Sechler 4 Mar 1824]
100 A improved land, 208 unimpr, valued at $700

695.711 Joseph C GRAHAM 26 M NC farmer 640
    Grizzy E. GRAHAM   28 F NC

[MB:Joseph C Graham/Grizzy E Dobbins 19 Sept 1849]
3 slaves

696.712 Naomi N. DOBBIN 52 F TN 500
    Jemima   26 F NC
    Emily G.   31 F NC
    Nancy E.   17 F NC
    Joseph C.   15 M NC farmer
    Naomi W.   12 F NC

90 A improved land, 90 A unimpr, valued at $500
6 slaves

697.713 Nimrod M DOBBIN 24 M NC M surgeon
    Margaret E. DOBBIN 19 F NC M

[MB:Nimrod M Dobbin/Margaret E Graham 17 Apr 1850]

698.714 Polly C DOBBIN 53 F NC 1,200
    George W. REX   24 M NC M blacksmith
    Mary E. REX   18 F NC M

[MB:George W Rex to Mary E Dobbin 24 Jan 1850]
110 A improved land, 930 unimpr, valued at $1200
4 slaves

699.715 Emily ANDERSON 52 F NC 400
    Elisabeth A. TODD   23 F NC
    Laura A. WINDERS   10 F NC S

[MB:John Anderson to Emely Cowan 28 Dec 1836]
75 A improved land, 30 A unimpr, valued at $400
5 slaves

700.716 Aaron PINKSTON 71 M NC farmer
    Catherine PINKSTON   57 F NC (X)
    William H.   17 M NC

707.717 Thomas PINKSTON 38 M NC (X) farmer 800
    Catherine PINKSTON   43 F NC
    Nancy PINKSTON   10 F NC S
    Thomas   7 M NC S
    Jane BRIGS   21 F NC S
    Mary BRIGS   18 F NC S
    Angeline   16 F NC S
    James   14 M NC S

[MB:Thomas Pinkston/Catharine Briggs 30 Dec 1839]
110 A improved land, 113 A unimpr, valued at $400

708.718 Edmund BRIGS 49 M NC farmer 1,600
    Priscilla BRIGS   49 F NC
    Elisabeth   22 F NC
    Margaret A.   20 F NC
    Mary E.   18 F NC
    Hannah M.   16 F NC
    John   12 M NC S
    Nelly C.   10 F NC S
    Thomas   6 M NC S
    Hannah BRIGS   74 F NJ

[MB:Edmund Briggs to Prucilla Dobbins 27 Feb 1827]
110 A improved land, 245 A unimpr, valued at $1600

709.719 Richard JULIAN   33 M NC overseer 400
    Sophia JULIAN   24 F NC
    James F.   10 M NC S
    William H.   4 M NC
[157] Mary E. JULIAN   3 F NC

[WC:Richard Julian to Miss Sophia Creason of
Davidson Co., NC, 5 Mar 1840, Davidson Co.]

p.157, School District #17, 28 Aug. 1850

704.720 William H KINCAID 36 M NC farmer 400
    Eleanar KINCAID   26 F NC
    William   9 M NC S
    David   3 M NC
    John   1 M NC
    Thomas HOWARD   18 M NC S labourer

[WC: William H Kincaid to Miss Elenor Blackwell
 2 May 1839]
51 A improved land, 75 A unimpr, valued at $400

705.721 Danial MENAS   35 M NC farmer
    Elisabeth MENAS   31 F NC
    Mary   9 F NC S
    Jane   7 F NC S
    Margaret   3 F NC
    Elijah RICE   31 M NC turner & courrier

[MB:Daniel Menus to Elizabeth Turner 3 Aug 1835]
65 A improved land, 30 A unimpr, valued at $300

706.722 John BLACKWELL 25 M NC farmer 600
  Lucy L. BLACKWELL   31 F NC
  Elisabeth BLACKWELL 14 F NC S

  65 A improved land, 110 A unimpr, valued at $600
  1 slave

707.723 Mathew PLUMMER 45 M NC farmer
  Nancy PLUMMER   40 F NC (X)
  John L.   20 M NC (X)
  Margaret   18 F NC
  Elisabeth   16 F NC
  Mathew   12 M NC
  Mary   10 F NC
  William F.   8 M NC
  Ester   1/12 F NC

  [MB:Matthew Plummer/Nancy B Pinkston 11 Dec 1828]
  no land but livestock

708.724 Samuel SLOAN   62 M NC farmer 900
  Jemima   19 F NC
  Jane   17 F NC
  Margaret   15 F NC
  Henery   13 M NC
  Sally   11 F NC
  Martha   9 F NC S
  Thomas   7 M NC S
  John   5 M NC S
  Jerusha   4 F NC
  Parley S.WINDER   11 M NC
  Moses HETINGER   20 M NC (X) labourer

  100 A improved land, 98 A unimpr, valued at $900
  3 slaves

709.725 John CRESS 28 M NC farmer 550
  Leah CRESS   30 F NC
  Daniel A.   6 M NC
  Martha E.   5 F NC
  Sally C.   2 F NC
  John W.   1 M NC
  Calvin CRESS   26 M NC tanner

  [MB: John Cress to Leah Bost 6 May 1842]
  100 A improved land, 80 A unimpr, valued at $500
  1 slave

710.726 John BARGER   56 M NC farmer
  Leah BARGER   44 F NC
  Sally   23 F NC
  Monroe   21 M NC S
  Ester   19 F NC
  Margaret   15 F NC
  Daniel   12 M NC S
  Anna   10 F NC S
  Paul   7 M NC S

  200 A improved land, 330 A unimpr, valued at $2500
  30 slaves

711.727. Lucy BEAN 47 F NC (X)
  Lundy F.   22 F NC (X)   cont.

  Adeline S.   20 F NC (x)
  Jane M.   18 F NC S
  Mary C.   11 F NC S
  Susan F.   9 F NC S

712.728 Alexander BEAN 26 M NC farmer 500
  Caroline BEAN   23 F NC
  Alice   1 F NC

  [MB:Alexander Bean & Caroline Waggoner 19 Feb 1848]
  50 A improved land, 80 A unimpr, valued at $550

713.729 Willa KINCAID 55 M NC overseer
  Nancy KINCAID   24 F NC (X)
  Mathew   4 M NC
  John H.   1 M NC

  400 A improved land, 411 A unimpr, valued at $5000

714.730 Levi LORANCE 34 M NC wagon maker 300
  Emely LORANCE   34 F NC
  Mary E.   11 F NC S
  Angeline A.   9 F NC S
  Julia F.   6 F NC S
  William G.   3 M NC

  41 A improved land, 26 A unimpr, valued at $300

715.731 George R JOHNSON 55 M NC physician 1,500
  Sarah C. JOHNSON   32 F NC

  [MB:George R Johnston & Sarah C McCulloch 5 May
     1840] 8 slaves
  125 A improved land, 47 A unimpr, valued at $1500

716.732 Robert L. SMITH   35 M NC farmer
  Mary SMITH   38 F NC
  Margaret E. GRAHAM   14 F NC S
  Mary V. SMITH   5/12 F NC
  Margaret COWAN   67 F NC
  David F. COWAN   43 M NC labourer 700

  [MB:Robert L Smith & Mary Graham 1 May 1848]
  100 A improved land, 59 A unimpr, valued at $500
  4 slaves

717.733 George KRIDER   26 M NC overseer
  Loretta KRIDER   22 F NC
  John H.   5 M NC
[158] Ann E.   3 F NC
  Infant   0/12 M NC

  [MB:George H Crider & Loretta Verble 28 Mar 1844]

p. 158, School District #16, 29 Aug. 1850

718.734 James C McCONNAUGHEY 53 M NC farmer 5,000
  Caroline McCONNAUGHEY   41 F NC
  Margaret M.   20 F NC
  William A.   19 M NC S
  James A.   17 M NC S
  Joseph L.   16 M NC S
  George C.   12 M NC S

Mary C.   10 F NC S
Anna H.   2 F NC
Anna H. VANSICKLE   35 F NC

[MB:James C McConnaughey/Caroline Hall 23 Nov
1827] 32 slaves
  600 A improved land, 300 A unimpr, valued at $5000

719.735 Asa RODGERS   27 M NC farmer 600
  Jane A. RODGERS   26 F NC
  Margaret E.   5 F NC S
  Jane W.   3 F NC
  Mary J.   1 F NC

  31 A improved land, 67 A unimpr, valued at $600

720.736 Elizabeth BRANDON   50 F NC
  Rufus A.   24 M NC

  125 A improved land, 63 A unimpr, valued at $700
  3 slaves

721.737 Peter SLOOP 36 M NC farmer 500
  Nancy SLOOP   29 F NC
  Polly LITTLE   10 F NC S

[MB: Peter Sloop to Nancy Baker 2 Oct. 1841]
  55 A improved land, 38 A unimpr, valued at $500
  1 slave

722.738 John J LOUDER   28 M NC blacksmith 300
  Sarah L. LOUDER   19 F NC (X)
  Lunda M.   5/12 F NC

  31 A improved land, 47 A unimpr, valued at $300

723.739 John P. SMITH   36 M NC farmer 400
  William L SMITH   30 M NC farmer 400
  Sarah B. IRVIN   45 F NC
  Jane E. YOUNG   14 F NC S
  Sarah YOUNG   10 F NC S

  John P: 100 A improved land, 61 A unimpr, valued
    at $900, 3 slaves
  William L: 2 slaves
  Sarah B Irvin: 2 slaves

724.740 Henry J BARRINGER 36 M NC farmer 600
  Elisabeth BARRINGER   36 F NC M (X)
  Mary J.   11 F NC S
  William H.   9 M NC S
  Edmund F.   7 M NC
  John L.   4 M NC
  Rufus Monroe   1 M NC

  81 A improved land, 68 A unimpr, valued at $600
  1 slave

725.741 Catharine LOUDER 66 F NC (X) 100
  Milly   30 F NC (X)
  Catherine   21 F NC
  Daniel   18 M NC

726.742 Amos ELLER   51 M NC (X) farmer
  Elisabeth ELLER   50 F NC
  Leporios   21 M NC (X) labourer
  Greenberry   18 M NC
  Obediah   10 M NC
  Louisa   23 F NC (X)
  .743. Edward ELLER 27 M NC (X) farmer
  Eliza ELLER   23 F NC (X)
  Mary A.   12 F NC S
  Maria E.   3 F NC
  John R.   8/12 M NC

[MB: Amos Eller to Betsey Eller 17 July 1821
  Edward Eller to Eliza Eller 19 July 1845]
Amos: no land but livestock

727.744 George WILHELM   58 M NC blacksmith 600
  Susanna WILHELM   52 F NC
  William STILLER   14 M NC

[MB:George Wilhelm to Susanna Stiller 29 Jan 1819]
  120 A improved land, 81 A unimpr, valued at $600
  1 slave

728.745 Polly WILHELM   37 F NC
  Eliza   2 F NC
  Jacob STILLER   54 M NC labourer
  Margaret STILLER   18 F NC

729.746 James B GIBSON   38 M NC farmer 3,000
  Priscilla GIBSON   64 F NC
  Martha LOCKE   17 F NC
  Mary A. LOCKE   14 F NC
  Richard LOCKE   12 M NC S

  200 A improved land, 369 A unimpr, valued at $3000
  James B: 9 slaves
  Priscilla: 8 slaves

730.747 James Mc WILSON 28 M NC farmer 400
  Margaret WILSON   24 F NC

[MB:James M Wilson & Margaret T Smith 20 May 1846]
  45 A improved land, 39 A unimpr, valued at $400
  2 slaves

731.748 Sarah H. HOUSTON 44 F TN
  Mary A. MILLER   18 F NC
  Sarah J. MILLER   15 F NC
  Houston A. MILLER   8 M NC

732.749 James GRAHAM   56 M NC 1,000
  Elisabeth GRAHAM   62 F NC
  James   10 M NC S

  170 A improved land, 81 A unimpr, valued at $1000
  6 slaves

733.750 Fergus GRAHAM   59 M NC farmer 1,000
  Fergus M.   20 M NC S
  Joseph A.   14 M NC S
  John C.O.   8 M NC S
  Richard F.   7 M NC S   cont.

[MB:Fergus Graham to Sally Baker 22 Apr 1828]
60 A improved land, 100 A unimpr, valued at $1000
9 slaves

734.751 John CASPER 55 M NC 1,000
   Nancy CASPER   64 F NC

70 A improved land, 145 A unimpr, valued at $1000

735.752. Jacob SLOOP   51 M NC farmer
   Leah SLOOP   39 F NC (X)
   Mumford S. McK.   17 M NC S
   Clarisa S.   15 F NC S
[159] Maria E.   11 F NC
   Ellen S.   9 F NC
   Mary C.   8 F NC
   Frances R.   4 F NC
   Adleine R.   1 F NC

[MB:Jacob Sloop to Leah Peahel 13 Mar 1839]
1 slave

p. 159, School District #16, 29 Aug 1850

736.753. Alexander LORANCE 71 M NC farmer 250
   Jane LORRANCE   74 F NC
   Jane E.   38 F NC
   Lydia A.   35 F NC
   Samuel MILLER   19 M NC

60 A improved land, 60 A unimpr, valued at $250

737.754 John ALLBRIGHT 55 M NC wheelright 300
   Mary ALLBRIGHT   38 F NC
   Elizabeth   24 F NC
   Catherine   22 F NC
   Peter   20 M NC S farmer
   William R.   9 M NC S

65 A unimproved land, 28 A unimpr, valued at $300

738.755 John COOPER 45 M NC chairmaker
   Mary COOPER   47 F NC

739.756 Conrod LINGLE   56 M NC farmer 800
   Elisabeth LINGLE   57 F NC
   Anna L.   29 F NC
   Margaret A.   27 F NC
   Catherine C.   25 F NC
   Salome   23 F NC
   Sarah   21 F NC
   Wilson A.   19 M NC S labourer
   Mary E.   15 F NC S

90 A improved land, 111 A unimpr, valued at $800

740.757 Thomas B. SLOAN 24 M NC 800

152 A improved land, 151 A unimpr, valued at $1500
5 slaves

741.758 John L. SLOAN 25 M NC blacksmith cont.

Mary C. SLOAN   24 F NC
Laura M.   3/12 F NC

[MB: John L Sloan & Mary C Cowan 20 Dec 1848]
2 slaves

742.759 John LINGLE 34 M NC farmer 700
   Margaret LINGLE   28 F NC
   Isabella N.   5 F NC S
   Samuel J.   3 M NC
   Elizabeth M FITE   13 F NC S

[MB:John Lingle & Margarett Peeler 13 Mar 1841]
100 A improved land, 50 A unimpr, valued at $700

743.760 Brittina SLOAN 45 F VA
   Samuel A.   13 M NC S
   Joseph   14 M NC S
   Sarah J.   9 F NC S

[MB:James Sloan to Britania Smoot 29 Jan 1821]

175 A improved land, 116 A unimpr, valued at $1000
10 slaves

744.761 John M McCONNAUGHEY 50 M NC farmer 2,500
   Robert SLOAN   21 M NC overseer

200 A improved land, 217 unimpr, valued at $2500
11 slaves

745.762 Henderson F. SMITH 25 M NC overseer

746.763 Samuel KERR 50 M NC physician 20,000
   Francis M. LUCKEY   26 M NC physician
   Stanhope J. BROWN   21 M NC overseer

   Samuel Kerr: 70 A improved land, 800 A unimpr,
      valued at $3,000, 52 slaves
   flouring: 360 bbls valued at $1,400
   corn mill: 3,000 bu valued at $1,200
   saw mill: 60,000 ft of lumber valued at $600

747.764 James OWIN 56 M NC farmer 2,800

   250 A improved land, 240 unimpr, valued at $1800
   8 slaves

748.765 Frederick MENUS 55 M NC farmer 900
   Elisabeth MENIUS   48 F NC (X)
   James M. MENUS   26 M NC farmer
   Mary E. MENUS   24 F NC
   Amanda A.E.   0/12 F NC

[MB:Frederick Menius/Betsey Steller 10 Sept 1821]
70 A improved land, 42 A unimpr, valued at $600
2 slaves

749.766 Mary E. DANCY 36 F NC (X) 1,000
   Naphthali L.   12 M NC
   Margaret A.   10 F NC
   Alpheus L.   7 M NC   cont.

Mary DANCY   27 F NC
Anderson BROADWAY   27 M NC farmer

125 A improved land, 175 unimpr, valued at $1000

750.767 James J. WAGONER   24 M NC farmer
    Amanda M. WAGONER   17 F NC

751.768 Catharine WAGONER   47 F NC (X) 350
    Nancy E.M.   )twins   27 F NC
    Susana E.   )   27 F NC
    Carmi Joshua)twins   16 M NC labourer
    Mathew David)   16 M NC labourer

100 A improved land, 59 A unimpr, valued at $350

752.769 Alexander BROWN   42 M NC farmer 3,000
    Mary BROWN   42 F NC
    George H.   12 M NC S
    Stephen A.   10 M NC S
    Laura M.   8 F NC S
    Martha E.   6 F NC S
    Pleasant M.   4 M NC
    Robert L.   1/12 M NC
    Mary B. KISLER   75 F NC (X)

[MB:Alexander Brown & Mary Kistler 29 Sept 1835]
150 A improved land, 250 A unimpr, valued at $3000
7 slaves
flouring: 625 bbl valued at $2,600
corn mill: 3,125 bu valued at $1,131

753.770 Catharine KESLER   39 F NC 3,000
    Welington L.   16 M NC S
    Theophilus J.H   9 M NC S
    Virginia M.C.   4 F NC S
    Catherine BARRINGER   70 F PA (X)

[MB:Henry Kistler/Catharine Barringer 26 Mar 1832]
110 A improved land, 215 A unimpr, valued at $3000
4 slaves

754.771 Maria C.D. COWAN   F NC
    Richard H.   21 M NC
    Abel A.   16 M NC S
    Marie C.   14 F NC S
    Leonides   12 M NC S
[160] Charlote   10 F NC S
    Robert HARIS   23 M NC merchant
    Mary E. HARRIS   19 F NC

320 A improved land, 300 A unimpr, valued at $5000
27 slaves
corn mill: 3,800 bu cornmeal valued at $1,520

<u>p. 160, School District #10, 30 Aug. 1850</u>

755.772 John A. BRUMLY   33 M NC shoemaker
    Margaret M. BRUMLY   33 F NC
    Ozni R.   10 M NC S
    William C.   12 M NC S
    Martha C.   8 F NC S
    James C.   6 M NC S   cont.

Thomas W.   3 M NC

30 A improved land valued at $180

756.773 John GARDNER   58 M NC wagon maker
    Elisabeth GARDNER   30 F NC
    Ann   26 F NC
    Mary   23 F NC
    James   21 M NC
    Sarah   19 F NC

70 A improved land, 90 A unimpr, valued at $800

757.774 John C GILLESPIE 29 M NC 1,200
    Harriet GILLESPIE   28 F NC
    Richard T.   5 M NC S
    Samuel M.   7/12 M NC

[MB:John C Gillespie to Jane S. Graham 11 Oct.
1843. John C Gillespie to Harriet Marlin 17 Jan
1849]   4 slaves
114 A improved land, 100 A unimpr, valued at $1300

758.775 Catharine F THOMPSON 28 F NC 200
    Mary B. ROBISON   27 F NC 200
    Jane M. ROBISON   18 F NC

759.776 Ann GILLESPIE   39 F NC (X) 3,500
    Jane A.   16 F NC
    Elisabeth   12 F NC
    Richard L.M.   14 M NC

150 A improved land, 335 A unimpr, valued at $3500
8 slaves

760.777 William GRAHAM   26 M NC (X) farmer
    Elisabeth GRAHAM   27 F NC
    Joseph G.   5 M NC
    George W.   2 M NC
    John L.   4/12 M NC
    Sarah B. REX   20 F NC

[MB:William Graham to Elizabeth Rex 10 Apr 1844]

761.778 James ALEXANDER   47 M NC farmer 700
    Elisabeth ALEXANDER   51 F NC
    Sarah BOWERS   12 F NC S

90 A improved land, 59 A unimpr, valued at $700
6 slaves

762.779 William A. BRUMLEY   31 M NC
    Ann H. BRUMLEY   33 F NC
    Mary E.   5 F NC
    John   3 M NC
    Thomas   1 M NC

763.780 Peter BRUMLEY   65 M NC farmer
    Susan BRUMLY   48 F NC (X)

[MB:Peter Brumley to Susan Becket 19 Nov 1849]
1 slave

764.781 John HICKS   31 M NC farmer
    Catherine HICKS   34 F NC
    William J.   10 M NC S
    Thomas A.   8 M NC S
    Mary C.   6 F NC S
    Martha J.   4 F NC
    John   1 M NC

    30 A improved land valued at $150

765.782 Abram BELT   37 M NC (X) ditcher
    Nancy BELT   36 F NC (X)
    Martha A.   13 F NC
    Emeline R.   8 F NC
    Nancy T.   6 F NC
    John W.   5 M NC
    Laura M.   11/12 F NC

766.783 John F. FOARD   23 M NC physician 2,500
    Laura C. FOARD   22 F NC
    George P. McCONNAUGHEY 14 M NC S
    James C. McCONNAUGHEY   9 M NC S
    Hugh G. McCONNAUGHEY   23 M NC overseer

    [CW: Dr John F Foard to Laura C M McConnaughey
        25 Mar 1847]
     250 A improved land, 200 A unimpr, valued at
        $2500, 15 slaves

767.784 Elkanah D. AUSTIN   65 M VA farmer 1,000
    Margaret AUSTIN   62 F NC
    Caroline E. GILLESPIE   22 F NC
    Lucas M. GILLESPIE   1 M NC
    William A. POSTON   24 M NC OVERSEER 500

    [MB: E.D. Austin to Margaret Hall 22 Jan 1834
    Thomas C Gillespie to Caroline E. Austin 2 Aug
    1847; he d 21 Dec 1848 CW]
     Elkanah: 17 slaves; Caroline E: 7 slaves
     175 A improved land, 100 A unimpr, valued at $1000

768.785 Thomas TODD   55 M NC farmer 2,200
    8 slaves

769.786 Cathey RICE   38 M NC farmer
    Nancy RICE   33 F NC
    Phillip B.   6 M NC
    Thomas D.   4 M NC
    John H.)twins   1 M NC
    William)   1 M NC

    [MB:Cathew Rice to Nancy Hellard 11 Aug 1841]
    100 A improved land, 151 A unimpr, valued at $1000
    3 slaves

770.787 Jackson CRAWLEY 28 M NC shoemaker
    Minerva A. CRAWLEY   26 F NC (X)
    Mary E.   4 F NC
    Frances M.   2 F NC
    Charlotte FRAZIER   30 F NC

771.788 Zepheniah TURNER   37 M NC gunsmith
    Mary TURNER   37 F NC (X)
    Sarah J.   11 F NC S
    Doctor M.   10 M NC S
    Isaac   7 M NC s
[161] Mary E.   6 F NC
    Wilson   3 M NC
    John   1 F NC

    [MB:Zephaniah Turner & Mary S Cowan 5 Sept 1837]
    3 slaves

<u>p.161, School District #18, 4 Sept. 1850</u>

772.789 Noe LEWIS   38 M NC farmer
    Elizabeth M. LEWIS 33 F NC
    2 slaves

773.790 Isabella MARLIN 57 F NC
    Jane E.   20 F NC
    Margaret A. MARLIN 15 F NC
 .791. Priscilla ENES   53 F NC (X) 250
    Eliza   25 F NC
    William   16 M NC

    [MB:Samuel Marlin & Isabella Lowry 18 Apr 1820.
    Samuel Marlin d 18 Aug 1848 CW]
    Isabella: 120 A improved land, 175 A unimpr,
    valued at $1,000, 5 slaves
    Priscilla Enes: 45 A improved land, 25 A unimpr,
        valued at $250

775.792 Jacob A LINK   54 M VA shoemaker
    Mary M. LINK   52 F NC
    Elisabeth C.   29 F NC
    George F.   25 M NC
    Mary A.   23 F NC
    Rebecka J.   20 F NC S
    Jacob H.   18 F NC S labourer
    James M.   15 M NC S labourer
    Margaret L.   13 F NC S
    Martha E.   11 F NC S
    Nancy C.   7 F NC

    100 A improved land, 48 A unimpr, valued at $600

776.793 Joseph MINGUS 43 M NC farmer 3,000
    Sarah MINGUS   50 M NC
    Elisabeth FREELAND 16 F NC

    [MB: Joseph H Mingis to Sarah Cowan 1 Jan 1842]
    125 A improved land, 239 A unimpr, valued at $2200
    5 slaves

777.794 Jane LEWIS 50 F NC (X)
    Peter   25 M NC (X) labourer

778.795 George THOMASSON 42 M NC farmer 500
    Jane T. THOMASSON   37 F TN
    William T.   16 M NC
    James W.   14 M NC   cont.

Margaret R.	12 F NC
Jesse P.	10 M NC
Elisabeth C.	8 F NC

50 A improved land, 61 A unimpr, valued at $500

779.796 Jesse THOMASSON   29 M NC farmer
Harriet L. THOMASSON   26 F NC
Harriet C.   5 F NC

70 A improved land valued at $200
4 slaves

780.797 Wilford DENT 35 M NC (X) farmer 60
Rachel DENT   30 F NC
Esly A.   13 F NC
Sarah E.   11 F NC
James O.   5 M NC
Margaret R.   3 F NC

[MB: Wilford Dent to Rachael Smith 11 May 1837]

781.798 John McATTEE 50 M NC farmer 25
Margaret D. McATTEE 50 F NC
Sarah DENT   27 F NC (X)
Mary DENT   84 F VA (X)

[MB: John Macate to Margaret Dent 8 Sept 1825]
30 A improved land valued at $100

782.799 John M. FOSTER 38 M NC
Mary Jane   11 F NC
Martha A.   7 F NC
Margaret C.   6 F NC
Nancy MILLER   68 F NC (X)
Nancy THOMASSON   62 F NC 300
Thomas T. WATSON 5 M NC

783.800 Elisabeth FRALEY 62 F NC (X) 2,300
Thomas D.   28 M NC farmer
Eliza JACOBS   26 F NC (X)
Ranson JEANS   11 M NC Mu

111 A improved land, 200 A unimproved
1 slave

784.801 Humphry LINSTER 65 M NC farmer 600
Goodwin LINSTER   63 F NC
Elvira LINSTER   27 F NC
Frederick T.   19 M NC labourer

[MB: Humphrey Linnster & Goodin Ford 6 Apr 1816]
60 A improved land, 60 A unimpr, valued at $600
9 slaves

785.805 John B. FRALEY 30 M NC farmer 50
Margaret FRALEY   16 F NC
Pinkney WATSON   11 M NC S

[MB: John B Fraley & Margaret Monroe 28 Apr 1849]
60 A improved land, 152 A unimproved
2 slaves

786.803 Thomas R WALTON 39 M NC brickmason 700
Harriet WALTON   21 F NC
Jesse ENNIS   25 M NC labourer

[MB:Thomas R Walton to Harriet Hellard 10 Nov
     1847] 1 slave
160 A improved land, 132 A unimpr, valued at $700

787.804 Elisabeth ROBY 80 F MD (X)
Letitia OWEN   25 F NC

788.805 Joseph OWENS 46 M NC farmer 1,500
Mary G. OWENS   43 F NC
Jane E.   16 F NC
Joseph F.   14 M NC
Wiliam R.   10 M NC
Henry C.   8 M NC
James A.   2 M NC
Mary A. R.   0/12 F NC
Thomas B. OWENS   19 M NC labourer

[MB:Joseph Owens & Mary G Lowrance 10 Sept 1846;
    Thomas B d. 12 July 1850, CW] 3 slaves
300 A improved land, 300 A unimpr, valued at $3000

789.806 James HEILIG   38 M NC farmer
Rachel HEILIG   35 F NC
Phillip A.   7 M NC
Elias   4 M NC
James   2 M NC

25 A improved land, 30 A unimpr, valued at $110

<u>p. 162, School District #18, 5 Sept. 1850</u>

790.807 John R THORN   39 M NC farmer 700
Jane Clementine)twins 9 F NC S
Mary Emeline   )   9 F NC S
Jane T. THORN   30 F NC (X)

[MB: John R Thorn to Jane Trott 4 April 1839]
120 A improved land, 100 A unimpr, valued at 100

791.808 James THOMASON   39 M NC farmer 900
Margaret THOMASON 42 F NC
William   18 M NC S labourer
John P.   16 M NC S
Franklin W.   14 M NC S
Martha J.   12 F NC S
Mary Jane   10 F NC
Rufus M.   6 M NC

[MB:James Thomasson & Margaret Marlin 8 June 1830]
70 A improved land, 50 A unimpr, valued at $650
4 slaves

792.809 John LEWIS   30 M NC farmer
Mary A. LEWIS   25 F NC

150 A improved land, 150 A unimpr, valued at $100

793.810 Henery J LEWIS   -- M NC labourer
   Margaret Lewis   34 F NC

794.811 George O TARR   35 M NC farmer 1,500
   Maria M. TARR   34 F TN
   Francis M.   9 M NC S
   Elisabeth V.   7 F NC
   Nancy Susanna   5 F NC

[MB: G O Tarrh to Maria M Canady 20 June 1838]
85 A improved land, 190 unimpr, valued at $1500
1 slave

795.812 Jacob CORRELL   52 M NC farmer 7,000
   Alfred   26 M NC idiot
   Clarissa   24 F NC
   Jane C.   22 F NC
   Francis A.   20 F NC
   William W.   18 M NC S
   David H.   7 M NC S

[MB: Jacob Correll to Betsey Freeze 22 Feb 1819.
She d 16 Mar 1850 aged 51, CW]   18 slaves
275 A improved land, 728 unimpr, valued at $4500
flouring: 623 bbl flour valued at $3,115
corn mill: 3,125 bu valued at $1,260
saw mill: 150,000 ft of lumber valued at $1,125

796.813 James B. NOLLY   35 M VA farmer
   Elisabeth   12 F NC
   Margaret   10 F NC
   William   6 M NC
   James W.   10/12 M NC

30 A improved land valued at $150

797.814 Henery H. SAUCERMAN   50 M NC miller
   Christina   21 F NC
   Joseph A.   14 M NC S
   Sarah C.   11 F NC S

[MB:Henry H Sossaman & Sally Fisher 22 Apr 1822]

798.815 John C MILLER 39 M NC farmer
   Sophia   38 F NC
   Martin M.   16 M NC S
   Alfred A.   13 M NC S
   Henery G.   12 M NC S
   Susanah R.   10 F NC S
   William W.   9 M NC S
   Philosopher Columb   4 M NC
   Francis V.   2 M NC

[WC: John C Miller to Miss Sophia Propst 25 Apr
1833 in Cabarrus Co]   11 slaves

799.816 Jessee LITAKER 26 M NC blacksmith
   Julia A. LITAKER   26 F NC (X)
   Mary E.   4 F NC
   Nancy C.   2 F NC

[MB:Jesse W Litaker & Juliana Hall 22 May 1845]

799.817 John MARLIN   40 M NC farmer 1,800
   Sophia MARLIN   32 F NC
   Julia V.   4 F NC
   Sarah J.   1 F NC

[MB: John Marlin & Sophia Graham 12 Jan 1845]
150 A improved land, 430 A unimpr, valued at $200
10 slaves

800.818 John PINKSTON 30 M NC (X) farmer 1,800
   Elisabeth PINKSTON 24 F NC
   Mary Jane   1 F NC
   Mary SMITH   27 F NC

[CW:John Pinkston & Elizabeth Hellard 15 Sept
1847] 1 slave

801.819 John LUCAS   22 M NC labourer
   Sarah LUCAS   22 F NC
   Mary   2 F NC
   William F.   5/12 M NC

802.820 Jacob CORL   69 M NC 500
   Elisabeth CLINE   36 F NC
   Susanna   1/12 F NC

60 A improved land, 26 A unimpr, valued at $500

804.821 Hezekiah HEATHMAN 78 M MD farmer 1,000
   David HEATHMAN   38 M NC overseer

[Mary Ann, wife of Hezekiah Heathman, d 10 May
    1847; Hezekiah d 7 Aug 1852, CW] 9 slaves
110 A improved land, 253 A unimpr, value:$1000

805.822 Edmund RICE 46 M NC farmer 800
   Nancy E.   14 F NC S
   Alen G.   12 M NC S
   Lydia P.   10 F NC S
   Joseph A.   9 M NC S
   William G.   5 M NC
   Margaret SMITH   32 F NC (X)
   Nancy E.   9 F NC S

[MB: Edmund Rice & Jane Culbertson 3 June 1834]
1 slave

806.823 Tobias FILE   31 M NC millwright 2,500
   Sarah FILE   30 F NC
   Mary J.   4 F NC
   Augustus A.   2 M NC
   Sarah E. SMITH   13 F NC S

[MB: Tobias File to Sarah Eddleman 27 Nov 1843]
150 A improved land, 390 A unimpr, valued at $2500
saw mill: 150,000 ft of lumber valued at $1,125

p.163, School District #46, 6 Sept. 1850

807.824 Absalem THOMAS 35 M NC (X) labourer
   Sarah THOMAS   34 F NC (X)   cont.

Fanny E.	7 F NC	
William F.	5 M NC	
Mary C.	3 F NC	
Benjamin WRIGHT	26 M NC (X) farmer	

[MB:Absolom Thomas & Charity Parks 27 Jan 1837]

808.825 John B. BENSON 21 M NC (X) labourer
   Elisabeth BENSON   20 F NC (X)

[MB:John B Benson & Elizabeth A C Wright 17 Apr
   1850]

809.826 Spencer BENSON 50 M NC (X) farmer 450
   Nancy BENSON   42 F NC
   Issabella A.   17 F NC
   Samuel S.   12 M NC
   Lucy C.   10 F NC
   Nancy C.   7 F NC
   Robert L.   4 M NC
   Elizabeth Jane   10/12 F NC

[MB: Spencer Benson & Nancy Rice 26 Mar 1828]
50 A improved land, 50 A unimpr, valued at $450

810.827 Mary MARLIN 35 F NC 1,000
   John P.   16 M NC farmer
   Ealy A.   12 F NC S
   Elvira J.   10 F NC S

55 A improved land, 30 A unimpr, valued at $375
1 slave

811.828 Joseph TURNER 47 M NC farmer
   Ann TURNER   45 M NC
   David C.   15 M NC S labourer

[MB: Joseph Turner to Ann Gray 10 Feb 1828]

812.829 John BOND   30 M NC farmer
   Anna BOND   30 F NC
   Susanna L.   8 F NC S
   John F.   5 M NC
   Melissa L.   3 F NC

75 A improved land, 75 A unimpr, valued at $425

813.830 Joseph McKNIGHT 36 M NC farmer
   Mary K. McKNIGHT   31 F NC
   Martha J.   3 F NC
   Mary E.C.   1 F NC

[MB: Joseph McKnight & Mary Barber 26 Dec. 1841]
65 A improved land, 70 A unimpr, valued at $300
4 slaves

814.831 William T MARLIN 26 M NC farmer 700
   Margaret MARLIN   24 F NC
   Laura I.   1 F NC

[MB: William T Marlin to Margaret L Howard 30 Dec
   1847] 2 slaves
25 A improved land, 107 unimpr, valued at $600

815.832 Ellen COWAN 37 F NC Mu
   Mary C.   26 F NC Mu (X)
   Alexander H.   22 M NC Mu labourer

816.833 William REX   35 M NC
   Elisabeth FRAZIER   22 F NC (X)
   William R. REX   5 M NC
   Nancy REX   21 F NC
   William R. REX   1 M NC

817.834 Ann THOMSON   43 F NC 112
   Jane C.   14 F NC S
   Thomas F.   11 M NC S

818.835 Hannah DICKSON 63 F NC (X) 100
   Hannah M. BEEFLE   14 F NC S
   Mary J. DICKSON   9 F NC S

819.836 Sarah A. LUCKEY 35 F NC
   Martha E. DICKSON   6 F NC S

820.837 John CARSON 38 M NC farmer 2,500
   Mary CARSON   34 F NC
   William L.   10 M NC
   Simeon I.   4 M NC
   Mary E.   1 F NC

[MB: John Carson & Mary Thompson 29 May 1838]
175 A improved land, 225 A unimpr, valued at
   $2500, 11 slaves

821.838 Ann GILLEAN   44 F NC 300
   Mary E.   24 F NC
   Sarah L.   20 F NC
   John N.   17 M NC
   Abigail   15 F NC

[MB: Jesse Gillean & Ann Thompson 21 July 1824]
60 A improved land, 75 A unimpr, valued at $300

822.839 Eli POWLESS   26 M NC M farmer 400
   Margaret A POWLESS 22 F NC M

[MB: Eli Powlas & Margaret A Gillian 13 May 1850]
100 A improved land, 300 A unimpr, valued at $400

823.840 Moses W THOMPSON   32 M NC farmer
   Joseph H. THOMPSON   32 M NC labourer

50 A improved land, 50 A unimpr, valued at $2125

824.841 Margaret S THOMPSON 37 F NC 600
   James L.   19 M NC S farmer
   William A.   17 M NC S labourer

50 A improved land, 144 A unimpr, valued at $350

825.842 Thomas BARBER   48 M NC farmer
   Melinda BARBER   46 F NC
   Margaret C.   24 F NC
   Willaim   23 M NC
   Samuel S.   21 M NC   cont.

```
Catherine E.           19 F NC
Jane M.                14 F NC
Thomas S.              10 M NC S
Mary E.                 7 F NC S
```

100 A improved land, 109 A unimpr, valued at $1200
3 slaves

```
826.843 Margaret POWLASS 48 F NC (X) 300
   Mary C.              24 F NC
   Rachael              15 F NC
[164] John H.           9 M NC
```

p. 164, School District #46, 6 Sept. 1850

```
827.844 Isaac COWAN  52 M NC farmer 1,000
   Jane COWAN           52 F NC
   Charlotte THOMSON    18 F NC
   James                11 M NC
   Joseph T.             2 M NC
```

225 A improved land, 75 A unimpr, valued at $1000
2 slaves

```
828.845 Jessee BEEFLE  38 M NC farmer 211
   John BEEFLE          40 M NC 212
```

60 A improved land, 118 A unimpr, valued at $423
1 slave

```
829.846 Joseph GRAHAM  45 M NC (X) labourer
   Elisabeth GRAHAM     30 F NC (X)
   Richard S.           17 M NC S
   John S.               2 M NC
```

```
830.847 Thomas CLAMPET   30 M NC miller
   Elisabeth CLAMPET    29 D NC (X)
   Benjamin F.           1 M NC
   Amanda CLAMPET       18 F NC
```

[MB:Thomas Clampet/Elizabeth Pinkston 30 Apr 1840]

```
831.848 Thomas L THOMSON   38 M NC farmer
   Elisabeth THOMSON    37 F NC
   Isaac C.             18 M NC S labourer
   Joseph T.            16 M NC S labourer
   Thomas L.            14 M NC S
   John P.               8 M NC S
   Jane E.              10 F NC S
   Julius W.             6 M NC
   Harriet M.            3 F NC
```

[MB:Thomas Thompson/Elizabeth H Cowan 28 July
   1830]
65 A improved land, 36 A unimpr, valued at $300

```
832.849  Nancy ELLIOTT  50 F NC (X)
   Willis H. TROTT      30 M NC (X) 500
   Jackson TROTT        28 M NC (X) 600
   Clementine TROTT     19 F NC
   Sarah TROTT          17 F NC
```

100 A improved land, 150 A unimpr, valued at $500

```
833.850  Margaret LYERLA 50 F NC 500
   Jonathan             31 M NC
   Mary C. DICKSON       8 F NC S
```

40 A improved land, 120 A unimpr, valued at $500
1 slave

```
834.851 John W. LINK   31 M NC farmer
   Amy A. LINK          22 F NC (X)
   Sarah A.              4 F NC
   Maria C.              2 F NC
   Mary E.           5/12 F NC
   Williams BOWERS      12 M NC
```

[MB:John W Link to Amey Emberson 25 Apr 1844]
30 A improved land valued at $100

```
835.852 Julius NEELY   22 M NC 3,500
```
   [Note: son of Alexander and Margaret (Barber)
   Neely]
   300 A improved land, 100 A unimpr, valued at
   $2500, 8 slaves

```
836.853  Daniel J. WEBB    28 M NC farmer
   Catherine J. WEBB    24 F NC
   William A.            8 M NC S
   John P.              5 M NC
   David A.          7/12 M NC
837.854 George M LYERLA 32 M NC blacksmith 600
   Nancy C. LYERLA      30 F NC
   Margaret E.           7 F NC S
   Mary C.               4 F NC S
   Richard A.        5/12 M NC
   Alexander CLINE      13 M NC
   Michael B. DICKSON   21 M NC blacksmith
   Catherine REX        19 F NC
   Alexander UTZMAN     26 M NC tailor
```

[MB:George M Lyerly & A C Graham 11 Jan 1841]
100 A improved land, 224 A unimpr, valued at $1000
2 slaves
blacksmithing: various articles valued at $1,000

```
838.855 Mary A. FRALEY  51 F NC (X) 2,200
   Lucinda C.           31 F NC
   Mumford S.           27 M NC farmer
   Barbara C.           23 F NC
   Jacob L.             21 M NC S farmer
   Jesse R.             19 M NC S labourer
   Ashbell S.           16 M NC S labourer
   Mary C.              12 F NC S
```

[Note: This is the widow & family of John Fraley
   who d 1849]
200 A improved land, 300 A unimpr, valued at
   $2200, 1 slave

```
839.856. Hezekiah C. GILLEAN  25 M NC 350
   Martha J.            23 F NC
```

[MB:Hezekiah C Gillian & Martha J Reppult 12 June
   1850]
50 A improved land, 52 A unimpr, valued at $550

840.857. Zachariah THOMASON   46 M NC farmer 1,000
  Kitty THOMASON   45 F NC
  William T.   22 M NC teacher
  Nancy E.   17 F NC
  Ann E.   11 F NC S
  Jesse VOLENTINE   50 MB NC (X) labourer

[MB: Zachariah Thompson & Kitty Turner 21 Aug
  1826] 1 slave
65 A improved land, 250 A unimpr, valued at $1,000

841.858. Elisabeth LYERLA   31 F NC
  Margaret LYERLA   45 F NC
  Catherine LYERLA   42 F NC
  Harriet J. LYERLA   11 F NC S
  Thomas S. LYERLA   9 M NC S
  Susan S. LYERLA   5 F NC S

80 A improved land, 50 A unimpr, valued at $600
4 slaves

842.859. Mary CANE   35 F NC (X)
  John J.   14 M NC S
  Sarah E.   11 F NC S

843.860. Robert V. COWAN   40 M NC farmer
  Nancy COWAN   40 F NC (X)
  Mary E.   16 F NC S
  George H.   13 M NC S
  John M.   6 M NC S
  Robert L.   2 M NC

[MB: Robert V Cowan & Nancy Capels 18 May 1832]
no land but livestock, 4 slaves

844.861 Ruhanna COWAN   40 F NC 1,100
  Hannah E.   14 F NC S
  Mary Jane   12 F NC S
  Isaac A.   9 M NC S
  Nathan V.   7 M NC S
  Emely R.   5 F NC
  Upshaw D. ELLIOTT   21 M NC farmer
  William W. ELLIOTT   14 M NC S

[MB: William Cowan to Ruannah Cowan 31 Oct 1826
She is the dau of John Cowan, WB H:408, 1827]
70 A improved land, 196 A unimpr, valued at
  $1,100, 2 slaves

845.862 Peter BARGER   52 M NC farmer 1,900
  Margaret BARGER   52 F NC (X)
  Catharine   23 F NC (X)
  Caleb   20 M NC labourer
  John   16 M NC S
  Jacob   14 M NC S
  Sarah J.   11 F NC S

[MB:Peter Barger & Margaret Shuping 1 Oct 1822]
70 A improved land, 125 A unimproved
4 slaves

846.863 John LYERLA   45 M NC farmer 1,500
  Mary G. LYERLA   43 F NC
  Mary E.   8 F NC S
  Jane E.   5 F NC
  William C.   2 F NC
  Julia LYNCH   20 F NC

[MB: John Lyerla to Polly G. Cowan n.d.]
85 A improved land, 139 A unimpr, valued at
  $1,500, 2 slaves

847.864 Elisabeth ROBISON 52 F NC 100
  Sarah W.   28 F NC
  Eliza C.   16 F NC
  James H.   15 M NC labourer

848.865 Margaret WEBB   45 F NC
  Margaret L.   19 F NC
1 slave

849.866 John B TODD   63 M NC farmer 400
  Sarah TODD   50 F NC
  Martha A.   19 F NC S
  Mary E.   16 F NC S
  Maria L.   13 F NC

[MB: John B Todd & Sarah Dent 13 Feb 1823]
75 A improved land, 92 A unimpr, valued at
  $400, 1 slave

850.867 Jonathan BARBER 38 M NC farmer
  Jane C. BARBER   29 F NC
  Henry H.   10 M NC S
  Elisabeth C.   7 F NC S
  Margaret A.   4 F NC
  Jane C.   9/12 F NC
  Jane BARBER   40 F NC

[MB: Jonathan Barber to Jane Barber 2 Jan 1839]
1 slave

851.868 Christopher LYERLA 56 M NC (X) carpenter
                      & farmer 5,500
  Mary LYERLY   47 F NC
  Otho   22 M NC labourer
  John   20 M NC labourer
  America   16 F NC
  Susanna   14 F NC S
  Isaac   12 M NC S
  Louisa   10 F NC S
  Charlotte   8 F NC S
  Alexander   6 M NC
  Mary   3 F NC
  Pinkney M.   1 M NC

[MB:Christopher Lyerly/Polly Trexler 11 Apr 1818]
200 A improved land, 200 A unimpr, valued at $3500
15 slaves

852.869 Andrew GRAY   42 M NC farmer 500
  Mary E. GRAY   36 F NC
  William M.   13 M NC S   cont.

George A.   11 M NC S
Sarah E.   10 F NC idiot
James A.   8 M NC S
Mary C.   6 F NC S
Joseph G.   4 M NC
Margaret A.   1 F NC
Elisabeth H. ROBISON 46 F NC

[WC: Andrew Gray to Miss Mary E Robinson of
    Iredell Co. 26 Nov 1835]
30 A improved land, 30 A unimpr, valued at $500
1 slave
Elizabeth H. Robison: 1 slave

853.870 William GRAY   72 M NC farmer 800
   Sarah GRAY   69 F NC
   Margaret   40 F NC
   Elisabeth   36 F NC
   Isabella   33 F NC
   Hudson VALENTINE   16 M NC B
   James C. FREEMAN   16 M NC B

100 A improved land, 150 A unimpr, valued at $700

854.871 Susanna S CUBERTSON 48 F NC
   Richard   26 M NC farmer 600
   Samuel S.   20 M NC labourer
   Eliza FREEMAN   33 F NC B
   Harriet   6 F NC B
   Franklin   3 M NC B
   Julia   1 F NC B

[MB: Gillaspie Culbertson to Susanna S Gray 20
    Nov 1823. He d 1845, WB K:6]
70 A improved land, 95 A unimpr, valued at $600

855.872 Mary C GALES   37 F NC
   William F.   17 M NC S farmer
   Sarah A.   13 F NC S
   Phillip S.   11 M NC
   Pinkney H.   6 M NC
   Margaret C.   18 F NC deaf & dumb

30 A improved land valued at $190

856.873 John RICE   40 M NC farmer 2,000

John E. Rice: 110 A improved land, 145 A
unimpr, valued at $2000, 3 slaves

857.874 Anna REPULT   62 F NC 400
[166] John   26 M NC farmer
   Lydia   21 F NC
   Caroline   18 F NC
   William C.   2 M NC
   Alexander VALENTINE 8 M NC B

[MB: Joshua Repult to Ann Marland 30 Sept 1811]
125 A improved land, 44 A unimpr, valued at $400
1 slave

858.875 Lewis BIRD 20 M NC farmer, b'smith 400
   Lucetta BIRD   18 F NC (X)   cont.

   Martha C.   3 F NC
   James L.   2 F NC
   Ridley BIRD   16 M NC

859.876 Willis HARRIS 36 M VA (X) farmer
   Elisabeth HARRIS   38 F NC (X)
   William A.   15 M NC S labourer
   Catherine P.   12 F NC S
   Henery W.   9 M NC S
   Charles C.   10/12 M NC

40 A improved land valued at $200

860.877 Catherine WILES 36 F NC (X)
   Henry W.   22 M NC shoemaker

861.878 Sarah RICE 59 F NC
   Martha A.   32 F NC 500
   David HALL   22 M NC farmer

[Note: 1837 will of William Rice, WB I:6]
75 A improved land, 57 A unimpr, valued at
   $300, 1 slave

862.879 Thomas HELLARD 39 M NC farmer 800
   Anna HELLARD   32 F NC
   George R.   15 M NC S labourer
   Mary C.   13 F NC S

100 A improved land, 150 A unimpr, valued at $800
2 slaves

863.880 John CULBERTSON   47 M NC farmer
   Daniel CULBERTSON   36 M NC farmer 700

100 A improved land, 170 A unimpr, valued at $700
John: 2 slaves
Daniel: 6 slaves

864.881 David MARLIN   76 M NC farmer 500
   Leander GAITHER   24 M NC M
   Mary A.M. GAITHER   34 F NC M
   Anderson E. HIGHTOWER 18 M NC S

100 A improved land, 60 A unimpr, valued at $500

865.882 William P LANE 57 M NC labourer
   Lydia P. LANE   54 F NC
   Lydia L.   22 F NC

866.883 James WATSON   40 M NC farmer 400
   Mary WATSON   30 F NC
   James H.   9 M NC S
   John B.   8 M NC S
   William G.   3 M NC

125 A improved land, 95 A unimpr, valued at
   $700, 5 slaves

867.884 James J WRIGHT 30 M NC blacksmith
   Franes A. WRIGHT   21 F NC
   Mary Jane   7/12 F NC
   Amos SMITH   35 M NC B   cont.

[MB:James J Wright/Francerine R Wright 14 Nov 1848]
140 A improved land, 40 A unimpr, valued at $500

868.885 Rufus D JOHNSON 46 M NC farmer
    Robert Z.   15 M NC student
    James G.   11 M NC S
    Henrietta D.   9 F NC S
    Ealy U.   7 F NC S

    [Note: He is the son of Robert Johnson,
        WB I:121, 1841]
    390 A improved land, 200 A unimpr, value:
        $2500, 9 slaves

869.886 Lawson SEMON   22 M NC farmer
    Angeline SEMON   19 F NC

870.887 Annabella JOHNSTON 65 F IRE 2,500
    John D.   28 M NC
    Catherine N.   21 F NC

    John D: 180 A improved land, 60 A unimpr,
        valued at $2,500, 10 slaves
    Robert F: 125 A improved land, 163 unimpr,
        valued at $700, 6 slaves

871.888 Margaret ANDERSON 54 F NC 1,000
    Margaret C.   16 F NC S
    Margaret G. IRVIN   16 F NC
    Mary L. IRVIN   10 F NC
    Ann E. IRVIN   6 F NC

    185 A improved land, 60 A unimpr, valued at
        $1000, 10 slaves

872.889 Giles RAINY   28 M NC (X) overseer
    Lucinda RAINY   25 F NC
    William A.   5 M NC

873.890 David FLEMMING 20 M NC farmer 1,200
    7 slaves

874.891 Mary HELLARD   49 F NC 2,000
    Jane   29 F NC
    Nancy   19 F NC
    George   18 M NC S
    Thomas   17 M NC S
    Jessee   15 M NC S
    Richard   14 M NC S
    John   12 M NC S
    James B.   11 M NC S
    Doctor W.   9 M NC S
    Charles   8 M NC

    230 A improved land, 458 A unimpr, valued at
        $2000

875.892 Henery PENCE 49 M NC blacksmith
    Sarah M. PENCE   26 F NC (X)
    Margaret   14 F NC
    John H.   11 M NC
    Julia E.   7 F NC   cont.

    Amanda L.   2 F NC
    James SEAMON   20 M NC

    smithing:various articles valued at $1000

876.893 Giles TAYLOR   20 M NC M (X)
    Lucinda TAYLOR   22 F NC M (X)
    Nancy SEAMON   1 F NC

877.894 Henery H. RUDICAL   36 M NC
[167] Jane L. RUDICIL   31 F NC
    Laura E.   6 F NC S
    William G.   2 M NC
    John F.   3/12 M NC
    William TURNER   19 M NC labourer
    Susana SEAMON   15 F NC S

    75 A improved land, 90 A unimpr, valued at $800

<u>p.167, School District #7, 11 Sept. 1850</u>

878.895 Hiram DONAHOO   39 M NC farmer
    Margaret DONAHOO   37 F NC
    Henery F.   17 M NC
    Elisabeth   15 F NC
    Maria   14 F NC
    William   12 M NC
    David   11 M NC
    Mary Jane   8 F NC
    Margaret   6 F NC
    Newberry   4 M NC
    Milas   2 M NC
    Nathan   6/12 M NC

    [MB: Hiram Donoho to Margaret Beek 13 Mar 1832]
    25 A unimproved land valued at $120

879.896 John TURNER   50 M NC farmer 400
    Mary TURNER   36 F NC
    Jane E.   20 F NC
    John K.   15 M NC
    James H.   12 M NC
    Mary C.   )twins   9 F NC S
    Martha M.)twins   9 F NC S
    Sarah N.   6 F NC S

    [MB: John Turner to Mary Luckey 7 Nov 1826]
    40 A improved land, 50 A unimpr, valued at $400

880.897 Samuel FELCOR   57 M NC farmer 100
    Elisabeth FELCOR   59 F PA (X)
    Anna   21 F NC (X)
    Elisabeth   18 F NC S

    100 A improved land, 25 A unimpr, valued at
    $100

881.898 Franklin STEEL 50 M NC farmer
    Catherine STEEL   25 F NC (X)
    Mary A.E.   3 F NC
    Samuel F.   1 M NC

882.899 Henery LINCH 44 M NC (X) labourer
 Mary LINCH 26 F NC (X)
 John A. 25 M NC labourer
 Mary E. 11 F NC
 Nancy J. 6 F NC
 Sarah H. 2/12 F NC

883.900 Margaret HALL 59 F NC 1,000
 Margaret M. 26 F NC
 Mary M. 24 F NC
 William W. 21 M NC S farmer
 Isabella P. 17 F NC S
 5 slaves

884.901 John HENLY 63 M NC farmer
 Nancy HENLY 53 F NC (X)
 Lamira 22 F NC
 Richard V. 17 M NC S labourer
 Rebeca 14 F NC S
 Sanford 12 M NC S
 Rose HENLY 67 F NC (X)
 Nancy HENLY 65 F NC (X)

 150 A improved land, 150 A unimpr, valued
  at $700, 3 slaves

885.902 Reason CLAMPET 36 M NC labourer
 Nancy CLAMPET 34 F NC (X)
 Mary 17 F NC
 Ailsy 9 F NC
 Hiram N. 5 M NC
 Sarah E. 1/12 F NC

886.903 Maxwell HALL 47 M NC farmer 100
 Elisabeth HALL 49 F NC
 Isaac L. 14 M NC S
 Sarah TESTER 36 F NC (X)
 William DOBBIN 72 M NC

 20 A improved land, 30 A unimpr, valued at $100

887.904 William EMERSON 34 M NC millwright 500
 Elisabeth EMERSON 28 F NC
 John W. 6 M NC S
 Sarah J. 4 F NC
 William 3 M NC
 Martha A. 11/12 F NC
 Jack EMBERSON 17 M NC blacksmith
 George FELCOR 22 M NC blacksmith

 150 A improved land, 158 unimpr, valued at $500
 3 slaves
 William E: smithing, made various articles valued
  at $1,250

888.905 Thomas RENSHAW 72 M NC farmer 500
 Martha RENSHAW 70 F PA
 Margaret C. 32 F NC
 Thomas N. 25 M NC
 William M. C. EMBERSON 13 M NC S

 60 A improved land, 240 A unimpr, valued at $500

889.906 Susanah EVANS 24 F NC 700
 Martha C. 21 F NC
 Margaret A. 16 F NC S
 Samuel W. 14 M NC S
 Henery A. 11 M NC S
 Henry H. 6 M NC S

 120 A improved land, 191 A unimpr, valued at $700

p. 168, School District #7, 12 Sept. 1850

890.907 Ester C. MOCK 33 F NC
 Thomas M. 9 M NC S
 John A. 6 M NC S

891.908 Peter SAFRET 49 M NC farmer 200
 Catherine SAFRET 44 F NC (X)
 Clara Ann 24 F NC (X)
 Paul 20 M NC (X) labourer
 Ester C. 18 F NC
 William C. 13 M NC
 Charles 11 M NC
 Peter A. 8 M NC
 James A. 4 M NC

[MB:Peter Safret & Catharine Bostian 27 July 1821]
60 A improved land, 68 A unimpr, valued at $200

892.909 John CARTNER 31 M NC farmer
 Elisabeth CARTNER 27 M NC (X)
 Sarah S. 7 F NC S
 Charles A. 5 M NC S
 William F. 3 M NC
 Martha C. 10/12 F NC
 George W. SEAMON 15 M NC S

893.910 Frederick CARTNER 55 M NC (X) cooper
 Margaret CARTNER 45 F NC (X)
 Abner 22 M NC (X)

[MB:Frederick Cartner & Caty Felkir 2 Jan. 1815.
Frederick Cartner & Margaret Felker 12 Feb 1846]

894.911 William W CARTNER 29 M NC (X) cooper
 Margaret C. 26 F NC
 Elisabeth 20 F NC

895.912 Henery FELCOR -- M NC farmer 250
 Rosena FELCOR 49 F NC (X)
 Mary A. 26 F NC
 Henery 18 M NC
 Elisabeth 15 F NC
 Wila 13 M NC
 Rosena 11 F NC
 Aleander 8 M NC
 Sallie 7 F NC
 William 5 M NC

 50 A improved land, 90 A unimpr, valued at $250

896.913 Joseph A HAWKINS 31 M NC farmer 500
 Jane G. HAWKINS 32 F NC cont.

Mary C. HALL   15 F NC

[MB:Joseph A Hawkins & Jane G Hall 16 Mar 1844]
70 A improved land, 110 unimpr, valued at $500
2 slaves

897.914 Margaret NIBLOCK 58 F NC
   [Note: she is the widow of John Niblock, 1845 WB
K:2]

898.915 Jacob HARE   21 M NC (X) farmer 150
   Celia HARE   30 F NC
   Jane CAMPBELL   12 F NC
   Clementine REX   21 F NC (X)

   Jacob: 40 A improved land, 40 A unimproved,
       valued at $200

899.916 Nancy S WILSON 49 F NC 900

   [Note: widow of Robert F Wilson, 1850 WB K:107]
   50 A improved land, 90 A unimpr, valued at $900
   6 slaves

900.917 Wilson TURNER   55 M NC farmer 1,550
   Elizabeth TURNER   27 F NC
   John W. TURNER   24 M NC teacher
   John F. LEOPARD   16 M NC S labourer

   100 A improved land, 285 unimpr, valued at $1500
   6 slaves

901.918 John F. TOWEL   61 M VA shoemaker
   Mary TOWEL   53 F NC (X)
   Mary A.   19 F NC S
   William A.   16 M NC
   Henry B.   13 M NC
   Lucy C.   6 F NC

902.919 John LUCKEY 57 M NC blacksmith 3,500
   Mary LUCKEY   54 F NC
   William A.   30 M NC farmer
   David M.   28 M NC farmer
   Jane T.   26 F NC
   John A.   21 M NC S
   Jay C.   19 M NC S labourer
   Margaret C.   14 F NC S
   Mary M.   12 F NC S
   Samuel P.   10 M NC S

[MB:John Luckey & Mary Morrison 10 June 1818;
he is the son   of John Luckey, WB H:671, 1836]
290 A improved land, 450 unimproved, valued at
    $3,500, 10 slaves

903.920 John CURRENT   27 M NC distiller
   Anna B. CURRENT   30 F NC (X)
   America   4 F NC
   William P.   2 M NC
   Margaret M.   3/12 F NC

904.921 Samuel SMITH 60 M NC farmer 400
   Jane SMITH   45 F NC (X)   cont.

Mary Jane   9 F NC S
Temperance   6 F NC S
Matissa A.   4 F NC

60 A improved land, 61 A unimpr, valued at $400

905.922 Jessee HALL 49 M NC blacksmith
   Margaret Hall   32 F NC (X)
   Margaret E.   12 F NC
   Richard L.   10 M NC
   Sarah J.   8 F NC
   Mary   6 F NC

906.923 Stuart CAMPBELL 36 M NC farmer 100
   John A.   15 M NC S
   Richard F.   12 M NC S
   Margaret A.   3 F NC
[169] Sarah STEEL   76 F NC (X)

   30 A improved land, 30 A unimpr, valued at $100

p.169, School Districts #7 & #45, 12, 12 Sept. 1850

907.924 Jane GHEEN   53 F NC

908.925 Samuel LUCKEY 53 M NC farmer 6,300
   Rebecca LUCKEY   48 F NC
   Rebecca C.   19 F NC
   Margaret T.   16 F NC S
   Samuel A.   14 M NC S
   Laura M.   12 F NC S
   Catherine C.   9 F NC S
   James N. P.   4 M NC S

[MB:Samuel Luckey & Rebecca Neely 12 Nov 1822;
she was dau of Francis Neely, WB H:472, 1828]
500 A improved land, 800 A unimproved, valued
at $5,000, 20 slaves

909.926 Soloman HALL 72 M NC 6,000
   Amanda   16 F NC

   750 A improved land, 500 A unimpr, valued at
       $600, 68 slaves

910.927 Daniel S SHEEK 32 M NC clerk in store
   Willa SHEEK   28 M NC merchant
   Phillip N. DOOLIN   18 M NC S clerk in store

911.928 Jacob KRIDER   61 M NC farmer
   Sarah KRIDER   58 F NC
   Charles C.   23 M NC farmer
   Barnabas S.   21 M NC S
   Julia E.   16 F NC
   James H. YOUNG   22 M NC tailer

[MB: Jacob Krider to Sally Wood 29 June 1815; son
of Barnabas & Peggy Krider; she was dau of Daniel
& Mary (Anderson) Wood], 24 slaves
machinery - $475
corn mill: 4,200 bu valued at $1,500
corn mill: 3,300 bu valued at $1,200
flouring: 600 bbls valued at $3,040   cont.

saw mill: 6,000 ft lumber valued at $300
Young: tailoring, various articles valued at $875

912.929 William E BARBER 34 M NC overseer
  Margaret BARBER   25 F NC
  John G.   5 M NC S
  Jacob F.   1 M NC
  Jacob L. POOL   12 M NC S
  Charles B. DICKSON   19 M NC S labourer

[MB:William E Barber & Margaret Lively 5 May 1840]
1 slave

913.930 Sally LUCKEY 52 F NC
  William A.   21 M NC farmer
  Sarah E.   15 F NC S

  175 A improved land, 177 A unimpr, valued at
    $3,000, 12 slaves

914.931 Thomas HALL 56 M NC farmer 800
  William F.   23 M NC labourer

  100 A improved land, 129 unimpr, valued at $800
  5 slaves

915.932 Moses D KILPATRICK 58 M NC farmer 6350

[MB: Moses Dickey Kilpatrick to Jane Graham 27
Mar 1812. She d 27 Apr 1846; he d 1 Sept 1855,
CW.]
  150 A improved land, 62 A unimpr, valued at
    $6,350, 11 slaves

916.933 Robert CAMPBELL 60 M NC (X) farmer
  James N.   32 M NC farmer
  Hannah E.   28 F NC
  Joseph R.   26 M NC distiller
  Margaret M.   24 F NC
  John A.   22 M NC S labourer
  William J.   20 M NC S carpenter
  Nancy Viniza   18 F NC S
  Benjamin F.   16 M NC labourer
  Robert J.   14 M NC
  Rachel C.   12 F NC S

  James Campbell: 400 A improved land, 144
unimpr, valued at $3,500, 4 slaves

917.934 Thomas A BURK 36 M NC farmer 1,500
  Harriet A. BURK   30 F NC
  Mary C.   10 F NC S
  James P.   9 M NC S
  Maria C   3 F NC
  Joseph D. COWAN   13 M NC S
  Mary BURK   59 F NC

  140 A improved land, 160 A unimpr, valued at
    $1,500, 4 slaves

918.935 Porter BURK 38 M NC farmer
  Mary C. BURK   32 F NC
  Edmund BURK   24 M NC carpenter   cont.

Henery T. BURK   20 M NC student

William P Burk: 8 slaves

919.936 John G FLEMING 27 M NC farmer 2,300
  Margaret C. FLEMING   27 F NC
  Robert   2/12 M NC
  Mary C. FLEMING   18 F NC S 100

[MB:John G Fleming & Margaret C Krider 17 Mar
  1845]
  150 A improved land, 100 A unimpr, valued at
    $2,300, 13 slaves

920.937 Andrew J FLEMING 25 M NC surveyor
  Margaret E. FLEMING   23 F NC

[MB: Andrew J Fleming to Margaret E Graham 27 Apr
  1849]
  200 A improved land, 82 A unimpr, value: $2300
7 Slaves

921.938 Rufus R THOMPSON 24 M NC carpenter
  Mary C. THOMPSON   25 F NC
  Jesse H.   2 M NC
  William R.   1 M NC

922.939. Lucy RICE   64 F VA 75
  Thomas S. RICE   16 M NC
  Amos A. CAMPBELL   11 M NC
  .940. John G. RICE   23 M NC M farmer
  Elisabeth RICE   25 F NC M
  Adam M. BIRD   3 M NC

[Note: widow of Samuel Rice]
80 A improved land, 200 A unimpr, value:$800

923.941 Franklin S NEELY 24 M NC maneger 4,800
  Jeffry MURPH   29 M NC (X) miller

  7 slaves
  flouring: 1750 bbls valued at $8,750
  corn mill: 6250 bu valued at $1,895
  saw mill: 150,000 ft lumber valued at $1,500

924.942 Moses W THOMPSON 23 M NC labourer
  Sarah THOMPSON   25 F NC (X)

[MB:Moses W Thompson/Sarah S Murph 31 Oct 1848]

925.943 Jacob RAINY   50 M NC M farmer
  Sarah RAINY   32 F NC M (X)
  John   30 M NC (X) labourer
  Abner   25 M NC (X) labourer
  Angelina   23 F NC (X)
  Nancy   20 F NC (X)
  James P.   17 M NC labourer
  Margaret   15 F NC
  Henly   33 F NC

no land but livestock

926.944 Benjamin F. HYDE   36 M NC farmer
   Elisabeth HYDE   35 F NC
   James C.   9 M NC S
   Mary A.   4 F NC
   Lydia E.   2 F NC

   3 slaves
   smithing: various articles valued at $425

927.945 Thomas COWAN 32 M NC farmer 1,200
   Margaret COWAN   29 F NC
   Lucreacia A.   7 F NC S
   John Y.   6 M NC
   Maria C.   2/12 F NC
   Ellen YOUNG   17 F NC S

[MB: Thomas Cowan to Margaret Young 4 Aug 1841;
she was the dau of Jonathan Young, see 1849 will
of Catherine Neely, WB K:101]
   100 A improved land, 266 A unimproved, valued at
      $1,200, 14 slaves

928.946 Richard L BURRIS   36 M NC shoemaker

929.947 Kiziah WADE 52 F NC Mu

930.948 Andrew GRAHAM 30 M NC farmer 850
   Jane L. GRAHAM   30 F NC
   Laura Jane   3 F NC
   Ann L.   1 F NC

[MB:Andrew Graham & Jane L Young 13 Oct 1845]
1 slave

931.949 Ann CLODFELTER   37 F NC (X)
   Elisabeth A CLODFELTER 16 F NC S

932.950 Thomas S CHAMBERS 35 M NC farmer
   Mary M. CHAMBERS   22 F NC
   Mary J.   14 F NC
   Richard M.   11 M NC
   Laura E.   10 F NC
   Ann E.   5 F NC
   Ellen C.   2 F NC
   Margaret T.   1/12 F NC
   Mary J. BOSTIAN   5 F NC

[MB:Thomas S Chambers/Mary M Graham 30 Dec 1847]
80 A improved land, 98 A unimpr, valued at $1800
3 slaves

933.951 Luke BARBER 63 M MD farmer 2,600
   Nancy C. BARBER   48 F NC
   William L.   22 M NC labourer
   Sarah A.   16 F NC
   Joseph   15 M NC S labourer
   John R.   12 M NC S
   Edward T.   10 M NC S

[Note: son of Elias Barber, WB I:154]
90 A improved land, 100 A unimpr, value: $900
6 slaves

934.952 Caleb SETZER   35 M NC wagonmaker
   Rachel M. SETZER   24 F NC

935.953 Catharine BARBER   52 F NC
   Thomas   29 M NC carp?
   Jonathan   22 M NC farmer
   Robert J. M.   17 M NC S labourer

   144 A improved land, 10 A unimpr, value: $500
   9 slaves

936.954 Benjamin HARRISON 68 M MD farmer 600
   Anna HARRISON   61 F MD
   George Dougless   44 M NC labourer
   Mary A. E.   36 F NC
   Nathan   34 M NC labourer
   Bennet A.   31 M NC labourer
   James   29 M NC labourer
   Margaret   27 F NC

   100 A improved land, 60 A unimpr, value:$600

937.955 William GARDNER   28 M NC farmer
   Thomas GARDINER   35 M NC labourer
   Sarah GARDNER   49 F MD
   Elisabeth GARDNER   33 F NC
   Mary GARDNER   31 F NC
   Jane GARDNER   29 F NC

   Wm & Thos:150 A improved land, 110 A unimpr,
      valued at $1,000; Wm: 2 slaves

938.956 Alexander GRAHAM 35 M NC (X) farmer 400
   Mary A. GRAHAM   23 F NC
   Nelly E.   6 F NC S
   Elisabeth F.   5/12 F NC
   Robert H. COWAN   13 M NC S
   David A. BOSTIAN   6 M NC S
   Ann D. GRAHAM   39 F NC (X)

[CW: Alexander Graham to Mary Ann Cowan 9 Apr
1846]
120 A improved land, 50 A unimpr, value:$400

939.957 John M SMITH   35 M NC (X) overseer
   Mary A. E. SMITH   25 F NC
   Jefferson A.   8 M NC

   88 A improved land, 23 A unimpr, value:$450
   manager: 600 A improved land, 1800 A unimpr,
      valued at $5,000

940.958 William BARBER   68 M MD farmer
   Margaret A. BARBER   57 F NC
   Rachael   29 F NC
   Jacob F.   23 M NC
   James   13 M NC S

[MB:William Barber & Margaret Hughey 8 Apr 1816]
120 A improved land, 120 A unimpr, valued at
   [blank], 19 slaves

941.959 Thomas C HYDE 29 M NC farmer 2,000
   Jane C. HYDE   27 F NC
   William C.   4 M NC
   James C.   9/12 M NC

[MB:Thomas C Hyde to Jane C Burke 15 Jan 1845; he
is son of James & Lydia (Cowan) Hyde (WB I:220,
   K:110)]
   100 A improved land, 324 A unimpr, valued at
   $2,000, 6 slaves

942.960 Margaret HYDE   68 F NC
   Ann P.   41 F NC
   Jane C.   37 F NC
   Benjamin M.   35 M NC
   John S.   32 M NC
   Malvina   28 F NC
   James M.K.   22 M NC
   Richard S. GRAHAM   17 M NC
   Mary M. HYDE   10 F NC
   Margaret A.   8 F NC

   145 A improved land, 123 A unimpr, value:$1700

p. 171, School District #9, 14 Sept. 1850

943.961 Robert CHUNN   50 M NC farmer
   Maria CHUNN   35 F NC
   James F.   -- M NC
   Lydia C.   -- F NC
   Susanna C.   -- F NC
   William   5 M NC
   Mary E.   3 F NC

[MB: Robert Chunn to Maria Hide 27 May 1835; she
is granddau of James & Lydia Hyde. Robert Chunn's
will, Book K:119]
   150 A improved land, 80 A unimpr, valued at
   $1,900, 3 slaves

944.962 Thomas GREEN 52 M NC (X) shoemaker
   Elisabeth GREEN   50 F NC
   Margaret A.   24 F NC
   Richard L.   22 M NC (X) labourer

[MB:Thomas Green & Betsey Clotfelter 27 Feb 1819]

945.963 Demsy PAGE   30 M NC farmer
   Malinda PAGE   23 F NC
   Jane C.   5 F NC
   Mary A.   3 F NC
   Simon Peter   1 M NC

   60 A improved land, 30 A unimpr, valued at $500

946.964 Mary COWAN   62 F NC 600
   Arthur C. CHAMBERS 32 M NC
   Elisabeth L. COWAN 36 F NC

[Note:s he was the dau of William Cowan, Sr.]
50 A improved land, 49 A unimpr, valued at $600
2 slaves

947.965 Margaret HARISON 42 F NC 350
   Elisabeth A.   28 F NC
   Mary A.   20 F NC
   Sarah C.   14 F NC
   Margaret A.   11 F NC

[MB:Hezekiah T Harrison to Margaret A Cowan 16
Nov 1825; his   1839 will, WB I:60]

948.966 David COWAN   36 M NC farmer
   Ann S. COWAN   59 F NC
   Rebecca COWAN   38 F NC
   Mary COWAN   46 F NC

   60 A improved land, 113 A unimpr, valued at $800

949.967 Rebecca COWAN 49 F NC 1,500
   Rebecca C.   21 F NC
   Lucinda A.   19 F NC
   Margaret E.   16 F NC S
   David S.   13 M NC S
   Sarah J.   11 F NC S
   James F   6 M NC S
   Isaac COWAN   75 M NC

   124 A improved land, 126 A unimpr, valued at
   $1,500, 4 slaves

950.968 Richard D GRAHAM 56 M NC farmer 1,200
   Jane I. GRAHAM   45 F NC
   Grizza C. GRAHAM   36 F NC

   184 A improved land, 120 A unimpr, valued at
   $1,200, 1 slave

951.969 Jeremiah BARINGER 41 M NC farmer 5,900
   Sarah A.   15 F NC S
   John M. P.   12 M NC S
   Susan Jane   10 F NC S
   George W. SMITH   24 M NC (X) labourer
                              idiotic
   Charity SMITH   18 F NC idiotic

   204 A improved land, 474 A unimpr, valued at
   $4,000, 12 slaves

952.970 Samuel KNOX   50 M NC farmer 3,000
   Elisabeth S. KNOX 46 F NC
   James   22 M NC labourer
   Jane L. KNOX   16 F NC
   Samuel P.   13 M NC S
   Benjamin A.   9 M NC S

[MB:Samuel Knox to Elizabeth Burris 19 Mar 1821;
she was the dau of Allen Burroughs, WB I:184]
   250 A improved land, 500 A unimpr, valued at
   $3,000, 19 slaves

953.970 John P BURK   33 M NC farmer 1,400
   Elisabeth W BURK 28 F NC
   John L.   3 M NC
   Richard P.   1/12 M NC   cont.

[MB:John P Burke to Elizabeth W Barber 5 May 1843;
he was the son of William Burke, WB I:189]
70 A improved land, 70 A unimpr, valued at $1400
3 slaves

954.972 Drucilla BEEFFLE   39 F NC
  Sarah J.   17 F NC S
  Elisabeth C.   12 F NC
  William F.   10 M NC S
  Nancy J. A.   4 F NC

[MB:James Beffel to Drucilla Dickson 3 Oct. 1829]

955.973 Osborn G. FOARD 30 M NC farmer 10,000
  Ann F. FOARD   28 F NC
  Robert O.   2 M NC
  Ann E.   1 F NC

[MB: Osborn G Foard to Ann F. Cowan 6 Jan. 1848]
350 A improved land, 698 A unimproved, valued at
    $10,000, 26 Slaves

956.974 Christopher GRAHAM 62 M NC farmer 1,140
  Jane C. GRAHAM   56 F NC
  Flora M.   ) twin   28 F NC
  Jane F.   ) twin   28 F NC
  Caroline   26 F NC
  Melissa A.   25 F NC
  Thomas D.   21 M NC carpenter
  William   18 M NC labourer
  John W.   15 M NC labourer
  Matthew A. LOCKE   30 M NC physician

[MB: Christopher Graham to Jane Gillespie 18 Feb
1812; he was the son of Richard Graham, WB H:484]
90 A improved land, 138 A unimpr, value: $1,140
19 slaves

957.974 Benjamin BLACKWELL 31 M NC tailor 400
  Elisabeth H. BLACKWELL 34 F NC
  Mary Jane   3 F NC
  Sarah Ellen   1 F NC

[MB: Benjamin Blackwell to Elizabeth H Thomason
23 Feb 1843; he is the son of Eleanor Blackwell,
WB K:66]
30 A improved land, 76 A unimpr, valued at $400
1 slave

958.976 John L. GRAHAM -- M NC
5 slaves

959.977 James G GRAHAM 33 M NC carpenter 1,600
  Nancy S. GRAHAM   24 F NC
  Mary V.   5/12 F NC

[MB: James G Graham to Nancy S Burke 5 Jan 1848]
125 A improved land, 100 unimpr, valued at $1600
5 slaves

960.978 Jacob BAKER   53 M NC miller 3,700

cont.

Susanna BAKER   57 F NC (X)
[172] John BAKER   21 M NC S farmer
  Michael   12 M NC S
  Susanna E.   23 F NC S
  Ellen   19 F NC S
  Mary A.   17 F NC S
  Catharine   15 F NC S
  Margaret   8 F NC S
  James M. TURNER   13 M NC S

[Note: Jacob Baker to Susanna Oolmer, spinster,
n.d.(JWL note:her occupation was spinning)]
225 A improved land, 115 unimpr, value: $500
flouring: 1,208 bbls valued at $5,424
corn mill: 1,500 bu valued at $2,250
saw mill: 150,000 ft lumber valued at $825
spinning: wool worth $2,000

p.172, School District #9, 14 Sept. 1850

961.979 William BAKER   27 M NC Mu miller
  Lucinda BAKER   27 F NC Mu

962.980 Perry HAIR 26 M NC carpenter 100
  Mary HAIR   23 F NC (X)
  James M.   5 M NC
  William S.   2 F NC
  Mary DONAHOO   18 F NC

963.981 Margaret HOLOBAUGH 60 F NC (X)
  Margaret   23 F NC
  Susanna   19 F NC S
  John   17 M NC S
  Mary A. SWAN   3 F NC

964.982 Henry DENT 34 M NC millwright 1,000
  Paulina DENT   19 F NC
  Sarah WRIGHT   55 F NC
2 slaves

965.983 John S. CARSON 50 M NC 2,500
  Prudence CARSON   58 F NC

150 A improved land, 220 A unimpr, value:$2500
John S: 7 slaves; Prudence: 6 slaves

966.984 James G RAMSEY 26 M NC physician 1,000
  Sarah J. RAMSAY   22 F NC
  Margaret F.   1 F NC

100 A improved land, 100 A unimpr, valued at
    $1,000, 6 slaves

967.985 Jacob HUGHEY   57 M NC farmer 2,000
  Frances HUGHEY   50 F NC
  George E.   26 M NC carpenter
  Henry M.   25 M NC labourer
  John J.   22 M NC S labourer
  Thomas A.   20 M NC S carpenter
  Mary F.   17 F NC
  Martha J.   15 F NC S
  Martha C.   14 F NC S
  Sarah E.   12 F NC S   cont.

Jacob F.   8 M NC S

[MB: Jacob Hughey to Fanny Niblock 2 Mar 1819]
200 A improved land, 115 unimpr, value: $2,000
4 slaves

968.986 Mathew BARBER 27 M NC farmer
  Margaret C. BARBER   22 F NC
  Jane E.   3 F NC
  Margaret C.   2 F NC

[MB:Matthew Barber & Margaret C Knox 16 Aug 1845]
70 A improved land, 94 A unimpr, valued at $700
2 slaves

969.987 Thomas LIGHTELL 49 M NC
  Elisabeth C LIGHTELL   39 F NC

40 A improved land, 117 A unimpr, valued at $240
5 slaves

970.988 George GILLESPIE 48 M NC farmer 700
  Ann S. GILLESPIE   45 F NC
  Mary Jane   18 F NC
  Flora C.   17 F NC
  Thomas P.   12 M NC S
  Margaret E.   10 F NC S
  Nancy A.   6 F NC S
  Sarah A. Felicia   2 F NC
  John C.   15 M NC

[MB: George Gillespie & Ann S Cowan 17 Nov 1830]
70 A improved land, 159 A unimpr, valued at $700
6 slaves

971.989 Levi NIBLOCK 55 M NC farmer 1,400
  Molly NIBLOCK   50 F NC
  George G.   25 M NC S labourer
  Benjamin   23 M NC S labourer
  Franklin   21 M NC S labourer
  Alexander   19 M NC S labourer
  Thomas   10 M NC S
  Alburtes   8 M NC

[MB: Levi Niblock to Molly R Nooe 27 Jan 1823]
130 A improved land, 470 A unimpr, valued at
    $1,400, 4 slaves

972.990 Peter STILLER 63 M NC (X) farmer
  Catharine STILLER 54 F NC
  Mary A. M.   15 F NC S
  Charles M.   13 M NC S
  Julius M.   12 M NC S

50 A improved land valued at $200

973.991 Lenard GARVER 64 M NC (X) shoemaker 10
  Catharine GARVER   52 F NC (X)

974.992 Michael P WALKER 29 M NC farmer 100
  Sarah WALKER   29 F NC (X)
  Lenard A.   7 M NC   cont.

  Henry N.   5 M NC
  James V.   2 M NC
  William F. T.   8/12 M NC

975.993. Valentine GARVER 35 M NC (X) farmer
  Charlott GARVER   47 F NC (X)
  Jane C.   13 F NC S
  Benjamin T.   11 M NC S
  Polly   9 F NC S
  James   7 M NC

[MB:Volentine Garver/Charlotte Parish 9 July 1845]
45 A improved land valued at $100

976.994 Polly RICKARD 35 F NC
  William   10 M NC S
  Phillip W.   5 M NC

p. 173, School District #6, 17 Sept. 1850

977.995 Henery WILHELM 52 M NC farmer 900
  Elisabeth WILHELM   57 F NC (X)
  Susanna   21 F NC S
  Lewis A.   21 M NC S labourer
  Margaret   19 F NC S
  Mary   18 F NC S
  Jacob R.   16 M NC S labourer
  John   14 M NC S
  Henery V.   12 M NC S

[MB: Henry Wilhelm to Betsey Dean 4 Sept 1827]
150 A improved land, 275 unimpr, valued at $900

978.996 Nelson DRY —— M NC farmer 455
  Eve M. DRY   52 F NC (X)
  Michael A.   21 M NC S labourer
  Daniel M.   19 M NC S
  Amelia C.   16 F NC S
  Sally C.   12 F NC

  62 A improved land, 62 A unimpr, valued at $455

979.997 Richard O COWAN 35 M NC tailor,farmer 300
  Elisabeth L. COWAN   24 F NC
  Margaret H.   5 F NC
  Samuel B.   3 M NC
  Nenian L.   1 M NC

[MB:Richard L Cowan/Elizabeth L Irvine 7 Jan 1845]
60 A improved land, 77 A unimpr, valued at $300
5 slaves

980.998 Richard F CORZINE 39 M NC farmer 700
  Lydia M.   17 F NC
  John C.   3 M NC
  Ruanah CORZINE   47 F NC

[Note:Richard F is the son of Levi Corzin, WB
H:305; Ruanah is Levi's sister]
170 A improved land, 175 A unimpr, value: $700
1 slave

981.999 Henry BAKER 50 M NC wheelwright 1,500
    Nancy C.   23 F NC
    Henery F.   20 M NC S farmer
    Moses W.   17 M NC S
    Sarah L.   16 F NC S
    Mary A.   14 F NC S
    Sophia C.   9 F NC S

    90 A improved land, 185 A unimpr, value: $1500

982.1000 Robert W HUGHEY   29 M NC carpenter
    Elisabeth W. HUGHEY   24 M NC [sic]
    Sarah J.   3 F NC
    George L.   1 M NC

    [MB:Robert W Hughey/Elizabeth W Barber
       28 Jan 1845] 2 slaves
    100 A improved land, 106 A unimpr, value:$1200

983.1001 Mary ROSEBOROUGH 46 F NC 100
    Hetty   20 F NC

984.1002 Nancy HUGHS 43 F NC
    James C.   8 M NC

985.1003 Zilla COWAN 56 F NC
    Abigail COWAN   45 F NC

986.1004 Ruhanna COWAN   39 F NC 450
    Sarah C. PHIFER   22 F NC S
    Margaret M. COWAN   17 F NC
    Nancy A.   15 F NC
    Ruannah   12 F NC S
    Mary M.   9 F NC S
    John TOWEL   21 M NC labourer

    [MB: William Cowan to Ruhannah Cowan 31 Oct 1826,
    dau of John Cowan, WB H:408]
    Ruannah: 5 slaves, 90 A improved land, 30 A un-
    improved, valued at $450

987.1005 Daniel WEBB   39 M NC farmer
    Mary A. WEBB   39 F NC
    Caleb A.   18 M NC S labourer
    Nancy M. K.   13 F NC S
    Daniel T.   11 M NC S
    Emily Jane   8 F NC S
    Rebecca D.   7 F NC S

    [MB: Daniel Webb to Mary Ann Dent 22 Feb 1831]
    45 A improved land, 45 A unimpr, valued at $500

988.1006 Rebecca COWAN   43 F NC
    Mary A.   16 F NC
    Laura R.   15 F NC S
    Jane Z.   12 F NC S
    Rachel E.   10 F NC S
    Emily C.   7 F NC S

[Note:she is the widow of Aaron Varner Cowan, WB
E:106, who d 16 Jan 1850 CW; they m 31 July 1827]
143 A improved land, 210 A unimpr, value: $3,000
6 slaves

989.1007 Silas PHIFER 57 M NC farmer 1,000
    Matilda PHIFER   42 F NC
    Zilpha C.   24 F NC
    Margaret C.   22 F NC
    John C.   19 M NC S labourer
    Carmi   17 M NC idiotic
    William H.   15 M NC S labourer
    Benjamin W.   13 M NC S
    Mary Jane   10 F NC S
    Sarah E.   7 F NC S
    Martha M.   5 F NC
    Elisabeth A.   10/12 F NC
    Thomas PHIFER   13 M NC S 300

    [MB: Silas Phifer to Matilda Cowan 6 Dec 1823;
    she is the dau of John Cowan, WB H:408]
    90 A improved land, 126 A unimpr, value: $1,000
    4 slaves

990.1008 Nancy ELLIOTT 50 F VA
    Martha M.   15 F NC

991.1009 John PHIFER   57 M NC farmer
    Jane PHIFER   58 F NC
    Jacob W.   30 M NC labourer
    Maria   29 F NC
    Catharine   27 F NC
    Sarah   24 F NC
    John C.   22 M NC S labourer
    Leah   19 F NC
[174] Robert H.   17 M NC labourer

    [MB: John Phifer to Jane Hughey 5 June 1815]
    125 A improved land, 292 A unimpr, value:$800

p. 174, School District #6, 19 Sept. 1850

992.1010 Matthias PHIFER 79 M Switz 1,500
    Leah PHIFER   82 F NC
    Margaret A.   44 F NC
    Mary   42 F NC
    Jacob   38 M NC carpenter
    Lydia A. H. PHIFER   19 F NC 300
    Jacob F. PHIFER   7 M NC 300

    [Note: he d 30 May 1852 CW]
    100 A improved land, 212 A unimpr, valued at
       $1,500, 1 slave

993.1011 David F. KNOX 30 M NC farmer 610
    Margaret M. KNOX   31 F NC
    John F.   6 M NC
    Margaret E.   4 F NC
    James A.   1 M NC

    45 A improved land, 45 A unimpr, value: $610

994.1012 Elisabeth SMITH 39 F NC (X)
    Sarah A   15 F NC
    Rebecca   13 F NC S
    Henery   7 M NC S
    Margaret   5 F NC
    Elisabeth C.   3 F NC   cont.

```
    John S.                    1 M NC
    Mary C.                    62 F NC (X)


995.1013 Catherine BIRD   62 F NC 1,500
    John M.                    35 M NC farmer
    William                    30 M NC carpenter
    Margaret A.                32 F NC
    Ross                       20 M NC labourer


[MB: Michael Bird to Caty Foster 16 Mar 1812;
Michael Bird d 20 Oct 1844 CW. See RCR, Vol 7]
    140 A improved land, 124 A unimpr, value:$1500
    4 slaves


996.1014 Thomas L. KERR   38 M NC 3,500
    Elisabeth L. KERR          46 F NC


    200 A improved land, 135 A unimpr, value:$3500
    17 slaves


997.1015 Jane G. KERR    39 F NC 3,500
    James McK.                 15 M NC S
    Benjamin K.                13 M NC S
    Margaret C.                10 F NC S
    Lettitia L.                 8 F NC S
    Elisabeth M.                6 F NC S
    Jane C. STEEL              18 F NC
    Ruth HOSLER               50 F NC Mu


[Note: she is the widow of John Kerr who d before
22 Apr 1844 when his father James Kerr provided
for her, WB I:245]
    150 A improved land, 206 A unimpr, valued at
        $3,500, 14 slaves


998.1016 James KERR   41 M NC farmer 3,000
    Nancy Jane             8 F NC S


    130 A improved land, 229 A unimpr, valued at
        $3,000, 11 slaves


999.1017 John IRVIN   43 M NC farmer 2,325
    Ann J. IRVIN           44 F NC
    Joseph C.              11 M NC S
    Margaret A.             9 F NC S
    Harriet A.             13 F NC S
    Samuel J. YOUNG        21 M NC carpenter 800


[MB: John Irvin to Ann J Young 30 Jan 1837]
    309 A improved land, 160 A unimpr, value:$2,325
    9 slaves


1000.1018 William B WOOD 56 M NC farmer 13,000
    William A.             18 M NC student
    Thomas S.              15 M NC S
    Mary D.                13 F NC S
    Margaret L.            11 F NC S
    James H.                9 M NC S
    Susan C.                1 F NC


[MB: William B Wood to Margaret D Knox 22 Mar
1830; she d 30 Jan 1849 CW]
    480 A improved land, 810 A unimpr, valued at
        $13,000, 70 slaves
```

```
1001.1019 Daniel B WOOD 29 M NC physician
    Margaret McK. WOOD     17 F NC


[MB: D.B. Wood to Margaret M Cowan 31 Mar 1849]
    5 slaves


1002.1020 John W JOHNSON 48 M NC farmer 1500
    Caleb A.               20 M NC labourer
    James C.               18 M NC S
    Mary Jane              15 F NC S
    William L.              8 M NC S
    Joseph D.               6 M NC


    100 A improved land, 105 A unimpr, valued at
        $1,500, 1 slave


1003.1021 Moses LINGLE   36 M NC teacher 1,000
    Jane C. LINGLE             38 F NC
    William L. COWAN            9 M NC S
    Benjamin F.                 6 M NC
    Sarah Jane                  5 F NC
    James C. LINGLE          5/12 M NC


[MB: Moses Lingle to Jane C Cowan 4 Nov 1848]
    75 A improved land, 160 A unimpr, value:$1,000
    5 slaves


1004.1022 Mathew H BRANDON 35 M NC farmer 4,200
    Elisabeth M. BRANDON       29 F NC
    David C.                   11 M NC S
    Mary Jane                   9 F NC S
    Ellen C.                    5 F NC S
    James E.                    2 M NC


    160 A improved land, 177 A unimpr, value:$3,500
    12 slaves


1005.1023 Rufus M ROSEBOROUGH 41 M NC farmer 2500
    Lucy E ROSEBOROUGH         23 F NC
    Lucy Jane                   3 F NC
    Daniel B.                   1 M NC


    175 A improved land, 145 A unimpr, value:$2,500
    14 slaves


1006.1024 Jane C. KNOX   37 F NC 7000
    Jane L.                16 F NC S
    James A.               14 M NC S
    Henry B.               12 M NC S
    John G.                10 M NC S
    Joseph A                8 M NC S
    Margaret E.             5 F NC
    Alice I.                3 F NC
    Julia I.                2 F NC


[MB: James G Knox to Jane C Burke 14 July 1830.
James G Knox d 15 May 1849 CW, WB K:98]
    400 A improved land, 250 A unimpr, valued at
        $7,500, 9 slaves
```

<u>p. 175, School District #7, 21 Sept. 1850</u>

```
1007.1025 John E POSTON 28 M NC m overseer 600
    Matilda POSTON         25 F NC m           cont.
```

[MB:John E Poston & Matilda E Ramsey 23 Oct 1849]

1008.1026 John McHENRY 42 M NC farmer 900
  Mary McHENRY   50 F NC

[Note: he is son of Henry McHenry, WB I:35]
75 A improved land, 75 A unimpr, valued at $900
7 slaves

1009.1027 John W STEEL 22 M NC farmer
  William STEEL   20 M NC
  Matthew H. STEEL   12 M NC

[Note: these are sons of Matthew Locke Steele, WE
  K:22]
140 A improved land, 160 A unimpr, value:$2,000
9 slaves

1010.1028 William P GRAHAM 52 M NC farmer 8,000
  Mary R GRAHAM   42 F NC
  Sarah E.   20 F NC
  William B.   18 M NC S labourer
  Marietta   16 F NC S
  James P.   14 M NC S
  Jane L.   11 F NC S
  Eliza C.   8 F NC S
  Henry Clay   6 M NC S
  James F. WATT   21 M NC farmer

[MB: William P Graham to Mary K Barr 9 July 1825;
he is son of James Graham, WB H:701; she is dau of
William Barr, WBI:122]
250 A improved land, 601 unimpr, valued at $8,000
16 slaves
sales of leather worth $2,000;harnesses worth
$1,000, pieces of ? worth $300, skins worth $100

1011.1029 Mary A GRAHAM 50 F NC 4,000
  Zilpha H.   30 F NC
  John K.   28 M NC farmer
  Margaret A.   26 F NC

250 A improved land, 372 A unimpr, valued at
  $4,000, 15 slaves

1012.1030 Ann COWAN 74 F NC
  John M.   41 M NC farmer
  Mary S.   39 F NC

John M: 170 A improved land, 250 unimproved,
  valued at $1,200; Ann: 11 slaves

1013.1031 Anna GRAHAM 65 F NC 1,500
  Thomas C   37 M NC 600

[MB: Moses Graham to Ann Cowan 31 May 1804;he d 11
May 1848 CW, WB K:73]
Anna: 300 A improved land, 225 A unimpr, valued at
  $1,500, 18 slaves

1014.1032 Michael FILHOUR 37 M NC farmer 5,500
  Elisabeth   58 F NC
                           cont.

350 A improved land, 650 A unimpr, valued at
  $5,000, 15 slaves

1015.1033 James COOK 29 M NC blacksmith
  Jane M. COOK   25 F NC (X)
  Mary A.   6 F NC
  Robert S.   5 M NC
  Elvira   1 F NC

3 wagons, various articles

1016.1034 Gray BELT 39 M NC (X) farmer
  Martha BELT   30 F NC
  Silas   13 M NC
  Ruth   11 F NC
  Mary   7 F NC
  William   5 M NC
  James   2 M NC
  Charlotte BELT   19 F NC

[MB: Gray Belt to Martha Baxter 6 Feb 1843]
25 A improved land valued at $100

1017.1035 Jacob C GOODMAN 53 M NC farmer 1,100
  Cloe C. GOODMAN   49 F NC
  Richard   19 M NC S labourer
  Rosena A.   17 F NC
  Manlas M.D.   15 M NC S
  Sarah Jane   9 F NC S
  Pinkney O.   3 M NC

300 A improved land, 250 A unimproved, valued at
  $1,000, 17 slaves

1018.1036 Willa RUFTY 44 M NC (X) farmer
  Anna RUFTY   33 F NC (X)
  Clementine   18 F NC
  John   16 M NC S labourer
  Mary A.   14 F NC S
  William W.   14 M NC
  Fanny   13 F NC
  Samuel R.   9 M NC
  George H.W.   6 M NC
  Pleasant H.   2 M NC

[MB: Wilie Ruffty to Anna May 29 May 1832]
150 A improved land valued at $450

1019.1037 Jessee GASKEY 50 M NC labourer
  Barbara GASKEY   48 F NC
  Susanah   25 F NC
  Emeline   8/12 F NC
  Elisabeth   22 F NC
  Martha A.   20 F NC
  Lucinda   17 F NC S
  Isabella   14 F NC S
  Joshua   12 M NC S
  David   10 M NC S

40 A improved land, 70 A unimpr, value: $600

1020.1038 George A. GASKEY 23 M NC m
  Margaret C. GASKEY 20 F NC (X) m

1021.1039 Nathan H NEELY 29 M NC farmer 3,000
    Isabella C. NEELY   29 F NC
    Charles C. LEPARD   18 M NC S labourer

    [MB: Nathaniel H Neely to Isabella C Cowan 27 Oct
      1847; he is named in the will of his mother
    Margaret, WB K:51, widow of Alexander Neely, WB
    H:542; she was a Barber]
      125 A improved land, 145 A unimpr, valued at
        $3,000, 12 slaves

1022.1040 David H PATTERSON 47 M NC farmer 1400
    Rebecca PATTERSON   54 F NC
    Hannah PATTERSON   52 F NC
    Frances E.   31 F NC
    Jane L.   30 F NC S
    Frances H. OWEN   8 F NC S
    Josiah J. OWEN   6 M NC

    [Note: son of James Patterson, WB I:45]
    125 A improved land, 225 A unimpr, valued at
      $1,400, 6 slaves
    Patterson & Owen: flouring, 728 bbls flour valued
    at $2,712; corn mill, 6,600 bu valued at $1,380;
    saw mill, 50,000 ft of lumber valued at $375.

1023.1041 Jinsy GRAHAM 66 F NC
    William C. SPEAR   15 M NC labourer

    [Note: she is the dau of Thomas Cowan and widow
    of James Graham, WB G:505.
    140 A improved land, 10 A unimpr, valued at $300
    11 slaves

1024.1042 Robert KNOX 42 M NC farmer 1,800
    Catherine KNOX   36 F NC
[176] Jane H.   9 F NC S
    Margaret C.   7 F NC S
    John S.   5 M NC
    Sarah M.   2 F NC

    350 A improved land, 300 A unimpr, value:$1800
    18 slaves

<u>p.176, School District #4, 25 Sept. 1825</u>

1025.1043 Isaac WITHERSPOON 41 MNC carriagemaker
                                       800
    Ann WITHERSPOON   33 FNC
    Thomas J.   13 MNC
    Margaret E.   8/12 FNC
    Abel M.N. COWAN   20 MNC carriagemaker 20
    Sidney TROUTMAN   23 MNC S carriagemaker
    Ninian A. ROBISON   18 MNC S carriagemaker
    Margaret C. COWAN   16 FNC

    [MB:Isaac A Witherspoon/Ann McNeely 11 Nov 1834]
    95 A improved land, 165 A unimpr, valued at $800
    2 slaves
    3 finished jobs valued at $357, 8 unfinished jobs
      valued at $200, repairing valued at $485

1026.1044 Eavan HAGLAR 35 M NC mu blacksmith 200
    Eliza HAGLAR   26 F SC mu (X)
    Elisabeth R.   11 F NC mu
    Frances L.   9 F NC mu
    Eliza J.   6 F NC mu
    James F.   4 M NC mu
    Sidney MURDAH   25 M NC mu blacksmith

    two buggies, 1 ?, various articles

1027.1045 Tobias GOODMAN 35 M NC 1,000
    Ellen GOODMAN   23 F NC
    John T.   4 M NC
    Margaret E.   2 F NC

    [MB: Tobias Goodman to Ellen Turner 27 May 1844]
    100 A improved land, 177 A unimpr, value:$1,000
    1 slave

1028.1046 George KNOX 74 M NC farmer 1,800
    Nancy KNOX   35 F NC
    Frances KNOX   30 F NC

    George Knox's name is scratched through on the
      agriculture schedule
    2 slaves

1029.1047 Rufus R KNOX 38 M NC farmer 1,000
    Elisabeth M. KNOX   33 F NC
    Mary E.   9 F NC S
    Martha J.   6 F NC S
    James P.   4 M NC

    60 A improved land, 120 A unimpr, value:$1,200
    3 slaves

1030.1048 S[t]ephen F COWAN 36 M NC farmer
    Ann McV. COWAN   34 F NC
    Ninnian S.   5 M NC
    Jinsy COWAN   68 F NC 1,000
    Mary Jane STEEL   11 F NC

    [MB:Stephen F Cowan to Ann M Graham 21 Mar 1842]
    200 A improved land, 121 A unimpr, value:$1,000
    3 slaves

1031.1049 Archibald GILLESPIE 37 M NC farmer 700
    Drucilla S. GILLESPIE   27 F NC
    Charlotte R.   9 F NC S
    William T.   7 M NC S
    Flora E.   4 M NC
    James A.   2 M NC

    67 A improved land, 180 A unimpr, valued at $700
    3 slaves

1032.1050 Absalem OVERCASH 50 M NC carpenter
    Polly OVERCASH   44 F NC (X)
    Anderson   25 M NC
    William   21 M NC (X) S farmer
    Franklin   19 M NC
    Margaret   17 F NC S
    Elisabeth   14 F NC S

Lewis   12 M NC S
Amanda   2 F NC

66 A improved land, 5 A unimpr, valued at $200

1033.1051 James A McNEELY 30 M NC merchant 200
   Margaret McNEELY   28 F NC
   Samuel L.   4 M NC
   Mary E.   2 M NC
   Margaret A. CROSBY   14 F NC S
   3 slaves

1034.1052 Alfred N GOODMAN 31 M NC farmer 1,200

   50 A improved land, 204 A unimpr, value:$1,200
   1 slave

1035.1053 David GOODMAN 40 M NC farmer 1,500
   Mary GOODMAN   33 F NC
   John A.   11 M NC S
   Samuel L.   7 M NC S
   Sarah BUSTLE   16 F NC

   75 A improved land, 175 A unimpr, value: $1,500
   1 slave

1036.1054 Mary S. COOK 56 F NC
   Isabella C.   27 F NC
   Jane L.   19 F NC
   Moses W.   16 M NC farmer
   Mary T.   12 F NC S

   70 A improved land, 8 A unimpr, valued at $125

1037.1055 Amanda H STIKELEATHER 31 F NC
   John McK.   9 M NC S
   Mary A.E.   6 F NC S

[MB:Joseph Stikeleather/Amanda C Cook 27 Jul 1839]

1038.1056 David C FOSTER 48 M NC farmer 1,000
   Abigail G. FOSTER   34 F NC
   Mary A.A.   4 F NC
   Laura C.   1 F NC

[MB:David C Foster to Abigail Graham 3 May 1840]
140 A improved land, 180 A unimpr, valued at $600
8 slaves

1039.1057 David KETCHY 32 M NC (X) miller
   Margaret L. KETCHY   27 F NC (X)
   William   12 M NC S
   Levi   10 M NC S
   Noe   8 M NC S

[MB: David Ketchey to Margaret L Rix 25 Apr 1850]

1040.1058 George SOWERS 54 M NC cooper 200
   Catharine SOWERS   60 F NC (X)
   Catharine   25 F NC (X)
   Christena   23 F NC (X)
[177] Elisabeth   20 F NC   cont.

[MB: George Sowers/Catherine Kesler 4 Nov 1821]

<u>p.177, School District #3, 27 Sept. 1850</u>

1041.1059 Sophia HOUSTON 58 F NC 500
   Elisabeth   53 F NC

   [Note: these are daus of Elizabeth Houston, WB
     I:117]
   70 A improved land, 30 A unimpr, valued at $500
   11 slaves

1042.1060 Margaret HOUSTON 52 F NC 800
   Oni P.   22 M NC medical student
   James A.   19 M NC farmer

   [MB: John Houston to Margaret Barr 19 Sept 1823;
     he d 1839, WB I:56]
   120 A improved land, 80 A unimpr, valued at $800
   7 slaves

1043.1061 Susan POSTON 55 F NC 1,000
   Nancy   27 F NC
   Sophia   25 F NC
   Hial L.   22 M NC farmer
   Amos F.   19 M NC S labourer

   [MB: John J Poston to Susannah Rice 1 Aug 1817]
   50 A improved land, 65 A unimpr, valued at $1000
   1 slave

1044.1062 George M SHUFORD 47 M NC farmer 1,500
   Sophia SHUFORD   56 F NC
   Alphonza F.   19 M NC S
   Mary A.   17 F NC S
   Martha E.   15 F NC S

   100 A improved land, 105 A unimpr, value: $1500
   2 slaves

1045.1063 George A CLOTFELTER 32 M NC farmer 800
   Isabella CLOTFELTER   27 F NC
   John A.   1 M NC

   75 A improved land, 105 A unimpr, valued at $800
   2 slaves

1046.1064 Daniel D SHUFORD 33 M NC farmer
   Margaret G. SHUFORD   19 F NC
   Laura Jane   2 F NC
   Mary E.   9/12 F NC
   Elisabeth SHUFORD   66 F NC 400

   [Note: he is son of Daniel Shuford, WB I:53 1839;
     Elizabeth is his mother: Daniel Shuford to
   Elizabeth Savage 11 Jan 1800.]
   Daniel: 50 A improved land, 100 A unimpr, valued
      at $400

1047.1065 Cicero A MORE 42 M NC farmer 600
   Sarah MORE   36 F NC
   Margaret C.   16 F NC   cont.

William A.	14 M NC S	
Mary E.	12 F NC	
John H.	10 M NC S	
Jane C.	8 F NC	
Samuel M.	5 M NC	
James K.	3 M NC	
Sarah E.C	1 F NC	

56 A improved land, 100 A unimpr, valued at $600

1048.1066 Ruel McNEELY 50 M NC farmer
Eliza McNEELY   44 F NC
Mary A.   24 F NC
James K.   22 M NC
Hugh W.G.   20 M NC
Ester R.   16 F NC S
John R.   12 M NC S
Matilda E.   10 F NC S
Eleanor J.   2 F NC
Elisabeth   78 F NC

145 A improved land, 175 A unimpr, valued at $1,000, 4 slaves

1049.1067 Hugh GRAY 80 M NC farmer
Ester GRAY   75 F NC
Ester   28 F NC

1050.1068 Robert WILSON 45 M NC black smith
Elmira WILSON   29 F NC
James M.   6 M NC
SARAH C.   2 F NC
.1069. Rial NANNEY   24 M NC black smith
Mary NANNEY   22 F NC
William W.   4 M NC
Sarah E.   1 F NC

1051.1070 James CHRISTY 57 M NC farmer
Lettitia CHRISTY   38 F NC (X)
Sarah C.   8 F NC S
Emeline   7 F NC S
Mary A.   4 F NC
Else R.   2 F NC
James S.   1/12 M NC

[MB:James Christy/ Letitia McLaughlin 9 Jan 1839
13 A improved land valued at $30

1052.1071 Robert H McLAUGHLIN 63 M NC farmer 50
Elsa T. McLAUGHLIN   62 F VA
Mary A.   26 F NC
James H.   24 M NC labourer
Nancy H.   23 F NC
Silas M.   18 M NC labourer

166 A improved land, 170 A unimpr, valued at $500
1 slave

1053.1072 James K McNEELY 42 M NC farmer 800
Margaret McNEELY   42 F NC
Burgas   16 M NC S
Carmi K.   14 M NC S
James A.   18 M NC S

Maxwell L.R.   5 M NC
Thomas G.   20 M NC

140 A improved land, 140 A unimpr, valued at $800
4 slaves

1054.1073 Samuel McLAUGHLIN 27 M NC farmer 150
Margaret C. McLAUGHLIN   28 F NC (X)
Samuel D.R.   1 M NC
Elisabeth McLAUGHLIN   32 F NC (X)

[MB: Samuel W McLaughlin to Margaret C Korriker
     7 Feb 1848]
28 A improved land valued at $126

1055.1074 John H McLAUGHLIN 35 M NC farmer
Mary C. McLAUGHLIN   21 F NC
Margaret D.   2 F NC
Edward WILLAFORD   17 M NC labourer

28 A improved land valued at $168

1056.1075 James EARNHEART 61 M NC farmer 1,200
[178] David EARNHEART   31 M NC labourer
William   14 M NC S
Ester D.   18 F NC S

100 A improved land, 112 A unimpr, value:$1200
5 slaves

<u>p. 178, School District #3, 27 Sept. 1850</u>

1057.1076 John A CHRISTY 37 M NC (X) farmer
Albertine E. CHRISTY   27 F NC
John H. A. McLAUGHLIN   7 M NC S
Elisabeth L.   5 F NC S
Mary E. CHRISTY   2 F NC
William L.   1 M NC

[MB: John A Christy to Albertine E McLaughlin 30
Mar 1847]
20 A improved land valued at $100

1058.1077 John L FREEZE 32 M NC farmer
Margaret M. FEZE   31 F NC

[MB:John L Freeze/Margaret M Poston 12 May 1849]
70 A improved land, 121 A unimpr, valued at $800
1 slave

1059.1078 Adam FREEZE 57 M NC wagonmaker, partially
                                          insane
Kiziah FREEZE   52 F NC
Margaret E.   17 F NC

[MB: Adam Freeze to Cashiah Laurance 24 Feb 1814]

1060.1079 John M. LORANCE 50 M NC 2,000
Elisabeth LORANCE   47 F NC
Jane C.   21 F NC S
Rufus N.   19 M NC S
James C   17 M NC S   cont.

Darkus C.   15 F NC S
Martha A.A.   13 F NC S
Harriet N.   11 F NC S
William B.   9 M NC S
Samuel A.   6 M NC

125 A improved land, 228 unimpr, valued at $2000
8 slaves

1061.1080 Jane BAXTER   78 F NC
  Polly BAXTER   68 F NC
  Eleanor BAXTER   60 F NC

1062.1081 Joshua LOWRANCE 82 M NC 500
  Rebecca   43 F NC
  Jane E. MILLER   24 F NC

  126 A improved land, 70 A unimpr, valued at $500

1063.1082 William McCORMICK 53 M VA blacksmith
  Eleanor McCORMICK   51 F NC
  David G.   25 F NC
  Edwin C.   18 M NC S
  Hiram A.   14 M NC S
  Eleanor M.   11 F NC S

1064.1083 James NEAL 58 M NC farmer 2,000
  Mary NEAL   58 F NC
  Sarah M.   33 F NC
  Andrew M.   29 M NC
  Elisabeth M.   28 F NC
  James W.   26 M NC S student deaf mute
  John R.   24 M NC labourer
  Elim W.   22 M NC student deaf mute
  Martha C.A   14 F NC

  248 A improved land, 281 unimpr, value:$2,000
  7 slaves

1065.1084 John F CLOTFELTER 33 M NC farmer 1,200
  Jane C. CLOTFELTER   33 F NC
  Mary Jane   2/12 F NC

[Note: son of George Clotfelter, WB K:47]
100 A improved land, 114 unimpr, value:$2100
5 slaves

1066.1085 Nancy CLOTFELTER 67 F NC
  [Note: widow of George Clotfelter, WB K:47]
  3 slaves

1867.1086 Michael W GOODMAN 30 M NC farmer
  Mary A. GOODMAN   30 F NC
  Thomas D.F.   2 M NC
  James D.   5 M NC

[MB:Michael W Goodman/Mary Ann Graham 23 Apr 1842]
43 A improved land, 43 A unimpr, valued at $1,000
2 slaves

1868.1087 Magdalene CLOTFELTER 40 F NC (X) 400
  Mary C.   14 F NC S
  Martha P.   13 F NC S cont.

Wilamina A.   10 F NC S
John T.   7 M NC S
David F.   4 M NC
Peter F. WAGONER   24 M NC farmer

  75 A improved land, 55 A unimpr, valued at $400

1869.1088 Henry L SHOFF 28 M NC farmer 1,300
  Susan SHOFF   28 F NC
  Otho H.   6 M NC
  Mary J.E.   4 F NC
  Henry E.   10/12 M NC

  100 A improved land, 120 A unimpr, value:$1300
  1 slave

1070.1089. Moses CLOTFELTER   34 M NC farmer
  Jane E. CLOTFELTER   26 F NC
  Cornelia A.   4 F NC
  Martha J.   1 F NC
  Sarah A. FREEZE   19 F NC
  Miles N. FREEZE   15 M NC S

[MB:Moses Clodfelter to Jane E Frieze 1 Jan 1845;
son of George, WB I:29]
132 A improved land, 60 A unimpr, valued at $600

1071.1090 Alfred M GOODMAN 28 M NC farmer 750
  Elisabeth GOODMAN   28 F NC
  William M.   3 M NC
  Samuel D.   1 M NC

[MB: Alfred M Goodman to Elizabeth Clodfelter 19
    Dec 1845]
34 A improved land, 60 A unimpr, valued at $750
2 slaves

1072.1091 Barbara BARR 38 F NC (X) 1,500
  Margaret L.   18 F NC S
  Mary W.   17 F NC S
  Jane L.   15 F NC S
  Charlotte E.   13 F NC S
  Isabella F.   9 F NC S
  Malinda C.   7 F NC S
  William M. OVERCASH 12 M NC S
  Rachel MOOR   38 F NC
[179] John B. MILLS   62 M NC 100

[Note: she is the widow of John Barr, WB I:238]
66 A improved land, 110 A unimpr, value: $2,000
5 slaves

p. 179, School District #3, 28 Sept. 1850

1073.1092 David UPRIGHT 62 M NC farmer 1,000
  Elisabeth UPRIGHT   63 F NC
  Catharine   33 F NC
  Mary M.   32 F NC
  John   31 M NC
  Margaret   28 F NC
  Elisabeth M.   25 F NC
  Susanna   22 F NC   cont.

[MB:David Upright/Elizabeth Albright 9 Jan 1816]
75 A improved land, 140 A unimpr, value;$1,000
1 slave

1074.1093 James E ANDREW 39 M NC farmer 800
  Mary S. ANDREW   31 F NC
  George A.   10 M NC S
  James A. BRADSHAW   38 M NC teacher of vocal
                                        music

  70 A improved land, 70 A unimpr, valued at $800
  3 slaves

1075.1094 Samuel S UPRIGHT 28 M NC tailor
  Catherine UPRIGHT   25 F NC (X)
  Cornelius J. A.   3 M NC
  David B.   1 M NC
  James C. OVERCASH   13 M NC S

  [MB:Samuel S Upright to Catharine Sechler 29 Sept
     1844]

1076.1095 John F McCORKLE 46 M NC farmer 6,000
  Elisabeth B. McCORKLE   32 F NC
  Catharine T. McCORKLE   16 F NC S
  Sarah T.   11 F NC S
  Mary C.   9 F NC S
  Elisabeth V.   1/12 F NC
  Louisa A. KILPATRICK   20 F NC

  [MB:John F McCorkle to Jane C. Barr 26 Oct 1830;
   Jane d 23 Aug 1846 CW]
  250 A improved land, 204 A unimpr, valued at
     $3,000, 11 slaves

1077.1096 Thomas E DAVIS 33 M NC P Clergyman 200
  Harriet L. DAVIS   24 F TN
  1 slave

1078.1097 William J MILLER 31 M NC farmer 600
  Mary L. MILLER   26 F NC
  Margaret A.S.   1 F NC
  Joel M. FREEZE   21 M NC labourer

  50 A improved land, 50 A unimpr, value:$600

1079.1098 Andrew COOK 28 M NC overseer
  Mary COOK   22 F NC
  Mary Jane   2 F NC

  300 A improved land, 250 A unimpr, value:$3,400

1080.1099 Thomas K POSTON 27 M NC (X) labourer
  Maria POSTON   23 F NC (X)
  Mary   3 F NC
  Jane   1 F NC

1081.1100 Jacob F GOODMAN 27 M NC
  Mary B. GOODMAN   32 F NC
  Harriet L.   3 F NC
  John K.   8/12 M NC

[MB:Jacob F Goodman to Mary B Knox 14 Oct 1843]
30 A improved land, 23 A unimpr, valued at $1000
1 slave

1082.1101 James COWAN 52 M NC farmer 3,000
  Nancy L. COWAN   43 F NC
  John S.   14 M NC S
  Robert T.   12 M NC S
  James P.   9 M NC S
  Thomas L.   5 M NC S
  Jane R. GILLESPIE   31 F PA
  Laura E. GILLESPIE   12 F NC S
  Martha A.   10 F NC S
  Carmi GILLESPIE   37 M NC

  [MB:James Cowan to Nancy L Gillespie 22 Dec 1828;
   she is the dau of Robert Gillespie, WB I:152]
  200 A improved land, 225 A unimpr, valued at
     $3,000, 15 slaves

1083.1102 Levi A BOSTIAN 21 M NC blacksmith
  Catharine D. BOSTIAN   17 F NC
  Sarah HODGINS   49 F NC (X)
  Clinton HODGINS   15 M NC
  .1103. Samuel D RANKIN   28 M NC physician 3,000
  Mary E. RANKIN   28 F NC
  Samuel D.   3 M NC
  Sylvester C.   1 M NC
  Sarah GILLESPIE   68 F NC

  [MB:Samuel D Rankin/Mary E Gillespie 8 Nov 1843]
  S Rankin: 401 A improved land, 175 A unimproved,
     valued at $3,000, 19 slaves

1084.1104 Davey C FOSTER 38 F NC 1,500
  Mary E.   12 F NC
  George S.   4 M NC

  [Note: she is the widow of Jesse Foster, WB I:231
     and was a Cowan]   2 slaves
  116 A improved land, 80 A unimpr, value: $1,500

1085.1105 Hiram SLOOP 26 M NC farmer
  Matilda SLOOP   20 F NC
  Adolphus J.   1 M NC

1086.1106 Samuel BARR 58 M NC farmer 2,000
  Matilda BARR   58 F NC
  James S.   23 M NC divinity student
  John A.   19 M NC student

  250 A improved land, 250 A unimpr, valued at
     $2,000, 17 slaves

1087.1107 Samuel HART 56 M NC
  Frances M.C. HART   52 F NC
  Sarah A.G   22 F NC
  Margaret E.J.   18 F NC S
  John S.E.   16 M NC S
  Martha J.R.   13 F NC S
  John KESTLER   29 M NC stage driver

                    cont.   cont.

[MB: Samuel Hart to Francis Boocker 11 Jan 1825]
100 A improved land, 210 A unimpr, valued at
    $3,000, 2 slaves

1088.1108 Sarah D HART   25 F NC 800
    John L. HART   23 M NC
    Ester HART   21 F NC
    Martha A. HART   20 F NC S
    Andrew A. HART   19 F NC S
    Samuel A. D. HART   17 M NC S
[180] James M. S. HART   14 M NC S

Andrew A Hart: 80 A improved land, 40 A
unimproved, valued at $800

1089.1109 Joel CLOTFELTER 39 M NC farmer
    Elisabeth CLOTFELTER 38 F NC (X)
    Jane E.   15 F NC S
    Ann   13 F NC S
    George L.   11 M NC
    Margaret A.   4 F NC
    Samarinus   1 F NC

    50 A improved land, 250 A unimpr, value:$800

1090.1110 Thomas F BAITY 40 M NC physician 1,600
    Ruhama BAITY   37 F NC
    James N.   9 M NC S
    Ann Eliza   7 F NC S
    Mary Jemima   3 F NC
    Martha R.   10/12 F NC
    William OVERCAST   16 M NC S labourer

    150 A improved land, 110 A unimpr, value:$800
    4 slaves

1091.1111 Ephraim IRWIN   64 M NC blacksmith
    Mary IRWIN   55 F NC
    Isabella E.   34 F NC
    Jane A.   27 F NC
    Andrew B.   21 M NC S labourer
    William F.   19 M NC partially deaf
                            idiotic
    Margaret E.   17 F NC S
    Martha T.   12 F NC S

    50 A improved land, 50 A unimpr, value: $200

1092.1112 John M.W. BIGGERS 29 M NC farmer 250
    Sarah BIGGERS   26 F NC
    Martha J.   2 F NC
    Dorothy A.   5/12 F NC

    25 A improved land, 65 A unimpr, value: $250

1093.1113 Marcus E REESE 51 M NC farmer 600
    Dorothy C. REESE   53 F VA
    Cinthia C.   21 F NC S
    Thomas E.   20 M NC tutor

[Note: son of David Reese, WB H:376]
60 A improved land, 50 A unimpr, value:$600

1094.1114 William KESTLER 37 M NC farmer
    Elisabeth KESTLER   37 F NC
    Joseph B.   13 M NC S
    John W.   12 M NC S
    Sarah C.   8 F NC S
    Caroline M.C.   7 F NC S
    James C.K.   4 M NC
    Nancy C. BIGGERS   24 F NC

    30 A improved land valued at $180

1095.1115 John A LOWRANCE 39 M NC farmer
    Jane C. LOWRANCE   59 F NC
    William M.   14 M NC
    John M.   13 M NC
    Ruel W.   11 M NC
    James C.   9 M NC
    Franklin A.   6 M NC
    Samuel L.   4 M NC
    Doctor L.   1 M NC

    100 A improved land, 150 A unimpr, value
        $1,200, 1 slave

1096.1116 Joseph OVERCASH 36 M NC farmer 500
    Barbara OVERCASH   35 F NC (X)
    James W.   13 M NC S
    Mary A.M.   11 F NC S
    John S.   9 M NC S
    Ruben A.   8 M NC S
    Sarah C.   6 F NC S
    George F.   4 M NC
    Margaret A.   2 F NC
    Caroline E.   1 F NC
    Edwin WILLAFORD   19 M NC labourer

    65 A improved land, 48 A unimproved, value:$500

1097.1117 William NISLER 24 M NC farmer
    Mary A. NISLER   22 F NC (X)
    John L.   2 M NC
    Thomas M.C.G.   8/12 M NC

1098.1118 Sarah C McKNIGHT   69 F PA
    Hugh F. McKNIGHT   39 M NC 1,800
    Mary A. McKNIGHT   29 F NC
    Sarah C.   7 F NC S
    Dorothy C.   5 F NC S
    Margaret A.   3 F NC
    Eliza A.   1 M NC
    David H.   0/12 M NC

[MB:Hugh F McKnight & Mary Ann Reese 23 Sept 1841.
 See will of Hugh McKnight, WB K:59; he d 1 June
 1847 CW]
100 A improved land, 130 A unimpr, value: $1800
3 slaves

1099.1119 William F MARTIN 37 M NC farmer 400
    Matilda C. MARTIN   37 F NC
    Catherine E.W.   9 F NC S
    Joseph S.A.   6 M NC S   cont.

Levi A.C.   4 M NC
Samuel M.L.   3 M NC

1100.1120 Elisabeth JAMISON 70 F NC
  John E. JAMISON   32 M NC farmer 1,200
  Milas S.   27 M NC farmer 450

[Note: widow and sons of James Jamison, WB K:52]
John E: 90 A improved land, 175 A unimpr, valued
    at $1,200, 9 slaves
Miles S: 15 A improved land, 135 A unimpr, valued
    at $700

1101.1121 James F JAMISON 42 M NC farmer 1,000
[181] Margaret JAMISON   30 F NC
  Mary A.   8 F NC S
  Sarah J.   6 F NC S
  Margaret E.   3 F NC
  John McKNIGHT   32 M NC carpenter

[Note: son of James Jamison, WB K:52]
60 A improved land, 140 A unimpr, value: $1,000
5 slaves

<u>p. 181, School District #2, 1 Oct. 1850</u>

1102.1122 Eli M STUART 40 M NC (X) farmer
   15 A improved land, 7 A unimpr, value:$45

1103.1123 Alfred S GRAY 39 M NC farmer
  Zilah GRAY   38 F NC
  Robert T.   12 M NC S
  Edwin L.H.   10 M NC S
  John C.   8 M NC S
  James T.   6 M NC
  Hugh W.   4 M NC

1104.1124 Thomas S ATWELL 37 M NC blacksmith 850
  Elisabeth D. ATWELL   36 F NC
  William L.   16 M NC S
  Obadiah W.   14 M NC S
  David A.   13 M NC S
  Mary A.   12 F NC S
  John C.   9 M NC S
  Charles F.   8 M NC S
  Joseph L.   1 M NC
  George ANTHONY   16 M NC blacksmith

[MB:Thomas S Atwell to Anne E. Woodson 13 Sept
1832, to Elizabeth Shuping 31 Jan 1846. Ann
Eliza d. 17 June 1845 and is identified as wife
of Capt. Thomas A., <u>CW</u>] 3 slaves
   50 A improved land, 157 unimpr, valued at $700

1105.1125 David KILPATRICK 46 M NC farmer 4,000
  Nancy KILPATRICK   41 F NC
  Sarah A.   19 F NC S
  Agnus L.   17 F NC S
  William A.   15 M NC S
  John J. MK   10 M NC S
  Newton L.   6 M NC
  Mary L.N. KILPATRICK   7 F NC S   cont.

150 A improved land, 253 unimpr, value:$1,453
26 slaves

1106.1126 Alexander CROSBY 50 M NC insane

1107.1127 John T WILLAFORD 28 M VA farmer
  Rachel WILLAFORD   22 F NC (X)
  Elisabeth   4 F NC
  Martha A.T.   2 F NC
  William A.W.   7/12 M NC

   25 A improved land, 67 A unimpr, value:$600

1108.1128 Richard DAVIS 34 M NC farmer
  Elisabeth D. DAVIS   39 F NC
  Mary Jane   14 F NC
  William P.O.   9 M NC S
  Adelade A.C.   7 F NC S
  James M.A.   4 M NC S
  Richard J.B.   2 M NC

   50 A unimproved land valued at $200

1109.1129 John W ATWELL 41 M NC farmer 1,000
  Eleanor G. ATWELL   42 F NC
  Columbus F.   19 M NC S labourer
  Mary E.   17 F NC
  Nancy E.   15 F NC S
  Martha A.   12 F NC S
  Alphonso L.   9 M NC S
  George A.   7 M NC S
  Joseph E.   4 M NC S
  Sarah L.   2 F NC
  Louisa R.   3/12 F NC

[MB:John W Atwell to Ellen Clotfelter 9 Feb 1830]
   60 A improved land, 90 A unimpr, value: $1,000
4 slaves

1110.1130 Martha M MASTERS 72 F NC 100
  Mary F.   36 F NC
  Mary Jane   7 F NC S

1111.1131 John M BROWN 37 M NC (X) farmer 50
  Catherine C. BROWN   38 F NC
  William L.   14 M NC
  Joseph F.   11 M NC
  George A.   10 M NC
  John M.   7 M NC
  James L.   5 M NC
  Robert N.   4 M NC
  Margaret C.   1/12 F NC

   60 A improved land valued at $120

1112.1132 Assenith CROSBY 42 F NC 210
  Mary G. CROSBY   33 F NC 280
  Mary Jane   10 F NC S

[Note: see will of Sarah McKnight, WB H:362]

1113.1133 William ELLIS 60 M NC (X) shoemaker

1114.1134 Willis ELLIS 35 M NC farmer 200
    Mary A. ELLIS   27 F NC
    John W.   9 M NC S
    Mary M.   6 F NC
    Mary J.   1 F NC
    Margaret SMITH   50 F NC
    Sarah A.   15 F NC

    [MB: Willis Ellis to Mary A White 2 May 1840]
    55 A improved land, 25 A unimpr, value:$200

1115.1135 John W LEZER 32 M NC farmer 400
    Susan LEZER   34 F NC
    Julia A.C.   9 F NC S
    Corlena A.   7 F NC S
    Isabella A.   4 F NC
    George C.   4/12 M NC

    40 A improved land, 70 A unimpr, value:$400
    7 slaves

<u>p. 182, School District # 2, 2 Oct. 1850</u>

1116.1136 Elisabeth SMITH 84 F MD (X) 250
    Ann ADAMS   75 F NC (X)

1117.1137 Hiram SMITH 48 M VA (X) farmer 300
    Catherine SMITH   37 F NC (X)
    John J.   18 M NC
    Elisabeth   16 F NC
    Hiram M.   14 M NC
    Washington P.   12 M NC S
    William   10 M NC
    Margaret   8 F NC
    Ann   6 F NC
    Caroline B.   4 F NC

    50 A improved land, 34 A unimpr, value:$300

1118.1138 Richard A SMITH 21 M NC (X) m
    Elisabeth SMITH   21 F NC m

    [MB:Richard A Smith/Elizabeth Niceler 9 Apr 1850]

1119.1139 Jacob SLOOP 37 M NC tailer
    Mary SLOOP   34 F NC
    David A.   11 M NC S
    Phillip A.   9 M NC S
    Mary C.D.   4 F NC
    Columbus S.   1 M NC
    William A.A.   5/12 M NC

    62 A improved land, 130 A unimpr, value:$390
    3 slaves

1120.1140 Alexander SLOOP 31 M NC farmer
    Juda SLOOP   31 F NC
    Catherine E.J.   7 F NC
    Lorean F.S.   4 F NC

    [MB:Alexander Sloop & Judy Sechler 25 Apr 1842]
    18 A improved land, 20 A unimpr, value: $100

1121.1141 David K WOODS 29 M NC farmer 250
    Joshua B. WOODS   26 M NC 250
    Terissa WOODS   38 F NC 230
    Elisabeth WOODS   33 F NC 230
    Jane WOODS   30 F NC 230
    James CROSBY   13 M NC

1122.1141 John LEAZER 43 M NC farmer 2,500
    Isabella LEAZER   40 F NC
    Mary V.   14 F NC S
    Celestia   12 F NC S
    John C.C.   8 M NC S
    Augustus   7 M NC S
    [MB:John Leazer Jr/Isabella Jamison 1 Jun 1835]
    225 A improved land, 275 A unimpr, value:$2500

1123.1143 Christian SECKLER 27 M NC farmer
    Susan SECKLER   26 F NC
    Avarilla E.   2 F NC
    Lodenaia F.   2/12 F NC
    Fany SECKLER   20 F NC (X)
    Cornelius SECKLER   18 M NC S
    Sophia SECKLER   16 F NC S
    Elisabeth SECKLER   54 F NC (X) 200
    50 A improved land, 130 A unimpr, value:$500

1124.1144 Daniel LEAZER 41 M NC farmer 200
    William H.   15 M NC labourer
    Margaret A.   13 F NC
    50 A improved land, 120 A unimpr, value:$200

1125.1145 John BROADWAY 52 M VA
    Ferebe   29 F NC
    Thursa   25 F NC
    Elisabeth   12 F NC

1126.1146 Henry CORIHER 67 M PA (X) farmer 390
    Catherine CORIHER   55 F NC (X)
    Rufus A.   25 M NC
    Jane E.   23 F NC
    Harriet A.   20 F NC
    Clary A.   18 F NC
    [Note:will of Jacob Corriher, WB H:487;Henry
    Corriker to Catherine Coleman 17 Nov 1823]
    100 A improved land, 95 A unimpr, value:$390

1127.1147 George CORHIER 37 M NC farmer 225
    Sarah CORHIER   39 F NC (X)
    Nancy C.   15 F NC S
    William A.   14 M NC
    Jane H.   12 F NC S
    Henry C.   10 M NC
    James F.   9 M NC S
    Margaret C.   7 F NC S
    George W.   4 M NC
    Laton J.   2 M NC
    Thomas C.   1 M NC
    [Note:will of Jacob Corriher, WB H:487]
    60 A improved land, 39 A unimpr, value:$225

1128.1148 John LEAZER Senr 73 M PA farmer 600
    Elisabeth LEAZER   74 F NC (X)
    Jane   28 F NC

100 A improved land, 115 A unimpr, value:$600

1129.1149 Martin LEAZER 65 M PA farmer 250
    Catherine LEAZER   61 F NC (X)
    Levi A. LEAZER   29 M NC farmer
    Catherine LEAZER   28 F NC
    Martha J.V.   1/12 F NC

    [MB:Levi A Leazer & Catharine Upright 16 Aug 1848]
    54 A improved land, 22 A unimpr, value: $250

1130.1150 Truth WOODS   62 M NC
    Mary WOODS   70 F NC

    [Note: son of David Woods, see WB G:154]
    175 A improved land, 25 A unimpr, value:$500
    6 slaves

1131.1151 William WOODS 64 M NC farmer 2,000
    James M.   34 M NC farmer
    Tirza A.   28 F NC
    Richard L.   26 M NC farmer
    Helen L.   20 F NC

    200 A improved land, 145 A unimpr, valued at
        $2,000, 11 slaves

p. 183, School District #1, 3 Oct. 1850

1132.1152 William McLEAN 54 M NC tanner & currier
1,300
    Sarah McLEAN   54 F NC idiotic
    James I.   23 M NC farmer
    Sophia E.   25 F NC
    Calvin S.   18 M NC S tanner
    George W.   16 M NC S labourer
    Robert G.   15 M NC S labourer
    Sarah M.   13 F NC S
    Joseph F.   10 M NC S
    .1153. William B McLEAN 29 M NC farmer m
    Jane J. McLEAN   25 F NC m

[MB: William McLean & Sarah B Graham 26 Apr 1817;
William B McLean & Jane J Cochran 2 Oct 1849]

    150 A improved land, 196 A unimpr,

1133.1154 Tobias BEAVER 25 M NC farmer m
    Jemima P. BEAVER   19 F NC m

    [MB:Tobius Beaver & Jamima P Smith 25 Sept 1849]

1134.1155 Jacob GOUGER 59 M NC farmer
    Elisabeth GOUGER   59 F NC
    Gilbert MILLS   45 M NC farmer
    Sarah E. MILLS   34 F NC
    Theophilus C.   4 M NC
    Jacob   7/12 M NC

    100 A improved land, 50 A unimpr, value: $300

1135.1156 John A WILLIFORD 41 M VA farmer
    Ruth WILLIFOED   40 F NC (X)

Martha A.   16 F NC S
William H.   15 F NC S
Mary H.   11 F NC S
James T.   9 M NC S
Anderson J.   6 M NC
Franklin H.   3 M NC
Harry D.W.   2/12 M NC

75 A improved land, 47 A unimpr, value:$620

1136.1157 Elisabeth BROWN 75 F NC 400
    Nancy CROSBY   20 F NC

1137.1158 Mildred KERR 75 F NC
    John E. DEATON   25 M NC overseer

    [Note: widow of William H Kerr, WB I:232, 1844]
    no acreage but livestock, 12 slaves

1138.1159 Richard GRAHAM 37 M NC 1,000
    Pricilla E.   35 F NC
    William W.   11 M NC S
    George G.   8 M NC S
    Richard L.   2/12 M NC
    Maria L. GRAHAM   31 F NC

    [MB:Richard Graham & Priscilla Graham 11 Dec 1837]
    120 A improved land, 92 A unimpr, value: $1,000
    6 slaves
    Miss Maria L: 90 A improved land, 27 A unimpr,
        valued at $550, 11 slaves

1139.1160 Daniel RUMPLE 36 M NC miller
    Mary L. RUMPLE   32 F NC
    Mary C.   15 F NC S
    Nancy A.   13 F NC S
    Martha J.   7 F NC S
    William N.   6 M NC S
    Robert M.   4 M NC S
    George M.   1 M NC

1140.1161 John SMITH   47 M NC farmer
    Mary SMITH   36 F NC
    George A.   12 M NC S
    Mary N.   10 F NC S
    Martha A.   8 F NC S
    Joseph W.   5 M NC S
    Chas. L.   2 M NC
    Nancy J.A.   1 F NC
    Gains C.   5/12 M NC
    Margaret SHINN   53 F NC (X)

    45 A improved land, 105 A unimpr, value: $300

1141.1162 Enoch WATTS   43 M NC (X) shoemaker
    Margaret WATTS   51 F NC (X)
    Joel H.   14 M NC
    Margaret R.   13 F NC
    Rufus F.   12 M NC
    William G.   11 M NC
    Sarah H.   9 M NC
    Mary J.   8 F NC
    Jesse D.   6 M NC   cont.

Robert W.   4 M NC

30 A improved land valued at $100

1142.1163 John WOODSIDES 59 M NC farmer
  Lucy WOODSIDES   48 F NC (X)
  Aseenith   17 F NC S
  James R.   15 M NC S
  Nancy J.   9 F NC S

1143.1164 Mary WOODSIDES 56 F NC 100

1144.1165 Elias RAIMER 38 M NC (X) farmer
  Ann RAIMER   37 F NC (X)
  Mary S.   17 F NC S
  Jemima S.   15 F NC S
  Clarissa E.   13 F NC S
  Sarah C.   10 F NC S
  Margaret A.   3 F NC
  John M.C.   9/12 M NC

30 A improved land valued at $100

1145.1166 David A MAXWELL 33 M NC physician 1,000
  Mary A. MAXWELL   25 F NC
  John S. MAXWELL   27 M NC physician

77 A improved land, 190 unimpr, value:$1,000
5 slaves

1146.1167 John M JAMASON 81 M NC farmer 625

150 A improved land, 100 A unimpr, value:$625
8 slaves

p.184, School District #1, 4 Oct. 1850

1147.1168 Stephen A WINECOFF 36 M NC labourer
  Barbara WINECOFF   31 F NC
  David E.M.   6 M NC

1148.1168 Daniel COCHARAN 52 M NC farmer 500
  Sarah W. COCHARAN   45 F NC
  Robert A.   22 M NC labourer
  John F.   15 M NC S labourer
  Mary M.   13 F NC S
  Cyrus A.   10 M NC S
  Hiram S.   7 M NC S
  Nancy R.   3 F NC

[MB: William Cochran & Sarah Fleming 29 Mar 1824
William Cochran: 65 A improved land, 35 A
   unimpr, valued at $500

1149.1170 John F EDMISTON 25 M NC blacksmith 60
  Edith EDMISTON   25 F NC
  Sarah G.   6 F NC
  Robert P. BENSON   19 M NC blacksmith

[MB: John F Edmiston to Eady Ellis 5 Dec 1842]
4 wagons valued at $260

1150.1171 Cyrena EDMISTON 54 F NC 150
  Samuel R.   25 M NC blacksmith
  Mary A.C.   13 F NC S

[Note: dau of Allison Fleming, WB I:1. Samuel
Edmiston to Sirena Fleming 30 Oct 182]
1 buggy valued at $20, various other articles
   valued at $333

1151.1172 John RILEY 43 M NC wagonmaker 600
  Temperance RILEY   43 F NC
  Sarah A.   14 F NC
  Jane   11 F NC S
  John A.W.A.   7 M NC S
  Mary A.   3 F NC
  Columbus W.   9/12 M NC
  Eliza Elisabeth   22 F NC

45 A improved land, 87 A unimpr, valued at $600

1152.1174 Ezra WITHERSPOON 45 F NC farmer 2,000

75 A improved land, 125 A unimpr, valued at
   $2,000, 1 slave

1153.1175 William H ANDREW 32 M NC farmer
  Jemima ANDREW   31 F NC
  Smily   3 M NC
  Elisabeth   2 F NC
  James   9/12 M NC

1154.1175 Cornelia WOODSIDES 45 F NC
  Rufus W.   21 M NC
  James A.   17 M NC
  Martha P.   16 F NC
  Archibald   13 M NC S
  Benjamin   11 M NC S
  Margaret C.   8 F NC S
  John C.   6 M NC S

[Note: She d bef Aug 1850, WB K:114]
45 A improved land, 23 A unimpr, value:$200

1155.1176 Charles CAUBLE 49 M NC blacksmith 100

1156.1177 Hugh PARKS 58 M NC farmer 3,500
  Margaret PARKS   52 F NC
  John P.   14 M NC S
  David McK.   13 M NC S
  Elisabeth S.   7 F NC S
  Elisabeth PARKS   54 F NC 125
  John P. DEMASQUES   15 M NC S

[Note: Hugh & Elizabeth's mother was Jane Parkes,
WB H:642]
125 A improved land, 540 A unimpr, value:$2000
8 slaves
flouring: 234 bbl of flour valued at $1,023
corn mill: 3,960 bu cornmeal valued at $1,380

1157.1178 John M LEEZER 31 M NC millwright 1,000
  Mary LEEZER   57 F NC (X)
  William A. LEEZER   21 M NC student   cont.

150 A improved land, 100 A unimpr, value:$800

1158.1179 James S FLEMING 35 M NC farmer
  Margaret T. FLEMING   34 F NC
  Mary   9 F NC S
  Jane C.   7 F NC
  Margaret   5 F NC
  Upheme   1 F NC

[MB:James S Fleming/Margaret T Leazer 19 Feb 1840]
  50 A improved land valued at $100

1159.1180 Solomon BEAVER 28 M NC farmer
  Mary E. BEAVER   24 F NC
  Martha E.   3 F NC

  Julia A.   1 F NC

[MB:Solomon Beaver & Mary E Leazer 19 Mar 1846]
  30 A improved land valued at $100

1160.1181 John MILLER 44 M NC shoemaker
  Anna MILLER   41 F NC (X)
  Julius A.   16 M NC S farmer
  Mary A.   15 F NC S
  Jacob W.   14 M NC S
  Ebenezer H.) twin   12 M NC S
  Francis M.) twin   12 M NC S
  Ibzan A.   10 M NC S
  Andrew A.   8 M NC S
  Samuel A.   4 M NC

1161.1182 Henry LEEZER 55 M NC (X) farmer
  Elisabeth LEEZER   49 F NC (X)
  Nancy E.   20 F NC S
  Rachel T.   16 F NC S
  Dewey P.   14 F NC S
  William F.   12 M NC S
  David M.   6 M NC S

1162.1183 John BEAVER 49 M NC farmer 1,500
  Elisabeth BEAVER   54 F NC (X)
  Levi A.   19 M NC labourer
  Mary A.   16 F NC
  Delilah LIPE   30 F NC deaf mute

  100 A improved land, 250 A unimpr, value:$1,600

<u>p.185, School District #1, 4 Oct 1850</u>

1163.1184 Sarah MISENHEIMER 57 F NC (X)
  Leah   23 F NC (X)
  Amelia C.   17 F NC S
  Daniel L.   15 M NC S
  George A.N.   4 M NC

1164.1185 George SMITH 86 M PA farmer
  Nancy S.   57 F NC 40
  Elen   40 F NC 40
  Jane C.   15 F NC

  67 A improved land, 67 A unimpr, value:$600

1165.1186 George W SMITH 39 M NC farmer 600
  Susanna SMITH   34 F NC (X)
  Amos V.   12 M NC S
  Jacob S.   10 M NC S
  William H.   9 M NC S
  Henry C.   7 M NC S
  James I.   4 M NC
  Sarah E.P.   1 F NC

[MB: George W Smith to Susan Beaver 12 June 1837]
[agriculture scheduled copied as written]

1166.1187 Alexander DEAL 26 M NC farmer m
  Mary DEAL   27 F NC (X) M

[MB: Alexander Deal to Mary Lingle 12 Nov 1849]

1167.1188 Sidney H HART 24 M NC farmer 600
  Ester E. HART   22 F NC

[MB:Sydney H Hart & Esther E Baker 20 Dec 1849]
  35 A unimproved land valued at $141, 1 slave

1168.1189 Jacob SHULIBARINGER 40 M NC carpenter
1,000
  Mary A. SHULIBARINGER   29 F NC
  William S.   8 M NC S
  John L.   6 M NC S
  Sarah M.   3 F NC
  James E.   1/12 M NC
  Elisabeth C. BIGGERS   31 F NC
  Wilson H. McNEELY   16 M NC S labourer

  60 A improved land, 182 A unimpr, value:$1,000
  2 slaves

1169.1190 David R BRADSHAW 37 M NC carpenter 500
  Margaret BRADSHAW   44 F NC
  Leighton F.   15 M NC S
  Sarah E.A.   9 F NC S
  Laura L.   5 F NC S
  Julia A.V. CORRELL   12 F NC S

[MB:David <u>B</u> Bradshaw/Margaret Miller 4 May 1839]
  60 A improved land, 140 A unimpr, value:$500
  3 slaves
  flouring: 234 bbl vlaued at $1,170
  corn mill: 3960 bu valued at $1,386
  saw mill: 25,000 ft lumber valued at $500

1170.1191 Mary EVERETT   85 F VA (X)
  Frances B.   39 F VA (X)
  Nancy E.   36 F VA (X)

1171.1192 Mary McLAUGHLIN 56 F NC 100
  Anna McLAUGHLIN   51 F NC 100
  John W. SEERS   15 M NC S

[Note: these are daus of Samuel McLaughlin, WB
I:178]
  Mary & <u>Nancy</u> McLaughlin: 44 A improved land, 20
    A unimproved, valued at $200

1172.1193 John W McNEELY 43 M NC farmer 1,000
    Mary McNEELY   42 F NC

[MB:John W McNeely to Mary McNeely 24 Oct 1845;
he is son of Samuel McNeely, WB I:176]
    100 A improved land, 114 A unimpr, value:$1000
    8 slaves

1173.1194 George MENUS   50 M NC farmer
    Eveline MENUS   30 F NC (X)
    George M.   20 M NC S labourer
    John C.   18 M NC S labourer
    Nancy E.   19 F NC S
    Sally D.   16 F NC S
    Franklin E.   8 M NC
    William A.   5 M NC
    Fredrick M.   2 M NC

[MB: George Menius to Evaline Lamb 9 June 1841]
    116 A improved land, 50 A unimpr, value:$240

1174.1195 Fergus McLAUGHLIN 54 M NC farmer 1,000
    Elisabeth McLAUGHLIN   50 F NC
    Eli C.   17 M NC S
    Elisabeth L.   14 F NC S
    Marietta L.   12 F NC S
    Sarah C.   10 F NC S
    Terissa C.   7 F NC S
    James CARUTHERS   84 M NC
    Elisabeth CAROTHERS   77 F NC
    Martha McLAUGHLIN   53 F NC
    Julia U.   17 F NC

[MB: Fergus McLaughlin to Elizabeth Caruthers 22
Oct 1827; he is son of Samuel McLaughlin, WB
I:178]
    100 A improved land, 200 A unimpr, value:$1000
    Martha: 20 A improved land, 75 A unimpr, valued
        at $500

1175.1196 Elihu N POOL   31 M NC blacksmith 500
    Hannah N POOL   34 F NC
    Tirza M.K.   7 F NC S
    Margaret J.   3 F NC
    Tabitha A.A.   1 F NC

[MB:Elihu N Poole to Hannah M Freeze 28 Dec 1840;
he is grandson of John Van Poole, WB H:401]
    25 A improved land, 111 A unimpr, value: $500

1176.1197 David McNEELY   50 M NC farmer
    Ann McNEELY   49 F NC
    Jane M.   24 F NC
    Margaret C.   22 F NC
    Silas A.   17 M NC S
    John L.   13 M NC S

[MB: David McNeely to Ann Lorance 18 July 1825]
    no land but livestock

1177.1198 Joshua MILLER 25 M NC farmer 200
    Mary D. MILLER   21 F NC

[MB:Joshua Miller & Mary D Correll 15 Sept 1849]
    2 slaves

1178.1199 James H McNEELY 36 M NC farmer 800
    Rebecca A.   26 F NC
    James B.   6 M NC
    Jane E.   4 F NC
    John N. McNEELY   25 M NC teacher

[MB: James H McNeely to Rebeca Wilson 29 Sept
1840; James Harvey McNeely is son of James
McNeely, WB H:620]
    275 A improved land, 175 A unimpr, value:$800
    6 slaves

1179.1200 Samuel McLAUGHLIN 56 M NC farmer 200

    Ann McLAUGHLIN   61 F NC
    William H.   22 M NC labourer
[186]John M.   20 M NC S labourer
    Samuel COOPER   65 M NC farmer

[MB: Samuel McLaughlin Jr to Anny Cooper 20 Oct
1824; she is dau of William Cooper, WB G:170]
    125 A improved land, 75 A unimpr, value: $200

p. 186, School District #11, 7 Oct 1850

1180.1201 Elisabeth SILLIMAN 56 F NC
    John P. SILLIMAN   32 M NC farmer
    Mary MILLER   50 F NC
    William MILLER   19 M NC labourer

[MB:James Silliman/Elizabeth Miller 26 Mar 1817]

1181.1202 Samuel MILLER 54 M NC farmer 500
    Martha MILLER   57 F NC
    James   21 M NC
    Margaret   20 F NC
    Samuel L.   17 M NC S labourer
    Clarissa A.   15 F NC
    Rebecca MILLER   47 F NC

[MB:Samuel Miller & Martha Lowrance 14 Apr 1818]
    70 A improved land, 70 A unimpr, valued at $500

1182.1203 Henry BAKER 24 M NC miller 1,000
    Martha E. BAKER   27 F NC
    Laura L.   1 F NC

[MB:Henry Baker to Martha E Miller 27 Dec 1847]
    flouring: 345 bbl valued at $1,538
    corn mill: 2,062 bu valued at $613

1183.1204 William B REED   34 M NC
    Margaret REED   34 F NC
    Hugh R.   12 M NC S
    Samuel A.E.   10 M NC S
    Mary A.   5 F NC
    Alfred J.   1 M NC

cont.   cont.

[MB:William B Reed & Margaret C Laurance 11 May
    1836]
    30 A improved land, 40 A unimpr, value: $300

1184.1205 Nancy REED   60 F NC 200
    Mary E   33 F NC

1185.1206 Elisabeth HOUCK 62 F NC
    Mary M.C. HOUCK   32 F NC 80

[Note: Elizabeth Houck's will, prb. Nov 1850
mentions niece Mary C Houck and sister Mary M
Houck, WB K:122]

1186.1207 Margaret HOUCK 63 F NC 100
    William A. HOUCK   24 M NC teacher 100
    Hulda Julia   21 F NC

110 A improved land, 50 A unimpr, value:$260

1187.1208 Henry HOUCK 45 M NC farmer
    Mary A. HOUCK   44 F NC
    Margaret G. McCORKLE 37 F NC 100

[MB:Henry Houck to Mary A McCorkle 7 Dec 1824]
Margaret McCorkle: 35 A improved land value:$100

1188.1209 Edward SLOOP 23 M NC farmer 100 m
    Adaline C. SLOOP   28 F NC m

[MB:Edward Sloop/Adeline C Albright 7 Dec 1848]

1189.1210 John LORANCE   40 M NC farmer 300
    Elisabeth LORANCE   32 F NC
    Jane C.   9 F NC S
    Mary Anne   7 F NC S
    David A.)twin   5 M NC
    John S.)twin   5 M NC
    Sarah E.   5/12 F NC

[MB:John R Lowrance/Elizabeth Dickson 14 Aug 1839]
John R:15 A improved land, 40 A unimpr, value:$300

1190.1211 John CARIGAN 55 M NC farmer 1,000
    Sarah CARIGAN   52 F NC
    Margaret A.   23 F NC
    Elisabeth A.   21 F NC
    James F.   20 M NC S labourer
    Sarah C.   18 F NC S
    Mary Jane   15 F NC S
    Martha C.   12 F NC

[MB:John Carrigan & Sarah Caruthers 18 Sept 1822]
80 A improved land, 175 A unimpr, value:$1,000

1191.1212 Michael ALBRIGHT 47 M NC farmer 1,400
    Elisabeth ALBRIGHT   43 F NC (X)
    Mary A.   20 F NC
    Peter R.   18 M NC S labourer
    Susan E.   16 F NC
    Thomas A.   13 M NC S
    Catherine ALBRIGHT   65 F NC (X)   cont.

[MB:Michael Albright & Betsey Leatho 18 Aug 1828]
200 A improved land, 240 A unimpr, value:$1,400

1192.1213 Joseph B McNEELY 23 M NC farmer 1,800
    Mary A. McNEELY   22 F NC
    Mary McNEELY   64 F NC

[Note: Mary is widow of John McNeely, d 1846 and
    Joseph B is their son, WB K:43]
200 A improved land, 276 A unimpr, value:$1800
Joseph: 6 slaves; Mary: 6 slaves

1193.1214 Henry SECKLER 63 M NC farmer 1,800
    Catherine SECKLER   57 F NC
    John F.   27 M NC
    Elisabeth   22 F NC S
    Moses W.   21 M NC teacher
    Sarah C.   19 F NC S
    Amelia A.   17 F NC S
    Dove A.C.   15 F NC S

[MB:Henry Sechler & Catherine Fink 8 Feb 1813]
200 A improved land, 400 A unimpr, value:$1800

1194.1215 Mary M ALBRIGHT 55 F NC 300
    Mary ALBRIGHT   52 F NC (X)
    Elisabeth ALBRIGHT   46 F NC (X)
    Eliza ALBRIGHT   37 F NC (X)

1195.1216 Peter ALBRIGHT 59 M NC farmer
    Elisabeth ALBRIGHT   60 F NC
    Sarah   30 F NC
    William   20 M NC
    Mary E.   15 F NC S
    Cornelius KLUTTS   13 M Mu wagon maker 317

[MB: Peter Albright to Betsey Fink 12 Dec 1817]

1196.1217 Jacob W BOSTIAN 52 M NC
    Mary BOSTIAN   47 F NC
    Mary A.   18 F NC S
    Margaret   16 F NC S
    James A.   14 M NC S
    John H.   12 M NC S
    George W.   7 M NC S

50 A improved land, 1 A unimpr, value:$317

p. 187, School District #12, 8 Oct 1850

1197.1218 Caleb SHUPING 33 M NC farmer 650
    Sarah SHUPING   32 F NC
    Jacob A.   3 M NC
    Alfred F.   2 M NC
    Andrew J. LYNCH   21 M NC S labourer
    Judith LYNCH   60 F NC (X)

[MB: Caleb Shuping to Sarah Cope 22 Dec 1845]
100 A improved land, 160 A unimpr, value:$650

1198.1219 John FREEZE 23 M NC farmer m
    Rebecca M. FREEZE   28 F NC m

1199.1220 Alexander BOSTIAN 41 M NC farmer 400
  Easter C. BOSTIAN   35 F NC (X)
  Lydia Relena   16 F NC S
  Sarah E.   15 F NC S
  Hetha D.   13 F NC S
  Cynthia   7 F NC
  John M.   5 M NC
  Amos A.   3 M NC
  William J.   1 M NC

   80 A improved land, 88 A unimpr, value:$400

1200.1221 Samuel SECHLER 68 M PA farmer 200
  Rachel SECHLER   53 F NC
  James P.   19 M NC

1201.1222 Michael ALBRIGHT 44 M NC farmer 500
  Rachel ALBRIGHT   45 F NC (X)
  John J.   19 M NC S labourer
  Jesse H.   15 M NC S labourer
  Elisabeth   11 F NC S

   60 A improved land, 90 A unimpr, value:$500

1202.1223 Noah A FREEZE 25 M NC farmer 150
  Martha A. FREEZE   17 F NC

[MB:Noah A Freeze/Martha Ann Sechler 10 Aug 1848]

1203.1224 Peter UPRIGHT 61 M NC farmer 1,400
  Barbara UPRIGHT   58 F NC (X)
  Polly) twin   25 F NC (X)
  Sally) twin   25 F NC (X)
  Maria   22 F NC (X)
  William   18 M NC S labourer
  David   16 M NC S labourer
  Eli   11 M NC S

[MB: Peter Upright to Barbara Frees 4 Jan 1813]
  200 A improved land, 258 A unimpr, value:$1,400

1204.1225 James A ATWELL 33 M NC farmer 600
  Jane M. ATWELL   34 F NC
  Gasper L.   9 M NC S
  Martha J.   7 F NC S
  George L.   6 M NC
  William A.   3 M NC
  Mary E.A.   1 F NC

[MB:James A Atwell & Jane M Masters 24 July 1839]
  75 A unimproved land, 132 A unimpr, value:$600

1205.1226 Mary E ATWELL 62 F VA (X) 700
  William L. ATWELL   16 M NC S labourer
  Martha BROWN   77 F MD (X)

[Note: widow of Lock Atwell, WB I:243]
  75 A improved land, 145 A unimpr, value:$700
  5 slaves

1206.1227 Margaret PENNY 77 F NC 300
  Adeline OVERCASH   38 F NC (X)
  Eli OVERCASH   4 M NC   cont.

  Lock J.   1 M NC
  1 slave

1207.1228 Caleb HAMPTON 39 M NC farmer
  Sarah HAMPTON   42 F NC (X)
  Easter L. EAGLE   13 F NC S

[MB:Caleb Hampton to Sarah Ritchie 17 Mar 1838]
  55 A improved land, 43 A unimpr, valued at $200

1208.1229 Barbara FESTERMAN 45 F NC (X)
  Sarah   19 F NC
  Levi   17 M NC S labourer
  Rose A.E.   14 F NC
  Amelia S.   12 F NC
  John F.N.   10 M NC

1209.1230 Mary W DUKES 49 F NC (X) 50
  John M.   16 M NC
  Martha A.   14 F NC
  Jacob J.   5 M NC
  Mary L.   3 F NC

1210.1231 David FOUTS 35 M NC farmer 200
  Christiana FOUTS   30 F NC (X)
  William H.   9 M NC S
  John D.   8 M NC S
  Sarah E.   6 F NC
  James S.   4 M NC
  Margaret E.   2 F NC

   35 A improved land, 600 A unimpr, value:$300

1211.1232 George KARIKER 24 M NC farmer
  Mary A. KARIKER   26 F NC
  Margaret J.C.   1 F NC

   25 A improved land valued at $75

1212.1233 Philip KARRIKER 63 M NC farmer 300
  Mary KARRIKER   61 M NC (X)
  Jacob L.   22 M NC labourer
  Delila C.   19 F NC S

   50 A improved land, 117 unimpr, value:$300

1213.1234 John W KARIKER 30 M NC
  Sarah KARIKER   32 F NC (X)
  William A.   9 M NC S
  Jacob P.   7 M NC S
  Daniel M.   6 M NC
  John Z.A.   5 M NC
  Mary A.E.   2 F NC
  [188] George   3/12 M NC

[MB: John Karrker to Sarah Beaver 29 June 1840]

<u>p.188, School District #12, 9 Oct. 1850</u>

1214.1235 John A MORIS 34 M NC brickmason
  Mary A. MORIS   24 F NC (X)
  Catherine   7 F NC
  Noah   3 M NC   cont.

Jane E.   1 F NC

[MB:John A Morris to Mary Ann Leazer 4 Mar 1843]

1215.1236 Alexander BOST 29 M NC farmer 200
    Catherine R. BOST   28 F (X)
    Jacob A.   1 M NC

[MB:Alexander Bost/Catharine R Leazer 13 Sep 1847]
    88 A improved land, 30 A unimpr, value: $200

1216.1237 William COOPER 46 M NC blacksmith 500
    Sarah COOPER   40 F NC (X)
    Mary A.   19 F NC
    David M.   17 M NC farmer
    John C.   13 M NC S
    William C.   10 M NC S
    Nancy C.   7 F NC S
    George A.   6 M NC S
    Joseph W.   4 M NC S
    Amelia C.   2 F NC
    Delila KEISTLER   17 F NC

    40 A improved land, 124 A unimpr, value:$500

1217.1238 Margaret COLEMAN 65 F NC (X)
    Sarah A.   24 F NC
    George P. COLEMAN   25 M NC trapper 300
    Mary COLEMAN   26 F NC (X)
    Margaret C. RAMSEY   32 F NC
    John F.   1 M NC

    George P: 50 A improved land, 13 A unimproved,
        valued at $130

1218.1239 John OVERCASH 54 M NC (X) farmer 900
    Ester OVERCASH   52 F NC (X)
    Marie   26 F NC (X)
    Emeline   25 F NC (X)
    Alexander   23 M NC (X) labourer
    Alison   21 M NC (X) labourer
    Margaret   19 F NC S
    Catherine   16 F NC S
    John M.   14 M NC S
    Noah   10 M NC S

[MB: John Overcast to Easter Beaver 10 June 1822]
    50 A improved land, 282 unimpr, valued at $900

1219.1240 Martin YOST 34 M NC farmer
    Mary YOST   35 F NC (X)
    Christiana R.   13 F NC S
    Susanna   10 F NC S
    Mary L.   8 F NC S
    Noah Abraham   5 M NC S
    Lena E.   3 M NC

    35 A improved land, 95 A unimpr, valued at $400

1220.1241 Henry DEAL 55 M NC farmer 1,000 m
    Nancy M. DEAL   28 F NC (X) m
    Susanna   25 F NC (X)
    Margaret   23 F NC (X)   cont.

John L.   21 M NC S labourer
William E.   18 M NC S labourer
Franklin W.   16 M NC S labourer
* James I.   8 M NC
William R.   5 M NC

[MB: Henry Deal to Mary Upright 18 Mar 1818; Henry
    Deal to Elizabeth Lingle 10 Aug 1850]
115 A improved land, 140 A unimpr, value:$1,000

1221.1242 James HAMPTON 35 M NC labourer
    Elisabeth HAMPTON   33 F NC
    John W.   10 M NC S
    David   8 M NC S
    Laura   6 F NC

[MB:James Hampton to Elizabeth Richey --1840]

1222.1243 Noah RITCHIE 37 M NC farmer 140
    Sarah RITCHIE   27 F NC (X)
    Mary A.   10 F NC S
    Nancy C.   7 F NC S
    John D.   4 M NC
    Barbara E.   11/12 F NC

    30 A improved land, 20 A unimpr, value:$140

1223.1244 John M RITCHIE 39 M NC farmer 400
    Margaret RITCHIE   30 F NC
    Mary E.   9 F NC S
    John R.   4 M NC

[MB:John M Ritchey to Margaret Linn 6 Apr 1840]
    70 A improved land, 100 A unimpr, value:$400

1224.1245 John DEAL 59 M NC farmer 2,900
    Mary DEAL   57 F NC
    Solomon   29 M NC (X) labourer
    William A.   22 M NC labourer
    Levi A.   16 M NC S labourer
    Elisabeth   24 F NC

[MB:John Deal to Mary Lingle 29 Jan 1816]
    160 A improved land, 595 A unimpr, value:$2000

1225.1246 Jacob DEAL 31 M NC farmer
    Mary M. DEAL   30 F NC
    William Elkanah   4 M NC
    Henry O.   2 M NC

[MB: Jacob Deal to Mary M Seckler 9 Apr 1844]
    30 A improved land, 100 A unimpr, value:$500

1226.1247 Jacob BOSTIAN   32 M NC farmer
    Sarah BOSTIAN   35 F NC (X)
    William W.   10 M NC S
    Margaret S.   8 F NC S
    James M.   6 M NC S
    Moses A.   4 M NC
    Sarah L.   2 F NC
[189] Emeline E.   2/12 F NC

                                          cont.

[MB: Jacob Bostian to Sarah Ramer 13 June 1839]
this name usually appears as Rymer or Rimer]
30 A improved land, 110 A unimpr, value: $300

<u>p.189, School District #12, 10 Oct. 1850</u>

1227.1248 Daniel W REAMER 27 M NC farmer 1,000
    Ann REAMER   26 F NC
    Elen V.   3 F NC
    Emeline L.   1 F NC
    Hannah ELLIOTT   18 F NC
    Simeon BEAVER   21 M NC

    100 A improved land, 136 A unimpr, value:$1000

1228.1249 Michael SHUPING 42 M NC farmer 700
    Amelia SHUPING   40 F NC
    Absalem A.   16 M NC
    Lydia H.   14 F NC
    John A.   11 M NC
    Noah R.   9 M NC
    Amanda C.   6 F NC
    Henery W.   6/12 M NC

[MB: Michael Shuping to Milly Freeze 16 Mar 1830]
50 A improved land, 200 A unimpr, valued at $700

1229.1250 James S FREEZE 30 M NC farmer
    Eliza L. FREEZE   25 F NC

[MB: James S Freeze to Eliza L Lingle 10 Nov 1849]

1230.1251 Henry FREEZE 46 M NC farmer 500
    Mary M. FREEZE   46 F NC
    Alfred A.   22 M NC labourer
    Hiram A.   20 M NC labourer
    Elmira E.   18 F NC
    Eliza C.   15 F NC
    Mathew   13 M NC
    Sarah R.   11 F NC
    Cynthia C.   8 F NC
    Henry J.   3 M NC

    61 A improved land, 70 A unimpr, value:$300

1231.1252 Thomas FREEZE 32 M NC farmer 350
    Lavina FREEZE   35 F NC
    Joel J.   12 M NC

[MB: Thomas Freeze to Lavina Locke 28 Feb 1837]
25 A improved land, 35 A unimpr, value:$350

1232.1253 John FREEZE 53 M NC farmer 258
    Anna FREEZE   43 F NC (X)
    Elisabeth M.   20 F NC S
    Mary J.   18 F NC S
    Jeremiah   7/12 M NC
    Henery E. FREEZE   22 M NC
    Cynthia C. FREEZE   23 F NC
    John W.S.   5/12 M NC

                    cont.

[MB:Henry E Freeze & Synthia C Sloop 6 Nov 1848]
50 A improved land, 37 A unimpr, valued at $258

1233.1254 Barbara FREEZE 60 F NC (X) 250
    Martha Rose   39 F NC (X)
    Margaret E.   19 F NC S
    John A.   17 M NC
    Elias FREEZE   39 M NC (X)

    35 A improved land, 57 A unimpr, value:$250

1234.1255 George CORIHER 35 M NC farmer 650
    Martha CORIHER   33 F NC
    Clarissa E.   10 F NC S
    Washington A.   7 M NC S
    Catherine A.   5 F NC S
    Sarah E.   4 F NC
    Henry J.J.   1 M NC
    Elisabeth CORRIER   73 F PA

    40 A improved land, 98 A unimpr, value:$650

1235.1256 Mary H. SHUPING 34 F MC (X) 500
    Margaret E.   11 F NC S
    Andrew F.   9 M NC S
    Hetta C.   8 F NC S
    Sarah M.   5 F NC S
    Crawford L.   3 M NC

1236.1257 David CORRIER 73 M PA (X) farmer
    Catherine CORRIER   69 F NC (X)
    John BOSTIAN   50 M NC (X)
    Elisabeth BOSTIAN   30 F NC (X)
    Mary   10 F NC S
    Catherine   4 F NC
    Delila   2 F NC
    Sarah CORRIER   15 F NC

    40 A improved land, 60 A unimpr, value:$1,500

1237.1258 George SLOOP 54 M NC farmer 150
    Joel G.   7 M NC S
    Hetta S.   19 F NC S
    George W.   17 M NC S labourer
    Henry O.   15 M NC S labourer
    Margaret E.   13 F NC S
    Jane A.   9 F NC S

    60 A improved land, 42 A unimpr, value:$150

1238.1259 James COBURN 35 M NC carpenter 400
    Nancy COBURN   26 F NC (X)
    Amos L.   10/12 M NC
    William ASHBY   6 M NC

[MB: James Coburn to Nancy Rimer 4 Feb 1841]
10 A improved land, 63 A unimpr, value:$400

1239.1260 Michael RAMER 69 M NC farmer 200
    Margaret RAMER   67 F NC (X)

    10 A improved land, 23 A unimpr, value:$200

1240.1261 Hezekiah SECKLER 29 M NC farmer 300
   Mirneva SECKLER   25 F NC
   Jacob W.   2 M NC

   [MB:Hezekiah A Sechler to Manerva Anthony 14 Apr
     1846]
   40 A improved land, 160 A unimpr, valued at $300

1241.1262 John CORRIER 44 M NC farmer 238
   Mary CORRIER   40 F NC (X)
   Catherine L.   16 F NC S
[190] Richard A.   14 M NC S
   Thomas W.   12 M NC S
   John A.   10 M NC S
   Mary E.   4 F NC
   Emelina A.   1 F NC

   50 A improved land, 69 A unimpr, value:$238

<u>p.190, School District #13, 12 Oct 1850</u>

1242.1263 Jeremiah INGOLD 32 M NC clergyman
   Margaret C. INGOLD   36 F NC
   Alice E.   2 F NC
   John R. RAMSOUR   11 M NC
   1 slave

1243.1264 Daniel CORRIER 38 M NC farmer 1,500
   Cynthia CORRIER   36 F NC
   Mary A.M.   11 F NC S
   Amos B.   8 M NC S
   Loretta E.   6 F NC S
   Silas H.   4 M NC
   Flora C.   2 F NC
   John C.   5/12 M NC
   Rufus R. ROBISON   22 M NC cabinetmaker

   40 A improved land, 300 A unimpr, value:$1500

1244.1265 Henry CORRIER 37 M NC
   Christiana CORRIER   36 F NC
   Joel   14 M NC S
   Rudolph J.   13 M NC S
   Dovey E.   11 F NC S
   Barbary E.   9 F NC S
   Mary A.R.   8 F NC S
   Benjamin L.   6 M NC
   Henry S.   3 M NC
   Margaret V.   2 F NC

   [MB:Henry Corriker/Christena Seckler 23 Mar 1835]
   100 A improved land, 150 unimpr, valued at $900

1245.1266 James BAUGHN 42 M VA Sarvyer? 625
   Sarah A. BAUGHN   28 F NC
   Henery C.   13 M NC S
   Caroline M.   12 F NC S

   60 A improved land, 103 A unimpr, value:$1000
   1 slave
   saw mill: 250,000 ft lumber valued at $2,000

1246.1267 John M COLEMAN 34 M NC farmer 625
   Jane COLEMAN   34 F NC
   1 slave

1247.1268 John DEAL Jr 33 M NC farmer 250
   Mary M. DEAL   33 F NC
   Andrew   6 M NC
   Alfred   4 M NC
   Levi   2 M NC

   [MB: John Deal to Mary M Seckler 9 Apr 1844]
   43 A improved land, 118 A unimpr, value:<u>$620</u>

1248.1269 Allen ROSE 47 M NC farmer 756
   Elisabeth ROSE   37 F NC
   Sarah E.   13 F NC S
   Margaret A.   12 F NC S
   John A.   9 M NC S
   Rufus A.   7 M NC S
   Mary L.   5 F NC S
   William C.   2/12 M NC

   [MB:Allen Rose & Elizabeth Eddlemon 26 Mar 1835]
   42 A improved land, 147 A unimpr, valued at $756
   1 slave

1249.1270 Jones OVERCASH 25 M NC farmer
   Mary A. OVERCASH   20 F NC (X)
   Barbara A.C.   0/12 F NC
   Margaret S. OVERCASH   9 F NC

   [MB:Jones W Overcash & Mary Ann Upright 5 Jan
     1849]
   17 A improved land valued at $50

1250.1271 William T.F. PLASTER 38 M NC farmer 625
   Sophia E. PLASTER   34 F NC
   John W.   13 M NC S
   William L.   10 M NC S
   Ann H.   7 F NC S
   Sarah J.   4 F NC
   Edmund R.G.   2 M NC
   Mary A. OVERCASH   29 F NC (X)

   30 A improved land, 126 A unimpr, value: $625

1251.1272 Mary PLASTER 45 F NC 245
   Margaret PLASTER   38 F NC
   John F. PLASTER   8 M NC S

   22 A improved land, 40 A unimpr, value:$245

1252.1273 Jacob OVERCASH 57 M NC farmer 1,300
   Catherine OVERCASH   59 F NC (X)
   Abraham   21 M NC S labourer
   Davon J.   18 M NC S labourer
   Reuben G.   15 M NC S labourer

   100 A improved land, 400 unimpr, value:$1,300

1253.1274 Francis OVERCASH 53 M NC saddler

cont.

Mary OVERCASH   50 F NC
Solomon W.   21 M NC farmer
Israel M.   20 M NC labourer
Catherine L.   18 F NC
Henry W.   15 M NC S
Mary A.   13 F NC S
John O.   10 M NC S

[MB: Francis Overcast to Mary Beaver 22 Nov 1819;
he is the son of Jacob and Susannah Overcash, WB
I:111]
    85 A improved land, 115 A unimpr, valued at $627

1254.1275 Margaret OVERCASH 49 F NC (X) 500
    Samuel   21 M NC farmer
    Polly C.   19 F NC
    Solomon W.   16 M NC S labourer
    Eliza E. UPRIGHT   9 F NC S

    100 A improved land, 180 unimpr, valued at $500

1255.1276 Charls BLACKWELDER 35 M NC 300
[191] Catherine BLACKWELDER 31 F NC (X)
    Henry C.   6 M NC S
    Catherine S.   1 F NC

[MB:Charles Blackwelder to Catharine Teele 3 Oct
    1842]
    24 A improved land, 82 A unimpr, value: $300

1266.1278 Christian BLACKWELDER 77 M NC farmer 200
    Mary BLACKWELDER   53 F NC

[MB:Christian Blackwelder to Mary Willeford 28
    Oct 1844]
[On the agricultural schedule next to Charles
Blackwelder is Christian Overcash: 60 A impr-
oved land, 20 A unimpr, valued at $200]

1267.1279 Martin F RODGERS 48 M NC farmer 200
    Catherine RODGERS   38 F NC
    Margaret E.   20 F NC
    George R.   18 M NC
    Lenard F.   16 M NC
    Sally C.   13 F NC S
    Barbara A.   11 F NC
    Laura C.   9 F NC S
    Mary L.   7 F NC
    Phebe L.   4 F NC
    Huldah S.   1 F NC

    65 A improved land, 35 A unimpr, value:$200

1268.1280 Henry OVERCASH 43 M NC farmer
    Catherine OVERCASH   41 F NC (X)
    Milcah D.   16 M NC
    Phillip N.   11 M NC
    Mary C.   4 F NC
    Henry A.   2 M NC

    25 A improved land valued at $75

1269.1281 Milcah OVERCASH 40 M NC 300
    Philip J.   18 M NC
    Cozby R.   16 M NC
    Iscah M.   14 M NC S
    Elen L.   11 F NC S
    Mary S.   9 F NC S

    30 A improved land, 50 A unimpr, value:$300

1270.1282 Phillip OVERCASH 49 M NC farmer 2,000
    Mary OVERCASH   50 F NC (X)
    Ira   21 M NC labourer
    Susanna   20 F NC
    Joseph J.   18 M NC labourer S
    Mary D.   15 F NC S
    Phillip L.   13 M NC S
    Daniel   11 M NC S
    Jacob LIPE   76 M NC farmer

1271.1283 Leonard OVERCASH 72 M PA (X) farmer 975
    Catherine OVERCASH   66 F NC (X)
    Solomon OVERCASH   28 M NC
    Sophia OVERCASH   23 F NC

    50 A improved land, 228 A unimpr, value:$556

1272.1284 Leonard OVERCASH 34 M NC farmer
    Christiana OVERCASH   34 F NC
    Paul S.   11 M NC S
    Margaret C.   9 F NC
    John M.   7 M NC
    Mary A.   5 F NC
    Elen M.   3 M NC
    Lena A.   2 F NC
    Andrew J.   3/12 M NC

    50 A improved land, 50 A unimpr, value:$224

1273.1285 Mary PATTERSON   43 F NC
    Harriet C.   18 F NC S
    Elisabeth C.   16 F NC S

1274.1286 Christiana FREEZE 63 F PA (X)
    Barbara   28 F NC (X)
    Adaline   25 F NC (X)
    William F.   20 M NC S

    20 A improved land, 20 A unimpr, value:$100

1275.1287 Henry BEAVER 45 M NC farmer
    Sophia BEAVER   41 F NC
    Simeon J   16 M NC S
    Allen A.   14 M NC S
    Mary C.   12 F NC S
    Anna A.   11 F NC S
    John W.   9 M NC S
    Sarah C.   6 F NC
    William A.   4 M NC
    Polly C.   2 F NC

    no land but livestock

1276.1288 Mary A BEAVER 71 F NC (X) 400
    Anna   31 F NC (X)

1277.1289 Eli F SHERILL 23 M NC farmer
    Esther N. SHERRILL   20 F NC
    Sarah E.   7 F NC
    Lydia M.A.   4 F NC
    Leah U.   2 F NC
    Catherine F.   )twins 0/12 F NC
    Jane Azanetta)   0/12 F NC

    80 A improved land, 90 A unimpr, value:$150

1278.1290 Henry W GOODNIGHT 29 M NC farmer
    Anna M. GOODNIGHT   25 F NC
    William A.   8 M NC
    James M.   5 M NC

    15 A improved land, 25 A unimpr, value:$80

1279.1291 Daniel OVERCASH 44 M NC (X) farmer
    Mary A. OVERCASH   47 F NC (X)
    Margaret C.   23 F NC (X)
    Terrissa E.   21 F NC (X)
    [192] Cornelius A.   19 M NC S labourer
    Darkus A.   17 F NC S
    Elizabeth C.   15 F NC S
    George R.   13 F NC S
    Hampton J.   10 M NC
    Siles A.   9 M NC

    3 slaves

p. 192, School District #13, 12 Oct 1850

1280.1292 Christopher OVERCASH 40 M NC farmer 112
    Jemima OVERCASH   28 F NC (X)
    Hervey W.   11 M NC S
    Terrissa A.   9 F NC S
    Hiram F.   8 M NC S
    Stanhope W.   5 M NC
    Sidney C.   3 M NC
    Christopher J.   9/12 M NC

    [MB:Christopher Overcash to Jemima Pahel 16 Sept
    1837]
    70 A improved land, 80 A unimpr, value:$300

1281.1293 Jacob OVERCASH 79 M PA blacksmith 200
    Sophia OVERCASH   76 F NC (X)
    Mary   37 F NC (X)

1282.1294 John OVERCASH 49 M NC (X) farmer
    Elisabeth OVERCASH   42 F NC (X)
    Mary   26 F NC
    Leah E.   14 F NC S
    John A.   11 M NC S
    Margaret L.   8 F NC
    James M.   6 M NC

    100 A improved land, 40 A unimpr, value:$300

1283.1295 Michael OVERCASH 48 M NC farmer 417
    Barbara OVERCASH   49 F NC
    Martin L.   25 M NC
    James P.   19 M NC
    William A.   16 M NC
    Jacob M.   14 M NC
    Mary MILLER   21 F NC (X)

    65 A improved land, 112 A unimpr, value:$419

1284.1296 Joseph S BAKER 64 M NC farmer 1,060
    Margaret BAKER   49 F NC
    Clarissa E.   16 F NC S

    80 A improved land, 397 A unimpr, value:$1,108
    9 slaves

1285.1297 James T BAKER 28 M NC farmer
    Mary A. BAKER   27 F NC
    Joseph N.   8 M NC
    Franklin C.   6 M NC
    Margaret A.   4 F NC
    Ann E.   2 F NC
    Hetta N.   6/12 F NC
    Prudence M. SIMS   19 F NC

    40 A improved land valued at $90

1286.1298 John YOST 22 M NC farmer
    Elisabeth YOST   19 F NC
    David M.   8/12 M NC

    18 A improved land valued at $90

1287.1299 Paul YOST 65 M NC farmer 885
    Catherine YOST   61 F NC
    Franklin M.   24 M NC
    Anna   21 F NC
    Margaret   18 F NC
    Amelia   15 F NC S
    Sophia   13 F NC S
    John R.   4 M NC

    [MB: Paul Youst to Caty Beairn 8 Feb 1815]
    100 A improved land, 195 A unimpr, value:$885

1288.1300 Robert A PATTERSON 48 M NC farmer 319
    Salome PATTERSON   33 F NC (X)
    Simpson G.   18 M NC S
    Mary A.   16 F NC S
    Margaret E.   14 F NC S
    Elisabeth   12 F NC S
    Sarah J.   9 F NC S
    Ibson F.   7 M NC S
    John E.   4 M NC

    34 A improved land, 70 A unimpr, value: $312

1289.1301 Noah PEATHEL 24 M NC farmer
    Mary A. PEATHEL   27 F NC
    William F.   1 M NC
    Jacob J.   0/12 M NC   cont.

[MB: Noah A Pahel to Mary Ann Cotton 21 Dec 1841]
30 A improved land valued at $120

1290.1302 John PAHEL 35 M NC
    Mary M. PAHEL   29 F NC S
    Margaret L.   9 F NC
    Adolphus J.   7 M NC
    Joseph G.   5 M NC
    James F.   4 M NC
    Samuel G.   1 M NC

[MB: John Pahel to Mary M Sloop 27 Jan 1842]
60 A improved land, 20 A unimpr, value:$200

1291.1303 John PAHEL 56 M NC (X) farmer 500
    Susanna PAHEL   65 F NC (X)
    Conrad M.   19 M NC

100 A improved land, 100 A unimpr, value:$200

1292.1304 Soloman PAHEL 25 M NC (X) 40
    Ann PAHEL   27 F NC (X)
    Flora, Luther, Lucinda, Elen 2 F NC

[MB: Solomon Pahel to Ann M Overcash 19 Oct 1846]
18 A improved land valued at $72

1293.1305 David BEAVER 80 M PA (X) farmer 7,000
    Jacob BEAVER   28 M NC (X) farmer
    Anna BEAVER   27 F NC (X)
    Theresa M.   6 F NC
    Edmund   2 M NC
    Nancy KETCHEY   32 F NC (X)

p.193, School District #13, 14 Oct 1850

1294.1306 Alison STIREWALT 37 M VA millwright 1,300
    Elisabeth STIREWALT   39 F NC (X)
    John C.   14 M NC S
    Jacob F.   12 M NC S
    Anne E.   8 F NC S
    Henry L.   5 M NC
    Mary Jane   2 F NC

    Rendleman & Stirewalt: 52,000 ft of lumber valued
       at $390
    Stirewalt & Rendleman: flouring: 667 bbl flour
       valued at $3,335; corn mill: 4,440 bu valued
       at $3,560

1295.1307 James MILLER 42 M NC labourer
    Mary MILLER   35 F NC (X)
    John R.   12 M NC
    Mary M.   6 F NC

1296.1308 Frederic WALKER   48 M NC farmer
    Delila WALKER   42 F NC (x)
    Polly M.   22 F NC
    Catherine E.   19 F NC
    Mary M.   17 F NC
    Lavinia   14 F NC
    Joseph M.   11 M NC   cont.

Jane S.   9 F NC
Sara A.   7 F NC
Laura   6 F NC
Henry Clay   4 M NC
Margaret E.   3 F NC
Susan R.   9/12 F NC
Flora D. BOST   5 F NC

100 A improved land, 100 A unimpr, value:$1,300

1297.1309 Levi PAHEL 26 M VA (X) wagonmaker
    Julia A. PAHEL   22 F NC
    Benjamin R.   4 M NC
    Thomas A.   1 M NC

[MB:Levi Pahel to Juliann Yarbrough 19 June 1845]
18 A improved land valued at $90

1298.1310 Daniel HESS 49 M NC farmer 900
    Mary M. HESS   45 F NC
    John A.   17 M NC S
    Jane Ashba   13 F NC S
    William N. COPE   13 M NC

40 A improved land, 109 A unimpr, value:$900

1299.1311 Daniel BEAVER 38 M NC farmer 620
    Jemima BEAVER   36 F NC
    Margaret I.   12 F NC S
    Nancy T.   11 F NC S
    George F.S.   9 M NC S
    Sarah A.   7 F NC S
    Jacob M.   6 M NC
    William W.   3 M NC
    Susan C.   9/12 F NC

20 A improved land, 105 A unimpr, value:$620

1300.1312 Charles A ROSE 37 M NC 1,000
    Sarah ROSE   33 F NC
    James W.A.   10 M NC S
    Sarah T.   8 F NC S
    Julia A.J.   5 F NC S
    Laura V.   4 F NC
    Maria E.   1 F NC

[MB:Charles A Rose to Sarah Carriker 20 Feb 1837]
75 A improved land, 190 A unimpr, value: $1,000
1 slave

1301.1313 William ROSE 77 M VA (X) farmer 430
    Polly BEAVER   40 F NC (X)

132 A improved land, 12 A unimpr, value:$4<u>50</u>
5 slaves

1302.1314 Peter KESLER 40 M NC farmer 600
    Uphrana KESLER   34 F NC
    Margaret D.   9 F NC S
    John A.   6 M NC S
    Elisabeth A.   4 F NC
    Peter J.   2 M NC   cont.

```
        George C.              2/12 M NC
        Jacob KESLER           12 M NC
```

[MB:Peter Kesler & Phreany Corriher 12 Feb 1839]
     60 A improved land, 140 A unimpr, value: $600

```
1303.1315 Benjamin SECHLER 40 M NC farmer 750
        Elisabeth SECHLER      37 F NC
        Elisabeth              10 F NC
```

     40 A improved land, 114 A unimpr, value:$300

```
1304.1316 Solomon SECHLER 47 M NC farmer 750
        Jesse                  24 M NC labourer
        Sarah                  21 F NC
        Lydia                  18 F NC
        Priscilla              14 F NC S
```

     50 A improved land, 180 A unimpr, value:$750

```
1305.1317 Henry BEAVER   -- M NC (x) farmer
        Mary E.                57 F NC (X)
        Mary M.                14 F NC S
        Catherine              11 F NC S
```

```
1306.1318 David E BEAVER 25 M NC farmer
        Polly BEAVER           24 F NC (X)
        Laura S.               2 F NC
        Henry A.               1/12 M NC
```

```
1307.1319 David LINN 23 M NC farmer 500
        Sophia R. LINN    29 F NC (X)
        Margaret J.        7 F NC S
        Harvey A.          3 M NC
        Columbus A.        1 M NC
```

     [MB: David Linn to Sophia R Correl 4 Feb 1840]
     30 A improved land, 95 A unimpr, value: $500
     2 slaves

```
1308.1320 Michael BEAVER 65 M NC (X) farmer 400
        Elisabeth BEAVER       59 F NC (X)
[194] Catherine               31 F NC (X)
        Moses                  25 M NC (X)
        Eli M.                 19 M NC
```

     70 A improved land, 69 A unimpr, value: $400

<u>p.194, School District #14, 15 Oct 1850</u>

```
1309.1321 Alexander BEAVER    34 M NC blacksmith 375
        Sarah BEAVER           40 F NC
        Riniholo E.            12 M NC S
        Levi A.                10 M NC
        Michael N.             8 M NC
        Adaline A.             6 F NC
        Emeline C. JOHNSON     16 F NC
```

[MB:Alexander Beaver & Sally Ketchey 5 June 1835]
     30 A improved land, 72 A unimpr, valued at $395

```
1310.1322 Sally BEAVER 37 F NC 300
        Moses                  21 M NC
        Catherine              19 F NC
        Sophia                 16 F NC
        Polly                  14 F NC S
        Martin                 12 M NC S
        John                   10 M NC S
```

     50 A improved land, 139 A unimpr, value:$300

```
1311.1323 Catherin SLOOP 68 F NC 150
        Catherine              27 F NC (X)
        Sarah SLOOP            13 F NC S
        John ROGERS            27 M NC farmer
        Wilhelm M. ROGERS      25 F NC (X)
        Mary C.                3/12 F NC
```

     [MB: John Rodgers to Wilhelmene Sloop 23 Oct 1848]
     60 A improved land, 15 A unimpr, value: $150

```
1312.1324 Polly PAHEL  45 F NC (X)
        Jacob                  14 M NC S
```

```
1313.1325 George ROSE 56 M NC farmer 1,000
        Sarah ROSE             56 F NC (X)
        Elisabeth              34 F NC 34
        Emeline                28 F NC
        Jemima                 21 F NC
        Jane                   12 F NC S
        Washington             6 M NC S
        Thomas DENTON          14 M NC S
        Catherine BOSTIAN      76 F PA (X)
```

     60 A improved land, 147 A unimpr, value:$<u>650</u>

```
1314.1326 Richard F ERVIN 30 M NC blacksmith 500
        Jane E.                24 F NC
        Elisabeth L.           7 F NC
        Charles A.             4 M NC
        Mary J.                1 F NC
```

     31 A improved land, 79 A unimpr, value:$500
     1 slave

```
1315.1327 Aaron L GOODNIGHT 25 M NC farmer 650
        Sarah J. GOODNIGHT     22 F NC
        Margaret J.            11/12 F NC
```

     35 A improved land, 105 A unimpr, value:$650

```
1316.1328 John SLOOP 40 M NC tanner & farmer
        Christiana SLOOP   38 F NC
        Susanah M.A.       14 F NC S
        Elisabeth L.       12 F NC S
        Nehemiah J.        10 M NC S
        Julia A.E.C.       8 F NC S
        Martin L.S.        5 M NC
        Frances C.         2 F NC
        Charles A.W.       7/12 M NC
```

[MB: John Sloop to Christiana Correll 13 Feb 1835]
     80 A improved land, 165 A unimpr, value: $700

1317.1329 Christiana SECHLER 56 F NC 400
  Eanos   15 M NC S farmer
  William ROGERS   25 M NC farmer
  Christiana C. ROGERS   20 F NC
  William J.A.   3 M NC
  Eanos F.   7/12 M NC

  30 A improved land, 70 A unimpr, value:$400

1318.1330 Henry SLOOP 37 M NC farmer 300
  Rosina SLOOP   29 F NC
  Mena D.A.E.   10 F NC S
  Henry O.   15 M NC S
  William J.A.   7 M NC S
  Abraham E.A.   3 M NC

[MB: Henry Sloop to Rosena Sechler 10 Oct 1838]
28 A improved land, 60 A unimpr, value: $300

1319.1331 Abraham SLOOP 21 M NC farmer 75
  Delila SLOOP   20 F NC
  Abraham W.   7/12 M NC

[MB:Abraham Sloop to Telilah Bostian 27 Nov 1848]

1320.1332 Adam KETCHY 29 M NC (X) farmer
  Ann M.   27 F NC (X)
  Glovy E.   4 F NC
  Greenberry F.   1 M NC

[MB:Adam Ketchey to Ann M Beaver 20 Jan 1843]
48 A improved land, 48 A unimpr, value: $250

1321.1333 Franklin M PAHEL 21 M NC (X) farmer 200
  Susanah L. PAHEL   35 F NC (X)
  Henry M.   1 M NC

1322.1334 Jacob CORRELL 65 M NC (X) shoemaker
                            disabled
  Christiana CORRELL   37 F NC (X)

1323.1335 Levi CORRELL 33 M NC farmer 3,000
  Mary E. CORRELL   29 F NC
  Adam M.   9 M NC S
  Mary C.   4 F NC
  Clary A.A.   1 F NC

120 A improved land, 226 A unimpr, value:$3000
6 slaves

1324.1336 Henry OVERCASH 42 M NC farmer 500
  Mathew A.   16 M NC S labourer
  Terrisa A.   15 F NC S
  Mary A.   14 F NC S
[195] William   11 M NC S
  Sarah C.   13 F NC S
  Mary A.   9 F NC S
  Nancy BOSTIAN   44 F NC 400

[MB:Henry Overcash to Polly Bostian 1 Apr 1831]
55 A improved land, 55 A unimpr, value:$440

1325.1337 Peter DEAL 61 M NC farmer 1,800
  Catherine DEAL   55 F NC (X)
  Margaret   29 F NC
  John   24 M NC
  Elisabeth   19 F NC
  Charles   17 M NC S
  Jacob   15 M NC S
  Levi   9 M NC S
  Jacob DEAL senr   87 M PA farmer

116 A improved land, 186 unimpr, value:$1,790

1326.1338 Peter DEAL jr 27 M NC farmer
  Mary A. DEAL   32 F NC (X)
  Frances C.   2/12 F NC

[MB:Peter Deal to Mary Ann Correll 11 Dec 1848]
20 A improved land valued at $80

1327.1339 John CORRELL 61 M PA farmer 850
  Elisabeth CORRELL   57 F NC
  Charles   35 M NC farmer 200
  Daniel   33 M NC labourer

[MB:John Correll to Betsey Custer 19 July 1810]
70 A improved land, 209 A unimpr, value:$850

1328.1340 John FINK 35 M NC farmer
  Mary A. FINK   30 F NC

20 A improved land, 80 A unimpr, value:$300

1329.1341 Samuel DEAL 35 M NC (X) farmer 800
  Mary M. DEAL   37 F NC (X)
  John D.M.   3 M NC

[MB: Samuel Deal to Polly Beaver 27 Sept 1845]
50 A improved land, 150 A unimpr, value:$420

1330.1342 Edward M CORRELL 23 M NC farmer 750
  M.E. CORRELL   25 F NC

flouring: 435 bbl flour valued at $2,235
corn mill: 2,750 bu valued at $462

1331.1343 Daniel BEAVER 39 M NC farmer
  Leah BEAVER   39 F NC
  William A.   10 M NC S
  Adam M.   7 M NC S
  Delila   5 F NC
  Reuben I.   3 M NC
  Charles   1 M NC

60 A improved land, 141 A unimpr, value:$1165

1332.1344 John A BEAVER 70 M NC (X) farmer
  Eve E. BEAVER   20 F NC
  Daniel   19 M NC
  Anna M.C.   13 F NC S

153 A improved land, 100 A unimpr, value:$600
1 slave

1333.1345 John Jacob SHUPING 84 M PA farmer 700
    Sarah   48 F NC (X)
    Margaret   44 F NC (X)
    Susana   30 F NC
    Frederick A. BUHMANN   21 M GER labourer
    Augustus W. BUHMANN   16 M GER labourer
    Leah KLUTTS   33 F NC (X)

    72 A improved land, 175 A unimpr, value:$700

1334.1346 Mumford S BEAVER 23 M NC blacksmith
    Sarah BEAVER   23 F NC
    Wesley A.   2 M NC
    Caroline   19 F NC S

    [MB: Montford Beaver to Sarah L Linn 18 Oct 1847]

1335.1347 Robert LINN 62 M NC farmer 500
    Christiana LINN   57 F NC (X)
    Moses   20 M NC S labourer
    Anna L.   17 F NC S

    45 A improved land, 55 A unimpr, value:$500

1336.1348 John ROBISON 43 M NC labourer
    Mary ROBISON   43 F NC (X)
    Benjamin C.   2/12 M NC
    Sarah D.   17 F NC S
    Henry A.   14 M NC S
    Margaret M.A.C.   10 F NC S
    Michael M.   8 M NC S
    Samuel J.   5 M NC

1337.1349 John LINN 34 M NC blacksmith 750
    Mary LINN   32 F NC
    James R.   10 M NC S
    Mary C.   8 F NC
    Margaret E.   5 F NC
    Rachel C.   2 F NC
    Mary HEITHCOCK   18 F NC

    33 A improved land, 65 A unimpr, value:$700

1338.1350 Mary LITAKER 55 F NC (X) 700
    Jacob   24 M NC (X) idiotic
    Anna   18 F NC
    Michael LITAKER   32 M NC (X) farmer
    Mary Ann LITAKER   29 F NC
    Margaret A. McK.   1 F NC
    John D. LITAKER   1 M NC
    William LITAKER   37 M NC cabinetmaker

    Michael LITAKER: 40 A improved land, 65 A
      unimpr, valued at $700

1339.1351 George BEAVER 44 M NC farmer
    Christina BEAVER   43 F NC (X)
    Wila   22 M NC labourer
    Simeon   20 M NC labourer
    Catherine M.   18 F NC
    Monroe   16 M NC S
    Delila   14 F NC S   cont.

    Joel   13 M NC S
    [196] Elisabeth   9 F NC S
    Obediah   3 M NC
    Elias A.   1 M NC

<u>p.195, School District #14, 16 Oct 1850</u>

1340.1352 Phillip A CORRELL 21 M NC farmer 2,200
    Jemima CORRELL   22 F NC
    Mary A.   1/12 F NC

    100 A improved land, 450 unimpr, value:$2200
    1 slave

1341.1353 Catherine PORTER 59 F NC 1,500
    Isabella TAYLOR   30 F VA

    350 A improved land, 200 A unimpr, value:$1800
    11 slaves

1342.1354 Sophia BOSTIAN   -- F NC
    Catherine   F NC
    Sarah   F NC
    Margaret   F NC
    Andrew   M NC

1343.1355 William N GILLON 35 M NC farmer 1,500
    Penelope GILLON   30 F NC
    Michael M.   8 M NC S
    Jemima C.   7 F NC S
    Mary J.P.   4 F NC
    Albertine S.   1 F NC
    Caleb SMITH   27 M NC (X) farmer m
    Sophia SMITH   20 F NC m
    David FREEZE   22 M NC farmer 1,500
    John FREEZE   12 M NC S labourer

    [MB:Caleb Smith to Sophia Freeze 1 Jan 1850]
    Wm GILLON & David FREEZE: 200 A improved land,
    200 A unimpr, value:$1,600
    Gillon: flouring: 500 bbl flour valued at $2,201
    D. Freeze: 2,200 bu cornmeal valued at $881
    Gillon & Freeze: saw mill, 9,000 ft lumber valued
      at $282

1344.1356 John GILLON   37 M NC miller
    Eleanor GILLON   34 F NC
    Mary J.   13 F NC S
    Sarah J.   11 F NC S
    Hugh L.   8 M NC S
    Nancy E.   6 F NC S
    William H.   3 M NC

1345.1357 Margaret WEAVER 35 F NC
    Ann WEAVER   33 F NC
    Jane B.   10 F NC S

1346.1358 Martha SECKLER 40 F NC
    Joseph   11 M NC S
    Henry J.   2 M NC

    24 A improved land, 60 A unimpr, value: $300

1347.1359 John McCULLOCKS 66 M NC farmer 1,800
  Yancey S. DEAN   30 M NC physician 150
  Martha A. DEAN   28 F NC
  William E. HOWARD   8 M NC
  Martha J. DEAN   5/12 F NC

[MB: Y S Dean to Martha A Howard 2 Apr 1849]
150 A improved land, 163 unimpr, value:$1800
14 slaves

1348.1360 Charles L PARTEE 37 M NC 2,500
  Laura A.   22 F AL
  Catherine L.   5/12 F NC

300 A improved land, 160 unimpr, value:$2,500
29 slaves

1349.1361 Solomon SMITH 47 M NC shoemaker
  Margaret SMITH   48 F NC (X)
  Cynthia C.   18 F NC
  Sarah A.M.   16 F NC
  Clarissa E.   11 F NC S
  Amanda R.   8 F NC S

1350.1362 William HOLLBROOKS 41 M NC X farmer 1000
  Sarah   8 F NC S
  Martha   6 F NC S
  John   1 M NC
  Elam HOLBROOKS   13 M NC S

100 A improved land, 166 A unimpr, value:$400
saw mill: 75,000 ft of lumber, valued at $600

1351.1363 Jacob SHUPING 57 M NC farmer
  Elisabeth SHUPING 59 F NC
  Louisa   29 F NC (X)
  Mary A.   24 F NC (X)
  Margaret   16 F NC S
  Noah P. CORRELL   17 M NC
  Mumford C. SHUPING 19 M NC S

200 A improved land, 500 A unimpr, value:$2000

1352.1364 Daniel CORRELL 50 M NC labourer
  Eleanor CORRELL   48 F NC
  Catherine   23 F NC
  Lydia   14 F NC
  John A.   20 M NC
  Eleanor S.   12 F NC
  Jane E.   10 F NC
  Julia A.   4 F NC

[MB:Daniel Correll & Nelly Pence 28 Oct 1822]

1353.1365 Michael ALBRIGHT 29 M NC farmer
  Leah ALBRIGHT   31 F NC
  Amanda E.   0/12 F NC

[MB:Michael Albright & Leah Lipe 30 Nov 1847]
20 A improved land valued at $100

1354.1366 George ALBRIGHT 29 M NC farmer
  Catherine ALBRIGHT   30 F NC (X)

12 A improved land valued at $50

1355.1367 Jacob FELKER 51 M NC labourer
  Archibald   24 M NC labourer
  Susana   20 F NC (X)
  Lydia   10 F NC S
  Anna   8 F NC S

1356.1368 Rose MENUS 78 F NC (X) 275
  James LEAZER   24 M NC S
  Elisabeth LEAZER 38 F NC (X)

1357.1369 Henry MENUS 30 M NC (X)
[197] Nancy MENUS   28 F NC (X)
  Jemima   5 F NC
  James   9/12 M NC

175 A improved land, 35 A unimpr, value:$275

<u>p.197, School District #15 18 Oct 1850</u>

1358.1368 Margaret FELKER 82 F PA (X)
  Mary   35 F NC (X)
  Susana   32 F NC (X)
  Mary M.C.   13 F NC S

1359.1369 Catherine GARVER 35 F NC (X)
  Catherine A.E.   17 F NC S
  William D.   15 M NC S
  Susana   11 F NC S
  John M.   9 M NC S
  Leonard B.   7 M NC
  Flora M.   4 M NC

90 A improved land, 60 A unimpr, value:$421

1360.1370 Margaret T TURNER 20 F NC 15
  Sarah A. TURNER   17 F NC 15

1361.1371 Abraham SECHLER 54 M NC farmer
  Mary SECHLER   49 F NC (X)
  General Andrew Jackson 19 M NC S labourer
  Benjamin C.   17 M NC S labourer

[MB:Abraham Sechler & Polly Freeze 22 May 1817]

1362.1372 John A CRESWELL 47 M NC merchant
  Mary M. CRESWELL 42 F NC
  Sophia L.   16 F NC
  Sarah A.E.   13 F NC
  Rose P.   9 F NC
  William C.   5 M NC
  Frederick G.   3 M NC

125 A improved land, 175 unimpr, value:$700

1363.1373 George FREEZE 42 M NC farmer 300
  Sophia FREEZE   42 F NC (X)
  Mary A.   20 F NC   cont.

Peter   18 M NC S
Caleb   16 M NC S
Penelope   15 F NC S
Sarah   14 F NC S
Mary   12 F NC S
Margaret   10 F NC
William M.   3 M NC
Flora   8/12 F NC
Jessee BOST   37 M NC (X) labourer

[MB:George Freeze & Sophia Bost 16 July 1827]
77 A improved land, 20 A unimpr, value:$300

1364.1374 Caleb FREEZE 40 M NC farmer 400
Polly FREEZE   38 F NC (X)
Lydia S.   18 F NC S
Catherine E.   15 F NC S
George   13 M NC S
Martha   11 F NC S
Michael   9 M NC
Moses   7 M NC
Daniel   5 M NC
Elisabeth   3 F NC
Peter   1 M NC
Albertine   7/12 F NC
Penelope FREEZE   82 F PA (X)

[MB:Caleb Freeze to Polly Wilhelm 15 Jan 1828;
Penelope is Caleb's mother, widow of Peter
Freeze, WB K:76]
68 A improved land, 40 A unimpr, value:$400
2 slaves

1365.1375 George H BAKER 41 M NC farmer 400
Lydia BAKER   34 F NC (X)
William T.   13 M NC S
Barbara E.   10 F NC S
John M.   8 M NC S
Mary C.   3 F NC
Harriet J.   1 F NC

40 A improved land, 79 A unimpr, value:$400

1366.1376 Barbara FREEZE 70 F PA (X)
Mary   45 F NC (X)
Catherine   40 F NC (X) 175
Noah   37 M NC farmer 390
Abraham   35 M NC farmer 390

N. & Abraham FREEZE: 100 A improved land, 160 A
unimproved, valued at $780

1367.1377 Daniel LIPE jr 39 M NC farmer 600
Eliza LIPE   38 F NC (X)
William A.   15 M NC S
Jacob S.   14 M NC S
Elijah I.   12 M NC S
Mary E.   11 F NC S
Caleb J.   10 M NC S
Sarah A.C.   8 F NC
John M.   6 M NC
Nancy E.   4 F NC
Milla A.   2 F NC   cont.

Laura J.   1 F NC

75 A improved land, 110 A unimpr, value:$600

1368.1378 Aaron LIPE 47 M NC Farmer 400
Catherine LIPE   44 F NC
Simon J.   20 M NC S labourer
Alexander   18 M NC S labourer
Mary S.   16 F NC S labourer
Margaret E.   13 F NC S
Felix E.   11 M NC S
[198]Leah P.   6 F NC
Julia A.   3 F NC
Flora H.   1 F NC

[MB: Aaron Lipe to Caty Overcash 28 Sept 1827]
50 A improved land, 117 unimpr, value:$500

p.198, School District #13, 19 Oct 1850

1369.1379 Sarah LIPE 61 F NC (X) 300
Daniel   39 M NC farmer
Lydia   37 F NC (X)
Delane   26 F NC (X)
Jacob   24 M NC labourer
John   22 M NC labourer

45 A improved land, 55 A unimpr, value:$300

1370.1380 Daniel COPE 28 M NC (X) labourer
Sally COPE   24 F NC (X)
Mary Jane   4 F NC
John   2 M NC

1371.1381 David J CORRELL 23 M NC farmer 750
Flora G. CORRELL   20 F NC
Abraham A.S.   2 M NC
Mary A. Lee E.   1 F NC

15 A improved land, 110 A unimpr, value:$250

1372.1382 Lawson BOSTIAN 22 M NC m
Eliza BOSTIAN   20 F NC (X)
Sarah Bostian   19 F NC

1373.1383 John FREEZE 22 M NC 200
Elisabeth FREEZE   18 F NC (X)
Mary P.   1 F NC
Calin E.   2/12 M NC

1374.1384 William J HULEN 38 M NC 130
Louisa M. HULEN   28 F NC 65

1375.1385 Richard HARIS 56 M NC farmer 5,000
Mary HARIS   63 F NC
Charles H. McKINZIE   15 M NC S
22 slaves

1376.1386 Henry MILLER 39 M NC farmer
Christiana MILLER   39 F NC
Emeline   15 F NC S
Margaret M.   13 F NC
Henry   11 M NC   cont.

```
Charles                 9 M NC
John                    7 M NC
Susan                   4 F NC
Luther                  10/12 M NC
```

[MB:Henry Miller & Christina Shuping 9 Dec 1834]
no land, 1 slave

```
1377.1387 Andrew SHUPING 26 M NC farmer
  Mary L. SHUPING       29 F NC (X)
  Henry J.              4 M NC
  Jacob                 3 M NC
  William               1 M NC
  Sarah SHUPING         48 F NC (X)
```

[MB:Andrew Shuping & Polly L Cruse 23 Dec 1844]
70 A improved land, 190 A unimpr, value:$1100
  flouring: 333 bbl valued at $1,339
  corn mill: 825 bu valued at $837

```
1377.1388 Jacob SHUPING 50 M NC farmer 1,000
  Margaret C. SHUPING  48 F NC (X)
  Margaret S.          18 F NC S
  Hetta L.             16 F NC S
  Ellen L.             11 F NC S
  Joice C.S.           1 F NC
```

50 A improved land, 100 A unimpr, value:$1000
  saw mill: 62,500 ft lumber valued at [illeg]

```
1378.1389 Moses GOODMAN 43 M NC farmer 2,500
  Elisabeth GOODMAN    38 F NC
  Montfort M.          18 M NC S
  Rose A.              16 F NC S
  Julius V.            13 M NC S
  William SHUPING      21 M NC labourer
```

[MB:Moses Goodman & Elizabeth Josey 28 Mar 1829]
150 A improved land, 1100 unimpr, valued at
  $2,500, 5 slaves

```
1379.1390 Barbara TRIFFINER 45 F NC (X)
  Mary                 28 F NC (X)
  Alexander LAMB       38 M NC labourer
```

```
1380.1391 John MENUS   46 M NC farmer
  Nancy MENUS          24 F NC
  John                 11 M NC
```

90 A improved land, 78 A unimpr, value:$700

```
1381.1392 Sarah CRESS 55 F NC (X) 300
  Mary A.              30 F NC (X)
  Sarah                23 F NC
  Sophia               20 F NC S
  Catherine A.         17 F NC S
  Thomas               15 M NC S labourer 300
```

```
1382.1393 Reuben CRESS 31 M NC farmer 300
  Elisabeth CRESS      25 F NC
  Clara L.             5 F NC
  John N.              2 M NC
  Jeremiah             2/12 M NC        cont.
```

100 A improved land, 103 A unimpr, value:$900
  2 slaves

```
1383.1394 Samuel WILHELM 47 M NC farmer 200
  Polly WILHELM        54 F NC (X)
  Margaret A.E.        16 F NC S
  Montfort S.          12 M NC S
  William A.           10 M NC
  Mary J.C.            4 F NC
  George H.            1 M NC
  James M.             20 M NC farmer
```

25 A improved land, 38 A unimpr, value:$200

```
1384.1395 Jacob WILHELM 40 M NC farmer
  Elisabeth WILHELM    38 F NC (X)
  William L.           22 M NC
[199] Jacob B.         20 M NC
  Mary S.              17 F NC
  Catherine C.         15 F NC S
  Leah D.              13 F NC S
  Margaret R.          11 F NC
  John C.C.            9 M NCS
  Martha A.L.          7 F NC
  Sarah J.             5 F NC
  Jessee P.W.          2 M NC
```

60 A improved land, 100 A unimpr, value:$600

<u>p 199, School District #15, 19 & 20 Oct 1950</u>

```
1385.1396 John A WILHELM 23 M F NC farmer 150 m
  Nancy M. WILHELM     20 F NC (X) m
```

[MB:John Wilhelm & Nancy Bostian 19 Nov 1849]

```
1386.1397 Michael BOSTIAN 49 M NC
  Sarah BOSTIAN        43 F NC
  Margaret D.          18 F NC S
  John A.              15 M NC S
  Hetta L.             12 F NC S
  Daniel M.            10 M NCS
  Jacob J.             8 M NC
  David E.             1 M NC
```

80 A improved land, 210 A unimpr, value:$1000

```
1388.1398 Moses WILHELM 37 M NC (X) farmer 200
  Penelope WILHELM     30 F NC (X)
  Michael              11 M NC S
  Mary M.              9 F NC S
  Margaret E.          7 F NC
  John L.              5 M NC
  Salome C.            3 F NC
  Penelope             9/12 F NC
  Margaret WILHELM     79 F PA (X)
```

[MB:Moses Wilhelm & Penny Lytaker 29 Jan 1838]
40 A improved land, 69 A unimpr, value:$200

```
1389.1399 Hervey BLUSTER 31 M NC farmer 220
  Sarah BLUSTER        30 F NC
  Mary A.              8 F NC        cont.
```

Sarah E.   3/12 F NC
Mary MENUS   60 F NC (X)

[MB:Hervy Bluster to Sally Menis 9 Apr 1839]
40 A improved land, 26 A unimpr, value:$220

1390.1400 Andrew MENUS 31 M NC farmer 200
Polly W. MENUS   28 F NC

40 A improved land, 20 A unimpr, value:$200

1391.1401 Serena HOLBROOKS 42 F SC (X)
Joshua   21 M NC (X)
Martin   18 M NC
Catherine   16 F NC
Elisabeth H.   13 F NC
Green A.   12 M NC
John F.   10 M NC
Camilla J.   7 F NC
Polly   5 F NC
Margaret A.   3 F NC

40 A improved land, 140 A unimpr, value:$820

1392.1402 Jacob LITAKER 32 M NC carriage maker 135
Margaret A LITAKER   29 F NC
Jane E.   7 F NC

60 A improved land, 47 A unimpr, value:$300
1 slave

1393.1403 Elisabeth LITAKER 60 F NC
George E. LITAKER   23 M NC 135
Mary A. LITAKER   3 F NC 67

20 A improved land, 3 A unimpr, value:$300
1 slave

1394.1404 Catherine BOSTIAN 28 F NC (X)
Daniel BOSTIAN   46 M NC farmer
Margery Bostian STILLER   8 F NC S

Daniel BOSTIAN: 86 A improved land, 30 A unimpr, valued at $350

1395.1405. George M RITCHIE 31 M NC farmer 300
Leah L. RITCHIE   27 F NC (X)
Henry V.   1 M NC
Jacob M. RITCHIE   18 M NC labourer

25 A improved land, 25 A unimpr, value:$300

1396.1406 Jesse P WISEMAN 38 M NC 2,000
Mary WISEMAN   39 F NC
Julia Ann   7 F NC S
Nancy K.   5/12 F NC
George C. HICKS   18 M student 800
Rosetta HICKS   20 F NC
Mary J. CROWEL   10 F NC S

[MB:Jesse P Wiseman to Mary Hicks 27 Apr 1841]
1078 A improved land, 45 A unimproved, valued at

$1,200, 9 slaves

1397.1407 Salah P DONNELL 36 M NC blacksmith 450
Mary D. DONNELL   31 F NC
James I.   6 M NC

40 A improved land, 35 A unimproved, valued at
$450, 1 slave

1398.1408 William C BRANDON 26 M NC farmer
Savannah BRANDON   28 F NC (X)
Mary E.   8 F NC S
Julia A.C.   2 F NC

65 A improved land valued at $150

1399.1409 Charles N MILLER 31 M NC farmer 1,300
Catherine MILLER   31 F NC
Pleasant M.   11 M NC S
Henry C.   9 M NC S
Jane C.   5 F NC S
Lunda M.   3 F NC
Rose S.   9/12 F NC

[MB:Charles M Miller & Catherine Redwine n.d.]
85 A improved land, 245 A unimpr, value:$1300
5 slaves

1400.1410 John GARDNER 44 M NC farmer 400
Nancy GARDNER   29 F NC (X)
William G.   4 M NC
Rose A.   1 F NC

[MB:John Gardner to Nancy Coon 25 Sept 1845]
68 A improved land, 70 A unimpr, value:$400

1401.1411 Richard GARDNER 36 M NC farmer
[200].1412. James CAUBLE   45 M NC farmer
Polly CAUBLE   48 F NC (X)
Richard   18 M NC S
Henry   16 M NC S
Edward   14 M NC S
Maria   12 F NC
Nancy   10 F NC S

Richard GARDNER: 30 A improved land, 70 A
unimproved, valued at $600
James CAUBLE: 30 A improved land valued at $100

p 200, School District #22, 24 Oct 1850

1402.1413 Henry MILLER 60 M NC farmer 3,825
Jesse W.   22 M NC labourer
Sophia   24 F NC
Catherine   20 F NC
Christiana   18 F NC

150 A improved land, 388 unimproved, valued at
$2000, 10 slaves

1403.1414 Catherine BEAVER 44 F NC
George W.   18 M NC farmer cont.

48 A improved land, 85 A unimpr, value:$400

1404.1415 John BEAVER   42 M NC 600
  Elisabeth BEAVER   38 F NC
  Alexander   17 M NC S labourer
  Crawford   15 M NC S labourer
  Susanna   13 F NC S
  Lavinia E.   11 F NC S
  Catherine   8 F NC S
  Margaret   6 F NC
  Mary S.   3 F NC
  John   3/12 M NC

70 A improved land, 56 A unimpr, value:$600

1405.1416 James BEAN 23 M NC m
  Hetty BEAN   19 F NC m

[MB:James W Bean to Betty Beaver 16 Feb 1850]

1406.1417 John HARTMAN 49 M NC farmer 350
  Polly HARTMAN   54 F NC (X)
  Sally OVERCASH   70 F NC (X) 100

110 A improved land, 60 A unimpr, value:$350

1407.1418 John HARTMAN   36 M NC (X)
  Margaret HARTMAN   34 F NC (X)

50 A improved land, 50 A unimpr, value:$300

1408.1419 Abraham HILL 44 M NC farmer
  Lydia HILL   29 F NC
  Sarah E.   10 F NC
  Abigail I.   5 F NC
  Mary J.   2 F NC

55 A improved land, 55 A unimpr, value:$300

1409.1420 Nelson SAFRET   32 M NC farmer
  Amelia SAFRET   29 F NC (X)
  Salena   10 F NC
  Jacob   8 M NC
  Rufus   6 M NC
  Calvin   3 M NC
  Charles   2 M NC
  Cornelius   0/12 M NC

no land but livestock

1410.1421 Christiana A MISENHEIMER 20 F NC
  Jemima J.   3 F NC
  Sophia L.M.   2/12 F NC
  Mary A. KLUTTS   24 F NC

48 A improved land valued at $200

1411.1422 John COON   38 M NC (X)
  Susan C. COON   35 F NC (X)
  William   13 M NC S
  Margaret A.   11 F NC S   cont.

Jane E.   9 F NC
Richard M.   6 M NC
George H.   2 M NC

[MB:John Coon to Susan Casper 19 Nov 1835]
  38 A improved land valued at $150

1412.1423 Saloma HEILIG 42 F NC 400
  George M.G.   22 M NC (X)
  Julius M.   20 M NC
  William J.   18 M NC S
  Charles M.   13 M NC S

120 A improved land, 115 unimpr, value:$3000

1413.1424 Montfort S McKINZIE 42 M NC farmer 7,000
  Margaret G. McKINZIE   36 F NC
  William W.   13 M NC S
  Montfort S.   10 M NC S
  John W.   6 M NC S
  Mary S.   3 F NC
  Margaret N.M.   1/12 F NC

200 A improved land, 300 A unimpr, value:$2800
17 slaves

1414.1425 John C RODGERS 23 M NC overseer
  150 A improved land, 250 A unimproved, valued
    at $2,500

1415.1426 William CRANFORD 36 M NC farmer 600

  75 A improved land, 75 A unimpr, value:$600
  3 slaves

1416.1427 William COLE 48 M NC (X) shoemaker
  Jane   17 F NC S
  John   14 M NC
  Brandon   12 M NC
  Mary   10 F NC
  Elisabeth COLE   70 F NC blind

1417.1428 Volentine STIREWALT 25 M NC farmer 6,000
  Sarah A. STIREWALT   28 F NC
  Walter H.   8/12 M NC

200 A improved land, 200 A unimproved, valued
    at $2,800, 6 slaves
  flouring: 600 bbls flour worth $3,000
  corn mill: 660 bu corn meal worth $1,980
  saw mill: 83,000 ft of lumber worth $850

1418.1429 James N RODGERS 27 M NC
  Elisabeth RODGERS   25 F NC
  Mary E.   2 F NC
  John K.   7/12 M NC

[MB:James N Rodgers to Elizabeth Stirewalt 13 Apr
  1846]

1419.1430 Henry SPECK 23 M NC farmer
  Sophya SPECK   20 F NC   cont.

[201] John H. RODGER   7/12 M NC

<u>p.201, School Districk # 21, 25 Oct 1850</u>

1420.1431 Phillip OWENS   47 M NC farmer 1,500
 Nancy OWENS   37 F NC <u>S</u>
 Amanda J.   15 F NC S
 David   14 M NC S
 Eliza   12 F NC S
 Margaret   10 F NC S
 Martha   7 F NC S
 Burges   5 M NC
 Christiana   2 F NC
 John H.   1/12 M NC

 [MB: Phillip Owens to Nancy Smith 15 Mar 1833]
 225 A improved land, 106 A unimproved, value:
  $1,450, 8 slaves

1421.1432 Sheppard COLE 52 M NC (X) farmer
 Penelope COLE   32 F NC (X)
 Julius A.   7 M NC
 Mary E.   1 F NC

 [MB: Sheppard Cole to Pene Cope 13 Jan 1847]
 255 A improved land, 75 A unimpr, value:$600

1422.1433 Catherine ROGERS 51 F NC (X)
 Solomon C.   26 M NC teacher
 Margaret E.   19 F NC
 Mary C.   11 F NC
 Solomon F. EAGLE 15 M NC

 80 A improved land, 42 A unimpr, value:$500

1423.1434 Barbara E ROGERS 26 F NC
 Henry M.) twins   5 M NC S
 Margaret) twins   5 F NC S
 William E.   2 M NC
 Lydia BOSTIAN   49 F NC

1424.1435 Henry STIREWALT 59 M NC blacksmith 700
 Elisabeth STIREWALT 59 F VA (X)
 William M.   31 M NC blacksmith
 Jacob   26 M NC blacksmith
 Emeline S.   19 F NC

 [MB:Henry Stirewalt & Betsey Recard 23 Dec 1812]
 80 A improved land, 170 A unimpr, value: $700

1425.1436 Adam STIREWALT 33 M NC farmer
 Judith C. STIREWALT 30 F NC
 Mary A.E.   9 F NC S
 Jane L.   4 F NC
 Sarah   1 F NC

 [MB:Adam Stirewalt to Judy C Shulibarger 3 Jan
  1840], 15 A improved land valued at $72
 blacksmith: other articles worth $273, ?? worth
  $275

1426.1437 Georg E. BOST   25 M NC farmer 800
 Margaret C. BOST 21 F NC
 Rose E.   2 F NC

 51 A improved land, 145 A unimpr, value:$800

1427.1438 John BOSTIAN 51 M NC farmer 2,000
 Mary BOSTIAN   51 F NC (X)
 Jeremiah E.   22 M NC
 Polly C.   13 F NC S
 Leah E.   24 F NC
 Margaret A.E.)twins 18 F NC
 Alpheus I.   )twins 18 M NC S
 Martha BUTNER   50 F NC (X)

 [MB: John Bostian to Mary Duke 17 July 1820]
 22 A improved land, 250 A unimpr, valued at
  $2,000, 2 slaves

1428.1439 William C MILLER 38 M NC farmer 1,000
 Mary A. MILLER   38 F NC (X)
 George W.   17 M NC S
 John L.   10 M NC S
 Richard A.   6 M NC S
 Knox Polk   4 M NC
 Mary C. AXIUM   11 F NC S idiotic

 [MB: William C Miller to Mary Ann Albright 9 Sept
  1830]   60 A improved land, 30 A unimproved,
  valued at $700
 tannery: [illeg] various articles worth $1,165

1429.1440 Jacob BOSTIAN 39 N NC farmer
 Mary L. BOSTION 25 F NC
 David W.   1 M NC
 Andrew BOSTIAN 67 M NC farmer 800

 [MB:Jacob Bostian to May L Lynn 22 Apr 1848]
 50 A improved land, 115 A unimpr, value:$800
 sawmill: 6,000 ft timber worth $800

1430.1441 Rineholt KETCHEY 45 M NC blacksmith 1,200
 Jane M. KETCHEY 36 F NC
 Polly S.   13 F NC S
 William R.   11 M NC S
 Sarah A.   9 F NC S
 Amanda   6 F NC
 Miles M.   4 M NC
 John D.   1 M NC
 Nancy Duke   76 F NC (X)
 Peter WEAVER   21 M NC blacksmith

 [MB:Rinehold Ketchy to Jane M Duke 20 Jan 1837]
 150 A improved land, 187 A unimpr, value: $1200

1431.1442 Jacob SETZER 45 M NC wagonmaker 2,000
 Mary A. SETZER   28 F NC
 Jason D.   8 M NC S
 William SAFORT   22 M NC wagonmaker

cont.

200 A improved land, 276 unimproved, valued at
    $2,000, 4 slaves
wagon shop: wagon & various article worth $500

1432.1443 John SPECK 46 M NC (X) farmer 400
   Sally SPECK   50 F NC (X)
   Monroe   21 M NC labourer
   William   19 M NC labourer

   40 A improved land, 60 A unimpr, value:$500

1433.1444 Valentine PROBSTS 50 M NC (X) farmer
   Elisabeth PROBSTS   50 F NC (X)
   Valentine, Junr.   24 M NC labourer
   Daniel W.   20 M NC S labourer
   Henry M.   17 M NC S labourer
   Thomas P.   14 M NC S
   Anna L.   9 F NC S
   Adolphus   7 M NC
   Sally E.   9 F NC S

   no acreage but livestock, grain

<u>p.202, School District #22, 26 Oct 1850</u>

1434.1445 Susan SAFORT 56 F NC (X) 800
   Moses   24 M NC
   Eliza   17 F NC
   Eli   15 M NC
   John   13 M NC
   Catherine BLACKWELDER 40 F NC
   George SAFORT   66 M NC 300
   William J. SLOOP   22 M NC miller
   Robert WILHELM   20 M Mu

   131 A improved land, 151 unimpr, value:$500

1435.1446 David J KLUTTS 28 M NC farmer 600
   Margaret KLUTTS   24 F NC
   William S.   4 M NC
   Rose Ann   1 M NC
   Jane HAIR   15 F NC

   55 A improved land, 84 A unimpr, value:$600

1436.1447 Catherine GARNER 68 F NC (X) 544
   Molina   41 F NC (X)
   Jacob F.   40 M NC labourer
                          slightly idiotic
   Sally   37 F NC
   Susanna   36 F NC
   Elisabeth   30 F NC
   Ealy M.   26 F NC

   100 A improved land, 172 unimpr, value:$500

1437.1448 Solomon KETCHEY 39 M NC farmer 400
   Catharine KETCHEY   33 F NC
   Ealy A.   12 F NC
   Susan S.   9 F NC
   Franey C.   3 F NC

                                    cont.

[MB:Solomon Ketchey to Catherine Garner 27 Mar
   1837]

1438.1449 John BOSTIAN 26 M NC farmer 275
   Polly E. BOSTIAN   26 F NC (X)
   Camilla C.   ) twin   2 F NC
   Margaret D.) twin   2 F NC
   Lowrance J.   1/12 M NC
   Lunda M. HAIR   19 F NC

[MB:John Bostian & Polly Eliza Yost 23 Dec 1844]
   50 A improved land, 125 unimpr, value:$275

1439.1450 Andrew CASPER 48 M NC (X) farmer 2,000
   Elizabeth CASPER   35 F NC (X)
   Adam M.   17 M NC
   James C.   14 M NC
   Ambrose   8 M NC
   Caroline   13 F NC
   Catharine CASPER   65 F NC (X)

[MB:Andrew Casper & Betsey Waller 26 Mar 1831]
   55 A improved land, 153 A unimpr, value:$1200

1440.1451 George RENDLEMAN 40 M NC farmer 1,500
   Eliza RENDLEMAN   32 F NC
   Andrew H.R.   13 M NC
   Catherine J.   11 F NC
   Lawson M.   9 M NC
   Robert   1 M NC
   Jessee PHILLIPS   35 M NC B labourer

[MB:George Rendleman & Eliza Roseman 8 Oct 1834]
   100 A improved land, 129 A unimpr, value:$1000
   10 slaves

1441.1452 Jacob LINGLE 54 M NC farmer 650
   Elisabeth LINGLE   46 F NC (X)
   Christina SEAFORD   80 F NC (X) 150
   Margaret S. BEAVER 12 F NC S
   Henry DEAL   22 M NC

   Jacob LINGLE: 60 A improved land, 134 A
      unimproved, valued at $650

1442.1453 John LINGLE 59 M NC farmer 125
   Catharine LINGLE   45 F NC (X)
   Moses   15 M NC S
   Mary A.   13 F NC S
   Alfred   10 M NC S
   Rachel C.   7 F NC
   Sarah M.   4 F NC

   60 A improved land, 61 A unimpr, value:$125

1443.1454 Michael BOSTIAN 31 M NC blacksmith 600
   Catharine BOSTIAN   32 F NC
   Mary A.C.   6 F NC
   Jacob A.   4 M NC
   David L.   1 M NC

   70 A improved land, 71 A unimpr, value:$600
   4 slaves

1444.1455 Phillip CASPER 66 M NC (X) farmer 400
    John   35 M NC (X)
    Alexander   33 M NC
    David   31 M NC
    Daniel   16 M NC
    Elisabeth   13 F NC S

    110 A improved land, 75 A unimpr, value:$400

1445.1456 Elisabeth OVERCASH 56 F NC (X)
    Henry OVERCASH   22 M NC labourer

1446.1457 Mary STIREWALT 70 F NC 400

1447.1458 William HORNBARRIER 42 M NC cabinetmaker
                                          50
    Mary HORNBARRIER   29 F NC (X)
    Elisabeth   9 F NC S
    Jacob   5 M NC
    John A.   2 M NC
    Jeremiah   2/12 M NC
    Catharine HORNBARRIER 60 F NC (X)

1448.1459 James MELTON 37 M NC labourer
    Elisabeth MELTON   37 F NC
    Lydia L.   15 F NC S
    Mary C.   12 F NC S
    William S.   9 N NC S
[203] Levi A.   7 M NC S
    James A.   4 M NC
    Susan J.   1/12 F NC

<u>p.203, School District #22, 29 Oct 1850</u>

1449.1460 Henry PLESS 45 M NC farmer
    Sarah PLESS   37 F NC
    Uriah M.   18 M NC S
    Harriet L.   16 F NC S
    Jacob I.   12 M NC S
    Henry J.   9 M NC S
    John L.A.   5 M NC

    no acreage but livestock, grain
    8 slaves

1450.1461 Caleb STIREWALT 39 M NC farmer 750
    Michiel STIREWALT   35 F NC
    Charles M.   13 M NC S
    Harriet L.   11 F NC S
    Mary A. E.   8 F NC S
    Amanda C.   3 F NC

    60 A improved land, 62 A unimpr, value:$750

1451.1462 Daniel FINK 48 M NC wagonmaker 600
    Rosana P. FINK   42 F NC
    John M.   19 M NC S labourer
    Jacob C.   17 M NC labourer
    William T.   14 M NC S
    Daniel C.   12 M NC S
    Henry H.   10 M NC S
    James F.   8 M NC S

    Sarah R.   5 F NC S
    Mary A.E.   3 F NC

    100 A improved land, 117 unimpr, value:$600

1452.1463 Charles BOSTIAN 28 M NC carpenter
    Seno BOSTIAN   23 F NC
    Sophia L.   1 F NC
    Mary A. EAGLE   12 F NC S

[MB:Charles Bostian to Cena Eagle 10 Feb 1846]
    22 A improved land valued at $66

1453.1464 John EAGLE 60 M NC carpenter 1,120
    Sophia EAGLE   55 F NC
    Maria   20 F NC S
    George W.   18 M NC S farmer
    Daniel M.   16 M NC S labourer
    William CASTOR   7 M NC S

    113 A improved land, 200 A unimpr, valued at
       $1,124, 2 slaves

1454.1465 David EAGLE 34 M NC farmer 350
    Charlotte EAGLE   28 F NC (X)
    Charlotte S.   10 F NC S
    William A.   8 M NC S

    25 A improved land, 63 A unimpr, value:$350

1455.1466 Daniel STIREWALT 47 M NC blacksmith 593
    Sarah C.   18 F NC
    Daniel B.   15 M NC labourer
    Anderson G.   13 M NC

    100 A improved land, 121 unimpr, value:$5<u>75</u>

1456.1467 George EAGLE 51 M NC farmer 850
    Sarah EAGLE   48 F NC (X)
    Margaret B.   24 F NC
    John P.   19 M NC S labourer
    Louisa A.   16 F NC S
    Catherine N.   14 F NC S
    Moses J.   8 M NC S
    Mary E.S.   5 F NC

    100 A improved land, 146 A unimpr, value:$850

1457.1468 John LIPPARD 59 M NC farmer 1,500
    Sarah LIPPARD   49 F NC (X)
    John W.A.   23 M NC labourer
    Eli S.P.   19 M NC S labourer
    Eliza S.   17 F NC
    Cleodora A.   13 F NC S
    Alison S.J.   8 M NC S

    190 A improved land, 195 unimpr, value:$1500

1458.1469 George RITCHEY   55 M NC farmer 180
    Elisabeth RITCHEY   55 F NC (X)
    Margaret C.   21 F NC
    John   19 M NC   cont.

```
Charles                    17 M NC
George W.                  15 M NC
Polly E.                   13 F NC

50 A improved land, 22 A unimpr, value:$180

1459.1470 George BASINGER 31 M NC tanner 162
  Anna BASINGER            23 F NC (X)
  Mary C.                   5 F NC S
  Joseph M.                 2 M NC
  Martha M.              9/12 F NC

1460.1471 Elisabeth BASINGER 61 F NC (X) 600
  Joseph                   24 M NC farmer 250
  Caleb                    21 M NC labourer
  James                    19 M NC S labourer
  Peter REDWINE             9 M NC S

40 A improved land, 220 A unimpr, value: $520

1461.1472 Charles Basinger 34 M NC farmer
  Mary BASINGER            34 F NC (X)
  Andrew                    9 M NC S
  George H.                 7 M NC S
  Mary A.                   6 F NC
  Sarah S.                  5 F NC
  Margaret E.               4 F NC

110 A improved land valued at $80

1462.1473 John BASINGER 38 M NC blacksmith 350
[204] Nancy BASINGER       36 F NC (X)
  Joseph J.                14 M NC
  Daniel M.                12 M NC S
  Julia A.C.               10 F NC
  John A.                   7 M NC
  William                   1 M NC

11 A improved land valued at $22
cutting: various articles worth $30
```

<u>p. 204, School District #24, 30 Oct 1850</u>

```
1463.1474 Michael BROWN  24 M NC (X) farmer 250
  Creasa BROWN            22 F NC (X)

10 A improved land, 90 A unimpr, value:$250

1464.1475 Adam CRUSE    31 M NC farmer
  Catharine CRUSE        22 F NC
  William J.A.            4 M NC
  Jacob H.C.             1 M NC

60 A improved land, 42 A unimpr, value:$205

1465.1476 Melcher TROUTMAN 73 M NC (X) wagonmaker

1466.1477 John CRUSE     29 M NC farmer  172
  Mary CRUSE             43 F NC (X)
  Esther RIGHT           10 F NC
  Catharine CARCAR       72 F NC (X)

61 A improved land, 40 A unimpr, value:$175
```

```
1467.1478 George SEAFORD 56 M NC farmer 33
  Elisabeth                27 F NC
  Christiana L.            25 F NC
  Sophia                   23 F NC
  Henry A.                 21 M NC labourer

28 A improved land, 5 A unimpr, value:$33

1468.1479 Martin JOSEY 44 M NC farmer 400
  Margaret JOSEY          43 F NC (X)
  Mary                    18 F NC S
  Theophilus              15 M NC S
  Lafett                  13 M NC S
  Margaret                11 F NC S
  Fielding                 9 M NC S
  Martin M.                7 M NC S
  Lunda                    3 F NC

100 A improved land, 120 A unimpr, value:$600

1469.1480 Daniel CRUSE 24 M NC farmer
  Maria CRUSE             22 F NC (X)
  Alexander M.          9/12 M NC
  Julia A. MOWRY          12 F NC

1470.1481 David CAUBLE  37 M NC (X) labourer
  Sophia CAUBLE           34 F NC (X)
  Emily                   13 F NC

1471.1482 Henry TROUTMAN  44 M NC (X) farmer
  Maria TROUTMAN          40 F NC (X)

1472.1483 Michael SHUPING 69 M NC (X) farmer 500
  Miles                   24 M NC

31 A improved land, 190 A unimpr, value:$500
1 slave

1473.1484 Caleb SHUPING  34 M NC farmer 550

20 A improved land, 66 A unimpr, value:$550

1474.1485 Moses A SHUPING 32 M NC farmer 1,000
  Elisabeth C. SHUPING    32 F NC (X)
  Michael                 11 M NC S
  Maria                    9 F NC S
  Flora                    2 F NC

31 A improved land, 83 A unimpr, value:$1000
sawmill: 60,000 ft lumber valued at $510

1475.1486 Jacob HOLTSHOUSER 26 M NC (X) famer 100
  Catharine HOLTSHOUSER   24 F NC (X)
  John R.                  7 M NC

25 A improved land valued at $200

1476.1487 David BROWN   36 M NC miller
  Christiana R. BROWN    31 F NC
  Peter A.                14 M NC
  Eliza M.                11 F NC S
  Henry                    9 M NC S
  Lawrence                 5 M NC S    cont.
```

Samuel C. FULKER   19 M NC labourer

45 A improved land, 129 unimpr, value:$1,300
flouring: ? bbls flour worth $3,750
corn mill: ? bu corn meal worth $2,760

1477.1488 Wilson A LENTZ 24 M NC tailor 700
  Mary C. LENTZ   26 F NC
  John P.   2 M NC
  Mary A.   4/12 F NC

58 A improved land, 129 A unimpr, value:$700

1478.1489 Henry KLUTTZ   44 M NC tailor 1,100
  Sarah KLUTTZ   42 F NC (X)
  Archibald M.A.   18 M NC S
  Alfred W.   16 M NC S
  Amey   14 F NC S
  Leah   18 F NC S
  Mary E.   8 F NC S
  Rose A.   5 F NC
  Rufus H.   3 M NC

50 A improved land, 160 A unimpr, value:$1,000

1479.1490 John P RIMER 36 M NC farmer 1,750
  Edith RIMER   38 F NC (X)
  Catharine   16 F NC S
  Mary A.   14 F NC S
  Christiana J.   9 F NC S
  Alexander   4 M NC

  150 A improved land, 102 A unimproved, value:
      $1,000, 1 slave

1480.1491 Jacob PROBTS 52 M NC farmer 660

  120 A improved land, 100 A unimpr, value:$660
  7 slaves

1481.1492 Jessee THOMAS 28 M NC labourer
  Dilla THOMAS   27 F NC (X)
  Daniel   10 M NC S
  Archibald   5 M NC

1482.1493 Paul A SEAFORD 42 M NC farmer 3,200
  Margaret P. SEAFORD   41 F NC
  [205] Eve Ann   19 F NC S
  Miles H.   17 M NC
  Margaret   15 F NC S
  Sarah E.   13 F NC S
  Moses A.   11 M NC S
  Mary L.   9 F NC S
  John M.   7 M NC S
  Louisa M.   4 F NC
  Jeremiah L.   2 M NC
  Margaret CASTER   10 F NC
  Jane   9 F NC

  100 A improved land, 225 A unimpr, valued at
      $2,500, 2 slaves

<u>p. 205, School District #24, 31 Oct 1850</u>

1483.1494 David ROSEMAN   41 M NC farmer 2,000
  Maria ROSEMAN   31 F NC
  Flora E.E.   7 F NC
  Theodore A.P.   5 M NC
  Zuingley W.   2 M NC

  100 A improved land, 70 A unimpr, valued at
      $2,500, 2 slaves

1484.1495 John CASTER   61 M NC 650
  Polly R.   18 F NC
  Henry M.   15 M NC S labourer
  Christiana E.   14 F NC S
  Jacob F.   12 M NC S

  60 A improved land, 60 A unimpr, value:$500

1485.1496 Adam ROSEMAN   57 M NC farmer 2,000
  Elisabeth ROSEMAN   47 F NC
  Miles A.J.   20 M NC medical student

  150 A improved land, 350 A unimproved, value:
      $1,500, 2 slaves

1486.1497 Moses SEAFORD 26 M NC farmer
  Sarah A. SEAFORD   26 F NC

1487.1498 Anna M.B. GRABER   54 F NC
  Louisa R.H.   18 F NC
  Anna E.M.   16 F NC
  Mary Salome Florentine   12 F NC
  John M.   19 M NC
  Thomas HOUSE   7 M NC

1488.1499 Jacob PHILLIPS 33 M NC farmer 400
  Catharine PHILLIPS   30 F NC (X)
  Julius A.   11 M NC S
  Mary A.C.   10 F NC
  Jacob M.   7 M NC S
  Charles L.F.   5 M NC
  Sarah C.   3 F NC
  Lawson J.   1 M NC

1489.1500 Moses FINK   34 M NC (X) labourer
  Catharine FINK   32 F NC (X)
  Mary E.   11 F NC S
  Margaret J.A.   9 F NC S
  John M.   3 M NC

1490.1501 Peter KEINER   30 M NC farmer 1,500
  Nancy KEINER   23 F NC
  Nancy A.C.   9/12 F NC
  John W.   6 M NC

  160 A improved land, 120 A unimproved land,
      valued at $1,500, 7 slaves

1491.1502 Nancy ROSEMAN 50 F NC
  Mary L.   23 F NC 200
  Edward H.   21 M NC 200

  90 A improved land, 50 A unimpr, value:$800

1492.1503 Frederick STIREWALT 44 M NC 1,200
    Catharine STIREWALT   42 F NC (X)
    Frederick A.   18 M NC
    Eve C.   8 F NC S
    Moses J.) twins   3 M NC
    David M.) twins   3 M NC

    100 A improved land, 900 A unimpr, value:$1200

1493.1504 Jacob STIREWALT 22 M NC farmer
    Catharine STIREWALT   26 F NC (X)
    Rufus A.   9/12 M NC

1494.1505 Moses BOGER 29 M NC farmer 173
    Anna M. BOGER   27 F NC
    George A.   6 M NC S
    Mary A.J.   2 F NC
    Sophia WRIGHT   12 F NC S

    15 A improved land, 39 A unimpr, value:$775

1495.1506 James C ROSEMAN 34 M NC farmer 4,000
    Christiana ROSEMAN   26 F NC
    Rufus   5 M NC
    Margaret   4 F NC
    Mary L.   7/12 F NC

    200 A improved land, 350 unimpr, value:$775
    12 slaves
    corn mill: 5,300 bu corn meal valued at $2200
    saw mill: 60,000 ft lumber valued at $510

1496.1507 John F KEIFNECK 58 M NC
    Sophia KEIFNICK   33 F NC (X)
    Rosana E.   10 F NC S
    Mary S.   9 F NC S
    Margaret M.   6 F NC
    Monro A.   3 M NC

1497.1508 Paul STRICKLER 32 M NC (X) farmer 350
    Polly STRICKLER   30 F NC (X)
    Jacob   6 M NC infirm
    Mary   4 F NC
    Rufues J.)twins   1 M NC
    Thomas M.)   1 M NC

    Paul STRIKLER: 37 A improved land, 38 A
      unimproved, valued at $350

<u>p. 206, School District #24, 31 Oct 1850</u>

1498.1509 Mary SHAVER 50 F NC
    Salene   17 F NC
    Rebecca   15 F NC
    John   13 M NC
    Paul J.   11 M NC

1499.1510 Jacob A. SMITH 22 M NC labourer
    Leah SMITH   20 F NC
    Jacob A.   9/12 M NC

1500.1511 Jacob YOST 54 M NC farmer 800
    Margaret YOST   54 F NC (X)   cont.

    Jacob A.   24 M NC labourer
    Alexander   22 M NC labourer
    Sena   17 F NC S
    Paul   14 M NC S
    Levi   10 M NC S

    80 A improved land, 144 A unimpr, value:$600

1501.1512 Alexander POWLAS 21 M NC farmer
    Rachel POWLAS   22 F NC (X)
    Clarissa   1 F NC
    Catharine POWLAS   52 F NC (X) 800

    90 A improved land, 100 A unimpr, value:$800

1502.1513 Daniel RIMER 34 M NC farmer 1,000
    Eve RIMER   38 F NC (X)
    James W.   14 M NC S
    Alexander M.   12 M NC S
    Eve A.C.   7 F NC S
    Daniel J.   2 M NC
    Susana RIMER   50 F NC (X)

    90 A improved land, 60 A unimpr, value:$800

1503.1514 John RIMER 47 M NC (S) wheelwright 1000
    Sophia RIMER   46 F NC (X)
    David A.   21 M NC farmer
    Jacob W.   19 M NC labourer
    Catharine L.   16 F NC S
    Samuel M.   13 M NC S
    Eve M. A.   9 F NC S
    Sophia M.   6 F NC S
    Mary C.   11/12 F NC

    100 A improved land, 25 A unimpr, value:$1,000

1504.1515 George BOST 72 M NC (X) hatter 1,500
    Catharine BOST   69 F NC
    Nancy   40 F NC
    Moses A.   24 M NC
    Ruben W.   22 M NC
    Catharine L. SEAFORD 12 F NC S

    100 A improved land, 240 A unimpr, value:$1,500

1505.1516 Elias BEAVER 38 M NC farmer
    Nelly BEAVER   38 F NC
    Jessee   18 M NC S
    William   16 M NC S
    Rachel   14 F NC S
    Susan   10 F NC S
    Elizabeth   7 F NC S
    Polly   4 F NC S
    David   1 M NC
    Peter COON   65 M NC labourer

    100 A improved land, 117 A unimpr, value:$600

1506.1517 Martin BARGER 33 M NC
    Catharine BARGER   30 F NC
    Moses J.   10 M NC
    George A.   6 M NC   cont.

45 A improved land, 92 A unimpr, value:$1,000

1507.1518 George H BARGER   24 M NC farmer 700 m
  Rebecca C. BARGER   17 F NC m
  Jessee BARGER   23 M NC farmer
  Elisabeth C. BARGER   23 F NC 300
  John M.   7/12 M NC

  George H & Jesse Barger: 65 A improved land, 35
  A unimproved, valued at $700

1508.1519 Moses BARRINGER   22 M NC miller 2,500
  Mary C. BARRINGER   30 F NC
  Elisha SMITH   36 M NC physician

  100 A improved land, 186 A unimproved, valued at
      $1,500, 5 slaves
  flouring: 200 bbl flour valued at $900
  corn mill: 3,300 bu corn meal valued at $2,230

1509.1520 Edmund FESPERMAN   25 M NC farmer
  Margaret D. FESPERMAN 23 F NC (X)
  Martha L.E.   1 F NC

1510.1521 John FESPERMAN   48 M NC farmer 1,150
  Sophia FESPERMAN   48 F NC (X)
  Eliza L.   21 F NC
  Elisabeth A.   17 F NC
  Willa M.   15 M NC S
  Simeon G.   13 M NC S
  Margaret C.   10 F NC
  Sarah L.   8 F NC
  John A.   4 M NC

  75 A improved land, 454 A unimpr, value:$1,085

1511.1522 John A CASTER 19 M NC labourer m
  Mary A.E. CASTER   22 F NC (X) m

1512.1523 Enoch E PHILLIPS 49 M NC stone cutter 400
  Charlotte E.   14 F NC S
  John L.   13 M NC S
  Calvin   12 M NC S
  Adam B.   10 M NC S
  Joseph   8 M NC S
  Ellen   7 F NC S
  [207] Jane   4 F NC
  Solomon   3 M NC
  Sally JEANS   40 F NC (X)
  Margaret   3 F NC Mu

  100 A improved land, 110 A unimpr, value:$400

<u>p.207, School District # 25, 1 Nov 1850</u>

1513.1524 John HOLTSHOUSER   55 M NC (X) stone
                                      cutter 250
  Christiana HOLTSHOUSER   36 F NC (X)
  Willa   18 M NC
  Washington   16 M NC
  Moses   14 M NC
  Mary A.   12 F NC   cont.

  John   9 M NC
  Green   7 M NC
  Catharine   4 F NC
  James L.   2 M NC
  Henry C.   5/12 M NC

  ?, 27 Gol Grinders value: $540

1514.1525 Caleb YOST   44 M NC farmer 600
  Margaret YOST   39 F NC (X)
  Elisabeth L.   17 F NC S
  Alexander W.   14 M NC S
  Solomon M.   12 M NC S

  50 A improved land, 80 A unimpr, value:$600

1515.1526 John YOST   36 M NC farmer 700
  Sarah YOST   26 F NC (X)
  Leah F.   7 F NC
  Margaret S.   4 F NC
  Mary YOST   62 F PA (X)
  Margaret D.   24 F NC (X)
  Mary A.   21 F NC

  133 A improved land, 130 A unimproved, value:
      $700, 1 slave

1516.1527 Montford HOLTSHOUSER 38 M NC collier
  Penelope HOLTSHOUSER   33 F NC (X)
  Louisa   10 F NC
  Catharine P.   7 F NC
  Sarah M.   2 F NC

1517.1528 George RUSHER   58 M NC farmer 800
  Mary RUSHER   55 F NC (X)
  Miles   34 M NC labourer
  Jacob   26 M NC blacksmith
  John   23 M NC blacksmith
  Moses A.   20 M NC S partially
                               idiotic
                               & defective
  Edward   17 M NC S blacksmith
  Alfred   )twins   15 M NC S labourer
  Eve Maria   )   15 F NC S
  Anna   18 F NC

  100 A improved land, 83 unimpr, value: $800
  Jacob & John Rusher: smithing: ? valued at $200,
  other articles valued at $200, wagons valued at
  $440

1518.1529 Margaret BROWN   32 F NC (X) 500
  George M. DUKE   6 M NC
  Rose FESPERMAN   65 F NC (X)
  George FESPERMAN   30 M NC farmer

  George Fesperman: 60 A improved land, 75 A
      unimproved, valued at $500
  Margaret Brown: 1 slave

1519.1530 Phillip CRUSE   60 M NC farmer
  Elisabeth CRUSE   50 M NC   cont.

Rose   20 F NC (X)
Rebeca   18 F NC
Moses   15 M NC S
Sophia   13 F NC S
Mary A.   5 F NC

30 A improved land valued at $100

1520.1531 Alexander JOSEY 38 M NC labourer
  Sally JOSEY   38 F NC (X)
  Elisabeth D.   16 F NC S
  Laura   10 F NC S

1521.1532 John L RENDLEMAN 47 M NC farmer 1,500
  Nancy RENDLEMAN   46 F NC
  Jacob A.   16 M NC S
  George R.   14 M NC S
  Maria C.   10 F NC S
  Lawrence T.   9 M NC S
  John L.   7 M NC S
  Mary A. L.   9/12 F NC

175 A improved land, 215 unimproved, value:
    $1,500, 15 slaves

1522.1533 Paul MISENHIMER 50 M NC farmer 2,000
  Malinda MISENHIMER   50 F NC
  Alison   24 M NC labourer
  Malisa C.   22 F NC
  Salina   19 F NC
  Elisabeth   16 F NC S
  Jacob   11 M NC S
  Lodemia   9 F NC S
  Richard W. McFARLAND   18 M NC S

196 A improved land, 160 A unimpr, value:$2000

1523.1534 Henry HILL 50 M NC farmer 400
  Jane HILL   50 F NC (X)
  Sarah J.   20 F NC
  Lydia A.   16 F NC S
  Margaret E.   13 F NC S
  Hannah P.   9 F NC S
  Henry W.   24 M NC

60 A improved land, 37 A unimpr, value:$400

1524.1535 Hiram BLACKWELDER 50 M NC (X) farmer
  Susana BLACKWELDER   39 F NC (X)
  Allison A.   19 M NC labourer
[208] Jemima L.   17 F NC S
  Leah M.   15 F NC S
  Alexander W.   13 M NC S
  Jacob C.   11 M NC S
  Sampson T.   3 M NC

40 A improved land, 160 A unimpr, value:$1000

<u>p.208, School District #25, 2 Nov 1850</u>

1525.1536 Bartlet G ALLEN 19 M VA (X) farmer 1000
  Amelia A. ALLEN   31 F NC (X)
  Mary J.   5/12 F NC   cont.

Nancy ELLER   10 F NC
George H. HILL   3 M NC

60 A improved land, 180 unimpr, value:$1,000

1526.1537 Michael FESPERMAN 39 M NC farmer 200
  Cyntha FESPERMAN   37 F NC
  William T.   14 F NC S
  Mary L.   11 F NC S
  Joseph H.   8 M NC S
  Cynthia C.   4 F NC

1527.1538 John HEILIG 46 M NC farmer 200
  Margaret L. HEILIG   29 F NC (X)
  Elisabeth   17 F NC
  George H.   15 M NC S
  Barbara M.   13 F NC S
  James M.   11 M NC S
  John F.   9 M NC S
  Margaret S.   7 F NC
  Julius A.   5 M NC
  Elias L.   3 M NC

60 A improved land, 75 A unimpr, value:$300

1528.1539 William W WEAVER 28 M NC farmer 400
  Anna WEAVER   25 F NC (X)
  David J.   3 M NC
  Susana WEAVER   47 F NC (X)
  Catharine L. WEAVER   23 F NC

31 A improved, 400 A unimpr, valued at $400

1529.1540 John S GRAHAM -- M NC farmer 1,000
  Sarah GRAHAM   55 F NC
  Richard   20 M NC labourer
  Thomas   18 M NC S labourer
  Frances WINDERS   10 F NC S

150 A improved land, 166 unimproved, value:
    $1,000, 11 slaves

1530.1541 Margaret COOK 60 F NC
  Charlotte   30 F NC

1531.1542 Peter KEINER sr.-- M NC farmer 1,000
  Elisabeth KEINER   49 F NC
  Catharine   26 F NC
  Henry   24 M NC
  Elisabeth   21 F NC
  Susan Sena   18 F NC
  John Peter   15 M NC S
  Margaret S.   11 F NC S
  Mary Ann   9 F NC S

65 A improved land, 250 unimproved, value:
    $1,000, 1 slave

1532.1543 Dawalt KEINER 62 M NC farmer 1,000
  John KEINER   27 M NC
  Barbara M.   19 F NC S
  Susana E.   16 F NC
  Margaret A.   9 F NC S   cont.

60 A improved land, 100 A unimpr, value:$1000

1533.1544 John A SMITH   45 M NC farmer
  Susana SMITH   40 F NC
  Samuel J.   22 M NC S
  John W.   19 M NC S
  Christiana C.   12 F NC S
  William HENRY   12 M NC S

1534.1545 Michael OVERCASH   58 M NC Farmer
  Christiana OVERCASH   57 F NC
  Christiana C.   29 F NC
  Mary A.   20 F NC
  Eli SULLIVAN   14 M NC
  Sophia OVERCASH   40 F NC

1535.1546 John LONG   68 M NC farmer 400
  Margaret LONG   63 F NC
  John S.   25 M NC
  Margaret A.   20 F NC

100 A improved land, 380 unimproved, value:
  $400, 2 slaves

1536.1547 Phillip YOST   31 M NC farmer 500
  Margaret YOST   30 F NC
  Jacob D.   5 M NC
  Margaret A.S.   3 F NC
  Jeremiah   1 M NC

1537.1548 David BOSTIAN   38 M NC farmer 800
  Elisabeth BOSTIAN   40 F NC
  Peter A.   18 M NC S
  Margaret L.   15 F NC S
  Eve E.A   13 F NC S
  John M.   8 M NC S

50 A improved land, 145 unimpr, value:$800

1538.1549 Catharine SEAFORD   42 F NC (X)
  Temperance L.   16 F NC S
  Mary A.   12 F NC S

1539.1550 John SMITH sr. 68 M NC farmer 400
  Catharine SMITH   63 F NC

<u>p.209, School District #30, 20 Aug 1850</u>

1540.1551 Rachael EARNHART 24 M NC (X) labourer
  Caroline EARNHART   28 F NC (X)

1541.1552 Ann LINEBARGER 33 F NC (X)
  Elisabeth LEACH   30 F NC (X)
  .1553. Richard LEACH   43 M NC labourer

1542.1554 Charles KLUTTS 30 M NC farmer
  Christina KLUTTS   28 F NC (X)
  George A.   8 M NC
  Miles I.   4 M NC
  .1555. Maria BLACK   23 F NC (X)
  David BLACK   24 M NC labourer

100 A improved land, 150 A unimpr, value:$1,500
  2 slaves

1543.1556 James D SMITH   40 M NC farmer 500
  Margaret SMITH   44 F NC
  Jane C.   15 F NC
  Moses A.   14 M NC
  Mary A.E.   11 F NC
  Laura R.   5 F NC
  Euphemia L.   3 F NC

25 A improved land, 25 A unimpr, value:$<u>3</u>00
  1 slave

1544.1557 George TREXLER   50 M NC teacher
  Nancy   22 F NC
  Alexander   18 M NC
  John   16 M NC
  Warren   12 M NC
  Marcus   10 M NC
  Adren   8 M NC

1545.1558 Daniel SHAVER   31 M NC blacksmith
  Lucy N.   30 F NC
  Sarah D.   5 F NC
  Margaret E.   2 F NC
  James B.   9/12 M NC

20 A improved land, 25 A unimproved, value:
  $200, 3 slaves

1546.1559 Ranson JACOBS 28 M NC overseer 300
  Sarah JACOBS   26 F NC
  Mary F.   1 F NC

1547.1560 Robert R BRADSHAW 41 M NC farmer 3,000
  Jane BRADSHAW   21 F NC
  Elisabeth   19 F NC
  Henry   16 F NC labourer
  Julia   14 F NC
  Laura   2 F NC

100 A improved land, 400 unimproved, value:
  $3,000, 11 slaves

1548.1561 William LOCKE 38 M NC farmer 5,000
  Jane A. LOCKE   30 F NC
  Mary A.   4 F NC
  Eliza W.   2 F NC
  Mary LOCKE   64 F NC

120 A improved land, 400 A unimpr, value:
  $<u>4</u>,000, 12 slaves

1549.1562 James E. PUGH   45 M NC blacksmith
  Lydia   27 F NC (X)
  John H.   12 M NC
  Virginia   9 F NC
  James A.   3 M NC

1550.1563 Maria MORRISON 48 F IRE 100
  Julia A.M.   22 F NC

cont.

1551.1564 James DEATON   39 M NC bricklayer
  Susanna   19 F NC
  Phebe T.   22 F NC
  Mary Ann   18 F NC
  John C.   16 M NC
  William WEST   3 M NC deaf & dumb

1552.1565 William H FOLTZ 61 M NC constable
  Elizabeth FOLTZ   52 F NC
  Mary   35 F NC
  Peter   26 M NC farmer 400
  William   21 M NC
  James H.   16 M NC

  Peter: 10 A improved land, 6 A unimproved,
      valued at $200

1553.1566 WILLIAM WEST   25 M NC labourer
  Margaret WEST   60 F NC

1554.1567 Albert T POWE   33 M NC physician 3,500
  Erasmus T.   27 M NC school teacher
  Charles T.   23 M SC druggist
  William E.   21 M SC farmer
  Hugh T.   19 M NC S
  Martha A.   17 F NC S
  Samuel S.   15 M NC S
  Mary L.   13 F NC S

  350 A improved land, 300 A unimproved, value:
      $3,500, 34 slaves

1555.1568 William STONER 28 M NC (X) labourer 500

1556.1569 Henry A WALTON 27 M NC farmer 500
  Ann C. WALTON   30 F NC
  Susan E.   8 F NC
  James H.   6 M NC idiot
  Louis A.   22 M NC labourer 300

  12 A improved land, 60 A unimpr, value:$100

1557.1570 George A WALTON 25 F NC 300
  Sarah W. WALTON   21 M NC
  James A.   4/12 M NC
  Miles I.   20 M NC S labourer 300
  Catherine GALLIMORE   21 F NC S

  10 A improved land, 60 A unimpr, value:$100

<u>p.210, School District #30, 21 Aug 1850</u>

1558.1571 Benjamin WALTON 30 M NC farmer 800
  Sarah   22 F NC (X)
  Juliana   18 F NC

  30 A improved land, 86 A unimpr, value:$500

1559.1572 Jacob G SMITH 70 M NC (X) farmer 1200
  Ritta   43 F NC (X)
  Anna   38 F NC
  Maria   15 F NC
  John D.L.   7 M NC   cont.

  Martha A.   4 F NC
  Austin STEEL   35 M NC B labourer

  75 A improved land, 125 A unimproved, value:
      $1,000, 1 slave

1560.1573 George W SMITH 36 M NC waggoner 300
  Matilda A.   35 F NC
  Harriet N.   12 F NC S
  Susanna W.   10 F NC S
  Elisabeth P.   7 F NC S
  Eleanor M.   5 F NC 300
  Peter M. WALTON   17 M NC

  75 A improved land, 100 A unimproved, value:
      $500, 1 slave

1561.1574 David M BUTNER 28 M NC farmer 1200
  Susan   19 F NC
  Henry L.   1 M NC

  75 A improved land, 75 A unimpr, value:$1,000
  5 slaves

1562.1575 William SMITH Sr. 72 M NC farmer 1000
  Elisabeth   70 F NC
  Eliza   20 F NC

  70 A improved land, 320 A unimpr, value:$1,000

1563.1576 Elizabeth KRIDER 70 F PA 250
  Peter WILLIAMSON   40 M NC farmer
  Elizabeth   30 F NC
  Sarah BLACKWELDER   14 F NC S
  Rebecca BLACKWELDER   4 F NC

1564.1577 Matthias RITCHIE 30 M NC labourer
  Elisabeth   35 F NC
  Linda M.   5 F NC
  Eve Ann   3 F NC
  Michael I.   1 M NC

1565.1578 Wendell KLUTTS   54 M NC farmer 1500
  Christina   42 F NC
  Caleb   26 M NC blacksmith
  Samuel   24 M NC farmer
  Michael   21 M NC S blacksmith
  Jessee   16 M NC S farmer
  Elisabeth   14 F NC
  Henry   11 M NC S
  Jacob   9 M NC S
  Christina L.   8 F NC S
  Catherine R.   5 F NC
  Sophia   4/12 F NC

  100 A improved land, 200 A unimpr, value:$1,000

1566.1579 John H VERBLE   28 M NC farmer 1000
  Nancy   38 F NC
  William I. SMITH   21 M NC labourer
  Mary A. SMITH   23 F NC
  Elisabeth SMITH   22 F NC   cont.

Harriet VERBLE   7 F NC

100 A improved land, 70 A unimpr, value:$1,000

1567.1580 Thomas E BROWN   27 M NC farmer 3150
    Eleanora BROWN   24 F NC
    Lewis   8 M NC
    Stephen W.   6 M NC
    Franklin   4 M NC
    Charles VERBLE   49 M NC lunatic

100 A improved land, 175 A unimproved, value:
    $1,000, 9 slaves
2 saw mills: 120,000 ft lumber valued at $1,200

1568.1581 George SMITHDEAL 53 M NC farmer
    Joseph   25 M NC labourer
    Sarah   20 F NC
    Lavinia   17 F NC S
    William   8 M NC S
    Anna   22 F NC

1569.1582 Daniel VERBLE   20 M NC labourer m
    Anna   22 F NC m

1570.1583 Catharine VERBLE 49 F NC (X) 100
    Anna   22 F NC
    Joseph G. CAUBLE   5 M NC
    Sylvester   2 M NC
    James   4/12 M NC
    2 slaves

1571.1584 Polly SANDERS   48 F NC (X)
    Eliza   25 F NC Mu

1572.1585 Peter KERNS   64 M NC farmer 5500
    Elisabeth   36 F NC
    Maria   16 F NC S
    Ebenezer   14 M NC S
    Juliana   12 F NC S
    Anderson   9 M NC S
    John   1 M NC

37 A improved land, 600 A unimproved,
    $2,500, 38 slaves

1573.1586 Margaret STONER 22 F NC
    Jacob   19 M NC
    Jane   17 F NC
    Angelina   14 F NC
    Joanna   12 F NC

<u>p.211, School District #31, 22 Aug 1850</u>

1574.1587 Daniel CAUBLE   47 M NC bricklayer
    Catharine CAUBLE   48 F NC
    Joicy   21 F NC
    Fanny   18 F NC S
    Selena   16 F NC S
    Augustus   15 M NC S
    Loveless   13 M NC S
    Daniel   10 M NC S

1575.1588 Maxwell CHAMBERS 30 M NC

1576.1589 George COPE 28 M NC (X) labourer
    Polly   28 F NC (X)
    Zachariah   14 M NC labourer

1577.1590 Zachariah ELLER 43 M NC (X)
    Christina   50 f nc (x)

1578.1591 John S REID 30 M NC farmer 1000
    Louisa REID   22 F NC
    Sarah Jane   6/12 F NC
    Noah REID   28 M NC schoolteacher
    Rufus TREXLER   11 M NC

100 A improved land, 75 A unimproved, value:
    $1,000, 1 slave

1579.1592 Charles L TORRENCE 48 M NC farmer 8000
    Philadelphia M.   35 F NC
    Catherine E.   10 F NC
    Margaret H.   9 F NC
    Jane M.   7 F NC
    Charles L.   6 M NC
    Albert F.   1 M NC

300 A improved land, 955 unimpr, valued at
    $5,000, 47 slaves

1580.1593 Conrad ELLER 53 M NC (X) labourer
    Mary   52 F NC (X)
    Lucy   26 F NC (X)
    Jemima   24 F NC (X)
    Polly   18 F NC
    Jackson   12 M NC
    Jacob   9 M NC
    Joseph   7 M NC
    Juliana   3 M NC
    Joicy   1 F NC
    1 slave

1581.1594 Rachel RAINY   32 F NC
    William   16 M NC S
    David   11 M NC S
    Letitia   7 F NC S
    John   5 M NC
    Loretta   1 F NC
    Joseph TREXLER   28 M NC (X)
    Delilah   19 F NC S (X)

1582.1595 Amos R. RICE   31 M NC farmer 1700
    Lucinda   35 F NC
    Robert A. STRANGE   12 M NC S
    Sarah Ann BROWN   10 F NC S
    Charles BROWN   5 M NC
    Jane O. BROWN   2 F NC

185 A improved land, 360 A unimpr, value:
    $1,700, 3 slaves [recorded twice]

1583.1596 Scythe BROWN   57 F NC (X)
    Alexander   34 M NC (X)
    Frances   23 F NC (X)   cont.

There are two listings for 1582-1591: see pp. 108 & 109 for 1582, 1583. Two listings p. 109 for 1584-1588; two for 1589, 1591 on pp. 109, 110.

Adam   21 M NC (X) labourer

1584.1597 Alexander SHAMMELL 25 M NC farmer 100
  Catherine   22 F NC
  Lucinda I.   3 F NC

1585.1598 Joel REID 41 M NC farmer 2500
  Sally   28 F NC
  Nancy I.   17 F NC S
  William P.   13 M NC S
  Charity E.   10 F NC S
  David C.   8 M NC S
  James A.   4 M NC
  Joicy A.   2 F NC
  Jacob W. COGGINS   17 M NC labourer

  300 A improved land, 390 A unimpr, value:
      $2,200, 7 slaves

1586.1599 Isaac KESLER 34 M NC farmer 6000
  Eliza   44 F NC
  Robert J. LINN   19 M NC S labourer
  Elisabeth   16 F NC S
  Laura C.   10 F NC S
  James H.   9 M NC S
  William A.   7 M NC S
  Joicy A.   5 F NC
  Augustus KESLER   23 M NC labourer 50

  [MB:Isaac Kesler to Eliza Lynn 19 July 1848]
  500 A improved land, 1300 unimpr, valued
      $4,200, 19 slaves

1587.1600 Peter HARTMAN   45 M NC overseer
  Senia   40 F NC (X)
  Henry L.   17 M NC S labourer

  [MB:Peter Hartman to Seany Brown 5 Aug. 1828]
  1 slave

1588.1601 Jacob MILLER 38 M NC farmer 500
  Mary   28 F NC
  Margaret   10 F NC S
  MaryAnn   9 F NC S
  Charles C.   7 M NC S
  Sophia   5 F NC
  James & Thomas D.   2 M NC

  100 A improved land, 150 unimpr, value:$500
  3 slaves

p.212, School District #32, 23 Aug 1850

1589.1602 Tobias ELLER 28 M NC (X)labourer m
  Margaret ELLER   24 F NC (X) m

1591.1605 Catharine ELLER 45 F NC (X)
  Eve   22 F NC (x)
  Adam   18 M NC
  Joshua   14 M NC
  Caleb   12 M NC
  Benjamin   10 M NC
  William   8 M NC

1582.1606 Mary MYRES 77 F NC (X)
  Elisabeth   40 F NC (X)

1583.1607 Miles AREY 28 M NC farmer 2200
  Ann AREY   18 F NC
  Ellen I.   6 F NC S
  Benjamin C.   1 M NC

  200 A improved land, 200 A unimpr, value:
      $2,200, 9 slaves

1584.1608 George PEELER 30 M NC farmer 800
  Rachel   34 F NC
  Sarah A.E.   7 F NC S
  Julius A.   1 M NC
  Jesse ELLER   20 M NC S labourer
  Richard ELLER   16 M NC S labourer
  Matilda ELLER   11 F NC S

  125 A improved land, 40 A unimpr, value:$800

1585.1609 John S BUTNER 25 M NC farmer 1000
  Susan   21 F NC
  Joicy ELLER   15 F NC S

  80 A improved land, 136 A unimpr, value:$1,000
  2 slaves

1586.1610 Nathan JOHNSON 40 M NC (X) farmer 200
  Cornelia   30 F NC (X)
  Elisabeth   9 F NC
  Benjamine   8 M NC
  Daniel   7 M NC
  Rhoda   4 M NC
  Catharine   2 F NC
  Margaret   6/12 F NC

  30 A improved land, 143 unimpr, value:$200

1587.1611 Catherine EDDINGER 47 F NC (X)
  Nathan   25 M NC
  Adam   22 M NC (X)
  John   20 M NC
  Sally   19 F NC
  Anna L.   15 F NC S
  Levi   12 M NC S
  David A.   9 M NC S
  .1612. Henry I.   5 M NC S
  Elisabeth MILLER   34 F NC 400
  David A.   11 M NC S

  120 A improved land, 100 A unimpr, value:$500

1588.1613 David BOGER 44 M NC farmer 950
  Mary BOGER   39 F NC
  Ali C.   15 F NC S
  Sarah L.   13 F NC S
  Mary A.M.   11 F NC S
  James W.   9 M NC S
  Janet M.   4 F NC

  80 A improved land, 70 A unimpr, value:$550

There are two listings for 1582-1591: see pp. 108 & 109 for 1582, 1583. Two listings p. 109 for 1584-1588; two for 1589, 1591 on pp. 109, 110.

1589.1614 Sarah EARNHART   31 F NC
    Samuel   10 M NC S
    Aaron   9 M NC S
    John E.   7 M NC S
    Flavius E.   6 M NC S
    Mary E.   3 F NC
    Robert W.   1 M NC
    Rachel MULL   20 F NC

    Edward EARNHART: 50 A improved land, 100 A
      unimproved, valued at $500

1590.1615 Daniel BOGER   34 M NC farmer 400
    Edith BOGER   32 F NC
    Louisa   10 F NC S
    Calvin M.   8 M NC S
    Sarah E.   5 F NC
    David A.   1 M NC

    15 A improved land, 75 A unimpr, value:$400

1591.1616 Jessee MAHALA   30 M NC farmer 350
    Susan MAHALA   30 F NC
    Julius   1 M NC

    45 A improved land, 85 A unimpr, value:$400

1592.1617 David MAHALA   26 M NC
    Elisabeth MAHALA   25 M NC 90

    40 A improved land, 63 A unimpr, value:$400

1593.1618 Catharine MULL 38 F NC 200
    Robert M. JONES   20 M NC school teacher
    John M. JONES   17 M NC S labourer
    Lewis P.   14 M NC S
    Margaret JARRETT   23 F NC
    Ellen J.   7/12 F NC

    40 A improved land 64 A unimpr, value:$200

1594.1619 Edward MULL   28 M NC labourer
    Caroline MULL   25 F NC
    Chrissa   4 F NC
    Mary Jane   1 F NC

1595.1620 John KITCHIE   37 M NC farmer 500
    Anna KITCHIE   36 F NC
    Jane L.   13 F NC S
[213] Mary R.   11 F NC S
    John A.   8 M NC S
    Joseph M.   2 M NC

    40 A improved land, 90 A unimpr, value:$500

<u>p.213, School District # 32, 24 Aug 1850</u>

1597.1621 John BRINGLE   39 M NC labourer
    Christina BRINGLE   35 F NC
    Loretta M.   16 F NC S
    Michael A.   13 M NC S
    David L.   11 M NC S
    John H.   9 M NC S   cont.

    Lorenza D.   6 M NC S
    Julius C.   4 M NC

1598.1622 Maria M. BISHERER 53 F GER
    Margaret   21 F NC
    John B.   21 M NC labourer
    Orrelia B.   17 F NC
    Christina B.   15 F NC
    Louisa B.   11 F NC

    50 A improved land, 100 A unimpr, value:$500

1599.1623 Sophia BISHERER 25 F NC
    Esau TYER   16 M NC

1600.1624 Fredrick VARNER 55 M NC miller
    Christina   29 F NC
    James R.   3 M NC
    Amanda E.   1 F NC

1601.1625 Laura A HUDSON   30 F NC 130
    Mary R.   12 F NC S
    Macon V.   8 M NC S
    Without a name   2 M NC

    9 A improved land, 4 A unimpr, value:$130
    3 slaves

1602.1626 Rebecca HUDSON   64 F NC 200
    Robert S.   16 M NC S labourer
    Harriet L.   12 F NC S

1603.1627 Edward D. WADE   43 M NC farmer 600
    Anna R. WADE   38 F NC
    Benjamin   19 M NC S
    Julia A.   17 F NC S
    Edward   16 M NC S
    Clementine   12 F NC S
    Atha   10 F NC S
    Lucius P.   8 M NC S

    70 A improved land, 60 A unimpr, value:$600

1604.1628 Elam F. MILLER   34 M NC labourer
    Sally L. MILLER   32 F NC (X)
    Charlotte L.   10 F NC S
    Margaret L.   8 F NC S
    Elisabeth R.   4 F NC
    Samuel C.   1 M NC

1605.1629 Sophia WALTON   54 F NC 200
    Benjamin F.   25 M NC
    Floro Virtus   22 F NC
    Isabella S.   20 F NC
    Richard   17 M NC S labourer
    Martin L.   14 M NC S
    Benjamin R. KETCHIE   4 M NC

    50 A improved land, 11 A unimpr, value:$200

1606.1630 William A WALTON 34 M NC farmer 400
    Ann D. WALTON   40 F NC
    Lucinda H.   11 F NC S cont.

There are two listings for 1582-1591: see pp. 108 & 109 for 1582, 1583. Two listings p. 109 for 1584-1588; two for 1589, 1591 on pp. 109, 110.

Lorenza W.   9 M NC S
Malinda F.   7 F NC S

50 A improved land, 100 A unimpr, value:$400
3 slaves

1607.1631 Henry AGNER 52 M NC (X) farmer 100
Sally A.   23 F NC (X)
Moses   16 M NC
Eve Ann   11 F NC
Mary Ann   1 F NC

50 A improved land, 50 A unimpr, value:$100

1608.1632 John SMITHDEAL   27 M NC farmer 300
Margaret SMITHDEAL   25 F NC
Eve Ann   3 F NC
Catherine E.   1 F NC
Samuel SMITH   8 M NC

90 A improved land, 110 A unimpr, value:$300

1609.1633 Henry TREXLER 57 M NC farmer
Elisabeth TREXLER   51 F NC
Henry M.   25 M NC labourer
Sophia C.   23 F NC
Jesse L.   21 M NC S labourer
Jacob   19 M NC S labourer
Polly L.   17 F NC
Mary Ann KERR   15 F NC
Amelia M.   12 F NC S

1610.1634 Moses TREXLER   32 M NC farmer
Margaret TREXLER   27 F NC
Henry A.   9 M NC S
Sophia K.   8 F NC S
Sarah Jane   4 F NC
Mary E.   2 F NC

48 A improved land valued at $260

1611.1635 David BARINGER 37 M NC farmer 6,000
Mary   33 F NC
Eugenia   5 F NC S
[214] Paul M.   2 M NC
infant   2/12 F NC
John L. KETCHIE   11 M NC

200 A improved land, 400 A unimproved, value:
    $4,000, 10 slaves
saw mill: 200,000 ft lumber valued at $1,900
grist mill: 600 bbl flour valued at $2,795; ? bu
    meal valued at $277

<u>p.214, School District #32, 26 Aug 1850</u>

1612.1636 Jacob MISEMER   29 M NC miller
Edith MISEMER   25 F NC (X)
Henry   4 M NC
Elisabeth   3 F NC

1613.1637 Peter L BARRINGER 28 M NC farmer 1800
Rose A. BARRINGER   26 F NC   cont.

Mary R.   6 F NC S
David M.   5 M NC S
Henry M.   2 M NC

170 A improved land, 113 A unimpr, value:$1,800
3 slaves

1614.1638 Moses CAUBLE 23 M NC
Polly CAUBLE   19 F NC
Catharine M.   1 F NC
Mary HOLSHOUSER   40 F NC

Moses A Cauble: 100 A improved land, 128 A
    unimpr, value:$100, 2 slaves

1615.1639 Alexander RUSHER 24 M NC
Maria RUSHER   20 F NC
Fanny EARNHART   16 F NC

1616.1640 Charles WISE 43 M NC
Sophia WISE   36 F NC (X)
Malinda   17 F NC
Benjamin   15 M NC
Maria   8 F NC
Sarah Ann   5 F NC
Pleasant   3 M NC
Caleb   2 M NC
John FRANCIS   57 M NC lunatic

75 A improved land, 300 A unimpr, value:$1,000

1617.1641 Charles WALLER 43 M NC
Polly WALLER   36 F NC
Lewis A.   14 M NC S
Jane M.   9 F NC S
Mary Ann   8/12 F NC

85 A improved land, 65 A unimpr, value:$800

1618.1642 George LYERLA 30 M NC farmer 1000
Elisabeth LYERLA   30 F NC
George L.   9 M NC S
Henry Adam   4 M NC
Mary L. CAUBLE   12 F NC S
George A. CAUBLE   10 M NC S

164 A improved land, 150 A unimpr, value:$1,000
1 slave

1619.1643 Catharine BULLAND 59 F NC (X) 75
Angeline   23 F NC
Mary L.   20 F NC
Sarah Ann   9 F NC S
Margaret   6 F NC
Isabella   4 F NC
Clayton   1 M NC
Maria   15 F NC Mu

12 A improved land, 20 A unimpr, value:$75

1620.1644 Elisabeth OWENS 30 F NC
Henry   7 M NC S cont.

James   5 M NC
George   4/12 M NC

1621.1645 Mary Ann BULLAND 23 F NC
  Thomas L.   2 M NC

1622.1646 William L BULLAND 23 M NC miner
  Eliza BULLAND   28 F NC
  Jane R.   4 F NC

1623.1647 Alexander KESLER 29 M NC farmer 1000
  Catherine KESLER   24 F NC
  John L.   6 M NC S
  William L.   5 M NC
  Laura F.   6/12 F NC
  Susan TREXLER   10 F NC

  90 A improved land, 70 A unimpr, value:$900

1624.1648 Sophia BLACKWELL 50 F NC
  Christa   25 F NC (S)
  Eliza   21 F NC
  Catharine   18 F NC
  Jane   18 F NC
  John   15 M NC S
  George   11 M NC S
  Jinny   4/12 F NC

1625.1649 John WISE 43 M NC farmer 700
  Christina L. WISE 39 F NC
  Ann L.   21 F NC
  Edward   19 M NC S labourer
  William A.   17 M NC S labourer
  Pelina R.   13 F NC S
  Delia V.   10 F NC S
  Mary S.   5 F NC S
  Joice E.   1 F NC

  120 A improved land, 26A unimpr, value:$700

1626.1650 Daniel MILLER 32 M NC farmer 600
  Elisabeth MILLER   29 F NC
  Caleb A.   12 M NC S
  Clementine M.   7 F NC
  Robert E.   5 M NC
  [215] Lucinda E.   5/12 F NC
  David A. KETCHIE   15 M NC S

  75 A improved land, 77 A unimpr, value:$600

<u>p.215, School District #33, 26 Aug 1850</u>

1627.1651 Charles EARNHART 44 M NC farmer 1000
  Catharine EARNHART   34 F NC
  Benjamine   21 M NC S labourer
  Edward   19 M NC S labourer
  Cruso   16 M NC S labourer
  Mary Ann   14 F NC S
  Malinda   9 F NC S
  Delia   8 F NC S
  Lettitia   6 F NC
  John   3 M NC
  Henry Miles   1 M NC   cont.

  Mary Ann MEYER   77 F VA

  50 A improved land, 29 A unimpr, value:$400

1628.1652 William MEYER 39 M VA (X) labourer
  Polly M. A. MEYER   28 F NS (X)
  Christiana AREY   49 F NC (X)
  Catharine FIGHT   19 F NC

1629.1653 Isaac B MILLER 34 M NC farmer 400
  Temperance MILLER   30 F NC
  Martha   7 F NC S
  Jane S.   6 F NC S
  Henderson V.   4 M NC
  Frances L.   2 F NC

  30 A improved land, 225 A unimpr, value:$500
  5 slaves

1630.1654 Benjamin BLACKWELL 31 M NC overseer 300
  Mary R. BLACKWELL   35 F NC
  William TREXLER   16 M NC labourer
  Hiram TREXLER   14 M NC
  Ellen S. TREXLER   9 F NC
  Julius V. TREXLER   5 M NC
  James P. TREXLER   5 M NC

  40 A improved land, 40 A unimpr, value:$500

1631.1655 John SHUMAN Jr. 44 M NC farmer 1,000
  Nancy SHUMAN   40 F NC (X)
  Mary Ann   20 F NC

  50 A improved land, 89 A unimpr, value:$1,000

1632.1656 Adam TREXLER 34 M NC carpenter
  Elisabeth TREXLER   30 F NC
  James M.   7 M NC S

1633.1657 Henry CAUBLE 44 M NC farmer
  Fanny CAUBLE   38 F NC (X)
  Maria   17 F NC
  William   15 M NC S
  John   12 M NC S
  Laura   10 F NC S
  Mary Ann   2 F NC

  13 A improved land, 31 A unimpr, value:$135

1634.1658 Elisabeth MESSEMER 50 F NC (X)
  Charles   21 M NC (X) labourer
  Dianah   23 F NC (X)
  Eveline   18 F NC S
  Calvin   13 M NC
  Miles RAINY   28 M NC (X) blacksmith
  Caroline RAINY   26 F NC (X)
  Sarah Ann   4 F NC

1635.1659 Margaret KLUTTS 51 F NC (X)
  Regina   26 F NC (X)
  Sarah   24 F NC (X)
  Margaret   22 F NC S (X)
  Anna   20 F NC S (X) cont.

Henry   16 M NC S
David   14 M NC

72 A improved land, 25 A unimpr, value:$211

1636.1660 Nancy HESS 43 F NC (X)
  William   24 M NC (X)
  Margaret   22 F NC (X)
  Chrissa   20 F NC
  Maria   18 F NC

1637.1661 Green REDWINE 45 M NC hatter
  Catharine REDWINE   42 F NC
  Jane M.   18 F NC
  Osborn   3 M NC
  Archibald   1 M NC
  Whitson KIMBELL   22 M NC labourer

1638.1662 David D PEELER 26 M NC farmer 400 m
  Camilla E. PEELER   20 F NC m

40 A improved land, 82 A unimpr, value:$400
1 slave

1639.1663 George M WALLER 43 M NC blacksmith 75
  Mary WALLER   35 F NC
  Jane M.   13 F NC S
  Cruso   12 M NC S
  George W.   9 M NC S
  Dr. Franklin   7 M NC
  Harriet L.   5 F NC
  Jonathan WALLER   4 M NC
  Whitson   1 M NC
  Jonathan WALLER   46 M NC (X) blacksmith
  Jacob A.W. Corl   22 M NC miner
  John FULENWIDER   19 M NC miner
  William McKANN   21 M MC Mu

<u>p.216, School District #33, 27 Aug 1850</u>

1640.1664 David PEELER Sr 44 M NC farmer 1,200
  Amelia PEELER   38 F NC
  Mary L.   18 F NC S
  Sally C.   15 F NC S
  Alexander   13 M NC S
  John R.   10 M NC S
  Camilla R.   7 F NC
  Henry C.   3 M NC

1641.1665 Charles KLUTTS 41 M NC blacksmith 1200
  Elisabeth KLUTTS   38 F NC
  Green E.   15 F NC S
  Jacob A.   13 M NC S
  Henry W.   11 M NC S
  Charles F.   9 M NC S
  Christina   7 M NC
  Julius A.   5 M NC
  Daniel A.   2 F NC

75 A improved land, 185 unimpr, value:$1,000

1642.1666 David ELLER 35 M NC labourer 400
  Nancy ELLER   29 F NC   cont.

Benjamin   8 M NC S

1643.1667 George CAUBLE 57 M NC farmer 1,000

  Rosina CAUBLE   49 F NC
  Mary   27 F NC
  Michael   25 M NC labourer
  Camilla R.   21 F NC S
  Peter   16 M NC S
  Clementine   16 F NC S
  Jane   11 F NC S
  Melinda   8 F NC S
  Nancy Klutts   8/12 F NC

100 A improved land, 150 A unimpr, value:$1,000

1644.1668 Caleb RIMER 30 M NC (X) farmer 370
  Catharine Folk   33 F NC (X)

50 A improved land, 40 A unimpr, value:$370

1645.1669 Matthias RIMER 37 M NC (X) farmer 370
  Anna RIMER   25 F NC
  Joseph   5 F NC
  Michael   2 M NC

15 A improved land, 20 A unimpr, value:$<u>100</u>

1646.1670 John RITCHIE 28 M NC miner 90 m
  Sarah RITCHIE   23 F NC (X) m

1647.1671 Isaac CAUBLE 31 M NC farmer
  Selena CAUBLE   29 F NC
  Adam A.   1 M NC
  Alexander AGNER   33 M NC farmer 600
  William   7 M NC
  Calvin   5 M NC

  Isaac CAUBLE: 50 A improved land, 150 A un-
    improved, valued at $800
  Alexander AGNER: 100 A improved land, 125
    unimproved, valued at $600, 3 slaves

1648.1672 Peter TREXLER 37 M NC farmer 2,000
  Elisabeth C. TREXLER 35 F NC
  Alfred M. TREXLER   11 M NC S
  Peter M.   6 M NC
  Crawford I.   3 M NC
  Julius B.   1 M NC

100 A improved land, 100 A unimpr, valued at
    $<u>1</u>,000, 6 slaves

1649.1673 Lewis AGNER   21 M NC farmer m
  Laura M. AGNER   20 F NC m
  Alexander HOLSHOUER   11 M NC S

1650.1674 Jacob LYERLY 60 M NC farmer 1500
  Catherine LYERLY   58 F NC
  Martin   22 M NC
  Charles   20 M NC
  Louisa   18 F NC
  Alexander   14 M NC   cont.

Joseph A. BROWN   3 M NC

71 A improved land, 100 A unimpr, value:$750

1651.1675 Paul MILLER 38 M NC farmer 3000
  Elisabeth MILLER   38 F NC
  George A.   15 M NC S
  Henry M.   13 M NC S
  Laura C.   11 F NC S
  Mary A.L.   9 F NC S
  John R.   6 M NC
  James A.   3 M NC

  150 A improved land, 90 A unimpr, value:$2,500
  5 slaves
  flouring mill: ? bbls flour valued at $3,625
  corn mill: 10,980 bu corn meal valued at $4,993

1652.1676 David KLUTTS 49 M NC farmer 700
  Salome KLUTTS   46 F NC
  Christina   22 F NC
  Adam   21 M NC S
  Dawalt   15 F NC S
  Andrew L.   10 M NC S
  Rufus   8 M NC S
  Moses A.   5 M NC

  125 A improved land, 77 A unimpr, value:$700

1653.1677 Mary BROWN   46 F NC 450
  Sarah A.S.   20 F NC
  Camilla C.   15 F NC S
  Elisabeth   13 F NC S
  Mary M.   9 F NC S

  60 A improved land, 116 unimpr, value:$450

1654.1678 Edward PAME 25 M NC farmer 100
  Margaret L. PAME   23 F NC
[217] Rose Ann   3 F NC
  infant   2/12 F NC

p.217, School District #36, 28 Aug 1850

1655.1679 Peter PEELER 56 M NC farmer 2,000
  Eve PEELER   46 F NC
  Lena L.   21 F NC
  Joseph A.   19 M NC S labourer
  Miles M.   15 M NC S
  Margaret L.   13 F NC S
  Moses   10 M NC S
  Daniel   8 M NC

  150 A improved land, 470 A unimpr, value:$2000

1656.1680 Adam TREXLER 28 M NC farmer 1000
  Margaret TREXLER   32 F NC
  Mary R.   2 F NC

  50 A improved land, 65 A unimpr, value:$500

1657.1681 John HOLSHOUSER   34 M NC farmer 170
  Pelina HOLSHOUSER   32 F NC   cont.

Laura R.   12 F NC S
Luretta   10 F NC S
Malinda   7 F NC S
Sarah L.   5 F NC
Margaret   2 F NC

  30 A improved land, 50 A unimpr, value:$200

1658.1682 Zacariah LYERLA 42 M NC farmer 480
  Rachel LYERLA   35 F NC
  Camilla   14 F NC S
  Sarah   12 F NC S
  Lavinia   8 F NC S
  Mary Ann   6 F NC S
  Tobias   3 M NC

  70 A improved land, 118 A unimpr, value:$480

1659.1683 Solomon BROWN 39 M NC farmer 1000
  Naomi   34 F NC
  Nathan   12 M NC S
  Sally L.   11 F NC S
  Calvin L.   9 M NC S
  Richard L.   8 M NC S
  Henry M.   5 M NC
  David L.   10/12 M NC

  60 A improved land, 90 A unimpr, value:$450

1660.1684 Leonard KINNEY 55 M NC (X) labourer
  Susan KINNEY   55 F NC (X)
  Lemuel SWINK   5 M NC

1661.1685 Henery BROWN 31 M NC 400
  Magdalena BROWN   25 F NC
  Peter M.   4 M NC
  Crawford L.   2 M NC

  40 A improved land valued at $400

1662.1686 Polly BLACK   35 F NC (X)
  Catherine BLACK   13 F NC S

1663.1687 Michael L BROWN 46 M NC farmer
  Elisabeth BROWN   39 F NC
  Elisabeth C.   16 F NC S
  Mary Ann   13 F NC S
  John D.A.   11 M NC S
  Sophia M.   10 F NC S
  Allen BROWN   5 F NC
  Simeon I.M.   3 M NC

  75 A improved land valued at $375

1664.1688 Sarah BROWN   67 F NC
  Sophia MILLER   6 F NC
  Daniel BROWN   27 M NC farmer 280
  Margaret Ruth   6/12 F NC

  50 A improved land, 120 A unimpr, value:$500
  3 slaves

1665.1689 George A BROWN   29 M NC
    Maria S. BROWN   26 F NC

1666.1690 Jacob BROWN 45 M NC farmer 500
    Anna BROWN   38 F NC
    Sarah L.   19 F NC S
    Mary C.   16 F NC S
    Margaret E.   13 F NC S
    Augustus T.   11 F NC S
    Jeremiah C.   9 M NC S
    Julia Ann   7 F NC S
    Jacob C.   2 M NC
    Jesse CADWELL   30 M NC labourer

    60 A improved land, 130 A unimpr, value:$600

1667.1691 Alexander EARNHART 32 M NC labourer
    Sally EARNHART   26 F NC (X)
    Partha C.   1 F NC

1668.1692 David ERONHART 34 M NC labourer
    Christa ERONHART   19 F NC

1669.1693 Asa RIBELIN 40 M NC farmer 700
    Susan RIBELIN   29 F NC
    Partha L.   7 F NC
    Annette E.   5 F NC
    Lewis I.   2 M NC
    Jane E.   5/12 F NC

    50 A improved land, 380 A unimpr, value:$630

1670.1694 Noah M. FRY 43 M NC
    Deborah FRY   37 F NC
    Amelia A.   18 M NC S
    Sarah Ann   16 F NC S
    Wiley T.   14 M NC S
[218] Noah W.   11 M NC S
    Pleasant S.   7 M NC
    William T.   4/12 M NC

<u>p.218, School District #26, 28 Aug 1850</u>

1671.1695 William M BROWN 33 M NC farmer 500
    Caroline BROWN   28 M NC
    Alice E.   5 F NC
    James Edwards   3 M NC
    Camilla L.V.   0/12 F NC

    30 A improved land, 53 A unimpr, value:$500

1672.1696 Alexander BROWN 44 M NC farmer 2,000
    Sophia C. BROWN   24 F NC
    Adam A.   10 M NC
    Mary M.   8 F NC
    Elijah VALENTINE   35 M NC Mu

    100 A improved land, 170 A unimpr, value:$2,000
    6 slaves

1673.1697 Henry W BROWN 31 M NC 37 farmer
    Moses A. BROWN   25 M NC farmer
    William A.   11 M NC S   cont.

    150 A improved land, 150 A unimpr, value:$700
    8 slaves

1674.1698 Catherine BULLAND 50 F NC
    William MORRISON   25 M NC labourer

1675.1699 James L BROWN 45 M NC farmer
    Sarah BROWN   43 F NC
    Laura M.   14 F NC
    3 slaves

1676.1700 Henry I HESS   41 M NC Mu labourer
    Mary HESS   47 F NC
    Mary Ann S.   13 F NC
    George H.B.   10 M NC
    Daniel L.A.   5 M NC

1677.1701 David HOLSHOUSER 51 M NC
    Eleanora HOLSHOUSER   45 F NC
    Margaret E.   21 F NC
    Julia Ann   19 F NC
    Jane L.   12 F NC S
    Ellen C.   9 F NC S
    Lewis D.   6 M NC

1678.1702 Jacob CASPER   58 M NC shoemaker
    Catharine C. CASPER   33 F NC
    William C.   2 M NC

1679.1703 Tobias HESS   52 M NC labourer
    Clementine HESS   40 F NC
    Christina HESS   22 F NC
    William D.   13 M NC

1680.1704 Margaret CORL 52 F NC (X)
    Polly Bird   28 F NC (X)
    Ann Elisabeth   18 F NC
    Margaret   16 F NC
    Daniel   12 M NC
    Sally   7 F NC

1681.1705 Sally ELLER 52 F NC (X)
    Fanny   21 F NC (X)
    Laura A.   17 F NC S
    John M.   16 M NC S

1682.1706 David BEAVER   33 M NC farmer 300
    Caroline BEAVER   39 F NC (X)
    Catharine BEAVER   12 F NC S
    Mary E.   10 F NC S
    Michael   8 M NC S

    40 A improved land, 35 A unimpr, value:$300

1683.1707 George M HARTMAN 69 M NC farmer 1000
    Charles A.   25 M NC labourer
    Matthew A.   22 M NC labourer

    50 A improved land, 140 A unimpr, value:$<u>8</u>00
    1 slave

```
1684.1708 George W HARTMAN 28 M NC farmer 187
    Catherine HARTMAN        39 F NC
    Laura                    25 F NC
    Catherine                 2 F NC
    Susan BEAVER             51 F NC

    40 A improved land valued at $187


1685.1709 Sarah ELLER  30 F NC (X)
    Augustus                  8 M NC
    Hamilton                  6 M NC
    Eliza                     4 F NC
    Barbara TARR             59 F NC (X)


1686.1710 George CAUBLE  54 M NC farmer
    Polly CAUBLE             50 F NC
    Catharine C.             27 F NC
    Polly L.                 22 F NC (X)
    George A.                18 M NC S labourer
    Jacob A.                 16 M NC S labourer
    Samuel                   14 M NC S
    Pleasant M.               9 M NC S
    Martha Ann BEAN           2 F NC

    110 A improved land, 150 A unimpr, value:$1000


1687.1711 H.C. JONES  51 M NC lawyer 2,100
    Eliza J. JONES           51 F NC
    Martha M.                24 F NC
    Julia H.                 22 F NC
    James M.                 16 M NC S engineer
[219] Alice I.              14 F NC S
    Hamilton C., Jr.         12 M NC S
    Edmund L.                10 M NC S
    Hiram CORRIHER           19 M NC Mu
    Selah PORTER             13 F NC Mu

    Hamilton C. Jones: 160 A improved land, 100 A
       unimproved, valued at $2,000, 8 slaves
```

<u>p.219, School District #26, 29 Aug 1850</u>

```
1687.1712 Margaret BENSON  57 F NC 400
    Roland H. WIATT          24 M NC

    140 A improved land, 200 A unimpr, value:$400
    8 slaves


1688.1713 Daniel PEELER  41 M NC (X) farmer 1200
    Sally PEELER             40 F NC
    Christina L.             19 F NC S
    Caleb E.                 17 M NC S
    Jacob Miles              15 M NC S
    Moses M.                 12 M NC S
    Luretta                  10 F NC S
    John C.                   7 M NC
    Margaret A.               3 F NC
    William KENNY            31 M NC labourer

    80 A improved land, 85 A unimpr, value:$1500
```

```
1689.1714 Jacob TREXLER 26 M NC farmer 1000
    Mary C. TREXLER          30 F NC
    Margaret M.               3 F NC
    David F.                  1 M NC
    Julia Ann STOCDON        22 F NC

    60 A improved land, 141 unimpr, value:$1,000


1690.1715 William B MISENHEIMER 25 M NC farmer 1000
    Eve Louisa MISENHEIMER   22 F NC
    Harriet M.                1 F NC
    Joseph A. MOOSE          16 M NC
    Mary R. MOOSE            14 F NC

    97 A improved land, 124 A unimpr, value:$1,000


1691.1716 Solomon KLUTTS  35 M NC farmer 500
    Barbara KLUTTS           26 F NC
    William C.                3 M NC
    Lucinda R.            7/12 F NC
    John F. MOOSE            18 M NC
    Charlotte E. MOOSE       11 F NC S
    David C. MOOSE            9 M NC S

    75 A improved land, 75 A unimpr, value:$500


1692.1717 Henry BARINGER 37 M NC (X) shoemaker
    Maria BARINGER           25 F NC (X)
    Ann L. HESS              21 F NC (X)
    Margaret E. BARINGER      7 F NC


1693.1718 John GLOVER  45 M NC shoemaker 200
    Elisabeth GLOVER         42 F NC
    Lydia                    21 F NC S
    Matilda                  16 F NC S
    Mary                     15 F NC S
    Avarilla                 12 F NC S
    Abraham                  10 M NC S
    John                      7 M NC S
    Jeremiah                  4 M NC S

    50 A improved land, 45 A unimpr, value:$200


1694.1719 Adam BROWN  52 M NC superintendent
                                of Poor House 600
    Frances BROWN            52 F NC (X)
    John C.                  20 M NC farmer
    Adam M.                  12 M NC S
    Susan PHILLIP             1 F NC

    65 A improved land, 70 A unimpr, value:$395


1695.1720 Inmates of the Poor House

    John MONROE 55 M NC pauper
    John FULTON 28 M NC lunatic, pauper
    John CRIESON 50 M NC idiot, pauper
    Temperance PHILLIPS 27 F NC pauper
    Priscilla EHERY  50 F SC pauper, insane
    Polly HESS 35 F NC Mu pauper, insane
    Ann KLUTTS 30 F NC pauper, insane
    Elisabeth WALTON  22 F NC pauper, epileptic
    William MOOR 3 M NC pauper        cont.
```

Burgess MOOR 3 M NC pauper
Harriet MOOR 1 F NC pauper
Sally BOSTIAN 38 F NC, pauper, insane
Jane WINDERS 32 F NC, pauper, insane
Sally EARNHART 28 F NC, pauper
Polly FOLK 27 F NC, pauper
Mary Jane FOLK 2 F NC, pauper
Anna JOHNSON 43 F NC, pauper
Sophia LINEBARGER 40 F NC, pauper
Susan ELLER 40 F NC, pauper, idiot
Mary DARIT 27 F NC, pauper, insane
Rachel PEARCE 21 F NC, pauper, idiot
Jane ELLER 5 F NC, insane
Henry JOHNSTON 5 M NC, pauper
Anna JOHNSTON 3 F NC, pauper
Catharine BECKET 30 F NC, pauper, idiot
Ann REEDWINE 25 F NC idiot, pauper
Julia Ann REDWINE 5 F NC pauper
Elisabeth REDWINE 3 F NC pauper
Richman STEEL 50 M NC B pauper

1696.1721 Peter EAGLE 57 M NC farmer 700
  Polly EAGLE   51 F NC
  Mary Caroline   24 F NC
[220] George A.   22 M NC S labourer
  Catharine   19 F NC S
  Sarah M.   15 F NC S
  Margaret C.   11 F NC S

  75 A improved land, 90 A unimpr, value:$700

<u>p.220, School District #22, 30 Aug 1850</u>

1697.1722 Daniel EDDLEMAN 42 M NC millwright 1500
  Elisabeth EDDLEMAN   36 F NC
  Jeremiah A.   9 M NC S
  William C.   6 M NC S
  Louisa M.   3 F NC
  George M. RITCHIE   21 M NC millwright
  Eli KLUTTS   20 M NC millwright

  70 A unimproved land, 100 A impr, value:$1,400
  3 slaves

1698.1723 Phillip EDDLEMAN 66 M NC farmer 1000
  Sarah EDDLEMAN   59 F NC
  John M. EDDLEMAN   21 M NC labourer
  Alexander   14 M NC
  Elisabeth EAGLE   29 F NC
  Edward NORMAN   33 M GER physician

  60 A improved land, 74 A unimpr, value:$1,000
  2 slaves

1699.1724 David SHUPING 33 M NC blacksmith 50
  Leah SHUPING   27 F NC (X)
  Julia Ann I.   8 F NC S
  Flora I.S.   7 F NC S
  Jeremiah D.W.   6 M NC S
  David L.A.   4 M NC
  John L.C.   3 M NC
  William T.   1 M NC

1700.1725 Jacob BOSTIAN 54 M NC blacksmith 600
  Catharine BOSTIAN   54 F NC
  Moses   23 M NC labourer
  Alexander BOSTIAN   21 M NC
  Margaret A.   17 M NC

  75 A improved land, 81 A unimpr, value:$600
  2 slaves

1701.1726 Andrew BOSTIAN 41 M NC 600
  Sarah BOSTIAN   40 F NC
  Christina M.   17 F NC S
  Sarah E.   15 F NC S
  Michael J.   12 M NC S
  Jesse L.   8 M NC S
  Jane E.   2 F NC
  Mary D.   1 F NC
  Simeon SIDES   17 M NC

  50 A improved land, 38 A unimpr, value:$400

1702.1727 Elisabeth BOSTIAN 55 F NC
  James M. PATTERSON   25 M NC farmer 400 m
  Caroline   21 F NC m

1703.1728 Jacob DEAL jr. 37 M NC farmer
  Polly DEAL   45 F NC

  25 A improved land, 15 A unimpr, value:$400

1704.1729. Jacob G. BOSTIAN 57 M NC (X) farmer
                                           1000
  Elisabeth BOSTIAN   54 F NC
  Eli   19 M NC
  Aaron   15 M NC

  2 slaves

1705.1730 Christine BOSTIAN 40 F NC (X)

1706.1731 Jacob DEAL 63 M NC farmer 1000
  Sarah DEAL   61 F NC
  Elisabeth   24 F NC (X)
  Daniel   22 M NC (X) labourer
  Samuel   20 M NC S labourer
  Sarah   15 F NC S
  Eliza   8 F NC S
  Catharine CARTER   4 F NC

  40 A improved land, 74 A unimpr, value:$500

1707.1732 John DEAL 28 M NC labourer
  Anna DEAL   35 F NC (X)
  John   5 M NC
  Mary   8 F NC S
  Elisabeth   2 F NC
  Caleb E.   1/12 M NC

1708.1733 Henry DEAL 31 M NC (X) labourer
  Sally DEAL   41 F NC (X)
  Reuben I.   12 M NC S
  William M.   10 M NC S
  Jacob A.   8 M NC S   cont.

```
Sarah L.              5 F NC
Margaret A.S.         3 F NC
Elisabeth C.       9/12 F NC
```

1709.1734 Christina BOSTIAN 52 F NC
```
Michael  BOSTIAN                    24 M NC (X)
                                    cabinetmaker
Andrew BOSTIAN           22 M NC farmer
Rachel BOSTIAN           28 F NC
Christina S. BOSTIAN     17 F NC
Elisabeth E.             13 F NC
John Howard              12 M NC
Mary Sophia            1/12 F NC
```

1710.1735 George KETNER   29 M NC farmer
```
Mary L.               3 F NC
Susanna L.            2 F NC
Alfred HORNBARGER    10 M NC S
Eli HORNBARGER       22 M NC labourer
```

p. 221, School District # 25, 27 Nov 1850

1711.1736 Catharine BIRD 28 F NC
```
Catharine C.         11 F NC S
John A.               6 M NC (X)
Margaret E.           2 F NC (X)
Susanna BIRD         34 F NC
John A. BUTNER       23 M NC farmer
```

Caroline Bird: 40 A improved land, value:$80

1712.1737 Jane CORZINE   25 F NC
```
Theodore              2 M NC
```

1713.1738 John BIRD 67 M NC X carriagemaker 900 m
```
Nancy BIRD        31 F NC X m
David             44 M NC farmer
Mary C. ALLEN     15 F NC
Amanda M. ALLEN   14 F NC
Martha H. ALLEN   13 F NC S
Gasper N. ALLEN    7 M NC S
```

[MB: John Bird to Nancy Allen 11 Feb. 1850]
60 A improved land, 110 unimpr, value:$600

1714.1739 James BROMHAD   51 M NC (X) miller
```
John J.           20 M NC (X) labourer
Hannah C.         17 F NC
Sarah L.          25 F NC (X)
```

1715.1740 Henry FESPERMAN 25 M NC X stonecutter 40
```
Sally FESPERMAN      36 F NC X
Selena                8 F NC S
Camilla               5 F NC
Mary FESPERMAN       18 F NC S
William TREXLER      13 M NC S
```

1716.1741 Margaret HOLTSHOUSER 38 F NC (X) 1000
```
Rufus               9 M NC S
John                7 M NC S
Mary Ann            3 F NC
Maria Jane          1 F NC
Sarah HOLTSHOUSER  42 F NC    cont.
```

150 A improved land, 50 A unimpr, value:$500
corn mill: ? bu. meal valued at $600

1717.1742 John GARNER   61 M NC farmer
```
Margaret GARNER      47 F NC
Isaac R. RAINY       19 M NC labourer
Margaret E. RAINEY   18 F NC
```

110 A improved land, 178 unimpr, value:$1,000

1718.1743 Thomas RIMER   40 M NC (X) farmer 500
```
Sally RIMER          39 F NC (X)
Sarah A.E.           15 F NC S
Henry F.             14 M NC S
Thomas H.            12 M NC S
Reuben H.            11 M NC S
Rufus J.              1 M NC
```

1719.1744 Michael HEILIG 46 M NC farmer 1300
```
Sally HEILIG         49 F NC (X)
Mary A. HEILIG       19 F NC S
James H.             18 M NC S labourer
Richard A.           17 M NC S labourer
George S.            15 M NC S labourer
Allen H.             14 M NC S
Sarah E.             12 F NC S
Margaret K.          11 F NC S
Amanda J.             5 F NC
```

120 A improved land, 110 A unimpr, value:$1,300

1720.1745 George GARNER   57 M NC (X) farmer 500
```
Barbara GARNER )twins  67 F NC (X)
Elisabeth "    )       67 F NC (X)
Margaret               52 F NC (X)
```

125 A improved land, 160 unimpr, value:$600

1721.1746 Sarah FISHER   48 F NC (X) 2500
```
Peter A.             25 M NC farmer
David                23 M NC labourer
Daniel               21 M NC labourer
Leah L.              19 F NC
Catharine L.         16 F NC S
Sarah C.             14 F NC S
Sally E.             12 F NC S
Charles H.            9 M NC S
```

200 A improved land, 400 unimpr, value:$2,500

1722.1747 Margaret R GARNER   42 F NC 200
```
Martha E.            20 F NC
John W.              18 M NC farmer
Mary R.              16 F NC
Samuel F.            13 M NC
Margaret M.          12 F NC
Joseph E.             9 M NC
Jane A.               4 F NC
```

37 A improved land valued at $148

1723.1748 William LINEBARRER 22 M NC farmer m
  Nancy LINEBARRER   29 F NC (X) m
  Tobias LINEBARRER   16 M NC S labourer

1724.1749 Henry RITCHEY 54 M NC (X) blacksmith
  Margaret RITCHEY   49 F NC (X)
  Rose A.   22 F NC (X)
  Peter   20 M NC labourer
  Moses J.   17 M NC S labourer
  Henry W.   15 M NC S labourer
  William M.   11 M NC S
[222] Sophia M.   9 F NC S
  Margaret M.   7 F NC

30 A improved land valued at $60

<u>p.222, School District # 25, 28 Nov 1850</u>

1725.1750 Daniel KLUTTS 28 M NC farmer 300
  Catharine KLUTTS   29 F NC
  Lawson A.   2 M NC
  Lewis A.   1 M NC

16 A improved land, 84 A unimpr, value:$300

1726.1751 Daniel FRICK 40 M NC
  Margaret FRICK   33 F NC
  Mary A.   8 F NC
  Roamy   6 F NC
  Joseph A.   4 M NC
  John W.   2 M NC

30 A improved land, 110 unimpr, value:$600

1727.1752 Catharine MOWREY 65 F NC (X) 400
  Margaret   35 F NC (X)
  Polly   33 F NC (X)

60 A improved land, 158 A unimpr, value:$400

1728.1753 Michal SHUPING 47 M NC farmer 500
  Sally M.   40 F NC S
  Willa M.   17 M NC S
  Alfred A.   18 M NC S
  Catharine M.   19 F NC S
  Rachel SHUPING   45 F NC (X)

30 A improved land, 190 A unimpr, value:$500
100 A improved land, 230 A unimpr, value:$500

1729.1754 Polly MOWRY 37 F NC 100
  Barbara C.   18 F NC S
  Elisabeth   11 F NC S
  Sarah A.   9 F NC S
  Jacob A.R.   2 M NC

1730.1755 Samuel SHINN 35 M NC farmer 500
  Margaret SHINN   33 F NC
  William   13 M NC S
  Lamanda   9 F NC S
  Joshua   4 M NC

50 A improved land, 35 A unimpr, value:$500

1731.1756 Catharine MILLER 44 F NC (X) 75
  Julia A. MOWRY   11 F NC S
  Catharine C.   8 F NC S

1732.1757 Peter MOWRY 79 M NC farmer 350
  Mary MOWRY   60 F NC (X)
  Henry HOUSE   22 M NC (X) labourer

75 A improved land, 50 A unimpr, value:$350

1733.1758 Anna PEELER 42 F NC (X)
  Adam   20 M NC
  Eve L.   15 F NC S
  Sally   12 F NC S
  Simeon   9 M NC S
  Crawford   7 M NC

40 A improved land, 60 A unimpr, value:$100

1734.1759 Andrew HOLTSHOUSER 32 M NC farmer 1,000
  Sophia HOLTSHOUSER 29 F NC (X)
  Jacob R.   14 M NC S
  Alexander   12 M NC S
  Clementine   10 F NC S
  Chrisenberg   8 M NC S
  Tobias   6 M NC S
  Frederick   3 M NC
  Lawson   9/12 M NC

50 A improved land, 120 A unimpr, value:$600

1735.1760 Peter CASPER 52 M NC farmer 900
  Catharine CASPER   45 F NC
  Adam   23 M NC
  John   21 M NC S
  Charles   19 M NC S
  Moses   16 M NC S
  Daniel   13 M NC S
  Willa   11 M NC S
  Eve C.   8 F NC
  Simeon   6 M NC
  Margaret C.   4 F NC

100 A improved land, 170 A unimpr, value:$900

1736.1761 Moses LINGLE 24 M NC farmer 900
  Anna L. LINGLE   21 F NC (X)
  Mary E.   3 F NC
  John C.   4/12 M NC

50 A improved land, 110 A unimproved

1737.1762 Moses LINGLE 41 M NC farmer
  Margaret LINGLE   32 F NC
  Mary C.   11 F NC S
  Joseph M.   10 M NC S
  Loretta L.   8 F NC S
  John R.   6 M NC S
  Margaret M.   1 F NC

50 A improved land, 110 A unimpr, value:$600

1738.1763 John CANUP   41 M NC (X) farmer 100
   Christiana CANUP   40 F NC (X)
   Steven C. CAUBLE   14 M NC S
   Henry M.A. CANUP   10 M NC S

   40 A improved land, 30 A unimpr, value:$100

1739.1764 George TROUTMAN 47 M NC (X) farmer 800
   Catharine TROUTMAN   46 F NC (X)
   Margaret   16 F NC S
   Monro   14 M NC S
   Catharine   11 F NC S
   Nathan   7 M NC S
[223] Amelia A.   3 F NC

   55 A improved land, 75 A unimpr, value:$1,000.

p. 223, School District #34, 29 Nov 1850

1740.1765 James HOLTSHOUSER 24 M NC farmer 700
   Sally HOLTSHOUSER   20 F NC
   Crawford A.L.   2 M NC

   75 A improved land, 175 A unimpr, value:$700

1741.1766 Peter MILLER   44 M NC farmer 1300
   Mary MILLER   34 F NC (X)
   William   15 M NC S
   Sally L.   12 F NC S
   Augustus L.   10 M NC S
   John R.   8 M NC S
   Mary A.   6 F NC
   Miles   4 M NC
   George A.   2 M NC

   75 A improved land, 140 A unimpr, value:$1300

1742.1767 Catharine EARNHART 44 F NC
   Margaret EARNHART   28 F NC

1743.1768 Henry PEELER   47 M NC farmer 800
   Sophia PEELER   42 F NC
   Sarah A.   19 F NC
   Margaret L.   17 F NC S
   Tobias   14 M NC S
   Eliza L.   11 F NC S
   Lawrence A.   9 M NC S
   Mary M.   7 F NC S
   Lawson J.   2 M NC

   160 A improved land, 96 A unimpr, value:$700

1744.1769 Elihu HOLTSHOUSER 50 M NC 2255
   Polly HOLTSHOUSER   48 F NC (X)
   Caleb   26 M NC partially deaf
   Margaret   21 F NC
   Sarah   18 F NC S
   Daniel M.   15 M NC S
   Eli   12 M NC S partially
                                       deaf
   Alfred   9 M NC S

   277 A improved land, 150 A unimpr, value:
        $1,695, 1 slave

1745.1770 David HOLTSHOUSER 54 M NC wagonmaker 500
   Sally HOLTSHOUSER   33 F NC
   Paul   29 M NC farmer
   John   20 M NC S labourer
   Willa   21 M NC labourer
   Mary A.   17 F NC S
   Malinda   14 F NC S
   Emeline CRESWELL   24 F NC (X)

   71 A improved land, 100 A unimpr, value:$500

1746.1771 John PEELER   52 M NC farmer 500
   Elisabeth PEELER   54 F NC (X)
   Catherine L.   15 F NC S
   Monroe   4 M NC
   Henry PEELER   23 M NC m
   Anna PEELER   23 F NC m

   68 A improved land, 70 A unimpr, value:$500

1747.1772 Levi KLUTTS   26 M NC farmer
   Margaret KLUTTS   26 F NC (X)
   Carmi C.   4 M NC
   Jacob R.   1 M NC
   25 A improved land valued at $100

1748.1773 Milla PEACOCK 34 F NC (X)
   Green C.   12 M NC S
   Mary L.   9 F NC S
   Jacob W.   6 M NC

1749.1774 Catharine KLUTTS 64 F NC (X)
   Solomon   27 M NC (X) farmer
   Jacob   22 M NC labourer
   Peter   20 M NC S labourer
   Moses FESPERMAN   22 M NC miller

   90 A improved land, 20 A unimpr, value:$812

1750.1775 Henry KLUTTS 43 M NC farmer 250
   Susan KLUTTS   29 F NC (X)
   Caroline   19 F NC S
   Mary   17 F NC S
   Elisabeth   9 F NC S

   124 A improved land, 12 A unimpr, value:$920

1751.1776 David CASPER   42 M NC (X) farmer 800
   Simeon   12 M NC S
   Sophia   10 F NC S
   Julia A.   8 F NC S
   John   6 M NC
   Elisabeth CASPER   44 F NC (X)

   69 A improved land, 50 A unimpr, value:$800

1752.1777 James KLUTTS 49 M NC farmer 1400
   Martha KLUTTS   42 F NC
   Osborn M.   20 M NC labourer   cont.

cont.

Sarah L.   16 F NC S

60 A improved land, 40 A unimpr, value:$700
1 slave

1753.1778 Casper HOLTSHOUSER 64 M NC farmer 750
  Sarah HOLTSHOUSER   47 F NC (X)
  Margaret   21 F NC S
  Eliza   18 F NC S
  Amy   14 F NC S

  [MB:Casper Holshouser & Sally Barger 21 May 1811]
  90 A improved land, 64 A unimpr, valued at $650
  2 slaves

1754.1779 Charles HOLTSHOUSER 33 M NC farmer 500
  Elisabeth HOLTSHOUSER   33 F NC
  Emeline   10 F NC S
  Calvin   8 M NC S
  William P.   7 M NC
[224] Mary A.   5 F NC
  Osborn   3 M NC
  Maria   1 F NC

  [MB:Charles Holshouser & E Klutts 21 Aug 1838]
  45 A improved land, 79 A unimpr, value:$500

p.224, School District #34, 30 Nov 1850

1755.1780 Simeon KLUTTS 26 M NC farmer
  Eve A. KLUTTS   26 F NC (X)
  Jeremiah L.   4/12 M NC

  100 A improved land, 50 A unimpr, value:$800

1756.1781 Lenard KLUTTS 62 M NC 450
  Sophia KLUTTS   56 M NC (X)
  Rose A.   18 F NC S
  Catharine   15 F NC S

  75 A improved land, 50 A unimpr, value:$500

1757.1782 Moses JOSEY 35 M NC farmer 450
  Ann M. JOSEY   37 F NC
  Richard   7 M NC S
  Macedon   5 M NC S
  Robert   7/12 M NC
  Lewis RITCHEY   19 M NC S

  40 A improved land, 78 A unimpr, value:$450

1758.1783 Frederick JOSEY 78 M NC farmer 625

  90 A improved land, 43 A unimpr, value:$500
  8 slaves

1759.1784 Mary JOSEY 74 F PA (X)
  Anna L.   30 F NC (X)
  Jackson R. JOSEY   16 M NC S

1760.1785 John JOSEY Jr 34 M NC farmer 500
  Elisabeth JOSEY   34 F NC   cont.

Julia A.P.   10 F NC S
Elisabeth   8 F NC S
Wilson R.   6 M NC
Ellen J.   4 F NC

50 A improved land, 45 A unimpr, value:$500

1761.1786 John JOSEY Sr. -- M NC blacksmith 400
  Sarah JOSEY   37 F NC (X)
  Catharine L.   15 F NC S
  Ester C.   14 F NC S
  Christiana F.   12 F NC S
  Mary   9 F NC
  Valentine   5 M NC
  Jane R.   3 F NC
  Miles   1 M NC

  33 A improved land, 33 A unimpr, value:$420

1762.1787 John TROUTMAN 39 M NC (X) farmer
  Polly TROUTMAN   39 F NC (X)
  Noah B.L.   13 M NC

  20 A improved land valued at $75

1763.1788 Frederick HOLTSHOUSER 61 M NC blacksmith
                                            1600
  Paul   25 M NC farmer
  Leah   25 F NC

  80 A improved land, 100 A unimpr, value:$800

1764.1789 Nancy CORL 39 F NC (X)
  George H. CORL   18 M NC S
  Daniel N.   16 M NC S
  Rufus V.   13 M NC S
  Elisabeth   11 F NC S
  Julia A.L.   8 F NC S
  Martin CORL   28 M NC miller

  80 A improved land, 60 A unimpr, value:$1,800

1765.1790 Joseph MILLER 40 M NC farmer 1200
  Cornelia MILLER   32 F NC (X)
  Rufus   14 M NC S
  Tobias   12 M NC S
  Catharine   10 F NC S
  William LEFLER   10 M NC S

  78 A improved land, 75 A unimpr, value:$1,900

1766.1791 Christopher HARKEY 36 M NC farmer
  Rachel HARKEY   42 F NC (X)
  Maria   14 F NC S
  Clementine   12 F NC S
  Daniel   10 M NC S
  John   8 M NC S
  Mary Ann   4 F NC

  60 A improved land, 60 A unimpr, value:$650

1767.1792 John LANTZ 39 M NC clergyman   cont.

```
Nancy LANTZ          28 F NC
Ellen E.             2 F NC
Susan C.             1 F NC
Henrietta C.         2/12 F NC
```

100 A improved land, 60 A unimpr, value:$600
2 slaves

```
1768.1793 John SEAFORD    48 M NC farmer 600
  Elisabeth SEAFORD       45 F NC
  Joseph                  21 M NC labourer
  Lavinia B.              18 F NC S
  John P.                 16 M NC S
  Simeon                  10 M NC S
  BARBARA KLUTTS          80 F NC (X)
```

60 A improved land, 40 A unimpr, value:$600

```
1769.1794 George KLUTTS   37 M NC farmer 700
  Nancy KLUTTS            38 F NC
  Alexander               12 M NC S
  Jeremiah                11 M NC S
  Rose A.                  8 F NC S
  Rufus                    6 M NC S
  Jesse A.                 4 M NC
  Calvin                   2 M NC
  Susanna SEAFORD         74 F NC
```

70 A improved land, 50 A unimpr, value:$700

```
1770.1795  Samuel SEAFORD 43 M NC farmer 700
  Elisabeth SEAFORD       44 F NC (X)
[225] Mary A.             18 F NC S
  Sarah M.                16 F NC S
  Willa M.                13 M NC
  Edmund                  10 M NC
  David A.                 4 M NC
```

60 A improved land, 45 A unimpr, value:$700

<u>p.225, School District #35, 2 Dec 1850</u>

```
1771.1796 Andrew CRUSE    51 M NC blacksmith
  Sarah CRUSE             45 F NC (X)
  Sarah M.                23 F NC
  Leah                    21 F NC (X)
  Solmon                  19 M NC
  Catharine L.            18 F NC S
  Christiana L.           16 F NC S
  Elisabeth               14 F NC S
  Monroe                  10 M NC S
```

```
1772.1797 William BOST 42 M NC farmer 1650
  Elisabeth BOST          41 F NC (X)
  Lavinia                 19 F NC
  David A.                17 M NC S
  George M.               15 M NC S labourer
  Sophia                  13 F NC S
  Leah M.                 11 F NC S
  William H.               8 M NC S
  Allison                  6 M NC S
  Moses J.                 3 M NC        cont.
```

100 A improved land, 100 A unimpr, value:<u>$800</u>

```
1773.1798 Alexander CAUBLE 38 M NC (X)
  Margaret CAUBLE         42 F NC (X)
  Elisabeth HORNBARRIER   66 F NC (X)
```

6 A improved land valued at $25

```
1774.1799 Joseph FISHER   36 M NC farmer
  Barbara FISHER          30 F NC (X)
  Julia A.V.              10 F NC S
  John C.                  7 M NC S
  Henderson A.             4 M NC S
  Camilla E.               2 F NC
```

100 A improved land, 221 unimpr, value:$2,000
6 slaves

```
1775.1800 Mary M BARRINGER 42 F NC 1000
  Lundy M.                16 F NC S
  Polly C.                14 F NC S
  Nicholas R.             12 M NC S
  Joseph A.               25 M NC farmer 800
```

75 A improved land, 75 A unimpr, value:$1,000
4 slaves

```
1776.1801 Elisabeth LENTZ 45 F NC 1200
  Helena                  24 F NC
  John F.                 21 M NC farmer
  Matthias                20 M NC labourer
  Green                   17 M NC S labourer
  Camilla    )twins       14 F NC S
  Margaret   )            14 F NC S
```

125 A improved land, 175 A unimpr, value:$1,200

```
1777.1802 Daniel CORL    65 M NC wagonmaker 1800
  Daniel                  25 M NC S
  Sarah                   30 F NC (X)
  Jacob                   22 M NC (X)
  Joseph                  18 M NC
  William                 16 M NC S
  Alexander               12 M NC S
  Nancy CORL               7 F NC S
```

90 A improved land, 90 A unimpr, value:<u>$900</u>
3 slaves

```
1778.1803 John D LENTZ 38 M NC cabinetmaker 700
  Evelina LENTZ           36 F NC
  Eli C.                  13 M NC S
  Crissa A.C.             11 F NC S
  John C.                  7 M NC S
  Caleb A.                 5 M NC
  Mary S.J.                2 F NC
  Laura M.             8 /12 F NC
  Elisabeth C. MOZER      17 F NC S
  George MOZER            57 M NC shoemaker
```

David LENTZ: 58 A improved land, 50 A
   unimproved, valued at $700

1779.1804 Lawrence LINGLE 50 M NC farmer 1500
  Elisabeth LINGLE   49 F NC (X)
  John   22 M NC labourer
  Anna   18 F NC
  Louisa   15 F NC S
  Elisabeth   12 F NC S

  75 A improved land, 176 unimpr, value:$1,500
  1 slave

1780.1805 Jacob FISHER 54 M NC carpenter 1800
  Christiana FISHER   50 F NC (X)
  Christiana C.   19 F NC S
  Lawson A.   16 M NC S
  Jacob R.   14 M NC S
  Clodora   12 F NC S
  Lavinia   10 F NC S
  Iriva   6 F NC S

  58 A improved land, 47 A unimpr, value:$1,100

1781.1806 Samuel BEAVER 49 M NC farmer 1200
  Lydia BEAVER   39 F NC (X)
  Matilda   12 F NC S
  Tobias   17 M NC S
  Peter   14 M NC S

  100 A improved land, 234 A unimpr, value:$1,200

1782.1807 Jacob HOLTSHOUSER 24 M NC farmer m
  Anna M. HOLTSHOUSER   19 F NC m

  [MB:Jacob Holshouser & Anny Beaver 18 April 1850]

  p.226. School District #35, 2&3 Dec 1850

1783.1808 Simeon MILLER 36 M NC farmer 1050
  Anna M. MILLER   35 F NC (X)
  Mary C.   12 F NC S
  David L.   11 M NC S
  Anna L.   8 F NC S
  Uriah E.   6 M NC S
  Catherine E.   3 F NC
  Theodore E.   1 M NC

  40 A improved land, 73 A unimpr, value:$1,000

1784.1809 John J MILLER 29 M NC farmer 1000
  Mary A. MILLER   23 F NC
  Boyden A.R.   2 M NC
  Luther E.   1 M NC
  Elisabeth MILLER   73 F PA (X)

  63 A improved land, 35 A unimpr, value:$4,000

1785.1810 Caleb A HEILIG 28 M NC farmer 12000
  Mary A. HEILIG   28 F NC
  Martha A.C.   6 F NC S
  Sarah E.   3 F NC
  George A.   1 M NC

  200 A improved land, 233 A unimpr, value:$4,000
  6 slaves

1786.1811 Sarah HEILIG   46 F NC (X) 11000
  Lawson G.   18 M NC S 9500
  Rose S.C.   15 F NC S 8000
  Margaret HODGINS   21 F NC (X)

  140 A improved land, 157 A unimpr, value:$4,000
  Sarah HEILIG - 14 slaves
  Rose C HEILIG - 4 slaves

1787.1812 John BOST 30 M NC farmer 700
  Elisabeth BOST   25 F NC
  Jessee M.   6 M NC
  Mary M.   4 M NC
  Nancy L.   1 F NC

  100 A improved land, 65 A unimpr, value:$700

1788.1813 Jacob RENDLEMAN 27 M NC farmer 500
  Elisabeth RENDLEMAN   35 F NC (X)

  85 A improved land, 40 A unimpr, value:$500
  1 slave

1789.1814 Peter EARNHART 27 M NC farmer 550
  Catharine EARNHART   24 F NC
  Moses J.   3 M NC
  Loretta C.   1 F NC

  85 A improved land, 50 A unimpr, value:$551

1790.1815 Dawalt BEAVER 42 M NC
  Martha BEAVER   43 F NC
  Joseph   17 M NC S
  Henry A.   16 M NC S
  Eve L.   8 F NC S
  Caroline   19 F NC

  157 A improved land, 70 A unimpr, value:$700

1791.1816 Amelia BEAVER 29 F NC (X) 150
  Jacob   10 M NC S
  Mary   7 F NC S
[Note of Marshall: We have here one too many
houses, see page 176.]
  Cecelia   4 F NC
  Leroy   1 M NC

1791.1817 Margaret RIBLIN 40 M NC 600
  Clotilda   18 F NC
  Matitia   6 F NC S

  95 A improved land, 100 A unimpr, value:$600
  1 slave

1792.1818 Isaac EARNHART 43 M NC farmer
  Sarah EARNHART   39 F NC (X)
  Simeon   17 M NC S
  Louisa   14 F NC S
  Rebecca   12 F NC S
  Alexander   11 M NC
  Delila M.   2 F NC

  100 A improved land, 100 A unimpr, value:$800

1793.1819 Paul BEAVER   37 M NC tailer 950
  Delila BEAVER   34 F NC (X)
  Catharine E.   16 F NC S
  Charles W.   12 M NC S
  Rufus   8 M NC S
  Eve C.   6 F NC
  Massa L.   3 F NC
  Jane S.   1 F NC

  150 A improved land, 133 A unimpr, value:$700

1794.1820 Jacob TROUTMAN   53 M NC miller 3800
  Polly TROUTMAN   52 F NC (X)
  Anna ALMON   28 F NC (X)
  Amanda JACKSON   13 F NC S

  110 A improved land, 130 A unimproved
  3 slaves
  corn mill: ? bu valued at $1,386
  saw mill: 60,000 ft lumber valued at $529

1795.1821 John POWLASS   35 M NC farmer
  Amy POWLASS   27 F NC
  Moses C.   6 M NC
  Mary C.   3 F NC
  Joseph A.   4/12 M NC

  94 A improved land, 100 A unimpr, value:$600

1796.1822 Charles BARGER   42 M NC farmer
  Susanna BARGER   42 F NC (X)
  Tobias   18 M NC labourer
  John A.   12 M NC S
  Moses   16 M NC
  Julia   14 F NC S
  Mary A.   9 F NC S
  Lavinia   5 F NC
  Washington   3 M NC
  Lawson A.   7/12 M NC
  Catharine BARGER   82 F NC (X)

  40 A improved land valued at $200

1797.1823 David TROUTMAN 42 M NC (X) farmer 210
  Caroline   18 F NC
[227] Joseph   17 M NC S
  Mary   16 F NC
  Catharine   14 F NC
  Sarah   12 F NC S
  Nelly   10 F NC S
  Ester   8 F NC S
  Jefferson   6 M NC
  Mary A. TROUTMAN   80 F PA (X)

  50 A improved land, 28 A unimpr, value:$200
  1 slave

<u>p.227, School District #36, 4 Dec 1850</u>

1798.1824 Andrew TROUTMAN 65 M NC (X) farmer 2000
  Elisabeth TROUTMAN   65 F NC
  Samuel   22 M NC labourer cont.

60 A improved land, 100 A unimpr, value:$400

1799.1825 Elias CRANFORD 39 M NC labourer
  Jane CRANFORD   31 F NC (X)
  Mary S.   15 F NC S
  Lucy M.   14 F NC S
  Henry C.   10 M NC S
  William H.   8 M NC S
  Nancy A.   6 F NC
  Richard J.   4 M NC

1800.1826 Phillip EARNHART 66 M NC farmer 1000
  Eve EARNHART   66 F NC
  Mary   26 F NC
  Leah   24 F NC
  Mary A. FRICK   11 F NC
  Julius A. REED   1 M NC

  100 A improved land, 40 A unimpr, value:$600
  1 slave

1801.1827 David EARNHART 36 M NC farmer 1200
  Elisabeth EARNHART   34 F NC
  Calvin M.   12 M NC S
  Eli   10 M NC S
  Freeland A.   7 M NC

  150 A improved land, 180 unimpr, value:$1,200

1802.1828 William POWLASS 61 M NC (X) farmer 1000
  Catharine POWLASS   61 F NC
  Samuel   23 M NC

  100 A improved land, 150 A unimpr, value:$1,000

1803.1829 George EARNHART 50 M NC (X) farmer 375
  Leah EARNHART   40 F NC (X)
  Elisabeth   20 F NC (X)
  Abraham   17 M NC S
  Willa   13 M NC S
  Robert   10 M NC S
  Henry   4 M NC

  100 A improved land, 60 A unimpr, value:$250

1804.1830 Stephen BRADDY 40 M NC (X) farmer 100
  Christiana BRADDY   39 F NC (X)
  David   19 M NC
  Catharine   17 F NC
  Benjamin   15 M NC S
  Amy   12 F NC S
  Joseph A.   8 M NC
  Lewis M.   4 M NC
  Charles W.   1 M NC

  30 A improved land, 70 A unimpr, value:$70

1805.1831 John BRADDY   43 M NC (X) farmer 100
  Sarah BRADDY   41 F NC (X)
  Moses G.   13 M NC S
  Calvin M.   9 M NC S
  John   6 M NC
  Sarah S.   3 F NC   cont.

40 A improved land, 60 A unimpr, value:$100

1806.1832 James MASON   44 M NC farmer
  Sarah MASON   40 F NC (X)
  William   19 M NC S labourer
  Nathan H.   10 M NC S
  Emeline RUSELL   15 F NC

  75 A improved land, 75 A unimpr, value:$600

1807.1833 Catharine PEELER 44 F NC (X)
  Sophia L.   19 F NC
  Solomon   17 M NC S farmer

  100 A improved land, 50 A unimpr, value:$500

1808.1834 Asa MILLER   59 M NC farmer 330
  Mary M. MILLER   57 F NC (X)
  Daniel   26 M NC S
  Joseph   23 M NC
  Barbara B.   20 F NC
  Margaret S.   19 F NC

  50 A improved land, 62 A unimpr, value:$300

1809.1835 Samuel ROTHROCK 40 M NC L. clergyman
  Amelia ROTHROCK   37 F NC
  Lewis Hazelius   11 M NC S
  Charlotte L.J.   3 F NC

  40 A improved land, 67 A unimpr, value:$900
  4 slaves

1810.1836 Elisabeth GOODMAN 58 F NC 500
  George   31 M NC farmer 800
  William A.   17 M NC S labourer

  46 A improved land, 20 A unimpr, value:$500
  1 slave

1811.1837 Joseph T CUNNINGHAM 32 M NC physician
                                            1000
  Margaret A. CUNNINGHAM   21 F NC
  Martha J.   1 F NC
  Phebe CUNNINGHAM   43 F NC
  Elisabeth   41 F NC
  Rebecca   39 F NC
  Sarah   36 F NC
  Beersheba   30 F NC
[228] Abner SEERS   22 M NC B

  75 A improved land, 75 A unimpr, value:$1,500
  3 slaves

<u>p.228, School District #36, 5 Dec 1850</u>

1812.1838 Elen FRALEY   54 F NC 1500
  Susanna M.   17 F NC
  Hiram   13 M NC

  55 A improved land, 55 A unimpr, value:$1,500
  4 slaves

1813.1839 Moses KLUTTS 35 M NC farmer 300
  Leah KLUTTS   27 F NC (X)
  Margaret E.   2 F NC
  Mary KLUTTS   57 F NC (X)

  35 A improved land, 15 A unimpr, value:$300

1814.1840 Amelia MILLER 59 F NC 900
  Adam   30 M NC farmer
  Jessee   20 M NC labourer
  Eve A.L.   19 F NC
  Eli MILLER   23 M NC
  Elisabeth MILLER   23 F NC

  100 A improved land, 78 A unimpr, value:$850

1815.1841 Jacob MILLER   48 M NC farmer 1200
  Catharine MILLER   49 F NC (X)
  Charles A.G.   23 M NC labourer
  Alexander M.   20 M NC
  Clara A.   13 F NC S

  160 A improved land, 100 A unimpr, value:$1,400
  2 slaves

1816.1842 John MILLER 52 M NC farmer 1660
  Elisabeth MILLER   50 F NC (X)
  John D.   27 M NC labourer
  Margaret M.   21 F NC

  100 A improved land, 110 unimpr, value:$1,500
  2 slaves

1817.1843 Daniel MILLER   36 M NC farmer 1200
  Lavinia MILLER   36 F NC
  Crawford A.   13 M NC S
  Calvin L.)twins   11 M NC S
  Alfred W.)   11 M NC S
  Mary L.   9 F NC S
  John KLUTTS   15 M NC S labourer

  25 A improved land, 80 A unimpr, value:$1,000
  1 slave

1818.1844 Alexander HOLTSHOUSER 42 M NC farmer 2500
  Salome HOLTSHOUSER   42 F NC (X)
  Rufus J.J.   19 M NC S labourer
  Crawford H.   17 M NC S labourer
  Lawson G.   11 M NC S
  Margaret C.   3 F NC
  Louisa CASPER   18 F NC S

  200 A improved land, 200 A unimpr, value:$2500
  2 slaves

1819.1845 Jacob HOLTSHOUSER 43 M NC farmer
  Rachel HOLTSHOUSER   43 F NC (X)
  Miles A.   20 M NC S labourer
  Eli   16 M NC S labourer
  Otho   13 M NC S
  Benjamin   11 M NC S
  Calvin   9 M NC S cont.

Catherine L.   6 F NC

50 A improved land, 75 A unimpr, value:$1,000

1820.1846 Simeon LENTZ   33 M NC farmer 500
  Mary A. LENTZ   28 F NC
  Sophia   11 F NC S
  Henry   9 M NC S
  Franklin   4 M NC
  Georg MEYER   57 M NC shoemaker
  Alexander LENTZ   20 M NC labourer

25 A improved land, 25 A unimpr, value:$500

1821.1847 Samuel CANUP   25 M NC farmer 100 m
  Mary A. CANUP   19 F NC m

[MB:Samuel Canup to Mary Ann Keply 8 Mar. 1850]

1822.1848 Elisabeth CANUP   59 F NC (X) 600
  Margaret   37 F NC (X)
  Mary   39 F NC (X)
  Milly   31 F NC (X)
  Christiana   29 F NC (X)
  Noah   18 M NC

125 A improved land, 125 A unimpr, value:$600

1823.1849 Lafayette GREEN   24 M NC labourer
  Sarah GREEN   22 F NC (X)
  Elisabeth   1 F NC

1824.1850 Henry HOLTSHOUSER 38 M NC farmer 125
  Sarah   14 F NC
  John   9 M NC
  Jeremiah   6 M NC

25 A improved land valued at $75

1825.1851 Jacob HOLTSHOUSER 32 M NC farmer 400
  Delila HOLTSHOUSER   31 F NC
  Miles M.   7 M NC
  Jacob R.   5 M NC
  Crawford   3 M NC
  Adam   1 M NC

40 A improved land, 60 A unimpr, value:$400
2 slaves

1826.1852 William HOLTSHOUSER 21 M NC X labour 100
  Barbara HOLTSHOUSER   21 F NC (X)
  Catharine E.   1 F NC

1827.1853 Samuel LINN   56 M NC farmer 6500
  Elisabeth LINN   54 F NC (X)
  Joseph A. LINN   30 M NC L clergman 1800 m
  Margaret A. LINN   26 F NC m
  John F.   2 M NC
  Samuel B. WILLIAMS   30 M VA millwright
  Isaac WAGNER   28 M NC millwright
  Rufus HILL   30 M NC millwright
                                  cont.

Samuel Linn: 200 A improved land, 223
  unimproved, $4,500, 14 slaves
Flouring: 2,000 bbls flour valued at $9,000
corn mill: 11,000 bu meal valued at $2,850
saw mill: 180,000 ft. lumber valued at $2,170
Joseph A. LINN - 2 slaves

p.229, School District #37, 6 Dec 1850

1828.1854 Levi STONER 25 M NC (X) labourer
  Elisabeth STONER   25 F NC (X)
  Henry C.   4 M NC
  Julius F.   1 M NC
  Deberry A. CHANDLER   22 M NC labourer

1829.1855 Benjamin CHANDLER 24 M NC labourer
  Elisabeth CHANDLER   21 F NC (X)
  Henry W.   6 M NC
  John D.   4 M NC
  Margaret A.   2 F NC
  Julia F.   0/12 F NC

1830.1856 Henry HICKS 39 M NC farmer 500
  Jane HICKS   41 F NC
  James M.   14 M NC S
  William W.   12 M NC S
  Thomas F.   11 M NC S
  John H.   9 M NC S
  Richard D.   7 M NC S
  Elisabeth R.   5 F NC S
  Mary Jane   2 F NC
  Martha Lamanda   7/12 F NC

2 slaves

1831.1857 Charles EARNHART 30 M NC farmer
  Elisabeth L. EARNHART   29 F NC (X)
  Jane S.   8 F NC
  Drucilla E.   5 F NC
  Loretta S.   2 F NC
  Elisabeth HODGINS   22 F NC (X)

25 A improved land, value of farm $150

1832.1858 Rachel KEPLY   51 F NC 400
  Nancy Martilla   25 F NC (X)
  Miless A.   22 M NC farmer
  Jacob N.   18 M NC S labourer
  Jane C.   15 F NC S
  Crissa L.   13 F NC S
  Robert V.   11 M NC S
  George C.   7 M NC S

70 A improved land, 76 A unimpr, value:$150

1833.1859 James PORTER 35 M NC farmer 300
  Anna L. PORTER   32 F NC (X)
  Otho Nial   8 M NC S
  Lunda   3 F NC
  Ruben   11/12 M NC
  Phebe PORTER   36 F NC (X)
                                  cont.

44 A improved land, 44 A unimpr, value:$<u>400</u>

1834.1860 Christopher BAIM 30 M NC (X) labourer
  Anna BAIM   23 F NC (X)
  Mary C.   6 F NC
  Julia I.A.   3 F NC
  Samuel C.   1 M NC

1835.1861 Elisabeth SMITH 52 F NC
  George   21 M NC farmer 200
  Mary E.   18 F NC S
  Rose A.   16 F NC S
  Charles A.   12 M NC S

1836.1862 Daniel HOUSE   29 M NC
  Leah HOUSE   28 F NC
  Margaret S.   1 F NC
  James HOUSE   15 M NC
  John HOUSE   5 M NC
  George HOUSE   55 M NC labourer
  Margaret HOUSE   15 F NC

1837.1863 Joseph SHANK   37 M NC (X)
  Sophia SHANK   41 F NC (X)
  Barbara   9 F NC S
  Joseph A.   6 M NC
  Elisabeth S.   3 F NC
  Daniel A.   )twins   9/12 M NC
  Mary Jane   )   9/12 F NC
  Catharine PENINGER   16 F NC S

1838.1864 Nelson SIDES   34 M NC
  Sarah SIDES   24 F NC
  John D.   12 M NC
  Ruben A.   9 M NC
  James M.   4 M NC
  Moses S.   1 F NC
  Levi SIDES   21 M NC labourer

30 A improved land, 30 A unimpr, value:$150

1839.1865 Eli LANCASTER 25 M NC labourer
  Elisabeth LANCASTER   42 F NC
  Frederick KORF   12 M NC S
  Catharine KORF   9 F NC S
  Jacob KORF   8 M NC S
  John KORF   4 M NC

1840.1866 Jeremiah GRABER 25 M NC farmer 500
  Eve E. GRABER   36 F NC
  John M. EDLEMAN   11 M NC S
  William H. C. EDLEMAN   6 M NC S
  Laura R.P.   2 F NC
  Henry T. GRABER   2/12 M NC
  Robert WILHELM   19 M NC Mu labourer
  William J. SLOOP   22 M NC miller
  Elisabeth LINGLE   19 F NC

50 A improved land, 50 A unimpr, value:$500
2 slaves

<u>p. 230, School District #3, p. 230</u>

1841.1867 Milton CALVIN 30 M NC Mu labourer
  Julia A. CALVIN   25 F NC Mu
  William H.   1 M NC Mu

1842.1868. Polly VALENTINE 60 F NC Mu
  Catherine   18 F NC Mu
  Sandy SAWYERS   21 M NC Mu labourer

The names below were this day April 4th 1851
added by the request of the Asst Marshall
                                        DM

  Mary J. POOL   31 F VA 1,000
  John H.   8 M NC S
  Joseph A.   5 M NC
  James L.   7 M NC S
  Mary E.   3 F NC
  Anna V.H.   11/12 F NC
  Mary H. HARDIE 50 F VA
  Martha   23 F NC
  Susan E.   17 F NC
  Caleb   18 M Mu
  2 slaves

LEFTOVERS

There are people whose statistics were included in the special schedules who could not be identified on the population schedule. Herewith:

Caleb BEAVER
   70 A improved land, 79 A unimpr, value:$600

Daniel M BEAVER
   110 A improved land valued at $235

Samuel BEAVER
   30 A improved land, 19 A unimpr, value:$196

Michael BOSTIAN
   80 A improved land, 210 A unimpr, value: $1,000, 2 slaves

Newberry HALL
   170 A improved land, 375 A unimpr, value:$5,000

George H. KETNER
   25 A improved land, 50 A unimproved, valued at $500

Willa KIRK
   40 A improved land, 260 A unimpr, valued at $400

Solomon KLUTTS
   75 A improved land, 100 A unimpr, value:$400

LOCK & COWAN tannery: 600 pieces leather valued at $1200

William McCOY
   750 A improved land, 1850 A unimproved, valued at $12,000, 31 slaves

Henry A MILLER
   100 A improved land, 140 A unimpr, value: $1,000

Colward H. ROSEMAN
   2 slaves

Mary S ROSEMAN
   3 slaves

Jno SMITH, manager
   475 A improved land, 187 A unimproved, valued at $3,110, 19 slaves

John THOMPSON jr.
   4 slaves

1850 ROWAN COUNTY CENSUS: MORTALITY SCHEDULE

The arrangement of material has been altered by the compiler with Whites and Blacks listed separately and alphabetically. The listings are supposed to show persons who died during the year ending 1 June 1850, enumerated by E. D. Austin, Asst Marshall. Bear in mind that the year for the deaths occurring June - December will be 1849 and those for January - May will be 1850. [Some deaths recorded took place later than the time requirement.] The listings for deceased slaves is omitted because the owner's name is not shown and there is no way to identify the slaves. The information on free blacks and mulattoes is included. Abbreviations are obvious, m meaning the deceased was married at the time of death, w that the deceased was widowed at the time of death. The place given is the place of birth. MB: indicates an extant Rowan County marriage bond. CW is the newspaper Carolina Watchman, from which death notices are taken. Some records from tombstones and from the compiler's files are also included.

ALISON, Mary - 45 F NC w, d May, sudden
       [CW: Mary Allison, widow of Theophilus Allison, d. 7 May 1850
       and the age of about 40. Issue of 9 May 1850. MB: Theophilus
       Allison to Mary Evalina Graham 27 Mar. 1823.]
ALSON, John - 2 M NC, d Sept, fever, ill 4 days
BARGER, Alexander - 34 M NC, m, d Dec, labourer, pneumonia, ill 12
       days
BARGER, Margaret - 81 F PA w, d Feb, unknown, ill 5 days
       [Note: Born 6 Oct. 1769, d. 10 Feb. 1850, she was the wife of
       John Barger and is bur. at Lower Stone Reformed Church.]
BARRINGER, Elisabeth - 35 F NC m, d Nov, enlargement/spleen
       [CW: Elizabeth Barringer, wife of Jeremiah Barringer, d. 18
       Nov. 1849. Issue of 22 Nov. 1849. Jeremiah Barringer, b. 22
       Apr. 1809, d. 29 Nov. 1876, is bur. in the Old Lutheran Cem.
       in Salisbury. Elizabeth Smith was the first of his three
       wives.] See hh #951
BARRINGER, Rufus L - 11/12 M NC, d Jul, inflam of brain, ill 22
       days
BASINGER (C), Infant - 0/12 M NC, d Jan, consumption, ill 12 mos
BEAN, Elisabeth - 12 F NC, d June, dyspepsy, ill 100 days
BEAN, John - 14 M NC, d Sept, dropsy, ill 100 days
BEAVER, Infant of Tobias, - 2/12 M NC, d Mar, ill 2 mos.
BEAVER, Jane A - 20 F NC, b Oct
BEAVER, Mary - 41 F NC m, d Feb, typhoid/pneumonia, ill 3 wks
BELT, Amos - 8 M NC, d Oct, congestive chill, ill 5 days
BENSON, Catharine - 45 F NC w, d Sept, disease of liver, ill 14
       days
       [Note: Catherine, wife of Thomas Benson, is bur. at the Old
       Lutheran Cem. in Salisbury; she died 21 Sept. 1849 aged 45
       yrs, 10 mos., 8 dys. He d. 30 Oct. 1839 aged 41 yrs, 9 mos,
       28 dys. MB: Thomas Benson to Katharine Brown 10 Nov. 1829.]

130

BERRINER, Charles - 46 M NC m, d Feb, farmer, delerium tremens, ill
    1 week
BIRD, Mary - 27 F NC, d Oct, pneumonia, ill 14 days
BLACKWELL, Rufus E - 1 M NC, d Jan, croup, ill 1 day
BLUE, Infant - 2/12 F NC, d July, thrush, ill 2 days
BOSTIAN, Michael Jr - 53 M NC m, d Mar, farmer, pneumonia, ill 9
    days
BOSTIAN, Michael Sr - 78 M NC w, d May, blackmith, inflam/bowels,
    ill 5 days
BRINGLE, William - 5/12 M NC, d Oct, unknown, sudden
BROWN, Isabella M - 49 F NC m, d May, cancer, ill 360 days
    [CW: Mrs. Isabella Maria Brown, wife of Michael Brown, d. 2
    May 1850 at age 49. Issue of 16 May 1850. She was the dau.
    of Alexander Long and was born 22 Apr. 1801, d. 2 May 1850,
    bur. Old Lutheran Cemetery, Salisbury.]
BROWN, Michael - 51 M NC m, d Dec, blacksnith, consumption, ill 3
    yrs [CW: Michael S. Brown d. 28 Nov. 1849. Issue of 29 Nov.
    1849]
BROWN, Polly - 30 F NC m, d Feb, plurisy, ill 15 days
BUCHANAN, Infant - 0/12 M NC, ill 9 days
BULLEN, John - 50 F NC m, d Dec, farmer, breast disease, ill 13
    days
    [Note: Bur. at St. Matthews Lutheran Church, he was b. 24 Aug.
    1804, d. 7 Dec. 1849.]
BUTNER, William C - 25 M NC, d Nov, farmer, dropsy, ill 15 days
CAMPBELL, Margaret M - F NC m, d Jan pneumonia
CASPER, Alfred W - 19 M NC, d Jun, farmer, cholic, ill 7 days
CASPER, Ezra - 40 M NC m, d Feb, bronchitis, ill 3 days
    [CW: Ezra Casper d. 27 Feb. 1850, aged about 40. Issue of 28
    Feb. 1850.]
CATON, George - 23 M NC, d Jan, pneumonia, ill 9 days
    [CW: George Caten d. 12 Jan. 1850. Issue of 17 Jan. 1850.]
CHRISTY, Mary - 65 F NC, d Dec, disease unkn, ill 6 weeks
CLODFELTER, John L - 19 M NC, d Sept, fever, 14 days
COPE, Lithe Ann - 8/12 F NC, d Oct, spasms, ill 1 day
CORRELL, Elisabeth - 50 F NC, d Mar, typhoid fever, ill 9 days
    [CW: Elizabeth Correll, wife of Jacob Correll d. 16 Mar. 1850.
    Issue of 28 Mar. 1850. According to tombstones at St. Andrews
    Episcopal Church near Woodleaf, she was b. 16 Aug. 1799.
    Jacob was b. 19 June 1798, d. 27 Nov. 1867.] See hh #795
CORRELL, Simeon - 17 M NC, d Mar, labourer, ill 20 days
    [CW: Simeon Correll d. 23 Mar. 1850 (b.1833), son of Jacob &
    Elizabeth Correll. Issue of 28 Mar. 1850. He was b. 16 Aug.
    1823, also bur. at St. Andrews Episcopal Church.]
COUGHENOUR, Amandrus - 1 F NC, d July, bronchitus, ill 120 days
    [CW: Amandus Caroline Coughenour, infant daughter of Mrs.
    Caroline Coughenour, d. 21 July 1849 (b. Apr. 1848). Issue
    of 26 July 1849.]

1850 ROWAN COUNTY CENSUS: MORTALITY SCHEDULE

COWAN, Aaron V - 42 M NC m, d Jan, farmer, pneumonia, ill 13 days
     [CW: A. V. Cowan d. 16 Jan. 1850 (b. 1807). Issue of 31 Jan.
     1850.]
CRUSE, Elisabeth - 24 F NC, d Nov
CULBERTSON, Margaret M - 22 F NC, d Jul, ill 19 days
     [She d. 20 July 1849, bur. Unity Presbyterian Church in
     Woodleaf]
DEATON, Cornelius - 20 M NC, d Aug, labourer, pneumonia, ill 8 days
DAKES, Daniel M - 39 M NC, d Aug. wagonmaker, unkn, ill 9 days
DENT, Infant (Henry) - 4 da M NC, d Jul
DENT, Thomas H - 1/12 M NC, d Nov, dropsy/heart, ill 6 days
EARNHART, Alfred M - 3/12 M NC, d Jul
EARNHART, Edward - 39 M NC m, d Apr, farmer, pneumonia, ill 11 days
EARNHART, twin infants - 0/12 F NC, d Apr
EARNHART, William C - 6 M NC, d Sept, colic, ill 8 days
EDDLEMAN, Polly - 52 F NC, d Nov, pneumonia, ill 5 days
ELLIS, Mary - 60 F NC m, d May, breast disease, ill 9 weeks
FISHER, Elisabeth R - Salisbury, 26 F NC m, d Mar, fever, ill 90
     days [CW:Mrs. Elizabeth Ruth Caldwell Fisher, wife of Charles
     F. Fisher, d. 18 Mar. 1850 (b. 1824). Issue of 28 Mar. 1850.]
     See hh #542
FLEMING, Infant - 0/12 F NC, d Jan
FOSTER, Amy C - 41 F NC, d Jan, pneumonia
FRALEY, David - 62 M NC m, d Aug, farmer, pneumonia, ill 9 days
     [CW: David Fraley d. 2 Aug. 1849). Issue of 9 Aug. 1849. He
     was b. 30 Dec. 1788 and is bur. at LowerStone Reformed Church
     Cem. with his wife Eleanor, b. 16 Aug. 1796, d. 4 Feb. 1853.
     MB: David Fraley to Elenor Robinson 1 Apr. 1818.]   See hh
     #1812
FRALEY, James F - 18 M NC, d May, labourer, drowned, sudden
     [CW. James F. Fraley, son of David Fraley dec., d. 29 May
     1850. Issue of 6 June 1850. He was b. 5 Apr. 1830 and is
     bur. at LowerStone Reformed Church with his parents (above).]
FRALEY, Margaret - 75 F NC w, d Mar, palsy, ill 1 year, 359 days
     [CW: Mrs. Margaret Fraley, widow of George Fraley, dec., d.
     18 Mar. 1850. Issue of 21 Mar. 1850. MB: Georg Frolich to
     Margaret Agenor 15 June 1796.]
GRAHAM, James D - 23 M NC, farmer, typhoid fever
     [CW: James Dwight Graham d. 15 Aug. 1849 (b. 1826). Issue of
     23 Aug. 1849.]
GRAY, Lydia - 25 F NC, d July, typhoid fever, ill 17 days
     [Note: She d. 7 July 1849 and is bur. at Unity Presbyterian
     Church in Woodleaf.]
HARTMAN, Margaret K - 15 F NC, d May, dropsy, ill 3 yrs
HOLBROOKS, Greenbury - 44 M NC m, farmer, consumptiom, ill 3 mos
HOLBROOKS, Margaret - 28 F NC m, d Apr, cholera morbus, ill 1 day
     [CW: Mrs. Margaret Holbrooks, wife of William Holbrooks, d.
     29 Apr. 1850 (b. c1823). Issue of 9 May 1850.]

1850 ROWAN COUNTY CENSUS: MORTALITY SCHEDULE

HOLTSHOUSER, Christina - 56 F NC m, d Nov, bilious fever, ill 9
    days
HOLTSHOUSER, Wila - 40 M NC, d Jun,
    [CW: Wiley Holtshouser d. 28 Jan. 1850 (b. c1812). Issue of
    14 Mar 1850.]
HOLTSHOUSER, Nancy - 66 F NC w, d Jan, pneumonia, ill 8 days
HYDE, Jane - 43 F NC w, d Nov, sudden
    [CW: Mrs. Jane Hyde, widow of Joseph Hyde, d. 4 Nov. 1849.
    Issue of 8 Nov. 1849. They are bur. at Thyatira churchyard.
    Joseph T. Hyde d. 10 June 1845, aged 40 yrs, 2 mos., 20 dys.]
HYDE, Lydia - 70 F NC w, d Nov, dropsy, ill 12 mos
    [She is bur. at Thyatira churchyard, d. 20 Nov. 1849, wife of
    James Hyde.]
JACOBS, James - 23 M NC, d Jul, fever, ill 5 days
JOHNSTON, Mary A - 11 F NC, d May, inflam/brain, ill 2 days
JOSEY, Eli - 22 M NC, d Apr, farmer, cold plaque, ill 2 days
KEPLY, Peter - 58 M NC m, d Jun, farmer, dropsy, ill 6 mos
KETNER, Susanna - 24 F NC m, d Mar, pneumonia, ill 12 days
    [She d. 30 Apr. 1850 and is bur. at Phaniel Lutheran Church.]
KLUTTS, Ellen L - 1 F NC, d Feb, ill 8 days
KLUTTS, Infant - 10/12 M NC, d Nov, unknown, sudden
KLUTTS, Infant (Eli) - 0/12 M NC, d May, ill 10 days
KLUTTS, Samuel - 22 M NC m, d Jan, farmer, unknown, ill 4 mos
LOCKE, John F - 24 M NC m, d. Oct, consumption, ill 3 mos
    [CW: John F. Locke d. 16 Oct. 1849 (b. c1824). Issue of 18
    Oct. 1849]
LOCKE, Richard - 50 M NC w, d Nov, pneumonia, ill 9 days
    [CW: Richard Locke d. 28 Nov. 1849 (b. c1799). Issue of 29
    Nov. 1849. He is bur. at Thyatira churchyard.]
LOVE, Amanda J - 1/12 F NC, d Jan, sore throat, ill 7 days
LUCKEE, Jehiel - 30 M NC m, d Feb, labourer, pneumonia, 6 days
LUCKEY, Temperance A - 21 F NC, d June, typhoid fever, ill 21 days
McCRAY, John - 23 M NC m, d Oct, farmer, palsy, ill 3 days
McNEELY, Infant - 0/12 M NC, d Dec, ill 2 days
MADISON, Thomas E - 30 M VA m, d Apr, tobacconist, congestive
    fever, ill 14 days
MAHALA, Infant - 1/12 F NC, d Dec, convulsions
MAHALA, John L - 4 M NC, d Oct, cholera infanta, ill 5 days
MENIS, Nicholas - 19 M NC, d Mar, labourer, unkn, ill 1 day
MILLER, Christenberry - 1 M NC, d Aug, spasms, ill 1 day
MILLER, Infant (Peter) - 0/12 M NC, d Apr, dropsy, ill 8 mos
MISENHIMER, Lawrence - 27 M NC m, d Apr, farmer, pneumonia, ill 2
    days   .
MOWRY, Jacob - 75 M NC m, d Feb, farmer, congestive chill, ill 1
    day
MURPH, John - 60 M NC m, d Apr, cooper, pneumonia, ill 5 days
MURPH, Lodemia - 32 F NC, d Mar, pneumonia, ill 14 days

1850 ROWAN COUNTY CENSUS: MORTALITY SCHEDULE

NOLLY, Anna - 23 F NC m, d Mar, typhoid pneumonia, ill 8 days
    [CW: Mrs. Anna, d. 24 Mar. 1850 (b. c1805). Issue of 28 Mar.
    1850.]
OLFORD, Temperance - 74 F NC w, d Jul
OVERCASH, Margaret E - 26 F NC, typhus fever, ill 19 days
PARKS, Alla - 37 F NC, d Mar, spasmodic fits, ill 6 days
PENDLETON, Susan - 3 F NC, d Oct, unknown, ill 7 days
    [CW: Susan Pendleton, infant dau. of Richard B. & Mary
    Pendleton, d. 23 Oct. 1849 (b. July 1849). Issue 25 Oct.
    1849.]
PHIFER, Mattias M - 22 M NC m, d Jan, farmer, pneumonia, ill 10
    days
RAINY, Isam - 48 M NC, d Sep, farmer, pneumonia, ill 5 days
ROUGH, Amos - 31 M NC m, d Dec, farmer, pneumonia, ill 18 days
ROSENKRANTZ, Caroline - 3/12 F NC, d Sept, fever, ill 40 days
RUSSELL, Watson - 19 M NC, farmer, palsey, ill 4 mos.
    [CW: Watson Russell d. 10 June 1850 (b. 1831). Issue of 20
    June 1850.]
SAWYER, James - 30 M NC, d Apr, blacksmith, disease of the head,
    ill 3 days
    [CW: James Sawyers d. 17 Apr. 1850 (b. 1816). Issue of 9 May
    1850.]
SECKLER, Moses - 45 M NC m, d Jan, pneumonia, ill 9 days
    [He was b. 15 Sept. 1804, d. 9 Jan. 1850, bur. Mt. Zion
    Lutheran Church, China Grove.]
SEERS, Jane A - 12 F NC, d Oct, epidemic, ill 1 day
SHUPING, Anna C - 79 F NJ m, d Nov, pareletic stroke, ill 4 wks
SHUPING, Leah - 4 F NC, d Dec
SMITH, Elisabeth - 9 F NC, d Dec, inflam brain, ill 5 days
SPECK, Infant (Henry) - 0/12 M NC, d Feb, white swelling, ill 16
    days
STARNES, Martin - 50 M NC, d Aug, farmer, pneumonia, ill 28 days
STILLER, Matthew A - 21 M NC, d Mar, labourer, pneumonia, ill 7
    days
STOKES, Julia - 8 F NC, d Jan, dropsy, ill 5 days
STONER, Barbara - 55 F NC w, d May, dropsy, ill 6 mos
SWAN, Zedekiah - 44 M NC w, d Jan, blacksmith, pneumonia, ill 8
    days
    [CW: Z. Swan d. 16 Jan. 1850 (b. 1806). Issue of 31 Jan.
    1850.]
TANNER, Virginia - 8 F VA, d Sept, congestive chill, ill 2 days
    [CW: Virginia Tanner, dau. of Byrd L. & Jane Tanner, d. 22
    Sept. 1849. Issue of 4 Oct. 1849.]
THOM, William D - 5 M NC, d Apr, pneumonia, ill 15 days
THOMPSON, Menly C - 1 F NC, d Sept, typhoid fever, ill 30 days
THOMPSON, Providence - 71 F NC m, d Nov, jaundice, ill 4 days
TOWNSLEY, John - 12 M NC, d May, labourer, pneumonia
    [CW: John Townsley, Jr., d. 3 May 1850 (b. 1829). Issue of
    9 May 1850.]

1850 ROWAN COUNTY CENSUS: MORTALITY SCHEDULE

TREXLER, Catharine - 20 F NC, d Jul, inflam brain, ill 3 days
TREXLER, Elisabeth - 25 F NC m, d Dec, dropsy, ill 21 days
TREXLER, George - 16 M NC, d Feb, labourer, pneumonia, ill 7 days
TREXLER, Robert F - 6/12 M NC, d June, diarrhea, ill 7 days
TURNER, Burrage C - 10 M NC, d Jan, congestive fever, ill 1 day
UPRIGHT, Joshua - 26 M NC, d Sep, labor/cripple, rheumatisa, ill
     1 mos
UPRIGHT, Peter - 13 M NC, d Oct, Rheumatisa, sudden
UPRIGHT, William - 51 M NC m, d Nov, farmer, pneumonia, ill 8 days
WAGONER, Infant - 1/12 M NC, d Nov
WALTON, William F - 1 M NC, d Mar, ill 14 days
WATSON, Henry W - 37 M NC m, d June, fever, ill 30 days
WILHELM, John - 30 M NC m, d Jun, farmer, epidemic, ill 2 days
     [CW: John Wilhelm d. 28 June 1850 (b. Oct. 1819). Issue of
     11 July 1850.]
WILHELM, Sophia - 30 F NC m, d Apr, ill 1 day
     [She is bur. at St. Matthews Lutheran Church Cem. (1819-1850)]
WISENHUNT, Marcus L - 35 M NC, d Jan, pneumonia, ill 4 days
WOODS, Mary - 61 F NC m, d Aug, unkn, ill 7 wks
     [She d. 4 Aug. 1849, age 61 yrs, 4 mo., 24 dys and is bur.
     with her husband William Woods (b. 18 June 1785, d. 1 Sept.
     1852) at Prospect Presbyterian Church Cem.] See hh #1131
WYITT, Rachel - 60 F NC w, d May, chronic consumption
YOST, Phillip - 72 M NC m, d Mar, pneumonia, ill 8 days
     [CW: Phillip Yost, d. 12 Dec. 1849 (b. 1777). Issue of 20
     Dec. 1850.]

BLACKS

GRAHAM, Stephen - 22 M NC Mu, d Jan, blacksmith, white swelling,
     90 days
OLFORD, Eliza - 8 F NC Mu

```
total of white males      4,844
total of white females    5,058
total number of whites    9,902

total of male slaves      1,894
total of female slaves    1,957
total number of slaves    3,851

free negro males                63
free negro females              52
total free negroes             115
```

<u>p. 254</u>
Real estate valued at $921,455
Personal Estates valued at $2,187, 916
Total $3,009,371
How valued? by assessors
True valuation, valued truly

```
Annual taxes: State tax - $2,457 - cash
              County -       1,673 - cash
              Poor -           549 - cash
              School -       1,498 - cash
              Court of E        24 - cash
              CSL               27 - cash
              CC                53 - cash
```

Colleges, Academies and Schools

   Number: 1 academy, 1 teacher, 40 pupils, $800 from other sources
      43 common schools, 43 teachers, 2,362 pupils, $645 from
      endowment, $1,498 from taxation, $1,682 from public funds,

Libraries: No., Kind, No. of Volumes:

```
1) Law & M, 1,400 vols          9) SSME, 152 vols
2)    "       700 vols         10) M,    100 vols
3)    "       500 vols         11) M,    175 vols
4) Divinity & M,  181 vols     12) M,    114 vols
5)    "            550 vols    13) M,    150 vols
6)    "            389 vols    14) M,    650 vols
7) SS Press        150 vols    15) M,    600 vols
8) D & M            75 vols    16) M, 1,040 vols
                               17) M,     25 vols
```

<u>p. 257</u>
```
1) Divinity   210 vols          8)  M      125 vols
2)    "        150 vols          9)  M       95 vols
3)    "        175 vols         10)  M       75 vols
4) Misel        70 vols         11)  Med     75 vols
5)    "         50 vols         12)  Med     52 vols
6)    "         50 vols         13)  Med & M  200 vols
7)    "        300 vols
```

[JWL note: M is apparently Miscellaneous; SS Pres, according to Bill Bennett, would be "Sunday School, Presbyterian"; SSME would, then, be "Sunday School, Methodist".]

Newspapers and Periodicals:

<u>Carolina Watchman</u>, Whig, weekly, subscription 800

Religion:

	no persons who can be accomodated	value of church property
1) P. Episcopal	300	$4,000
2) Pres. D.S.	500	$4,000
3) E. Lutheran	700	$2,500
4) ME South	500	$1,200
5) Pres D.S.	700	$2,500
6) "	400	450
7) "	400	300
8) "	500	600
9) "	300	300
10) ME South	400	500
11) "	250	350
12) "	250	150
13) "	400	250
14) "	200	100

No. of churches?
Denomination: Baptist (1); E & L (3), M.E. South (4), P.E. (2), E.Latius (6), G. Reformed (2)

<u>p. 256</u>.

1) E.L.T. Synod	650	500			
2) "	250	350			
3) "	650	300			
4) Baptist	200	150			

<u>p. 257</u>

6) M.E. South	400	200			
7) "	150	150			
8) "	100	50			
9) "	200	50			
1) P.E.	600	800			
2) "	500	800			
1) E Lutheran	700	2000			
2) "	600	600			
3) "	700	800			
4) "	600	1000			
5) "	800	1000	1) G Reformed	325	2000
6) "	500	1000	2) "	700	2000

What crops are short? wheat
Average crop: 6 bushels
Pauperism: 30 natives whose cost of support is $1,000

Criminals - 1

Average monthly wages to farm hand with board - $6.00
Average to a day labourer with board - $4
Average to a day labourer without board - $7
Average to a carpenter without board - $7

1850 ROWAN COUNTY CENSUS:SLAVE SCHEDULE

The following statistics are given for the schedule: name of slave owner; number of slaves with age, sex, and colour of each; fugitives from the state; number manumitted; whether deaf & dumb, blind, insane, or idiotic.

For purposes of this compilation, only the number of slaves is listed.

1850 ROWAN COUNTY CENSUS:AGRICULTURE SCHEDULE

Agriculture schedule provides the name of the owner or manager of the farm, the number of acres of improved land, of unimproved land, and the cash value combined; the value of farming implements and machinery; number of horses, asses and mules, milch cows, working oxen, other cattle, sheep, swine; value of livestock; number of bushels of wheat, rye, Indian corn, oats, lbs of rice, tobacco; number of bales of cotton, lbs of wool; number of bushels of pease & beans, Irish potatoes, sweet potatoes, barley, buckwheat; value of orchard products; gallons of wine, value of produce; number of pounds of butter and chees, tons of hay, bushels of clover, bushels of other grain seeds, pounds of hopps, tons of dew rotted hemp, tons of water rotted hemp, pounds of flax, bushels of flaxseed, lbs of silk cocoons, maple sugar, cane sugar; gallons of molasses, lbs of honey and beeswax, value of home-made manufacture, value of animals slaughtered.

In the present compilation only the number of acres of improved land, of unimproved land, and the total cash value of that land is included with the population schedule. Readers must turn to the agriculture schedule itself for the other details.

Schedule 5. Products of Industry in Rowan County, North Carolina, during the year ending 1 June 1850:

Names of Corporations, Companies, or Individuals producing Articles to the Annual value of $500:

Names of Businesses, Manufactures or Products

Capital invested in Real and Personal Estate in the Business: $215,455

Raw Material used, including Fuel, including Quantities, Kinds, Values: $181,538

Kind of motive power, machinery, structure, or resource

Average number of hands employed, male and female: 427-1/2 male, 72 female

Wages: Average monthly cost of male labour: $6,584
       Average cost of female labour: $514

Annual Product:
     Quantities, Kinds, Values: $334,920

In this compilation only the names of the companies and the values of the specific products are included. Many households appear to have been overlooked in this schedule, but it is possible that the manufacture amounted to less than $500 in value.

p. 253.   [Closing notation by Ass't Marshall, Elkanah D. Austin]

Schedule No. 1 filled up 238 pages and 10   10,006
         No. 2   45   72   3,864
         No. 3   5   27   202
         No. 4   34   11   1,118
         No. 5   5   containing 108 mills & shops

Certification dated 22 Dec. 1850

Index

Unless preceded by p., numbers are for household, not page

-A-

Adams, 388
Adderton, 62, 87, 222
Agle, 52
Agner, 329, 343, 569, 658,
    1607, 1647, 1649
Airy, 228
Airy see also Arey
Albright, 737, 1073, 1188,
    1191, 1194, 1195, 1201,
    1353, 1354, 1428
Alexander, 761
Allen, 407, 1525, 1713
Allison, 476
Allison, p. 129
Almon, 277, 321, 193, 1794
Alson, p. 129
Anderson, 132, 674, 699,
    871
Andreus, 166
Andrew, 1074, 1153
Anthony, 1104, 1240
Arey, 56, 295, 302, 1583,
    1628
Arey see also Airy
Arey see also Ehery
Arnell, 96
Aronheart see Earnhart
Ashby, 1238
Atwell, 1104, 1109, 1204,
    1205
Austin, 103, 172, 767
Axium, 1428
Axum, 396

-B-

Badget, 215, 265
Baily, 579
Baim, 252, 347, 196, 1834
Baim see also Pame
Baity, 1090
Baker, 444, 489, 721, 733,
    960, 961, 981, 1167,
    1182, 1284, 1285, 1365
Barber, 813, 825, 850,
    912, 933, 935, 940, 953,
    968, 982, 1021
Barge, 396
Barger, 355, 690, 710,
    845, 1506, 1507, 1753,
    1796
Barger, p. 129
Barker, 468

Barnes, 647
Barnett, 403, 604
Barnhart, 160
Barnhart, Moos & Co., 160
Barr, 1010, 1042, 1072,
    1076, 1086
Barrett, 478
Barrier, 691
Barringer, 76, 296, 301,
    377, 724, 753, 951,
    1508, 1611, 1613, 1692,
    1775
Barringer see also
    Berriner
Barringer, p. 129
Bartlet, 122
Basinger, 3, 318, 332,
    510, 1459, 1460, 1461,
    1462
Basinger, p. 129
Bass, 149
Baughn, 1245
Baxter, 1016, 1061
Bean, 36, 234, 236, 244,
    711, 712, 1405, 1686
Bean, p. 129
Beard, 458, 459, 460, 483,
    530
Bearin, 1287
Beaver, 95, 253, 1133,
    1159, 1162, 1165, 1213,
    1218, 1253, 1275, 1276,
    1293, 1299, 1301, 1305,
    1306, 1308, 1309, 1310,
    1320, 1329, 1331, 1332,
    1334, 1339, 1403, 1404,
    1405, 1441, 1505, 1682,
    1684, 1781, 1782, 1790,
    1791, 1793
Beaver, p. 128 (3)
Beaver, p. 129
Becket, 763, 1695
Beefle, 641, 818, 828, 954
Beek, 878
Bell, 521, 554
Belt, 765, 1016
Belt, p. 129
Bencini, 482
Bennett, 114
Benson, 222, 427, 515,
    808, 809, 1149, 1687
Benson, p. 129
Berriner, p. 130
Bevins, 402
Biggers, 1092, 1094, 1168
Biles, 426, 636, 640

Bird, 102, 858, 922, 995,
    1711, 1713
Bird, p. 130
Bisherer, 1598, 1599
Black, 32, 224, 517, 1542,
    1662
Blackmer, 476
Blackwelder, 1255, 1266,
    1434, 1524
Blackwell, 553, 638, 704,
    706, 957, 1624, 1630
Blackwell, p. 130
Blalock, 79
Blue, 600, 619
Blue, p. 130
Bluster, 1389
Bodenhammer, 378
Boger, 432, 442, 1494,
    1588, 1590
Boggs, 11
Bolitho, 140
Bond, 812
Boocker, 1087
Bost, 205, 365, 581, 610,
    709, 1215, 1296, 1363,
    1426, 1504, 1772, 1787
Bostian, 891, 932, 938,
    1083, 1196, 1199, 1226,
    1236, 1313, 1319, 1324,
    1342, 1372, 1385, 1386,
    1394, 1423, 1427, 1429,
    1438, 1443, 1452, 1537,
    1695, 1700, 1701, 1702,
    1704, 1705, 1709
Bostian, p. 128
Bostian, p. 130
Bowers, 80, 418, 761, 834
Boyd, 171
Boyden, 124, 477
Braddy, 1804, 1805
Bradshaw, 1074, 1169, 1547
Brady, 31
Brandon, 396, 561, 720,
    1004, 1398
Briggs, 242, 707, 708
Bringle, 51, 211, 1597
Bringle, p. 130
Brinkley, 385
Broadway, 749, 1125
Bromhad, 1714
Brown, 26, 169, 301, 302,
    310, 323, 342, 371, 401,
    408, 411, 416, 422, 433,
    434, 441, 443, 449, 467,
    470, 482, 486, 497, 500,
    509, 512, 513, 515, 636,

Unless preceded by p., numbers are for household, not page

Brown (cont.)
746, 752, 1111, 1136,
1205, 1463, 1476, 1518,
1567, 1582, 1583, 1587,
1650, 1653, 1659, 1661,
1663, 1664, 1665, 1666,
1671, 1672, 1673, 1675,
1694

Brown & Baker, 441
Brown, p. 129
Brown, p. 130
Brumly, 755, 762, 763
Bruner, 124, 268, 272, 440
Bruner & James, 440
Bryant, 527
Buchanan, 204
Buchanan, p. 130
Buchart, 174
Buhman, 1333
Buis, 475
Bulland, 1619, 1621, 1622,
1674
Bullen, 190
Bullen, p. 130
Bunn, 182
Burk, 917, 918, 953
Burke, 449, 941, 959, 1006
Burket, 151
Burkhead, 551
Burrage, 237, 238
Burris, 382, 656, 928, 952
Burroughs, 952
Butner, 610, 612, 1427,
1561, 1585, 1711
Butner, p. 130
Byers, 676

-C-

Cadwell, 1666
Cairns, 388
Caldwell, 437, 439
Caldwell, p. 131
Calvin, 506, 1841
Camp, 40
Campbell, 30, 44, 100,
136, 693, 898, 906, 916,
922
Campbell, p. 130
Canada, 506
Canady, 794
Cane, 842
Canup, 16, 19, 42, 43, 56,
287, 668, 1738, 1821,
1822
Capels, 843
Carcar, 1466
Carigan, 1190

Carriker, 1300
Carroll, 136
Carson, 820, 965
Carter, 65, 1706
Cartner, 892, 893, 894
Caruthers, 1174, 1190
Casper, 152, 153, 154,
155, 156, 259, 273, 274,
283, 290, 389, 617, 734,
1411, 1439, 1444, 1678,
1735, 1751, 1818

Casper, p. 130
Caster, 1453, 1482, 1484,
1511
Castle, 142
Caton, p. 130
Cauble, 173, 345, 350,
351, 416, 495, 504, 528,
609, 615, 620, 621,
1155, 1401, 1470, 1570,
1574, 1614, 1618, 1633,
1643, 1647, 1686, 1773

Causey, 63
Cellars, 180
Chaffin, 446
Chambers, 397, 448, 476,
666, 679, 932, 1575
Chandler, 362, 363, 1828,
1829
Christy, 1051, 1057
Christy, p. 130
Chunn, 423, 517, 943
Clampet, 830, 885
Clark, 597
Clary, 420
Clemmons, 398
Clifford, 688
Cline, 802, 837
Clodfelter, p. 130
Clotfelter, 931, 944,
1045, 1065, 1066, 1068,
1070, 1071, 1089, 1109
Coaty, 476
Coburn, 1238
Cochran, 1132, 1148
Coffin, 162
Coffin, Worth & Co., 162
Coffman, 469
Coggins, 1585
Coldiron, 404
Cole, 637, 683, 1416, 1421
Coleman, 1126, 1217, 1246
Coltharp, 160
Cone, 526
Conrad, 455
Cook, 1015, 1036, 1037,
1079, 1530

Coon, 556, 595, 599, 1400,
1411
Cooper, 738, 1179, 1216
Cope, 594, 1197, 1298,
1370, 1421, 1576
Cope, p. 130
Corhier, 1127
Coriher, 1126, 1234, 1236,
1241, 1243, 1244, 1302,
1687
Corl, 607, 802, 1680,
1764, 1777
Correll, 425, 466, 600,
795(2), 1169, 1177,
1307, 1316, 1322, 1323,
1326, 1327, 1330, 1340,
1351, 1352, 1371
Correll, p. 130
Corzine, 980, 1712
Cotton, 1289
Coughenour, 401, 488, 517,
521, 592
Coughenour, p. 130, 795
Courtney, 462
Cowan, 371, 679, 699, 716,
741, 754, 771, 776, 815,
827, 831, 843, 844, 846,
917, 927, 938, 941, 946,
947, 948, 949, 955, 970,
979, 985, 986, 988, 989,
1001, 1003, 1012, 1013,
1021, 1023, 1025, 1030,
1082

Cowan, p. 131
Cox, 7, 317, 410, 415, 568
Cozart, 572, 625, 677
Craig, 579, 618, 623, 624
Cranford, 565, 682, 1415,
1799
Crawford, 546
Crawley, 770
Creason, 376, 709, 1695
Cress, 294, 396, 588, 709,
1381, 1382
Creswell, 1362, 1745
Crider, 110
Crider see also Krider
Crittenton, 514
Crook, 131
Crosby, 1106, 1112, 1136
Crossland, 434
Crotzer, 39
Crowell, 65, 223, 267,
1396
Crumo, 431
Cruse, 1377, 1464, 1466,
1469, 1519, 1771
Cruse, p. 131

Unless preceded by p., numbers are for household, not page

Cubertson, 854
Culbertson, 805, 854, 863
Culbertson, p. 131
Culp, 95, 125
Culverhouse, 480
Cunningham, 1811
Curkhead, 7
Current, 903
Custer, 1327

-D-

Dakes, p. 131
Dancy, 749
Daniell, 246
Darit, 1695
Davis, 96, 161, 266, 377,
    393, 1077, 1108
Deal, 1166, 1220, 1224,
    1225, 1247, 1325, 1326,
    1329, 1441, 1703, 1706,
    1707, 1708
Dean, 977, 1347
Deaton, 509, 1137, 1551
Deaton, p. 131
Demasques, 1156
Dennis, 179
Dent, 552, 630, 631, 632,
    780, 781, 849, 964, 987
Dent, p. 131
Denton, 1313
Dial, 85
Dickson, 522, 818, 819,
    833, 837, 912, 954, 1189
Dillow, 525
Dixmukes, 511
Dobbins, 656, 695, 696,
    697, 698, 708, 886
Doby, 270, 469
Doland, 462
Donahoo, 878, 962
Donnell, 1397
Doolin, 910
Dougherty, 420
Driver, 111
Dry, 978
Duke, 1427, 1430, 1518
Dukes, 1209
Dunin, 63
Dunn, 657
Dustan, 540

-E-

Eagle, 198, 401, 1207,
    1422, 1452, 1453, 1454,
    1456, 1696, 1698
Eagle see also Agle
Earnhart, 29, 33, 54, 120,
    125, 150, 175, 176, 177,

Earnhart (cont.)
    287, 288, 289, 333, 338,
    339, 341, 346, 357, 358,
    360, 361, 462, 491, 505,
    537, 605, 611, 683, 196,
    1056, 1540, 1589, 1615,
    1627, 1667, 1668, 1695,
    1742, 1789, 1792, 1800,
    1801, 1803, 1831
Earnhart, p. 131
Eddinger, 1587
Eddleman, 274, 806, 1248,
    1697, 1698, 1840
Eddleman, p. 131
Edmiston, 1149
Edward, 605
Edwards, 606
Ehery, 1695
Elias, 85
Eller, 17, 189, 269, 282,
    305, 306, 307, 308, 310,
    311, 312, 317, 328, 457,
    467, 534, 726, 1525,
    1577, 1580, 1584, 1589,
    1591, 1642, 1681, 1685,
    1695
Elliott, 63, 396, 649,
    654, 655, 660, 832, 844,
    990, 1227
Ellis, 462, 476, 1113,
    1114, 1149, 1150
Ellis, p. 131
Elwood, 89
Emberson, 834
Emerson, 887, 888
Ennis, 454, 476, 637, 681,
    773, 786
Ervin, 558, 1314
Evans, 506, 889
Everett, 1170

-F-

Faust, 464
Felcor, 880, 887, 895
Felker, 893, 1355, 1358
Felker see also Fulker
Felts, 97
Ferrand, 372, 544
Fesperman, 1509, 1510,
    1518, 1526, 1715, 1749
Festerman, 566, 667, 1208
Fight, 1628
Fight see also Fite
File, 221, 257, 271, 274,
    806
Filhour, 1014
Fink, 55, 1193, 1195,
    1328, 1451, 1489

Fisher, 66, 356, 542(2),
    608, 797, 1721, 1774,
    1780
Fisher, p. 131
Fite, 289, 293, 742
Fite see also Fight
Fleming, 873, 919, 920,
    1148, 1150, 1158
Fleming, p. 131
Fletcher, 166
Fo(a)rd, 576, 602, 640,
    766, 784, 955
Folk, 1695
Foltz, 1552
Foster, 387, 409, 578,
    653, 782, 995, 1038,
    1084
Foster, p. 131
Foutz, 2, 14, 1210
Fox, 466
Fraley, 21, 24, 165, 311,
    376, 389, 412, 475, 502,
    524, 571, 577, 783, 785,
    838, 1812
Fraley, p. 131
Francis, 1616
Frazier, 770, 816
Freeland, 776
Freeman, 142, 444, 853,
    854
Freeze, 152, 633, 694,
    795, 1058, 1059, 1070,
    1078, 1175, 1198, 1202,
    1203, 1228, 1229, 1230,
    1231, 1232, 1233, 1274,
    1343, 1361, 1363, 1364,
    1366, 1373
Frick, 202, 240, 254,
    1726, 1800
Frits, 344
Frolich, p. 131
Fry, 1670
Fulker, 1476
Fulker see also Felker
Fullenwider, 364, 365
Fulton, 1695
Furrer, 421

-G-

Gaither, 864
Gales, 855
Gallimore, 49, 92, 1557
Gardner, 756, 937, 1400,
    1401
Garner, 1436, 1437, 1717,
    1720, 1722
Garver, 973, 975, 1359
Gaskey, 1019, 1020
Gatlin, 68, 69, 71

Unless preceded by p., numbers are for household, not page

Gheen, 165, 379, 380, 424,
    582, 639, 644, 664, 670,
    684, 907
Gibbons, 566, 568
Gibson, 472, 729
Giles, 474
Gillean, 821, 822, 839
Gillean see also Gillon
Gillespie, 757, 759, 767,
    956, 970, 1031, 1082,
    1083
Gillon, 1343, 1344
Gillon & Freeze, 1343
Gillon see also Gillean
Glover, 303, 319, 379,
    1693
Godfrey, 504
Goodman, 40, 41, 185, 186,
    264, 276, 328, 330, 340,
    611, 1017, 1027, 1034,
    1035, 1067, 1071, 1081,
    1378, 1810
Goodnight, 1278, 1315
Gordey, 146
Gouger, 1134
Graber, 1487, 1840
Graham, 140, 666, 695,
    697, 716, 732, 733, 757,
    760, 799, 829, 837, 915,
    920, 930, 932, 938, 942,
    950, 956, 958, 959,
    1010, 1011, 1013, 1023,
    1030, 1038, 1067, 1132,
    1138, 1529

Graham, p. 129
Graham, p. 131
Graham, p. 134
Gray, 811, 852, 853, 854,
    1049, 1103
Gray, p. 131
Green, 635, 682, 944, 1823
Griffin, 78, 83, 155, 412,
    535
Groaner, 95

-H-

Hacket, 455
Haglar, 1026
Hains, 486
Hair, 962
Hall, 648, 718, 767, 799,
    861, 883, 886, 896, 905,
    909, 914
Hall, p. 128
Hampton, 464, 1207, 1221
Hannah, 62
Hannans, 534
Hardie, p. 127

Hare, 560, 898
Hargrave, 396
Harkey, 47, 184, 185, 187,
    261, 359, 1766
Harris, 476, 754, 859,
    1375
Harrison, 396, 427, 936,
    947
Hart, 1087, 1088, 1167
Hartley, 467, 674
Hartline, 359
Hartman, 26, 27, 183, 261,
    262, 264, 271, 281, 285,
    291, 322, 345, 486,
    1406, 1407, 1587, 1683,
    1684
Hartman, p. 131
Hawkins, 476, 896
Heathman, 630, 804
Hedinger, 309
Heilig, 62, 144, 789,
    1412, 1527, 1719, 1785,
    1786
Heilig, Barnart & Co, 160
Helfer, 383, 485
Hellard, 769, 786, 800,
    862, 874
Henderson, 435, 461, 476,
    477, 544
Henley, 20, 21, 22, 247,
    614, 669, 680, 884
Henry, 1533
Hess, 308, 482, 1298,
    1636, 1676, 1679, 1692,
    1695
Hethcock, 1337
Hetinger, 708
Hickman, 363, 540
Hicks, 267, 764, 1396,
    1830
Higdon, 578
Hightower, 864
Hill, 28, 186, 209, 224,
    313, 314, 315, 316, 414,
    1408, 1523, 1525, 1827

Hiltbrant, 418
Hipp, 172
Hodge, 198, 219
Hodges, 227, 229, 230, 543
Hodgins, 1083, 1786, 1831
Hoffman, 183, 188, 189,
    225
Hofner, 34, 60, 255, 672
Holbrooks, 1350, 1391
Holbrooks, p. 131
Holder, 447, 468
Holland, 484
Holmes, 125, 520
Holmes & Earnhart, 125

Holobaugh, 963
Holshouser, 367, 447, 469,
    562, 1475, 1513, 1516,
    1614, 1649, 1657, 1677,
    1716, 1734, 1740, 1744,
    1745, 1753, 1754, 1763,
    1782, 1818, 1819, 1824,
    1825, 1826
Holshouser, p. 132
Honeycut, 62, 77, 593
Hooks, 29
Hopman, 175
Horah, 393, 421
Hornbarger, 1710
Hornbarrier, 339, 365,
    1447, 1773
Hosler, 997
Hotchins, 347
Houck, 1185, 1186, 1187
House, 1732, 1836
Houston, 731, 1041, 1042
Howard, 458, 508, 553,
    579, 704, 814, 1347
Howlet, 585
Hudgins, 361
Hudson, 1601, 1602
Huffman, 325
Hughes, 389, 984
Hughey, 940, 967, 982, 991
Huie, 376, 381, 463
Hulen, 261, 263, 606, 609,
    663, 1374
Hunt, 555
Hyde, 926, 941, 942, 943
Hyde, p. 132

-I-

Icehour, 201
Idler, 85
Ingold, 1242
Irvin, 723, 871, 999
Irvine, 979
Irwin, 1091

-J-

Jackson, 50, 235, 244(2)
Jacobs, 494, 501, 563,
    582, 598, 641, 642, 645,
    783, 1546
Jacobs, p. 132
James, 353, 425, 444, 454,
    461
Jamison, 1100, 1101, 1122,
    1146
Jarrett, 482, 1593
Jeans, 783, 1512
Jenkins, 133, 371

Johnson, 91, 105, 396,
    450, 483, 627, 685, 715,
    868, 1002, 1309, 1586,
    1695
Johnston, 870, 1695
Johnston, p. 132
Jones, 53, 81, 82, 90, 94,
    169, 624, 1593, 1687
Josey, 671, 1378, 1468,
    1520, 1757, 1758, 1759,
    1760, 1761
Josey, p. 132
Julian, 472, 560, 572,
    574, 577, 709

-K-

Kariker, 1054, 1211, 1212,
    1213
Keifneck, 1496
Keller, 466
Kelly, 67
Kenny, 1688
Keply, 41, 1821, 1832
Keply, p. 132
Kerns, 115, 1572
Kerr, 445, 463, 483, 746,
    996, 997, 998, 1137,
    1609
Kesler, 189, 251, 286,
    292, 295, 323, 324, 325,
    334, 335, 345, 373, 399,
    407, 510, 513, 752(2),
    753, 1040, 1094, 1216,
    1302, 1586, 1623

Kester, 409, 469
Ketchey, 252, 287, 413,
    1039, 1309, 1320, 1430,
    1437
Ketchie, 1595, 1605, 1611,
    1626
Ketner, 1490, 1531, 1532,
    1710
Ketner, p. 128
Ketner, p. 132
Kilpatrick, 149, 171, 915,
    1076, 1105
Kimbell, 1637
Kincaid, 440, 561, 564,
    626, 652, 654, 665, 687,
    704, 713
Kinder, 529
King, 661, 662
Kingsbery, 123
Kinney, 234, 1660
Kirk, 2, 45, 46
Kirk, p. 128
Klutts, 340, 358, 671,
    469, 1195, 1410, 1435,
    1478, 1542, 1565, 1635,

Klutts (cont.)
    1641, 1652, 1691, 1695,
    1697, 1725, 1747, 1749,
    1750, 1752, 1754, 1755,
    1756, 1768, 1769, 1813
Klutts, p. 128
Klutts, p. 132
Knox, 575, 952, 968, 993,
    1000, 1006, 1024, 1028,
    1029, 1081
Knup see Canup
Korf, 1839
Krider, 534, 550, 575,
    610, 717, 911, 919, 1563

Krider see also Crider

-L-

Lamb, 106, 1173, 1379
Lambeth, 473
Lancaster, 1839
Lane, 865
Lantz, 1767
Laurance, 1059
Laurence see Lorance
Lawson, 402
Leach, 522, 1541
Leatho, 1191
Leazer, 1115, 1122, 1124,
    1128, 1129, 1157, 1158,
    1159, 1161, 1214, 1215,
    1356
Lee, 637
Leech, 431
Leers, 87
Lefler, 247, 385, 424,
    510, 1765
Lemly, 272, 476
Lentz, 1, 4, 144, 258,
    283, 304, 313, 326, 327,
    334, 402, 1477, 1776,
    1778, 1820
Leonard, 617
Leopard, 900, 1021
Leopard see also Lippard
Lessly, 396
Lewis, 772, 777, 792, 793
Lightell, 969
Linch, see Lynch
Linebarger, 1541, 1695
Linebarrer, 1723
Linebarrier, 284, 303,
    304, 450
Lingle, 739, 742, 1003,
    1166, 1220, 1224, 1229,
    1441, 1442, 1736, 1737,
    1779, 1840
Link, 73, 677, 775, 834
Linn, 377, 1223, 1307,
    1334, 1335, 1337, 1429,

Linn (cont.)
    1586, 1827
Linster, 784
Lipe, 1, 1162, 1353, 1367,
    1368, 1369
Lippard, 1457
Lippard see also Leopard
Lisk, 109
Litaker, 799, 1338, 1388,
    1392, 1393
Little, 466, 516, 721
Lively, 912
Lock & Cowan, p. 128
Locke, 548, 557, 729, 956,
    1231, 1548
Locke, p. 132
Logan, 678
Long, 433, 476, 485, 1535
Long, p. 130
Lookinbee, 624
Lopp, 5
Lorance, 714, 736, 788,
    1059, 1060, 1062, 1095,
    1176, 1181, 1183, 1189
Lord, 372
Lotwick, 200
Lotwick see also Ludewick
Louder, 722, 725
Love, 74, 526, 541
Love, p. 132
Lowry, 558, 773
Lucas, 801
Luckee, p. 132
Luckey, 167, 746, 819,
    879, 902, 908, 913
Luckey, p. 132
Ludewick, 100, 108, 199,
    319, 322, 192, 194
Ludewick see also Lotwick
Luther, 287
Lyerla, 291, 292, 356,
    480, 684, 833, 837, 841,
    846, 851, 1618, 1658

Lyerly, 476, 690, 691,
    693, 1650
Lynch, 846, 882, 1197

-M-

McAttee, 781
McCanless, 117
McCann, 374
McCarn, 70, 137
McCarnes, 145
McCay, 570
McCombs, 35
McConnaughey, 433, 718,
    744, 766
McCorkle, 85, 1076, 1187
McCormick, 1063

Unless preceded by p., numbers are for household, not page

McCoy, p. 128
McCrary, 639, 656
McCray, p. 132
McCulloch, 715, 1347
McDaniel, 554
McDonald, 396
McFarland, 1522
McHenry, 1008
McKay, 526
McKenzie, 1375, 1413
McKnight, 813, 1098, 1101,
    1112
McLand, 482
McLaughlin, 1051, 1052,
    1054, 1055, 1057, 1171,
    1174, 1179
McLean, 1132
McLendon, 13
McNeely, 371, 1025, 1033,
    1048, 1053, 1168, 1172,
    1176, 1178, 1192
McNeely, p. 132
Madison, 496
Madison, p. 132
Mahala, 297, 470, 531,
    1591, 1592
Mahala, p. 132
Makew, 570
Malt, 31
Mann, 137
Marland, 857
Marlin, 757, 773, 791,
    799, 810, 814, 857, 864
Martin, 157, 166, 1099
Mask, 93, 94
Mason, 1806
Masters, 1110, 1204
Matthews, 550
Maxwell, 284, 431, 1145
May, 331, 332, 336, 338,
    637, 1018
Melton, 1448
Menus, 547, 705, 748,
    1173, 1356, 1357, 1380,
    1389, 1390
Menus, p. 132
Meroney, 396
Meyer, 1627, 1628
Meyer see also Mires,
    Myers
Michael, 468
Michals, 331
Milea, 338
Miller, 4, 5, 6, 8, 25,
    57, 184, 217, 218, 220,
    231, 232, 251, 253, 256,
    298, 316, 370, 466, 668,
    731, 736, 782, 798,
    1062, 1078, 1160, 1169,
    1177, 1180, 1181, 1182,
    1283, 1295, 1376, 1399,

Miller (cont.)
    1402, 1428, 1588, 1604,
    1626, 1629, 1651, 1664,
    1731, 1741, 1765, 1783,
    1784, 1808, 1814, 1815,
    1816, 1817
Miller, p. 128
Miller, p. 132
Mills, 48, 136, 1072, 1134
Milton, 102
Miner, 424
Mingus, 776
Mires, 409, 412
Misemer, 92, 118, 257,
    262, 1612, 1634
Misenheimer, 257, 258,
    1163, 1410, 1690
Misenhimer, 249, 259, 1522
Misenhimer, p. 132
Mitchell, 63, 477, 487,
    540
Mock, 398, 890
Monroe, 467, 483, 618,
    785, 1695
Montgomery, 72, 414
Moody, 164
Moon, 467
Moor, 662, 1072, 1695
Moor see also More
Moose, 75, 469, 1691
More, 533, 1047
More see also Moor
Moreau, 149, 171
Morgan, 34, 38, 155, 201,
    203, 207, 208, 209, 214,
    221, 225, 257, 445
Morphis, 65, 121
Morris, 379, 562, 1214
Morrison, 902, 1550
Moseley, 87, 147
Mowry, 256, 382, 419(2),
    636, 672, 675, 1469,
    1727, 1729, 1731, 1732
Mowry, p. 132
Moyer, 163, 493
Moyla, 161
Mozer, 1778
Mull, 349, 1593, 1594
Murdah, 1026
Murph, 924
Murph, p. 132
Murphy, 421, 423, 476,
    517, 519
Murr, 507, 508
Myers, 476, 528, 612, 616,
    1582
Myers see also Meyer
Myers see also Mires

-N-

Nanney, 1050
Nash, 62, 112
Neal, 1064
Neely, 835, 908, 923, 1021
Nesbitt, 85, 437
Niblock, 897, 967, 971
Niceler, 1118
Nisler, 1097
Noah, 64, 104
Noble, 664
Nolly, 796
Nolly, p. 133
Nooe, 971
Norman, 1698

-O-

Olford, p. 133
Olford, p. 134
Oliver, 170
Oolmer, 960
Overcash, 401, 1032, 1072,
    1075, 1090, 1096, 1206,
    1218, 1249, 1250, 1252,
    1253, 1254, 1266, 1268,
    1269, 1270, 1271, 1272,
    1279, 1280, 1281, 1282,
    1283, 1292, 1324, 1368,
    1406, 1445, 1534
Overcash, p. 133
Overman, 447
Overman & Brown, 447
Owen, 119, 295, 396, 489,
    567, 637, 651, 747, 1022
Owens, 788, 1420, 1620

-P-

Pace, 471
Page, 492, 945
Pahel, 735, 1280, 1289,
    1290, 1291, 1292, 1297,
    1312, 1321
Pahel see also Peathel
Paine, 199
Palmer, 476
Pame, 39, 1654
Pame see also Baim
Pape, 66
Parish, 975
Park, 131, 219
Parker, 9, 10, 12, 15, 17,
    61, 397, 511
Parks, 205, 236, 242, 243,
    244, 248, 250, 271, 470,
    489, 807, 1156(2)
Parks, p. 133
Parnell, 98, 601
Partee, 1348

Unless preceded by p., numbers are for household, not page

Patterson, 1022, 1273,
    1288, 1702
Patterson & Owen, 1022
Peacock, 1748
Pearce, 1695
Peathel, 1289
Peathel see also Pahel
Peeler, 275, 293, 300,
    309, 342, 742, 1584,
    1638, 1640, 1655, 1688,
    1733, 1743, 1746, 1807
Pence, 110, 138, 599, 875,
    1352
Pendergrass, 97
Pendleton, 390, 391
Pendleton, p. 133
Peninger, 1837
Penny, 1206
Peters, 158, 167, 168
Peters & Martin & Co., 166
Peterson, 438
Phifer, 986, 989, 991, 992
Phifer, p. 133
Phillip, 1694
Phillips, 134, 155, 412,
    535, 625, 660, 1440,
    1488, 1512, 1695
Pierce, 261, 262, 516, 569
Pinkston, 514, 597, 622,
    664, 700, 707, 800, 830
Plaster, 1250, 1251
Pless, 1449
Plummer, 373(2), 707
Pool, 29, 30, 214, 280,
    285, 304, 316, 337, 351,
    415, 420, 431, 912, 1175

Pool, p. 127
Porter, 539, 1341, 1687,
    1833
Poston, 767, 1007, 1043,
    1058, 1080
Potts, 432
Powe, 1554
Powlass, 387, 686, 822,
    826, 1501, 1795, 1802
Probsts, 1433
Probts, 1480
Propst, 798
Pugh, 1549

        -Q-

Quilman, 581

        -R-

Rabon, 58
Raimer, 1144

Rainy, 574, 659, 661, 872,
    925, 1581, 1634, 1717
Rainy, p. 133
Ramer see Rimer
Ramsey, 476, 966, 1007,
    1217
Ramsour, 1242
Rankin, 1083
Reamer, 1227
Reamer see also Rimer
Recard, 1424
Redwine, 18, 296, 363,
    412, 1399, 1460, 1637,
    1695
Reed, 18, 63, 212, 213,
    217, 1183, 1184, 1800
Reese, 432, 1093, 1098
Reeves, 99, 399, 404, 453
Reich, 400
Reid, 1578, 1585
Rendleman, 1440, 1521,
    1788
Rendleman & Stirewalt,
    1294
Renshaw, 888
Reppult, 839
Repult, 857
Rex, 698, 760, 816, 837,
    898
Reynolds, 381
Ribelin, 52, 197, 1669,
    1791
Rice, 86, 705, 769, 805,
    809, 856, 861, 922,
    1043, 1582
Richards, 129, 398
Richey, 1221
Richwine, 162
Rickard, 976
Riggins, 101, 106
Right, 1466
Riley, 1151
Rimer, 406, 436, 664,
    1226, 1238, 1239, 1479,
    1502, 1503, 1644, 1645,
    1718
Rimer see also Reamer
Ringle, 85
Ritchey, 1458, 1724, 1757
Ritchie, 1207, 1222, 1223,
    1395, 1564, 1646, 1697
Rix, 1039
Robards, 396, 424
Roberson, 692
Roberts, 398
Robertson, 580
Robinson, p. 131
Robison, 689, 692, 847,
    852, 1025, 1243, 1336
Roby, 787

Rodgers, 719, 1414, 1418,
    1419
Rogers, 27, 1267, 1311,
    1317, 1422, 1423
Rosankrantz, 559
Rosankrantz, p. 133
Rose, 1248, 1300, 1301,
    1313
Roseborough, 983, 1005
Roseman, 286, 1440, 1483,
    1485, 1491, 1495
Roseman, p. 128 (2)
Rothrock, 116, 1809
Rough, 273, 335, 467, 603
Rough, p. 133
Rowzee, 427
Rowzee & Harrison, 427
Rudicil, 877
Rufty, 348, 1018
Rumpelt, 447
Rumple, 1139
Rusell, 1806
Rusher, 1517, 1615
Russell, p. 133
Rutherford, 664

        -S-

Safort, 1431, 1434
Safret, 891, 1409
Sanders, 587, 1571
Sappenfield, 384
Saucerman, 387, 797
Saucerman see also
    Sossamon
Savage, 1046
Sawyer, 170, 532, 569
Sawyer, p. 133
Sawyers, 499, 1842
Schoff, 1069
Scott, 128, 143
Scroggs, 451
Seaford, 1441, 1467, 1482,
    1486, 1538, 1768, 1769,
    1770
Seamon, 869, 875, 876,
    877, 892
Sechler, 694, 1075, 1120,
    1123, 1193, 1200, 1202,
    1225, 1240, 1244, 1247,
    1303, 1304, 1317, 1318,
    1346, 1361
Sechler, p. 133
Secrease, 407
Seers, 394, 538, 1171,
    1811
Seers, p. 133
Segraves, 419
Sells, 97
Setzer, 934, 1431

Unless preceded by p., numbers are for household, not page

Shammell, 1584
Shank, 1837
Shankle, 62
Sharpe, 401, 517
Shaver, 14, 208, 212, 216,
    223, 226, 405, 425, 476,
    482, 1498, 1545
Sheek, 910
Shemwell, 476
Sheppard, 114, 206, 211,
    233, 239, 240
Sherrill, 1277
Shinn, 1140, 1730
Shipton, 37
Shoaf, 386
Shoff, 385
Shuford, 1044, 1046
Shulibarger, 1425
Shulibaringer, 1168
Shuman, 375, 1631
Shuping, 845, 1104, 1197,
    1228, 1235, 1333, 1351,
    1376, 1377, 1378, 1472,
    1473, 1474, 1699, 1728
Shuping, p. 133
Sides, 95, 1701, 1838
Sikes, 424
Silliman, 1180
Simpson, 107, 482
Sims, 1285
Sitton, 407
Skeen, 247
Slate, 443
Slater, 447, 545
Sloan, 596, 708, 740, 741,
    743, 744
Sloop, 721, 735, 1085,
    1119, 1120, 1188, 1232,
    1237, 1290, 1311, 1316,
    1318, 1319, 1434, 1840
Smart, 113
Smith, 148, 293, 296, 417,
    429, 465, 468, 487, 488,
    490, 491, 503, 518, 520,
    557, 616, 716, 723, 730,
    745, 780, 800, 805, 806,
    904, 939, 951, 994,
    1114, 1116, 1117, 1118,
    1133, 1140, 1164, 1165,
    1343, 1349, 1420, 1499,
    1508, 1533, 1539, 1543,
    1559, 1560, 1562, 1835
Smith, p. 128
Smith, p. 129
Smith, p. 133
Smithdeal, 1568, 1608
Smoot, 743
Solomon, 139
Sossamon, 797

Sossamon see also
    Saucerman
Sowers, 1040
Spear, 1023
Speck, 1419, 1432
Speck, p. 133
Sriver, 619
Sroat, 597
Sroat see also Trote
Starnes, 86(2), 320
Starnes, p. 133
Starr, 687
Steel, 476, 544, 881, 906,
    997, 1009, 1030, 1559,
    1695
Steller, 748
Stenp, 335
Stevens, 159
Stidafor, 167
Stikeleather, 97, 1037
Stiller, 727, 728, 972,
    1394
Stiller, p. 133
Stirewalt, 1294, 1417,
    1418, 1424, 1425, 1446,
    1450, 1455, 1492, 1493
Stirewalt & Rendleman,
    1294
Stockton, 380
Stoker, 62, 172, 469
Stokes, 20, 23
Stokes, p. 133
Stoner, 43, 200, 269, 279,
    192, 1555, 1573, 1828
Stoner, p. 133
Stouck, 335
Strange, 1582
Strickler, 1497
Stuart, 1102
Sullivan, 101, 412, 476,
    1534
Summerell, 438
Sumpter, 519
Sutton, 456, 470
Swan, 963
Swan, p. 133
Swicegood, 127
Swink, 401, 412, 460, 483,
    494, 495, 499, 509,
    583(2), 584, 585, 586,
    587, 593, 596, 607, 613,
    629, 665, 1660
Swisher, 402, 595, 598,
    628

-T-

Tanner, 496
Tanner, p. 133
Tarr, 794, 1685

Taylor, 389, 876, 1341
Teele, 1255
Temples, 412
Tester, 886
Thom, p. 133
Thomas, 175, 299, 536,
    807, 1481
Thomason, 573, 575, 638,
    643, 645, 647, 664, 778,
    779, 782, 791, 840, 957

Thompson, 181, 430, 552,
    758, 820, 821, 823, 824,
    921, 924
Thompson, p. 128
Thompson, p. 133
Thomson, 210, 817, 827,
    831
Thorn, 790
Thrift, 141
Thyatira, 371
Tippett, 136
Todd, 549, 655, 699, 768,
    849
Tom, 476(2)
Tomlinson, 564
Tompkins, 179
Torrence, 1579
Towel, 681, 901
Townsley, 650, 673, 676,
    677, 678
Townsley, p. 133
Traloar, 161
Trexler, 38, 202, 205,
    357, 366, 367, 368, 369,
    377, 457, 493, 499, 501,
    686, 687, 851, 195,
    1544, 1578, 1609, 1610,
    1623, 1630, 1632, 1648,
    1656, 1689, 1715

Trexler, p. 134
Triffiner, 1379
Trote, 507
Trote see also Sroat
Trott, 488, 631, 790, 832
Troutman, 33, 59, 120,
    177, 1025, 1465, 1471,
    1739, 1762, 1794, 1797,
    1798
Troy, 437, 448
Tucker, 84, 402
Turner, 634, 705, 771,
    811, 840, 877, 879, 900,
    960, 1027, 1360
Turner, p. 134
Twopence, 461
Tyer, 1599

-U-

Unless preceded by p., numbers are for household, not page

Udy, 178
Umstead, 126
Upright, 1073, 1075, 1129,
    1203, 1220, 1249, 1254
Upright, p. 134
Utzman, 523, 837

-V-

Valentine, 461, 487, 539,
    853, 857, 1672, 1842
Vanderburg, 104
Varner, 1600
Verble, 717, 1566, 1567,
    1569, 1570
Vogler, 394, 400
Volentine, 130, 392, 840

-W-

Wade, 374, 390, 929, 1603
Wadesworth, 387
Wagoner, 646, 712, 750,
    751, 1068, 1827
Wagoner, p. 134
Walker, 974, 1296
Wall, 239, 373, 461
Wallace, 232
Waller, 204, 349, 350,
    351, 352, 354, 1439,
    1617, 1639
Walls, 123
Walter, 389
Walton, 135, 173, 376,
    503, 642, 786, 1556,
    1557, 1558, 1560, 1605,
    1606, 1695
Walton, p. 134
Wamack, 522
Warren, 386
Warrne, 386
Watkins, 604
Watson, 467, 504, 552,
    554, 631, 782, 785, 866
Watson, p. 134
Watt, 1010
Watts, 517, 1141
Weant, 110, 436, 479, 491,
    583, 589, 590, 591
Weaver, 413, 1345, 1430,
    1528
Webb, 84, 836, 848, 987
Wesct, 446
West, 391, 395, 412, 535,
    545, 590, 591, 1551,
    1553
Wheeler, 446
White, 272, 1114
Whitehead, 452
Whitlock, 62, 113

Whitman, 692
Wiatt see Wyatt
Wiles, 860
Wilhelm, 233, 275, 278,
    279, 314, 727, 728, 977,
    191, 1364, 1383, 1384,
    1385, 1388, 1434, 1840
Wilhelm, p. 134
Willaford, 1055, 1096,
    1107, 1135, 1266
Williams, 188, 396, 485,
    627, 1827
Williamson, 375, 428, 501,
    515, 516
Willis, 80
Wilson, 396, 476, 730,
    899, 1050, 1178
Wimbish, 435
Winder, 708
Winders, 565, 567, 621,
    626, 658, 699, 1529,
    1695
Winecoff, 1147
Wire, 389, 498
Wise, 115, 603, 665, 1616,
    1625
Wiseman, 399, 451, 1396
Wisenhunt, p. 137
Witherspoon, 1025, 1152
Wood, 480, 550, 911, 1000,
    1001
Woods, 1130, 1131
Woods, p. 134
Woodsides, 432, 1142,
    1143, 1154
Woodson, 502, 1104
Woolworth, 88, 464
Wormington, 360, 363, 364
Worth, 64, 125
Wren, 85
Wright, 807, 808, 867,
    964, 1494
Wright see also Right
Wyatt, 241, 245, 246, 248,
    257, 260, 653, 1687
Wyatt, p. 134

-Y-

Yarborough, 412, 1297
Yontz, 160
Yost, 1219, 1286, 1287,
    1438, 1500, 1514, 1515,
    1536
Yost, p. 134
Young, 550, 723, 911, 927,
    930, 999

DRAKE-ARRINGTON, WHITE-TURNER, LINN-BROWN AND TWO DOZEN RELATED SOUTHERN LINES: TREADWELL, SLADE, LACEY, HARRISON, CATHEY, REDWINE, KRIDER, WOOD, McNAIR,PEDEN, SANDEFUR, TOMPKINS, BENNETT, HODGES, GOODRICH, BECHINOE, WILLIAMS, BUSTIN, OUTLAW, FOX, SMITH, GEORGE, DOLL AND STAHLE. 490 pp., casebound, charts, maps, illus., copies of orig. documents, letters, Bible records, index $35.00.

THE GRAY FAMILY AND ALLIED LINES: BOWMAN, LINDSAY, MILLIS, DICK, PEEBLES, WILEY, SHANNON, LAMAR, McGEE. 660 pp., gold-stamped Kivar casebound, 126 illus., 7 maps, 2 fold-out charts, 8,000-name index. $27.50. Out of print.

PEOPLE NAMED HANES. 291 pp. casebound, 142 illus, maps, complete index. $25.00. Primarily Surry, Stokes, Forsyth, and Davie counties, NC. This is a Moravian lineage. Allied lines: Hauser, Legenauer, Zimmerman, Frey, Kerber, March, Sehner, Hinkle, Hodgin, Lassiter, Chatham, Booe, Poindexter.

THE ANCESTRY OF NATHALIE FONTAINE LYONS GRAY: LYONS, NUNES MIRANDA, LURIA, COHEN, HART, CLAYLAND, MAFFITT, BEACH. 260 pp., casebound, illus., charts, index, $25.00. The first five lines are Jewish. Clayland and Maffitt are Maryland lineages. Beach is Connecticut.

A MILLER FAMILY OF ROWAN COUNTY. 166 pp., casebound, illus, charts, index, $37.50. Descent from Wendle Miller, immigrant to Rowan Co., NC, through his son Jacob Miller whose daughter Sophia married Abraham Miller in Rowan 9 Jan. 1810.

THE DIARY OF ELIZABETH DICK LINDSAY. Facsimile edition of diary kept by the wife of Andrew Lindsay of Guilford County, NC, for the period 1837-1861. She was the daughter of Thomas and Jane Erwin Dick. A detailed introduction provides the lineages. Casebound, map, illus., $18.50.

A HOLMES FAMILY OF ROWAN AND DAVIDSON COUNTIES, NORTH CAROLINA. 336 pp., casebound, illus., maps, complete index, $25.00.

ABSTRACTS OF THE WILLS AND ESTATES RECORDS OF ROWAN COUNTY, NC, 1753-1805 AND ROWAN COUNTY TAX LISTS OF 1759 AND 1778. 220 pp., casebound, complete name index, slave index. $25.00.

ABSTRACTS OF THE DEEDS OF ROWAN COUNTY, NC, 1753-1785. 276 pp., casebound, map, complete index. $30.00.

ABSTRACTS OF THE MINUTES OF THE COURT OF PLEAS & QUARTER SESSIONS, ROWAN COUNTY, NC. casebound, complete index.
> Vol. 1: 1753-1762, 177 pp., $30.00 (second printing)
> Vol. 2: 1763-1774, 210 pp., $30.00 (second printing)
> Vol. 3: 1775-1789, 240 pp., $28.00

1815 ROWAN COUNTY, NORTH CAROLINA, TAX LIST. Soft cover, complete index, map, 64 pp., $12.00.

Ordering information: brochure and/or index search on receipt of SASE. Add $2.50 postage. NC residents add 6% sales tax. Order from Jo White Linn, Box 1948, Salisbury, NC 28145-1948.